Ritual Participation and
Interreligious Dialogue

Also available from Bloomsbury

Interreligious Studies, Oddjbørn Leirvik
Religion or Belief, Discrimination and Equality, Paul Weller, Kingsley Purdam,
Nazila Ghanea and Sariya Cheruvallil-Contractor
Loss and Hope, Edited by Peter Admirand

Ritual Participation and Interreligious Dialogue

Boundaries, Transgressions and Innovations

Edited by
Marianne Moyaert and Joris Geldhof

Bloomsbury Academic
An imprint of Bloomsbury Publishing Plc

B L O O M S B U R Y
LONDON · OXFORD · NEW YORK · NEW DELHI · SYDNEY

Bloomsbury Academic

An imprint of Bloomsbury Publishing Plc

50 Bedford Square	1385 Broadway
London	New York
WC1B 3DP	NY 10018
UK	USA

www.bloomsbury.com

BLOOMSBURY and the Diana logo are trademarks of Bloomsbury Publishing Plc

First published 2015
Paperback edition first published 2016

British Library Cataloguing-in-Publication Data
A catalogue record for this book is available from the British Library.

ISBN: HB: 978-1-4725-9035-0
PB: 978-1-3500-1237-0
ePDF: 978-1-4725-9036-7
ePub: 978-1-4725-9037-4

Library of Congress Cataloging-in-Publication Data
Ritual participation and interreligious dialogue : boundaries, transgressions, and innovations / edited by Marianne Moyaert & Joris Geldhof. – 1 [edition].
pages cm
Includes bibliographical references and index.
ISBN 978-1-4725-9035-0 (hardback)
1. Worship.   2. Interfaith worship.   3. Rites and ceremonies.
4. Religions–Relations.   I. Moyaert, Marianne, joint editor.
BL550.R58 2015
201'.5–dc23
2015007118

Typeset by Deanta Global Publishing Services, Chennai, India

CONTENTS

Part III
CHRISTIAN AND EAST ASIAN RELIGIOUS PERSPECTIVES

Part IV
JEWISH AND JEWISH-CHRISTIAN PERSPECTIVES

NOTES ON THE CONTRIBUTORS

Albertus Bagus Laksana teaches at Sanata Dharma University in Yogyakarta, Indonesia. His research interests and publications include topics in Muslim-Christian comparative theology (especially the role of pilgrimage, saints, and sacred space) and theology of religions, mission studies, theology and culture, and Asian theologies. He is the author of *Muslim and Catholic Pilgrimage Practices: Explorations Through Java* (2014).

Gavin D'Costa is Catholic Professor of Theology, University of Bristol. He acts as an advisor to the Roman Catholic Church in England and Wales and the Anglican Church on matters of interreligious dialogue and theology. He also advises the Pontifical Council for Interreligious Dialogue, Vatican City. His most recent publication is *Vatican II: Doctrines on Jews and Muslims* (2014).

James Farwell is Professor of Theology and Liturgy at Virginia Theological Seminary. He is the author of *This Is the Night: Suffering, Salvation, and the Liturgies of Holy Week* (2005) and has recently written a new version of the classic primer *The Liturgy Explained* (2013).

Joris Geldhof is Professor of Liturgical Studies and Sacramental Theology at the Faculty of Theology and Religious Studies, KU Leuven. Along with several articles in the domain of liturgical theology and philosophy of religion he published a monograph entitled *Revelation, Reason and Reality. Theological Encounters with Jaspers, Schelling and Baader* (2007). He is the editor-in-chief of the bilingual journal *Questions Liturgiques/Studies in Liturgy*.

Mark Heim is Samuel Abbot Professor of Christian Theology at Andover Newton Theological School. He is deeply involved in issues of religious pluralism, Christian ecumenism, and the relation of theology and science. He is author of *Salvations: Truth and Difference in Religion* (1995), *The Depth of the Riches: A Trinitarian Theology of Religious Ends* (2001) and, *Saved From Sacrifice: A Theology of the Cross* (2006).

Richard Kearney holds the Seelig Chair of Philosophy at Boston College and is author of several books on the philosophy of religion. These include *Anatheism: Returning to God after God* (2010), *The God Who May Be* (2001), *Strangers, Gods and Monsters* (2000) and as editor, *Traversing the Heart: Journeys in Interreligious Imagination* (2006) and *Hosting the Stranger: Between Religions* (2012). His forthcoming book is *Reimagining the Sacred: Debating God with Richard Kearney* (2015).

Ruth Langer is Professor of Jewish Studies (Comparative Theology) in the Theology Department at Boston College and Associate Director of its Center for Christian-Jewish Learning. Her publications include *Cursing the Christians? A History of the Birkat HaMinim* (2012).

Martha Moore-Keish is Associate Professor of Theology at Columbia Theological Seminary. Her research interests include Reformed theology, liturgical theology, and feminist theology. She also has interests in ecumenical theology and interfaith issues. She is currently coediting a book on Karl Barth and comparative Theology. In 2008 she published *Do This in Remembrance of Me: A Ritual Approach to Reformed Eucharistic Theology.*

Marianne Moyaert is the Fenna Diemer Lindeboom Chair of Comparative Theology and Hermeneutics of Interreligious Dialogue at the VU University Amsterdam. She recently obtained funding for a four-year research project Crossing Borders: Interreligious Ritual Sharing as a Challenge to the Theology of Interreligious Dialogue (2014–2018). Her latest book is *In Response to the Religious Other: Ricoeur and the Fragility of Interreligious Encounters* (2014).

Douglas Pratt is Professor of Religious Studies at the University of Waikato, New Zealand and Adjunct Professor (Theology and Interreligious Studies) at the University of Bern, Switzerland. Together with David Cheetham and David Thomas, he coedited the volume *Understanding Interreligious Relations* (2013) His most recent book is *Being Open, Being Faithful: The Journey of Interreligious Dialogue* (2014).

Anantanand Rambachan is Professor of Religion at Saint Olaf College, Minnesota, USA. Among his books are, *Accomplishing the Accomplished: The Vedas as a Source of Valid Knowledge in Śaṅkara* (1991), *The Limits of Scripture: Vivekananda's Reinterpretation of the Authority of the Veda* (1994), *The Advaita Worldview: God, World and Humanity* (2006). His latest book is *A Hindu Theology of Liberation: Not-Two is Not One* (2015).

Rachel Reedijk is a cultural anthropologist specializing in the dialogue between Jews, Christians, and Muslims. She works as a lecturer at the Amsterdam Center for the Study of Cultural and Religious Diversity (ACCORD), VU University Amsterdam. Her book is entitled *Roots and Routes: Identity Construction and the Jewish-Christian Muslim Dialogue* (2010).

Maria Reis Habito PhD, is the International Program Director of the Museum of World Religions and the Director of the Elijah Interfaith Institute USA. Her latest publication is *Heart to Heart. Buddhist-Muslim Encounters in Ladkah* (edited), Museum of World Religions (2012).

Anya Topolski is a postdoctoral fellow, (FWO-Flanders), at the Higher Institute of Philosophy, KU Leuven. Her current research involves the deconstruction of the discourse of Judeo-Christianity in relation to European identity formation and its symbolic role in propagating Islamophobia. Her most recent publications are *Arendt, Levinas and the Politics of Relationality* (2015) and the coedited volume *Is there a Judeo-Christian Tradition? A European Perspective* (2015).

André van der Braak is Professor of Buddhist Philosophy in Dialogue with other World Views, VU University Amsterdam, Faculty of Theology. His main publication is *Nietzsche and Zen, Self-overcoming without a Self* (2013). He is currently coediting a volume with Paul van der Velde and Aloys Wijngaards, titled *Buddhist Transformations*.

Walter Van Herck is Associate Professor of Philosophy of Religion at the University of Antwerp and guest professor at Ghent University. One of his most recent edited books is *The Sacred in the City* (ed. with L. Gomez, 2012). He is editor-in-chief of *International Journal of Philosophy and Theology* (Routledge).

Tim Winter is University Lecturer in Islamic Studies at the Faculty of Divinity, University of Cambridge, and Dean of the Cambridge Muslim College. His academic publications include many articles on Islamic theology and Muslim-Christian relations. He is the editor of the *Cambridge Companion to Classical Islamic Theology* (2008). His most recent book is *Commentary on the Eleventh Contentions* (2012).

Chapter 1

INTRODUCTION: EXPLORING THE PHENOMENON OF INTERRELIGIOUS RITUAL PARTICIPATION

Marianne Moyaert

Living in the midst of religious plurality, we are challenged to build relationships and understandings with believers of other faith traditions. Such encounters may take various forms, ranging from Jews, Christians, and Muslims meeting in Scriptural reasoning groups to grassroots initiatives revolving around interfaith peacebuilding; from religious leaders trying to establish diplomatic relations between their communities to spiritual interfaith encounters between Buddhist and Christian monks; from theological dialogues exploring complex doctrinal questions to the dialogue of life focused on building local communion across religious believers. As more and more people experience religious diversity firsthand and are touched by the vividness of other religious traditions and by the spiritual and moral wisdom of the "other," they also increasingly ask if they can celebrate religiously with believers belonging to other religious traditions. Both in the United States and in Europe, especially, we cannot but note the increasing impetus for shared ritual activity. The (r)evolution from monologue to dialogue seems to be continued in the domain of rituality. Many people feel that inter-riting is an important facet of taking dialogue to a deeper, more affective, and experiential level.

1 Types of ritual participation

Ritual participation is a multifaceted phenomenon that takes many forms, depending on (1) the context in which it occurs, (2) the intention that undergirds the sharing of ritual, (3) the nature of the ritual performed, and (4) the religious communities involved. Generally speaking, however, one may distinguish between two types: on the one hand, ritual sharing that is *responsive* and *outer-facing* and on the other hand ritual participation that is *inner-facing* and follows the pattern of *extending* or *receiving hospitality*.[1]

When ritual sharing is outer-facing, believers belonging to various faith traditions come together for prayer, celebration, or worship *in response to* some external event or challenge. This may be to address a global challenge (e.g. war prompting a prayer for peace), or to commemorate and mourn the victims of a national calamity (e.g. religious leaders standing shoulder to shoulder to remember the victims of 9/11) or to solemnly inaugurate a new academic year. (Inter)national days against discrimination and racism, national liberation days, and (inter)national women's days also can become occasions for an interreligious ceremony of some sort. These initiatives gather people together and address the need to create a "we" in the face of shared challenges.

Although some of these outer-facing gatherings are the result of political initiatives—supported by religious leaders attempting to contribute to the establishment of nonviolent pluralistic societies, for example—this is not always the case. Religious leaders may also clearly take the initiative in promoting these gatherings, as in the case of the World Day of Prayer for Peace in Assisi, initiated by Pope John Paul II in 1986 and continued by his successors Benedict XVI and Francis I. Gathering religious leaders from all over the world to pray in their own way, the Pope intends to show to the entire world that violence in the name of religion is never justified, and that all religions, despite their undeniable differences, together intend to bring peace and harmony to the world. It would seem that this recurring event with a stipulated pattern of action has become a new ritual in itself. Although many would agree that such prayerful and ceremonial expressions of interreligious solidarity are laudable, when listening to people actively involved in the process of setting up a context in which such an interreligious meeting can occur, it becomes clear just how challenging it is to find prayerful language, appropriate symbols and proper gestures that are meaningful for all participants. This difficulty, it could be argued, has to do with the nature of ritual: it is a set pattern of behavior which people receive rather than create. More than any other structured cultural behavior, rituality is traditional and resists change. This difficulty, however, does not utterly prevent new ritual patterns from emerging; new, meaningful, and evocative forms of ritual sharing or praying do arise, to the benefit of participants (cf. World Day of Prayer for Peace).

Ritual sharing, however, may also be inner-facing (Pratt, 60), following a paradigm of hospitality. If confessional worship reinforces particular religious identities and strengthens communal bonds, then extending hospitality to strangers by inviting them to visit, celebrate, or even participate in the ritual life of one's community symbolizes a desire to transcend confessional barriers. There is an understanding that dialogical openness or, if you will, interreligious hospitality, cannot come to full fruition if one is not prepared to receive "the other" in one's house of worship. A ritual framing of hospitality is thus not secondary to interreligious dialogue but shows precisely that, despite any real differences, including even disagreements and misunderstandings, a choice is being made for interreligious solidarity. Different from forms of ritual participation that are outer-facing, here we are speaking of ordinary rituals in which the "guest" can participate to a certain degree.

One may look at ritual hospitality from either of two perspectives: either one becomes a guest (e.g. a Christian) in one of the ceremonies (e.g. *Shabbat*) of another faith (e.g. Jewish) community, or one welcomes as a host (e.g. Hindu community) other believers (e.g. Christians) to participate in a ceremony of one's home tradition (e.g. *puja*). These ceremonies may happen both in the sacred space (e.g. a temple, synagogue, or church) of a religious community or at home. Though (minor) adjustments may be made, because of the presence of guests, usually the liturgical standards of the home tradition will be followed (Hoffman 1990: 11). The challenge for both guests and hosts is to find the right balance between loyalty to one's own tradition (and its set of rules) and openness to the tradition of the other (with its set of rules). Religious communities will have to provide their own legitimation and reasoning to engage in forms of ritual hospitality, e.g. a *Muslim* theology of sharing worship (Winter); a *Hindu* theology of ritual hospitality in a Hindu temple (Rambachan); or a *Catholic* theology of praying together (D'Costa).

Many of the contributors to this book testify to the complexity of negotiating between the do's and don'ts of ritual sharing; for both host and guest it is difficult to find the right balance between maintaining and transgressing certain boundaries, and between too much openness or too little. What some hosts may see as openness—e.g. offering the Eucharist to unbaptized guests—may be perceived by the latter as a form of "undue" transgression and even a potentially violent inclusion. What I wrote elsewhere about interreligious encounters taking place in a fragile hermeneutical and theological space, fraught with the risk of misunderstanding and failure, certainly holds true for ritual sharing across religious borders (Moyaert 2014b). Nevertheless, when the right balance is found, ritual hospitality may penetrate deeper than any other form of interreligious dialogue. Ritual sharing holds the promise of gaining access to the beating heart of another religion; it may touch people at a deep emotional level.

2 Reasons for ritual participation

There may be various reasons why people come to participate in the rituals of another faith community, the most common occasion probably being an invitation by family members, friends, or colleagues. In his chapter in this volume, Mark Heim names these "one-off" choices (Heim, 20). Usually, such invitations are extended within the context of the great life-cycle events, which are connected to particular rites of passage, e.g. birth, marriage, and burial. As Ruth Langer and Stephanie Perdew VanSlyke point out, "we attend one another's marriage and funerary rites, [and] honor one another's children by attending baptisms, bris and baby-naming ceremonies, bar and bat mitzvahs, first communions and confirmations" (Langer and VanSlyke 2011: 2). To accept such an offer can be a way to strengthen family connections, honor friendships, or express mutual respect.

Another context to which the question of inter-riting applies is that of mixed families in which both partners are committed to respect, preserve, and sustain each other's faith. Different from the "one-off" choices mentioned earlier, in the case of intermarriage, ritual negotiation is an ongoing endeavor calling for quite some ritual flexibility from the family members. Certainly when children are involved it may be quite challenging to navigate choices with regard to the great moments of life that are celebrated differently in faith traditions. In daily life too, couples need to find a way to organize and negotiate their religious practice(s). Some select a family religion to avoid confusion and so that the children are not confronted with the problem of conflicting loyalties. In other families both traditions are treated equally, with both parents holding on to their own religious perspective, trying to avoid undue mixture and allowing the children to have a taste of each religious practice. Though this may be a way to avoid the problem of syncretism, some couples report that not being able to share certain moments or events in a prayerful or ritual way puts an extra strain on their married life. Both for family interaction and for the transmission of faith to the next generation, rituals are very important. This is why some families, over time, develop their own ritual practices in which they try to extend as much hospitality as possible to the religion of their beloved ones (Crespo and Davide 2008). In this new territory, a balance needs to be found between tradition and innovation in such a way that the "recreated" rituals may speak to both partners (and their children). In her chapter in this volume, Jewish philosopher Anya Topolski relates how she and her Catholic husband made a promise, which they ritually inscribed in their *ketubah*, to support and enhance each other in their respective faith commitments and to raise their children as both Jews and Christians (Topolski, 196). Shared rituals that cross religious boundaries are conditional for being able to share both the grand and grievous moments of life *as a family*. Topolski's chapter makes it clear that not all religious communities are ready for this task.

Ritual participation is becoming more important also in a pedagogical setting. Many teachers committed to interfaith pedagogies see ritual sharing as an educational opportunity to visit a Christian community during the Eucharist, a Hindu temple for the puja ritual, or a Buddhist Sangha during its meditation sessions. Entering the sacred space of another religious community and being shaped by their rituals creates the possibility of deeper interreligious understanding rooted in real religious life. Stephanie Paulsell, who teaches at Harvard Divinity School, relates that her students actively look for new ways to gather for worship in this multireligious context:

> We want to be with each other as we truly are, they said. We want to be present for each other's prayers and rituals and practices. We want to be led in Torah study by the Jewish students, and in Friday prayers by the Muslims; to listen to a dharma talk with the Buddhist students and hear a sermon with the Baptists; to be with the Episcopalian students for the Eucharist and with the Hindus for puja; to light Advent candles with the Roman Catholics, offer prayers at the flaming chalice with the Unitarian Universalists, and keep silence with the Quakers. (Paulsell 2012: 35)

Students point to the transformative nature of ritual participation. Indeed, there is a sense that interreligious encounters that do not include the ritual dimension of religious life may have a limited scope (Maraldo 2010: 106). The primary religious language of traditions is closely connected to narrative traditions, concrete symbols, devotional practices, and small and great rituals, which constitute the beating heart of the teaching of a tradition and without which the teaching would also become meaningless. Deep understanding of another tradition's teachings, rituals, and narratives cannot be attained via discursive dialogue because that does not give access to the primary religious language, which is tacit and embodied. It requires not only dialogue and study but also participation in the life of a community and its religious outlook. Believers have a point when they expect to be able to learn something from ritual participation that they cannot learn from a discursive interreligious exchange (Moyaert 2014a).

Ritual sharing may also function as a way to express solidarity with another religious community that is in a difficult political position. I am thinking especially of Islam, which is confronted with a growing phenomenon of Islamophobia in Europe and elsewhere, resulting in contentious laws such as the prohibition of women wearing a headscarf in public spaces. Christian (and other) women have started to veil themselves in protest and to support the Muslim population, which is increasingly targeted for their appearance. Another context where ritual sharing takes the form of a sociopolitical act would be the tradition that has grown in the occupied West Bank city of Bethlehem, where Christians fast together with their Muslim brothers and sisters during the month of Ramadan. At stake is an expression of being in the proximity of the other.

Last but not least, some believers report that their presence and participation in the rituals of another religion is an expression of their ongoing personal spiritual journey. Today, believers in pursuit of their own spiritual development may decide to participate in the prayer and meditation practices of another tradition. Asian traditions and their methods of prayer and meditation seem to attract many Westerners. Christians practicing Zen meditation or yoga with the guidance of Buddhist and Hindu gurus is a well-known phenomenon (Amaladoss 2012: 88). While some tap into the ritual resources of another tradition to fulfill a spiritual lacuna in their own (Cornille 2013: 326), others, taking on a more pluralistic perspective, firmly believe that one may pray to and worship the same God under various names. Those who believe that religions differ in their creeds, rituals, symbols, and organization, but converge at the core of religious experience, would regard ritual sharing as an expression and enhancement of such a religious experience (Amalorpavadass 1988: 55–6). To engage in the worship practice of another tradition thus becomes a *means* to encounter the divine anew or to discover hidden or forgotten dimensions of the divine. From this perspective ritual participation may be an expression of the ongoing journey that religious life really is.

3 Shared belief as a precondition to inter-riting?

While ritual sharing may be a novel phenomenon in the West, which is the focus of this volume, in other parts of the world the idea that one should restrict oneself to one ritual tradition makes no sense. "Ritual polytropy" (Chau 2012; Carrithers 2000), or turning to different deities and ritual specialists, is indeed a major trend at the grassroots level in many Asian societies. In China, for example, while self-reported religious identities tend to be singular ("Buddhist," "Christian," "non-religious"), this does not necessarily pose restrictions to plurality in ritual performance (Colijn 2014). "Religion" and "religious identity" are modern phenomena in China, and people may adopt or self-report an exclusive religious identity parallel to their diverse ritual practices. According to Adam Chau (2006), this ritual polytropy in China is intertwined with a desire to maximize the result of ritual performances. Similarly, as Rose Drew explains in her book on dual belonging, "in India and Nepal … people pray at shrines connected with various religious traditions, deities and saints. And, in Japan, many visit Shinto shrines on auspicious occasions, Christian churches for weddings and Buddhist temples for funerals" (Drew 2011: 2). Interreligious theologian Peter Phan construes that "in Asia religions are not considered as mutually exclusive organizations but as having specialized functions responding to a division of labor, as it were, to different needs and circumstances in the course of a person's life" (Phan 2004: 62–3). What is at stake is not confessionality but rather efficacy; the only important thing is the question: does the ritual work? Religions and their symbolic practices are approached from a rather functional perspective: they are supposed to be useful means.[2]

In the West, on the other hand, ways of thinking about religion "as bounded traditions—ways closely connected to the theisms that have predominated in that region—have meant that one does not typically understand oneself to be involved in more than one tradition at a time" (Farwell, 166). Certainly with regard to those monotheist traditions of Middle Eastern origin (Judaism, Christianity, and Islam) that have prevailed in the West and that revolve around a single creed, a claim to final revelation, or an exclusive soteriology, to "belong" implies to "believe," which in turn means to commit oneself to the truth as it is conveyed by a tradition and ritually reenacted, transferred, and embodied. This intertwining of truth and ritual means that (certain) rituals may be performed only by those who *believe*, and this limits the possibilities of *inter-riting*. According to comparative theologian Catherine Cornille, "performance of ritual gestures without corresponding convictions may be experienced as disrespectful, or as trespassing of proper religious boundaries, and as lacking an essential ingredient for proper understanding: personal belief" (Cornille 2008: 155–6). Sharing some of the basic religious convictions central to one of these traditions seems to be conditional for participation in its rituals. Consider the following experience related by David Brown, a Christian scholar of Islam:

> My distance from Islam came home to me in a sad but profound way one evening in Khartoum, when I went to the home of a Muslim leader. There were some thirty men sitting at ease in his courtyard and for an hour or more we enjoyed a good and open discussion about religious matters. The time came for the night prayer, and they formed ranks to say it together. I asked if I might stand with them, but the Sheikh told me I could not do so, since I did not have the right

"intention" (*niyya*). I had to remain standing at the edge of the courtyard. Even though I have walked on the approaches of Islam for over thirty years I can only speak of it as a stranger. (Brown 1982: 47–8)

To participate in the rituals of another tradition assumes unity of belief; it is an expression of faith. Several of our contributors would corroborate this. Indeed, in his discussion about interreligious prayer (as distinguished from multireligious prayer), Catholic theologian Gavin D'Costa argues that co-intentionality is a necessary requirement for acts of interreligious praying (D'Costa, 96), and Jewish liturgical theologian Ruth Langer refuses to partake in the Eucharist, even when invited, because doing so "would constitute a symbolic gesture of our participation in fundamental Christian beliefs" (Langer, 210). The general sense is that by participating (bowing, kneeling, touching, eating), one expresses consent to the beliefs communicated by means of the ritual. If one participates in a ritual, the "truth" of which one cannot affirm, the ritual participant is guilty of *inauthenticity*, thereby making a mockery of both his own beliefs and those of the host community. According to this line of argument, belief (or the lack thereof) determines the possible level of participation in the rituals of another faith community.

Certainly for the monotheistic religions, belief and ritual are closely intertwined; the question *what can we do together* depends at least to a certain extent on doctrinal questions. Nevertheless, such a cognitive approach, according to which belief precedes practice, does not entirely do justice to the complexity of ritual. Clearly, beliefs are part of ritual, but one does not quite capture the specificity of ritual when one reduces its function to "an expression of the prior beliefs concerning supernatural beings shared by its celebrants." In his chapter Walter Van Herck rightfully attributes this "fallacy" to certain Enlightenment presuppositions, which lead to an impoverishment of ritual (Van Herck, 46). Lacking from this cognitive approach to ritual is an understanding of the performative dimension of rituality.

4 The transformative power of ritual performance

Ritual is a doing; it is performative through and through: *breaking* the bread and *drinking* from the wine (Eucharist); making the sign of the cross; touching the relics of a saint; kneeling before an altar; lighting candles; embarking on a pilgrimage; reading from the Torah scrolls; eating matzah and bitter herbs during the Passover meal; singing psalms; offering food and water (*prasada*) to a deity during worship (*puja*); sitting in *zazen* or chanting in a Buddhist temple. These ritual performances do more than express belief; they engage the entire person (not just the mind); they impact on all the senses (vision, hearing, smell, taste, and touch); they evoke powerful emotions (or soothe emotions that are too overwhelming); they stimulate religious experiences, stir the imagination, and attune the body to the divine. By engaging the person in her entirety, as an embodied mind or a minded body, ritual potentially has the power to transform the participant in the ritual, to mold her identity, not so much by altering the mind, but through rewriting the body (see Moore-Keish; van der Braak).

By performing symbolic practices, ritualists become deeply permeated by the truths conveyed in that tradition and acquire religious knowledge. This religious knowledge should not be mistaken for scholarly (theological) knowledge, which is *secondary* to the primary religious knowledge that is conveyed through symbolic practice and inscribed onto the body.[3] According to Van Herck, this primary knowledge "concerns the most tangible forms in which the religion is manifested. This language represents a symbolic universe in which the body is central: people bow and kneel, stride through the ship, smell the incense, sing the psalm in the choir, enter the holy place" (Van Herck 2003: 171–2). Believers learn to master this primary religious knowledge through ritual practice until they know through their body: they are introduced to a "tempo-spatial continuum" of concrete religious objects, festivities, ritual gestures, religious formula, customs, and values central to the tradition. Throughout this process particular convictions, aspirations, and experiences become interiorized and incorporated, thereby shaping and transforming the religious identity of the ritualist. Tradition becomes en-fleshed, its truth embodied (O'Donnell 2012). From this perspective we may understand Talal Asad when he says that "the inability 'to enter into communion with God' may well be a function of untaught bodies" (Asad 1993: 77). Thus embodied ritual practices are conditional to religious experiences and to the formation of religious identities, which may also include the affirmation of certain convictions.

Maybe the problem is not simply that by participating in the ritual of a foreign religious tradition one would seem to affirm beliefs of that religious community (implying inauthenticity); maybe the problem is rather that believers, sensible to the power of ritual, realize that "liturgy is the locus where belief is enacted, formed and enhanced."[4] The body plays a central role in establishing beliefs. Surpassing the mere expression of consent, ritual has the power to inscribe beliefs onto the body. That is something ritual scholars and cultural anthropologists know. Ritual is evocative, transformative, and compelling: one's beliefs may be altered by participation. For comparative theologian Bagus Laksana, the evocative and powerful nature of ritual is precisely what appeals to him. Inter-riting makes one vulnerable to change and transformation in a way that discursive dialogue (inter-texting) cannot do. Inter-riting enables him to enter into the sensory world of the religious other: "For the sensory experience of being near the other has the power to make us not only open but also vulnerable to their world, not primarily at the level of religious concepts, but rather at the deeper affective, emotional and experiential level" (Laksana, 111). However, the transformative power of ritual may also explain why people—even those who are deeply engaged in interreligious dialogue—may refrain from ritually crossing over (Moyaert 2014a). Certainly, for people who still have a strong symbolic sensibility, it may intuitively feel wrong to enter into a sacred space of another religion, let alone take part in a ritual central to another community of faith. Mark Heim relates below that this resistance sometimes has "a quality of almost physical recoil from the practice at hand." Elaborating on this hesitation, he attributes the reluctance of some of his students to a "kind of negative reverence for the sacred character of the place in question, a recognition that it represents and conveys real spiritual powers that are not identical with and may not be controllable by the student's own religious resources. They believe that real effects are exercised on a visitor by presence and practice in that place, regardless of the intention with which a visitor may enter" (Heim, 27). Participating in the rituals of another tradition is neither irreproachable nor without risk.

5 Ritual as identity marker

Rituality is formal, repetitive, and stable; it harks back to conventional practices established by fixed traditional rules handed down from one generation to another in a particular community, and its meaning transcends both momentary concerns and mere subjective personal sentiments. Rituals tend to resist change, even though rituals, like all cultural elements, do undergo change. Different from other human activities, novelty or expressing one's deep personal feelings does not have a place in the ritual domain; the ritualist rather acts in accordance with the prescriptions of the faith community. Instead of creativity, ritual performance implies conformity to traditional rules of stipulated patterns of behavior, clearly implying a resistance to innovation. The ritualist executes a fixed, predetermined, preexisting mode of action. Right performance—doing things *the way they should be done according to tradition*—is an important dimension of ritual. This focus on a fixed sequence of actions (potentially) frees the ritualist of being overly preoccupied with him- or herself, thereby enabling that person to become connected both to the community and to become part of a greater narrative: rituality binds people together into one religious community that shares a single destiny and a collective memory.

Rituals not only instill a sense of (collective and individual) identity; they also reinforce the distinction between "insiders and outsiders" by upholding certain strictures of participation, a theme developed in the chapter of cultural anthropologist Rachel Reedijk. From in-depth interviews (forty-four Jews, Christians and Muslims engaged in dialogue), she learned that ritual practices represent the bridges that are most difficult to cross. Religious rituals were understood as being holy, and her interviewees regarded them as definitive boundary markers establishing a clear demarcation line between "us" and "them" (Reedijk, 183).

This distinction between insiders and outsiders is symbolized preeminently by the so-called entrance rites. The latter usually follow after a long process of formation in which a person is taught by priests, gurus, or elders who initiate her in the religious (sometimes sacred) knowledge and acquaint her with the religious symbols and rituals. Not only is she gradually allowed access to the secrets of the community, she is also allowed little by little to enter into domains previously off-limits (Grimes 2002: 107). Formal entrance rituals "officially" demarcate the transition between standing outside and belonging to and (fully) participating in a community. One can imagine how various forms of inter-riting may be perceived as a challenge to "group identity and security" (Braybrooke 1989: 89).

This demarcation is also obvious with ceremonies that enable believers to address "the most sacred dimension of a religion, which is central to its self-definition, e.g. the cultic practices such as the Eucharist."[5] Participation in such cultic ceremonies is normally restricted to believers who have been (fully) initiated in the tradition, assent to its creed and live according to its rules. Religious others are generally speaking excluded; they do not take part in this tableau. Reflecting on the sacredness of rituals, systematic theologian Pim Valkenberg argues that lived faith possesses "in its ritual dimension a holiness which is difficult to break open in the contact with other religions. My tradition," he continues, "speaks of communicatio in sacris, the sharing of what is holy and that is in most cases forbidden" (Valkenberg 2001: 1). Even if "outsiders" are allowed to attend a religious ceremony, the chances are great that their participation would be restrained. They may be allowed to partake in some rituals, whereas others are simply off-limits for those who do not belong (Cornille 2011: 39). Conversely, not too many religious traditions would appreciate their members taking part in the ritual life of another religious community. From a more traditional perspective, the whole notion of cross-riting evokes notions such as idolatry and heteropraxis. It is out of order, out of place, it is an anomaly: it is a blurring of boundaries, a transgression of symbolic thresholds; it is a reaching across conventional religious borders (Vishanoff 2013: 351) that may threaten religious identities.

6 Changing patterns of religion

Today, the standard understanding of monoreligious worship is being challenged. In the West increasing numbers of believers are open to engaging the religious diversity that surrounds them by participating in the ritual practices of other faith traditions. They feel, at least to a certain extent, at ease to challenge the boundaries guarded by what Michelle Voss Roberts calls "the gatekeepers of religious traditions" (Voss Roberts 2010: 44). The very possibility of ritual participation seems to be illustrative of wider shifts in the contemporary religious landscape in the West. Sociologists of religion explain how processes of detraditionalization contribute to a much more reflexive dealing with tradition, commitment, and identity, even to the extent that sociologists and religious scholars nowadays speak of "flexible believers" and their "fluid affiliations." Since the transmission of tradition no longer happens naturally, identity is no longer given but must be constructed. Identity is continually being formed, and the believer can be involved in that process in a productive way. As a consequence, the emphasis is less on the objective pole of religious belonging (the authority of tradition) than on its subjective pole (Cornille 2013: 328). The formation of religious identity is increasingly freed from the rule of conformity. Moreover, when people engage in ritual traditions, what increasingly matters to them is if the ritual performed resonates within them and if they experience that ritual as an authentic expression of spirituality (Amalorpavadass 1988: 56). Sociologists call this the *subjective turn* (Woodhead and Heelas 2005: 2). The subject is called to exercise authority in the face of the great existential questions, and this opens up the possibility of experimentation, questioning, and exploring, also across religious boundaries. Taboos, claims to sacredness, religious hierarchies, and no-go zones are being challenged and the traditional (Western) understanding of religion as a unitary whole with fixed boundaries is being questioned (McGuire 2008). As the borders of religions become more permeable, religious identities multiply and ritual participation in some form becomes at least a possibility.

Today, many regard ritual participation as an expression of an ongoing spiritual journey which does not allow itself to be fixed in bounded traditions. After all, what is Ultimate transcends all human comprehension, and it may even be called a form of idolatry to try to capture the Ineffable in one ritual tradition. If one acknowledges that these "bounded" traditions are arbitrary constructs, historical-culturally determined products, it becomes more and more difficult to justify traditional and authoritative claims to exclusivity, which prevent religious communities and their believers from growing toward one another. Why not break through ritual boundaries and enrich one's religious perspective by means of interritual sharing? Maria Reis Habito, for example, relates in her chapter how, many years ago, she "took refuge in" the Buddha, the Dharma, and the Sangha, while nevertheless also remaining Catholic, celebrating the Eucharist on Sunday. She regards herself as someone "who personally has crossed boundaries, while at the same time remaining very sensitive to the necessity of respecting the boundaries of a given religious tradition in an interfaith context" (Reis Habito, 34).

In his chapter, while emphasizing his great respect for tradition, Richard Kearney shows himself to be particularly sensitive to the potentially violent nature of exclusionary traditions. He takes issue especially with the way dogmatic beliefs have functioned as ideological boundary markers, constructing dichotomies between "us" and "them." Speaking for his own tradition, Catholicism, he wonders how it is possible that

> the Eucharist, of all sacraments, rituals and gestures, could be the cause of such egregious hurt? "One Bread, One Body," my fellow Catholics chanted as they knelt to receive Holy Communion—but, according to official Church doctrine for centuries, that was *only* if you were members of the "True Church": Roman Catholicism, as dogmatically defined by the Congregation for the Doctrine of the Faith. The rest—non-baptized in the one true holy and apostolic Church— were "not" part of the One Body. (Kearney, 140)

Continuing this line of thought, Kearney argues for an open Eucharist, for permitting the most sacred Catholic cultic practice to become a locus of exuberant generous hospitality, welcoming strangers instead of excluding them.

7 Overview chapter by chapter

To this day the complexities of ritual participation remain under-theorized. Apart from various pastoral documents formulating guidelines for how to organize multi-faith prayers or interreligious weddings, there exists little academic literature that delves deeply into this phenomenon. Most *theological* approaches to interreligious dialogue are interested primarily in *high* tradition, which is discursive and propositional. The focus is on myths, creeds, and dogmas, which are written down in documents that can be subjected to various hermeneutical analyses that enable the disclosure of meaning and truth. The question of how to make sense of conflicting truth claims is regarded as one of the most important challenges for any interreligious dialogue. Liturgical theologian Martha Moore-Keish has a point when she states in her chapter that theologies of interreligious dialogue have basically "taken the approach of most of the wider field of theology: conceptual reasoning based on critical engagement with texts, on topics such as God/the divine/the Real, the human condition, the world, and the relationships among these" (Moore-Keish, 67). The prevailing theological approach is rooted in a *cognitive* understanding of religion: religion is associated primarily with the realm of beliefs and convictions, which in the opinion of most academics are translatable into doctrinal statements. The emphasis is on the formulation of *what* is believed, and not on what believers *do*. The practical dimension of religion, represented by rituals, prayers, prohibitions, and obligations, is regarded as secondary to the cognitive dimension of religion. This lack of interest from "interreligious" theologians is matched by a similar disinterest from liturgical theologians on the one hand and ritual scholars on the other hand. Ritual sharing is a phenomenon that has lacked sustained reflection; inter-riting seems to be a blind spot for theologians of interreligious dialogue, liturgical theologians, and ritual scholars.

This volume intends to delve deeper into the complexities and intricacies of interreligious ritual participation. To that end it presents scholars from different disciplines as well as from different faith traditions. Some of our contributors develop an internal theological reflection on the (im)possibility of either outer-facing or inner-facing forms of inter-riting, while others take on a more "distanciated" perspective, approaching this novel phenomenon as philosophers of religions or as cultural anthropologists. Many of our contributors however could be called *border-crossers*: their approach to religion, interreligious dialogue, and ritual participation does not allow itself to be clearly delineated or categorized. They span disciplinary fields and engage various traditions to establish conversations between them, and it turns out to be quite productive. Indeed, there is something to be said about James Farwell's claim that to understand the complex phenomenon of ritual sharing, one needs both an emic (which reflects the voice of religious believers) and an etic account of ritual. As a consequence, deciding upon a "clear and distinct" table of contents was probably the most difficult part of this project. As editors, we realize it may be contested.

We have divided our volume into four sections, as follows.

Part I: Philosophical, theological, and phenomenological observations

In the opening chapter Mark Heim immediately brings to light the intricate nature of ritual participation, considering the interaction of three elements—intention, intuition, and intellectual accounts—in relation to "doing what others do" religiously. Drawing upon various examples, he shows that the question whether one may or may not participate in the ritual tradition of another religious community is a contextual question to a certain extent. To further illuminate this, he considers some of the complexities in the intentions and rationales that can be involved in multiple ritual participation. Next, he focuses on the spontaneous physical and emotional reactions that (even the possibility of) inter-riting sometimes evokes. Such intuitive experiences of repugnance and discomfort receive little attention in the literature of religious pluralism, except as obstacles to be overcome. Heim sets out to gain more insight into these seemingly irrational reactions. He turns to the role that intellectual accounts play in the evaluation of the phenomenon of multiple ritual participation and argues that theologies of religious pluralism, whether explicit and elaborate or implicit, help coordinate understanding, intention, and intuition. He makes this concrete by showcasing how his "particularist" theology of religions has guided him in discerning both the possibilities and limits of ritual participation.

The second chapter is from Maria Reis Habito, who is deeply rooted in both Catholic tradition and Buddhism, and has a strong and long commitment to interreligious dialogue. In her chapter, she looks at ritual participation from the point of view of someone who personally has crossed boundaries, while remaining very sensitive to the necessity of respecting the boundaries of a given religious tradition. First, she examines ritual participation in a Buddhist context from different angles—from her experience as a Catholic Zen teacher facilitating retreats with Christians, Jews, and Muslims, and as a scholar engaged in interfaith dialogue. Next she looks at the issue in a Jewish-Muslim context as described by Yossi Klein Halevi. Concluding, she reflects on the implications of these individual examples of crossing boundaries and on whether and how the lessons learned from these can be applied to the wider field of interreligious relations.

Philosopher of religion Walter Van Herck develops a criticism of the phenomenon of cross participation. He focuses on the individualistic spiritual intentions undergirding ritual sharing. Cross participation wants to signal one's (individualist) spiritual journey which will lead one—it is hoped—beyond words and rituals. This attitude is typical of a mystical-experiential view of religion. Religion is thought to be a quest that detaches people of all materiality. In the end it also detaches of specific religions, institutions, traditions, symbols, and rituals. By cross participating one signals one has reached a stage which goes beyond the demarcations of traditional religious groups. Van Herck hopes to uncover and criticize the enlightened presuppositions of this practice.

The fourth chapter is written by theologian and scholar of religion Douglas Pratt, who focuses on one specific form of ritual participation, namely interfaith prayer. In particular, a specific case study of interreligious prayer is examined and some theological rationales for Christian engagement in such prayer are highlighted. Furthermore, as prayer is most typically a sensible locution—prayers use words, very often poetically—so different modes of language involved will be discussed, for language is the bearer of symbol and meaning for the one who is making the prayer. The chapter closes with a discussion of the dialogical implications of interfaith prayer.

Next, Martha Moore-Keish, a liturgical theologian engaged in ecumenical dialogue—which is a dialogue that reaches its limits precisely where rituality (the Eucharist) is concerned—responds to the question: What lessons can interreligious dialoguers learn from ecumenical dialogue? Are there analogies? Why is rituality so delicate from an ecumenical perspective, and what does this mean for practices of interreligious inter-riting?

Part II: *Muslim and Christian-Muslim perspectives*

Tim Winter, a Sunni Muslim scholar, develops an Islamic perspective on ritual participation. His chapter surveys classical Shari'a sources to ask whether non-Muslims can ever be welcome in the formal, canonical worship of the mosques. Does the majoritarian Sunni discourse offer genuinely informed and thoughtful guidance for mosques where non-Muslims wish to join congregations? He shows that a raft of difficulties, shaped by anxieties over purity, transgression, and identity, immediately present themselves and provide the major influence in shaping the jurists' verdicts. Yet, he argues, they do not appear to be entirely insuperable.

Gavin D'Costa also reflects on the (im)possibility of interreligious prayer between Muslims and Catholics, and he does so from a Catholic perspective. This chapter distinguishes various ways in which the term "pray together" might be understood. It distinguishes "interreligious prayer"—here meaning praying together, using the same words with two religious groups united in heart and mind—from "multi-religious prayer," which refers to prayer in the presence of another religious group. He argues that, in the early literature on the matter, there is a danger of conflating the two different types, and shows that some Catholic communities, following the initiatives of Pope John Paul II, have reached a consensus that interreligious prayer is problematic, while multireligious prayer is not. The chapter goes on to consider an essay by Joseph Ratzinger, which discusses the preconditions for interreligious prayer and is very skeptical about its possibility, except perhaps for Christians and Jews. Finally, one of Ratzinger's preconditions for interreligious prayer is used to examine the possible grounds for interreligious prayer between Christians and Muslims, concluding that the door is as yet neither closed nor open.

The final chapter in this section comes from the comparative theologian Bagus Laksana. Unlike most comparative theologians (Clooney, Cornille, Thatamanil), his work does not revolve around texts, but rather around practices (Christian-Muslim) of pilgrimage. In a way, he nuances the textual focus of comparative theology and opens up this field to nontextual approaches. But what does it mean, for a comparative theologian, to engage other religions ritually? This chapter will certainly help to open up the field of comparative theology.

Part III: *Christian and East Asian religious perspectives*

Anantanand Rambachan, a Hindu scholar, explains why ritual hospitality is part and parcel of what Hinduism, in his understanding, is about. He focuses on the Hindu ritual of *puja*: a hospitality ritual of sixteen offerings to God that includes food, incense, water, flowers, clothing, and light. He asks whether it is possible to participate in a temple or domestic *puja* ritual without sharing the orthodox theological assumptions. How do Hindus regard persons of other religions who wish to participate in *puja*? Are there forms of Hindu ritual that are more easily accessible for participation by persons of other traditions?

Philosopher of religion Richard Kearney argues for an interreligious understanding of the Eucharist. He offers his own ecumenical experience as an Irish Catholic growing up in a sectarian environment before exploring the prophetic examples of two twentieth-century pioneers of an "open communion"— Henri le Saux (Abhishiktananda) and Teilhard de Chardin. Kearney asks why any Christian, following Christ the host-giver of body and bread, would want to exclude any stranger from the greatest gift which he came to bring to all human beings? Surely not because the recipients should first be instructed in the approved doctrinal "word" or have copies of a baptismal certificate issued by the correct Christian Church (of which there is much dispute among Christians)? He then concludes with an outline of a series of "extending Eucharists," from the liturgical and ecclesiastical to the carnal and quotidian.

Buddhist scholar André van der Braak focuses on the practice of zazen meditation. This practice of sitting meditation is widely practiced in the West, and from a Western perspective such meditation practice is often seen as aimed at the improvement of several mental skills, such as the capacity for attention and focus. From a Japanese esoteric Buddhist perspective, however, this practice should properly be understood as a ritual performance in which the Buddha's enlightenment is enacted within the practitioner. Zen Master Dogen (1200–53) calls zazen "the practice-realization of totally culminated awakening." Rather than being a technique aimed at spiritual acquisition, zazen is the expression of Buddhahood itself. Van der Braak explores this discrepancy between Western antiritual perspectives of zazen and the Japanese understanding of zazen as ritual performance. Together with Robert Sharf, he posits that there is no precise Asian Buddhist analogue to the Western distinction between ritual and meditation (Sharf 2005: 160), and that this very distinction needs to be deconstructed.

James Farwell's chapter connects well with the preceding one. He provides an emic account of rituals in two traditions, focusing on Catholic/Orthodox traditions of Christianity and Soto Zen and esoteric forms of Buddhism, proffering a shared notion of ritual as embodied enactment of soteriological and moral ends. He then uses this shared account to hone the question of the validity of inter-religious participation in the case of Christianity and Buddhism, showing how legitimacy depends upon the particular traditions being examined; upon which rituals are in question; and upon specific theological, philosophical, and rhetorical strategies chosen by Christians and Buddhists to articulate the doctrinal dimension of their particular life-worlds.

Part IV: Jewish and Jewish-Christian perspectives

Empirical research forms the foundation for Rachel Reedijk's chapter. As a cultural anthropologist, she explores the limits and possibilities of ritual participation by following and interviewing Jews, Muslims, and Christians who are part of interreligious groups. What she brings to the surface is the ambiguity of the phenomenon of ritual participation: it both attracts people and in a way repels them. She examines the concrete religious motivations her interviewees give to reject or support ritual participation.

An example of the failure of ritual participation is given in Anya Topoloski's chapter. She is a Jewish philosopher with a Polish-Canadian background who married a Catholic. She explores, from a first-hand perspective, the unfortunate tensions which arise in relation to our attempts to create mourning rituals for a Jewish-Christian interfaith family. Recently she and her husband lost their daughter, and she writes about how inter-riting failed her the most in this time of need. She testifies to the almost insurmountable ritual obstacles she was confronted with in this difficult time.

Jewish liturgical theologian Ruth Langer argues that hospitality is required before interreligious participation can generate interreligious learning. The ability of host and guest to discern and meet each other's needs and expectations is critical for communication and ease of discourse to occur. What constitutes a genuine welcome requires a nuanced sensitivity, particularly on the host's part. This chapter reflects on these dynamics, drawing from personal experiences, positive and negative, focusing on examples of visits to others' liturgical settings, especially in the American context. It also addresses the challenges of sharing hospitality and constructing effective shared, interreligious prayer.

Each of the chapters in this volume offers an important contribution to a better understanding of ritual participation as a specific and irreducible form of interreligious encounter. Through the various chapters, it becomes clear that ritual participation is a complex and exciting phenomenon that definitely needs further exploration. This volume is only a first mapping of the field, and points to both the difficulties and the possibilities of inter-riting. I now invite the readers to delve into the book so that they may experience something of the richness and challenges of partaking in rituals across religious boundaries. I hope that this book may promote continued research and debate at the intersection of ritual participation and interreligious dialogue.

Part I

PHILOSOPHICAL, THEOLOGICAL, AND PHENOMENOLOGICAL OBSERVATIONS

Chapter 2

ON DOING WHAT OTHERS DO: INTENTIONS AND INTUITIONS IN MULTIPLE RELIGIOUS PRACTICE

Mark S. Heim

1 Introduction

In pluralistic and culturally fluid environments, people and their religious practices increasingly mix in patterns that do not match received structures of religious identity. This is an external fact, visible in sociological analysis. But it also raises questions about the rationale and intentions underlying such activities, questions that are to some extent addressed in theologies of religious pluralism. This chapter explores some of the complexities related to the subjective intentions of persons who undertake religious behaviors without necessarily seeking to adopt the univocal identity often associated with those behaviors. It then adds to this discussion of religious identities and intentions a consideration of religious intuitions, a dimension of this complexity that has been insufficiently appreciated in academic discussions.

Multiple religious participation is often discussed on the assumption that it involves people with fixed religious identities. We then ask on one hand what religious "hosts" find legitimate for guests to appropriate before crossing a line that transgresses on the hospitality and integrity of the host community. Or we ask on the other hand what visitors find legitimate for themselves to experience and endorse, before crossing a line that violates their fidelity to their home community or their own sense of identity. This "home and away" paradigm is not adequate to the full range of multiple religious participation.[1] There are people who may combine elements from several religious sources without identifying with any one in particular. And there are those who would claim more than one identity simultaneously, where the pattern of multiple religious participation rises to a point of multiple religious belonging. Such religious synergy might be a conscious composition, or it might be an unchosen hybridity, as in a child who grows up living in more than one extended faith family. Multiple religious belonging requires a certain kind of mutual recognition.[2] Multiple religious practice itself however does not require that participants "belong" in some definitive way to particular traditions. For the purposes of this discussion, multiple religious participation focuses less on the location of the practitioner than the rootedness of their practices. It is not that one necessarily defines oneself as a Hindu, so much as that in a certain behavior one follows models of what (some particular) Hindus do.

Multiple religious participation (MRP) as I understand it involves some continuing exercise of elements of behavior and belief which themselves are grounded in distinguishably different communities or traditions. This definition presumes that the practice in question is not a one-time event in the life of the participant. It presumes that she or he continues to look to particular religious sources beyond their own experience or intuition for guidance on the path of the practices in question. In that sense she or he has connections to distinguishable communities of practice, whether these are found in literal religious communities to which they attach themselves in some (perhaps tangential) way, in the instruction of individual teachers, or in textual sources. It is the quality of apprenticeship to different sources that makes such practice "multiple" in my view, as opposed to simply idiosyncratic. The ongoing nature of the apprenticeship is key: serial adherence to different faiths is not what I mean by multiple religious participation. In MRP we do one type of religiously located activity while being the same person who continues to do another type.

The landscape of MRP is a spectrum. Such participation has to start somewhere, and we often face "one off" choices. Shall we undertake this activity for the first time? If we already participate in multiple religious practices, shall we extend this to include something new? The question is not whether to regularly participate in Jewish ritual, but whether to accept a single invitation to attend a Passover meal with a Jewish friend. The question for people who already follow a faith is how far they will give themselves over fully to the experience of doing what the other does, and how far this is consistent with their continuing to be at the same time the religious person that they are otherwise. Because these individual events and decisions may stand alone, or because they may prove to be the door to a more fully elaborated MRP, I think it is helpful to look at such single cases against that wider background.

Theologies of religious pluralism bear both on the actions of individuals and on the discourse within and among religious communities about life in a diverse religious environment.[3] These theologies articulate the tension between commitment to one's own tradition and identity and openness to learning and dialogue with others. Though they were constructed without primary concern for MRP, increasingly these systems of thought both draw on such activities and are reshaped by them. The intellectual understanding embodied in such theologies may play a role in the intentions that people bring to their participation in the religious rites of the other. Subjective intentions are something individuals have and groups do not. But individuals also have certain religious intuitions that are significantly formed through participation in groups and their activities. Those intuitions are also an important aspect of MRP, though they often receive less attention than either intellectual explanations or personal intentions. I want to consider the interaction of these three elements—intention, intuition, and intellectual accounts—in relation to "doing what others do" religiously. I will conclude with a few comments on my own theology of religious pluralism and its relation to religious participation.

2 Practice and intention

Before we turn to the role of intuition, we will consider some of the complexities in the intentions and rationales that can be involved in MRP. We can observe from the outside how someone apportions bodily time and presence. It is much harder to understand the apportioning of inner attention and intention. Most religious activity presumes a subjective orientation on the part of the devotee. Religious texts are often explicit in expecting a certain kind of reader and reading, which may not be what academic study presumes (Griffiths 1999). So the question is unavoidable: To what extent, for instance, in behaving in a Hindu way am I (as a Christian) acting in one of the ways a Hindu (subjectively) might? What makes MRP *religious* depends largely on intention. Rote imitation of a Hindu religious ritual (as for instance for the purposes of a theater performance) does not amount to participation. My activity becomes participation when I not only act as a Hindu would but also share some of the same intention.

A number of complicated questions arise even in relation to this apparently straightforward point. First, from the point of view of those who study religion mainly in terms of ritual, "intention" is a very controverted term (see Bell 2009). "Intention" can suggest that a ritual exists for the sake of some causal effect that extends outside the ritual itself (e.g. to bring rain, to appease a god). If we look to the subjective disposition of those taking part in many traditional religious rituals there might not be anything that corresponds to that expectation. The intention might simply be to do what has long been done before, with no "explanatory" picture. The focus on the subjective can also suggest that the validity of the ritual depends on the attitude of those who perform it, rather than the performance itself. This arguably misunderstands at least some traditional rituals, which might be regarded as effective so long as rightly enacted, regardless of the attitude or understanding of the participants.

There are occasions of MRP where the issue of "intending what the other intends" is moot or clearly subordinate to other concerns. Association with or bodily practice of religious activities has an unavoidable social meaning. For instance, in a context where Jews are being persecuted, a non-Jew might participate in certain kinds of religious observance—she might wear a yarmulke or other distinctive dress, observe dietary regulations, attend temple services—as a simple act of solidarity. In such a circumstance, it is unlikely that the "host" community would regard the behavior as transgressive or presumptuous, even if it lacked religious sincerity in the sense of intending by these actions what Jews normally mean by them. The behavior could be lacking in specifically religious intention at all, or the religious motivation might flow entirely from the actor's adherence to her own tradition.

Brian McLaren, a prominent Christian pastor, author, and leader in the emergent church communities in the United States, recounts his decision to observe the Muslim fast of Ramadan, and his recruiting of a somewhat reluctant Muslim friend as a guide (McLaren 2012: 242–3). McLaren is clear that he saw this as a kind of witness, or rather a "with-ness," in which he primarily wished as a Christian to express his concern and respect for Muslims and their practice, within a society where many Christians did not express these things. It was a social act, expressing in a tangible way a neighborliness he understands to be an essential aspect of his Christian faith.

In both of these cases, the intention to do and mean religiously what others do and mean is no necessary part of the intention of the interfaith participant. Both behaviors mean to express support for the members of another religious community, if not for the validity of their religious observances. At the least, they reflect no fear of being contaminated by association with the other, or of violating the other's boundaries. On the part of the "host" community, the motive of solidarity behind the actions may (but might not) override hesitations about the appropriation of these practices by outsiders. A similar situation often seems to pertain to occasions of hospitality, when one community purposely invites members of another to visit with them and to be present for rituals or worship. Under these conditions, those in each party might relax general concerns about the sincerity of the religious intentions involved.

Intentions can be secondary in a more problematic sense. In Malaysia, a protracted court case, punctuated with public rallies and occasional violence, has addressed the legality of non-Muslims using the word "Allah" to refer to God. The most recent court ruling as of this writing held that Christians were forbidden to use this word, as it belonged to Muslim practice alone (*WSJ* 2013). Christians in this case are accused of multiple religious practice, of undertaking an essentially Muslim activity without being Muslim. Their subjective intentions might not have been at all to "do what Muslims do," but the behavior itself is taken as confusing, as blurring the line between the two traditions. "Behaving like a Muslim" was something McLaren did to express solidarity with Muslims, and many Muslims perceived it positively in that light. In Malaysia, "behaving like a Muslim" by using the Arabic word for God was something many Muslims condemned in Christians. It was seen as a deceptive strategy to lure converts with an implication that they would be worshipping the same God in the church as in the mosque.

Clearly, not all multiple religious behavior involves the desire to do subjectively "as the other does." There can be intentions that explicitly separate us from what we are participating in and that distinguish our disposition from that of those we otherwise emulate. Extreme examples are sometimes illuminating. In the sixteenth century, after bloody conflicts with the Christian authorities, large numbers of *moriscos* (Muslim converts to Christianity) were expelled from Spain. The accusations fueling the expulsion were that *moriscos* still held to their Muslim faith (dissembling in their Christian practice) and/or allied themselves with external Muslim enemies of the Spanish Christian states. In the case of particular *moriscos*, one or both of these assumptions may have been false, but this rarely won an exemption. As *moriscos* struggled with increasingly aggressive Christian rulers, they appealed for direction to the Grand Mufti Ahmad ibn Abu Jum'a of Oran. In a decree which drew upon the notion of *tqqiyyah* or "precaution," the Grand Mufti authorized extraordinary steps by which the *moriscos* could accommodate to participation in Christian practices:

> If at the hour of prayer you are compelled to venerate the Christian idols ... look at the idols when the Christians do, but think of yourself walking in God's path, even though you are not facing the *qibla* [the niche in a mosque indicating the direction of Mecca].

> If you are forced to drink wine, drink, but set yourself apart from all intention to commit evil.

> If you are forced to eat pork, do so, but with a pure mind and admitting its unlawfulness, as you must do for any other prohibited thing.

> If you are forced to take interest [forbidden under the laws of Islam] do so, purifying your intention and asking pardon of God.

> If you are being adjudged by infidels, and you can dissimulate, do so, denying with your heart what you are saying with your words, which are forced from you. (Wheatcroft 2003: 138–9)

This was a situation where every step of participation was experienced as a transgression, and conscious awareness of the transgression was a key to spiritual fidelity. People remained Muslim by living a double life, on the one hand maintaining the distinctive rituals of their faith as best they could without drawing attention to themselves, and on the other outwardly conforming to the behavior of a committed Christian while inwardly renouncing what they did or focusing their minds on another purpose. The decree went so far as to say that believers might even deny the Prophet Muhammad with their tongues, so long as they retained their adherence subjectively (advice that would find less agreement from other Muslim authorities).

I note this extreme example because it highlights the distinction between outward behavior and inward intention. Participation in religious ritual has an undeniable social meaning, apart from the subjective attitude of the participant. But the possible gap between the two was the source both of the suspicions of the Christian persecutors and of the hopes of the Muslim believers.

Let us put beside this picture a radically different one. A contemporary Christian, who follows an ordinary round of worship and prayer in her Christian community, is much interested in interfaith issues and becomes friends with a close circle of Hindu colleagues at her work place. She regularly goes to a nearby temple, where she offers gifts to the central deities, receives *prasad*, prostates herself before the images, circumambulates their shrines, and chants along with ritual festivities. She creates a small shrine at her home, originating with an image given to her as a gift, which differs from those of her friends only in its smaller scale and its inclusion of a large image of Jesus. Let us further stipulate—as the Christian tells us—that she wholeheartedly engages in all of these activities with one simple principle. In all that she does, she consciously and explicitly transposes Christ into the place of any of the deities or images. Her outward behavior is multiple, but to her understanding her inward intention is exactly the same in all her ritual or spiritual activities. In an ironic way, this situation mirrors the behavior counseled by the Mufti of Oran for the oppressed *moriscos*, with the obvious difference that it is impelled not by coercion but by affection. In both cases there is multiplicity in practice, but no multiplicity in intention. This Christian woman wants to share the practice but not the inner intentions of its devotees.

We have seen that from some perspectives it does not matter whether one has the subjective intention intrinsic to a practice: the multiple religious practice is approved or condemned on other grounds entirely. In other cases, there are explicit intentions that *separate* the practitioner from those aspirations typically associated with the act, as was the case with the *moriscos* and in another way with the Christian who gave no subjective space to devotion to the Hindu deities she outwardly revered. In some respects, multiple religious practice is in the eye of the beholder: Malaysian Christians are being told they are doing it, regardless of whether they desire to or not. In other respects, it is something that is only determined internally. The *moriscos* who were faithful Muslims did not wish to be multiple. They did not desire to practice Christianity in any way and, according to their intentions, they did not.

The more common case, however, is probably one in which the intentions are neither incidental to the behavior nor completely divorced from them. Instead the subjective intention represents what we might call a mixed aim. There is a kind of negotiation of the terms on which one adopts the guidance and goals of another's practice. To practice a certain type of Buddhist meditation, for example, it is necessary to follow the directions of a teacher and, insofar as that teacher directs you to take up a certain subjective attitude, to do so to the best of your ability. So far, one may say that one's intention differs in no way from those who "belong" to that tradition, even if you explicitly regard yourself as belonging to a different one. The person involved may simply defer the question of how this intention sits with other intentions that he may also adopt with sincerity when he prays to Christ or says the Creed. If a Hindu takes part in a Passover seder, she may well have some understanding or intention in mind that indicates how this observance relates to her existing convictions and practices. It is to such negotiation or deferral that theologies of religious pluralism may particularly speak.

To focus in this way on intention gives our discussion of MRP a heavily individualistic bias. It reinforces a view of MRP that sees it almost entirely as the product of personal choice, and that sees the purpose and benefits of religion through the lens of the individual alone. Group boundaries, authoritative rules, and communal solidarity are precisely what MRP may be seen to break down or problematize, perhaps as largely arbitrary constructs. But the reality of MRP, even at the individual level, cannot be appreciated without attention to these dimensions as well. It is to this topic that we turn in the next section.

3 Spiritual intuitions

When people enter the space or the practice of a religious "other," they often experience an inner repugnance or discomfort that is prior or even contrary to any conscious objection. These responses are frequently more powerful than those that attach simply to the culturally unfamiliar. Precognitive and at times almost bodily in character, such impulses receive little attention in the literature of religious pluralism, except as obstacles to be overcome. These responses may be contrasted with others that sometimes develop in those who regularly cross into the realm of a religious other, impulses of attraction or satisfaction that come from small, specific capacities to "do as others do" in these spaces—removing one's shoes or adopting a certain posture. These experiences deserve our attention.

In fact, such phenomena have attracted serious consideration from those who consider the interaction of emotion and cognition, particularly around morality. For instance, Jonathan Haidt (2012) has developed a model of moral intuitions that I think might be usefully extended to inform our reflection on spiritual intuitions.[4] His model identifies six categories of moral intuition, related to six sets of concerns: care/harm, fairness/cheating, liberty/oppression, loyalty/betrayal, authority/subversion, and sanctity/degradation. Some of Haidt's research explores peoples' responses to behaviors to which they have an intuitive repugnance. He constructed some hypothetical cases to present to his subjects. In one a family eats the meat of their deceased beloved pet. In another, two young unmarried adults, brother and sister, one of whom is sterile, have sexual relations with each other for a short time and subsequently live untroubled lives. Large majorities expressed distaste for the behaviors in question. Some were willing to ground that disapproval in appeals to authority or in assertions that the behavior was intrinsically degrading or expressed a kind of disloyalty. Others based their objection entirely on the insistence that persons were harmed or treated unfairly in some way, though the case descriptions were explicitly constructed so as to provide no evidence for this.[5]

Haidt's moral categories have no explicit religious reference, but the connections are plain. Some people may not see issues of purity, loyalty, or authority as properly moral questions at all. But it would be hard to miss the fact that these play significant roles in religious traditions, alongside issues of liberty, care, and fairness. In fact, religious traditions, like cultures, constitute somewhat distinctive accounts of all of these values. And these lead to somewhat different profiles as to what evokes revulsion under each of the categories.[6] Haidt notes that fairness, care, and liberty are values often expressed as rights of individuals to be enforced over against groups. Purity, loyalty and authority are values that have particularly to do with obligations or contributions of those within groups toward the health of those groups, as settings within which persons and their relationships can flourish.[7] These values are expressed by individuals, but they refer principally to communities. Religious traditions articulate these values explicitly. Haidt's point is that logical arguments about such values are rooted in moral or spiritual intuitions. These intuitions play more of a role in MRP than our somewhat atypical academic discussions allow.

Arvind Sharma has made the point that our ideas of religious freedom are themselves shaped by assumptions around these same issues. In a recent book (2011), he says that international and United Nations standards for religious freedom are heavily weighted toward the individual and toward the right to propagate a religion and to change from one religion to another. These assumptions are influenced both by monotheistic, missionary traditions and by a Western individualist perspective. But Sharma notes that many religions and cultures place great value on the right of a group to build a community of practice untroubled by contrary proselytism. Many, likewise, might reject the principle that choice to change religions is a necessary index of freedom, since they would deny that religions actually represent strict alternatives. In other words, existing ideas of religious freedom are intrinsic repudiations of some groups' religious intuitions about the nature of liberty and loyalty.

If we look at the case of the *moriscos* instanced above, we can see how powerfully the concerns of sanctity/impurity, loyalty/betrayal, and authority/subversion were at play. In terms of their religious liberty, the Muslims were plainly oppressed. They were forced unfairly to behave in a way contrary to their beliefs. But the unfairness of the situation and the necessity to comply in order to avoid harm were not sufficient to put their minds at rest. They still felt deeply that their behavior was impure, disloyal, and disobedient. Hence they appealed to a religious authority to set a standard for their conduct in this situation, searching for a way to manifest loyalty to their community and employing (subjective) practices by which to dispel the impurity or sacrilege that they experienced as intrinsic in these coerced Christian activities.

I find the consideration of spiritual intuitions illuminating for understanding MRP. For instance, although I have often taken *prasad* in various forms in Hindu temples in the United States, I have almost never done so in India. There is no universal principle by which I can explain this, and no reason I could see to adopt a different intention in participating in the act on one continent from another. But within the Christian community in India, for many believers to whom I have close connections, this activity is perceived (if not actively condemned) as a kind of betrayal. It is a practice that Christians, some very recently, have rejected at great personal cost as associated with forms of oppression they had experienced and as a submission to authorities they reject. This is particularly true among the low-caste Christian communities. This is much less so in the United States, where both Hindu and Christian communities with which I relate have a more positive view of this activity. My interreligious practice has been guided by a mix of intuitions that include intuitions of loyalty and authority which I find difficult to put into words, and which appear, in some sense, to have geographical limits. Both the promise and the limits of MRP come into fuller view when we recognize these dimensions of experience.

4 Spiritual intuitions and education

A friend of mine taught Jewish undergraduates in a very traditional Jewish environment. Her students questioned her about books she was assigning them in a class about religious diversity and many consulted their rabbis to ask, "Can we read these books?" The class expectation, which she regarded as commonplace, aroused a certain tension for these particular observant Jews. The question was significant for them, partly for reasons related to authority and purity, but it was particularly acute because in their own tradition of practice, study was itself a quintessentially religious act. To read a text from another religion was religious participation of the first order, in a manner that might not be true for the devout in all traditions. MRP is often discussed by analogy with fidelity within a family or between married spouses. One recognizes that other relationships are as precious as one's own, but this perception of equality does not mean that one presumes the same intimacy with other's kin as with one's own. However, as this example illustrates, what *counts* as intimacy may differ from one religious family to another.

When I go with my students to visit various religious sites (a Hindu temple, a mosque, a Buddhist monastery), the majority are enthusiastic, quite open to participation in other settings and rituals, and very slow to criticize the host tradition. The most common exception on the last point has to do with issues related to women (restrictions on their participation, requirements for their clothing, segregation in seating). Some students struggle over whether to conform to or respect these practices, which they view as violations of fairness and as intrinsically harmful (judgments that they readily apply to similar practices in their own faith communities). This is often not an abstract conviction, but has a quality of almost physical recoil from the practice at hand.

There are sometimes those for whom physical entry into the building or site itself is a matter of serious debate. This reaction is sometimes fueled by ignorance about the tradition involved or a prior demonization of it. But this is not always true: some of these students come from contexts where they have lived in close and amicable contact with the other religion. The hesitation reflects a stronger sensitivity toward the dimensions of loyalty, authority, and sanctity in religion, dimensions that they value in their own tradition and acknowledge in another. There is a kind of negative reverence for the sacred character of the place in question, a recognition that it represents and conveys real spiritual powers that are not identical with and may not be controllable by the student's own religious resources. They believe that real effects are exercised on a visitor by presence and practice in that place, regardless of the intention with which a visitor may enter. This conviction actually coheres with the understandings among some religious groups, who would affirm that to hear the chanting of a sutra or to physically circumambulate about a shrine or to stand before the image of the deity is necessarily to receive a benefit or karmic effect, independent of one's conscious purpose.

As educators we tend to have analogous assumptions. The mere fact of having entered another religious space, even if it is experienced as confusing or offensive in some ways, necessarily changes us. Its effects cannot be undone. Its colors, sounds, faces, and smells cannot be deleted from all our future engagement with the people and substance of this tradition. Given a visit to the right place at the right time, it is hard to avoid registering at some level the respect in which "another tradition"—a matter of text, history, philosophy, and culture—is also a living reality of faith for neighbors and friends.

In the social sciences, there are highly developed protocols for observation and observer-participation, though the only stated goal of these activities is the gathering of information and the advancement of academic understanding. Given the significantly murkier intentions of dialogue and interreligious learning (which would at least include informational "learning about" but almost always seek something potentially transformative and engaging), it could be argued that the use of religious site visits or the offering of opportunities for multiple religious participation ought to require waivers or approval for human subject research. I realize that my attitude toward site visits for my students has largely viewed the matter from the perspective of an individual. I entertained concerns largely under the headings of care and fairness. This is ironic, because when I consider the sensibility of the hosts for our visits, I attend to a wider range of Haidt's values. I will readily defer to even implicit appeals to authority, loyalty, and purity on their part.

This leads to another question. Some of my students fit a profile we discussed earlier. They have no specific or exclusive religious affiliation, at least none that they feel would bar them from entry into the life of the community they study. Is it the case then that half of Haidt's spectrum is irrelevant to them? Do issues of authority, loyalty, and purity arise only when one definitively belongs to a specific religious community that defines these things? If religious intuitions are shaped largely by factors other than conscious deliberation, then the matter is not so simple. These values continue to be significant, though they may appear in new guises. A "hybrid" person who grows up with family connections to both Islam and Christianity might not lack sensitivity to all the purity considerations of either tradition but instead register those from both. She might have the same repugnance for physical disrespect to the Qu'ran as for physical disrespect to the communion host. Someone who is sociologically a "none" in terms of religious belonging may have an extremely powerful sense of the sanctity of certain places, including traditional religious sites like Lourdes or the Meenakshi Temple in Madurai, even while being indifferent to the teachings of or affiliation with the traditions involved.

In regard to MRP, theology is often seen as a kind of border patrol whose role is to set boundaries and to keep people inside them. But if Haidt is right, intuitions related to authority, purity, and loyalty are not created by theoretical theological arguments. They are natural parts of religious life. Theology may reflect and enforce them. It may also reform them. But people with no religious affiliation have such intuitions. Indeed, it may be the development of alternative frameworks for grounding those intuitions that accounts for their indifference to established traditions.

We might take LGBT persons as an example. Some have struggled with an intuitive repugnance toward their own sexuality, fostered by a particular cultural and religious tradition. They may have experienced a wrenching move away from that outlook and come to a strong intuitive sense of the sanctity of that same sexuality (a sanctity of the sort dominant religious traditions ascribe to heterosexuality). This is a momentous change for an individual, and it seems virtually impossible without a strong group to support it. New, strong intuitions of loyalty and purity are generated in association with the community that enables this transformation of values. It is not that these values are not operational. They are simply not directed toward traditional or institutional religious communities.

It is true that we are all hybrids in some way, that religious traditions are internally diverse, and that boundaries and borders are somewhat arbitrary impositions on the full spectrum of experience. These points are often advanced with primary reference to individuals, with the express purpose of minimizing appeals to authority, loyalty, or purity. But the dialectic among these values is not so simple. There are certainly "hybrid" groups as well as individuals: we might think of Alawites or messianic Jews. Such groups (and the individuals within them) may place a very high value on the intuitions relating to loyalty or authority. This only reinforces the fact that lack of attention to these values may have more to do with a primary focus on autonomous individuals and static institutions than with the reality of hybridity itself.

5 Theology, intention, and intuition

Theologies of religious pluralism, whether explicit and elaborate or implicit, are an important part of the context for MRP. They help coordinate understanding, intention, and intuition. For those with explicit religious identities, such theologies are a way to negotiate or locate levels of MRP. It is the way we explain to ourselves and to those in our community how this activity comports with continued belonging (loyalty) to that community. We do this by reference to the sources of our shared tradition (its authorities). And in the process we may partly reshape the nature of our emotional response to the trappings of the other (our purity intuitions).

I think it is fair to say that the early wave of "pluralist" theologies of religion were largely driven by religious intuitions related to unfairness, harm, and oppression, negative dynamics whose power is multiplied when manifested by groups (Knitter and Hick 1987). The oppression associated with imperialistic forms of Christian mission, the unfairness of studies that compare the best of one tradition with the worst of another, the harm that comes from punishing individuals who deviate from a dogmatic orthodoxy—all these were reasons to attack exclusivist religious views. From this perspective, loyalty, authority, and purity are primarily criticized as tribal and retrograde concerns. "Pluralist" theologies emphasized liberty for the individual to choose among religious options, the fairness of treating all religions as of equal value, and the priority of avoiding any harm that might flow from religious differences. In fact, the entire agenda of this theological project might be seen as a "harm reduction" one.

The "post-modernist" or "post-liberal" theologies of religion on one hand took issue with these approaches along the same axes of thought, arguing for instance that the so-called pluralist views themselves unfairly flatten the various traditions and impose their own values or harm those seeking to preserve their distinctive cultures.[8] But postliberal approaches to religious traditions also take more account of the values of loyalty, authority, and purity themselves. These are integral to traditions as cultural-linguistic systems, helping to constitute distinctive practices and perspectives. The reciprocal relation in which groups form spiritual intuitions in individuals and those personal intuitions help build up religious communities is viewed more positively in these theologies. The project's dominant tenor might be viewed as "learning from difference."

I have written a rather extensive Christian theology of religious pluralism in this second vein, notable for its supposition that religious traditions might offer a variety of real but distinct religious ends (Heim 1995, 2001). From the Christian perspective, this diversity of ends and religious experience is rooted in a complex, Trinitarian God. The divine life has varied dimensions because of that inner complexity. This allows human interaction with the triune God to take different forms. God's channels of relation with creation are open on many frequencies. Human interaction with the divine can "tune" itself to one or more of these dimensions (Heim 2001). There is an ultimate ground for distinct loyalties and authorities that might attach to these distinctive dimensions. As this theology evolved, it provided me an understanding of how and to what extent I may hand myself over to the authority and direction of other religious traditions. It explains (at least to me) the way in which I intend to do what the other does religiously.

I will take Hinduism as a case in point. At the beginning of my career, I had a certain amount of academic knowledge of Hindu tradition and even some striking spontaneous spiritual experience (Heim 2012). However, I was very reserved in regard to any actual practice or participation in Hindu rites or activities. My rather *ad hoc* approach to Hindu practices was clarified as my theology developed, processing both the knowledge and the experience. The *bhakti* devotion to particular deities is rightly regarded as a point of strong similarity between Hinduism and Christianity. But ironically I found my own avenue to actual participation (as opposed to appreciation) through the Advaita tradition (see Rambachan 2006). That is, I approach my participation in the temple *puja* as a recognition and deepening of the pervasive immanence of a single ultimate reality. The overflowing multiplicity of the Hindu pantheon is for me a powerful, albeit different, window on the unitive immanence of God.

Particular devotion to a Hindu deity would intrude on space that I devote to Christ, and I intuitively avoid activities that would progressively define me as, for instance, a Vaishnavite and a particular devotee of Krishna. However, acts of reverence and worship directed at Hindu deities, particularly in their transpersonal character (their manifestations with multiple arms, or in "terrific" or animal forms) are for me an initiation into more radical realization of the "not twoness" of God's presence in all that is. It is in this respect that I believe I can take instruction and share intentions to a large degree with the Hindu worshipper of an Advaitan perspective. It is my identification of this dimension of unitive immanence by reference to Christian sources that allows me to "give over" to the instruction and realization of this spiritual practice. When I actively waft toward my face the light of the flame that has been offered before the image of the deity, I am not a polite guest going through motions that mean nothing to me subjectively. Nor am I simply replicating and relocating an inner intention that would be the same in any act of Christian devotion. My subjective intention is to do as others do, to receive *darshan*. The god whose *darshan* I receive is the one God whose presence is unimaginably varied.

Insofar as a Vaishnavite identifies Vishnu as truly the supreme Lord of all, whose devotees remain lovingly separate from him, I recognize a kindred spirit to my own theistic devotion. In fact, I endorse that theological structure more fully than that of the Advaitan view of the relation of Brahman and *Atman*. But I do not participate in the ritual on that (qualified nondualistic) assumption, precisely because its form more closely maps my own. I could only participate if I in some way substituted Christ for Vishnu, or if the two were jostling in the same space. The more that this framework has been clarified in my thinking outside the moments in the temple, the less conscious such ideas are and the more spiritually present I am in those moments.

When my participation faces toward Buddhism, the issues are different. Intensions come to the fore in Buddhism, for a great many of its practices clearly prescribe what your subjective attitudes and consciousness should be. To follow the *bodhisattva* path means at the very first stage (and throughout) one should generate the quality of mind that is *bodicitta*, or the desire for enlightenment for the sake of others. In temple *puja* an intention is distinct from the outward practice. In meditation, intention or focus is the practice. The intention to quiet and empty the mind of distractions is hard to carry out but not hard to understand, or to reconcile with any number of existing assumptions, religious or nonreligious. The intention to realize emptiness as the true nature of all apparent being is harder still to carry out, and is in direct conflict with some other religious aims (like that of the Advaitan). The intention to attain enlightenment for the sake of all sentient beings is one that may be impossible to form without a strong prior knowledge of the Buddhist elements of wisdom and compassion it combines, and it distinguishes some Buddhists from others. In the case of my own very modest Buddhist practice, experience followed thought, in that it was the development of my theology of religious pluralism that impelled me forward. It was concluding that the realization of emptiness (as opposed to simply calming the mind) was a real possibility, one rooted in a dimension of God's relation with the world, that led me to be able to pass over and more fully accept the authority of the superior wisdom and the instruction that is offered in this tradition. It cleared the way for me to want to desire the realization of emptiness.

These examples are illustrative, not normative. Tacit or explicit, our theologies play a dialectic role in an ongoing process. Our existing theologies of religious pluralism may allow or encourage study and experience of religious diversity. The study and experience then likely overflow the theology that authorized them.

Or it may work the other way around. Our cross-religious experiences may make us aware that we have no theology adequate to them. Either way, we shift the understanding and intentions we bring to religious practices, and over time this can also alter our intuitions. In both of the cases I just noted, my revised theology has partly reshaped my spiritual intuitions, and those altered intuitions have been the means to pass somewhat more fully into the practice of my religious neighbors. To do as the other does is to move in all three of these dimensions. It is in some measure to understand as they do, to intend what they intend, and to be attracted and repelled as they are.

Chapter 3

BOWING BEFORE BUDDHA AND ALLAH?
REFLECTIONS ON CROSSING OVER RITUAL BOUNDARIES

Maria Reis Habito

1 Introduction

"Can you make prostrations before the Buddha?" I was asked by my teacher, Master Hsin Tao, on the day I officially became his disciple by taking my refuge to the Threefold Jewel: the Buddha, the Dharma (the teaching), and the Sangha (the community). It was fall of 1983, and we had just entered the small temple on Ling Jiou Mountain on the east coast of Taiwan, overlooking the Pacific Ocean. To take refuge had not been my idea at all.

I had first met Shih-fu, as Master was called in Chinese, three years earlier, when he still lived in a tiny hermitage on Dragon Lake near the Eastern town of Yi-lan. I was twenty years old at the time and studying Chinese language and culture at Taiwan Normal University, hardly knowing anything at all about Buddhism. That would change in the course of my two-year stay in Taiwan, during which I frequently visited the hermitage on Dragon Lake, while also continuing to go to a Catholic Church on those Sundays that I did not spend at the hermitage. During those two years of intense interfaith encounters with Shih-fu, I realized how little I knew, not only about Buddhism, but more importantly about the Catholic faith in which I had been raised, and which I found difficult to explain in a clear and convincing way to this Buddhist hermit. Continuing my education at Munich University, I immersed myself in the studies of both Chinese Buddhism and philosophy, mainly taking courses offered at the Institut für Christliche Weltanschauung for the latter subject, writing most of my papers on comparative Buddhist-Christian topics. Following the advice of Shih-fu I had also started meditating, and was lucky enough to join Zen retreats that were offered by Father Hugo Enomiya-Lassalle, the pioneer Jesuit priest who had immersed himself in Zen as a missionary to Japan and then taught it to Christians in Europe and Japan.[1]

In 1983, Shih-fu moved from the hermitage near the lake to the mountain to continue his strict ascetic meditation in a cave for two years. "I know that you believe in God," he said to me on that particular morning, "but taking refuge will not bring you into any conflict with your faith. It will help you to always maintain a connection with me as teacher, and with the Buddhist teaching. And after making the prostrations," he continued "can you speak the words of refuge after me? You are not taking refuge to a being out there, but to your own mind of enlightenment, to the Buddha in your heart." And with these words of clarification, my resistance started to give way, and the barriers began to crumble. I made the prostrations and repeated the words of refuge. "I take refuge in the Buddha. I take refuge in the Dharma. I take refuge in the Sangha."

As I was going through the motions of the ceremony, the remainders of my initial doubt and resistance melted away completely, giving way to an experience of spiritual joy that was so deep and vibrant that it felt like a new birth. And yet this new birth did not cause me to give up my Catholic roots, as I have remained a practicing Catholic ever since.

For me, taking refuge was not an act of "converting" to Buddhism, but a further step on the path that had begun in my initial encounter with Shih-fu. This encounter, I reasoned, would not have happened without divine guidance, without providence. How likely was it for a young German Catholic woman to meet a Buddhist hermit in far-away Taiwan? Given this opportunity to visit and study with a Buddhist Master, would I rise to the challenge and take it up or not? I decided I should take it, and the sense of spiritual joy I experienced three years later during the refuge ceremony was a clear indication for me that I was on the right spiritual path (Reis Habito 2001: 7–51).[2]

The questions of whether or not one can take refuge in the Buddha and still remain Catholic, or of what dual practice entails, are not the subject of this chapter. These topics have been explored elsewhere.[3] Instead, I look at the topic of ritual participation from the point of view of someone who personally has crossed boundaries, while at the same time remaining very sensitive to the necessity of respecting boundaries of a given religious tradition in an interfaith context. My reflections are based on my personal experiences as dual practitioner of both the Catholic and Zen Buddhist traditions, and on the interfaith work I have been engaged in for many years as the International Program Director of the Taiwan-based Museum of World Religions[4] and think-tank member of the Elijah Interfaith Institute.[5]

In the first part of this chapter, I will examine the complex issue of ritual participation in a Buddhist context from different angles—from my experience as a Catholic Zen practitioner and teacher of the Sanbo (Three Treasures) Zen lineage,[6] facilitating retreats with Christians, Jews, and Muslims, and as a scholar deeply engaged in interreligious dialogue and friendship. I find the crossing of boundaries to be a deeply personal and transformative experience also reflected in the writings of my friend Yossi Klein Halevi, especially in his book *At the Entrance to the Garden of Eden* (2002), where he describes the phenomenon in a Jewish-Muslim context, one that is both religiously and politically more challenging, given the situation in Israel/Palestine. I include his inspiring example of crossing boundaries in differing religious traditions in part two of this chapter. This leads up to the concluding part three, in which I will reflect on the implications of the individual examples of crossing boundaries and on the question of whether and how the lessons learned from these can be applied to the wider field of interreligious relations.

2 Bowing to the Buddha

Raising one's palms and bowing before entering or exiting the meditation hall, before sitting down and after getting up from the cushion after meditation, is a basic ritual in a Japanese Zen retreat. This ritual was adapted in the retreats that I joined at the Franciscan monastery in Bavaria, where Father Enomiya-Lassalle was teaching. Raising one's palms is explained as a sign of respect to Western, non-Buddhist participants of a retreat. By raising our palms we honor the sacredness of the room that we enter and of the other people present. This ritual does not pose any difficulties to Christian or nonreligious participants in retreats who appreciate its gracefulness; it is not considered to be "bowing to the Buddha". Likewise, the full prostrations before the altar that, in the context of a Zen retreat are traditionally done before and after the teacher's talk and at the end of the day after the chanting, are explained as symbolizing "the Emptying of Self", not as prostrations before the Buddha. Since it is explained clearly that this act did not consist in bowing to a deity, Christian participants saw no problem in joining these prostrations, neither in the monastery in Germany (which in any case did not have a statue of the Buddha on the altar) nor at the Zendo in Kamakura, where Yamada Koun Roshi, teacher of Father Enomiya-Lassalle and other priests and nuns who now teach the Sanbo Zen lineage, held retreats. The third element, the chanting of Buddhist texts, was also easily adopted in those retreats, and various teachers added Christian passages to the chanting book, depending upon where the retreats were held.

But the ease with which many Christians adapt to these two basic rituals in a Zen retreat is not often shared by Jews and Muslims. In one retreat I held at the small temple at the Mahabodhi International Meditation Centre in Leh/Ladakh in 2010, a young Jewish woman was deeply troubled by the bowing and the prostrations, saying that she would not dare to imagine what other Jews would think if they saw her doing this. I understood her perfectly—there were Buddhist statues on the altar, and even with the explanation that bowing and making prostrations is nothing but an acknowledgment and expression of our enlightened nature, she did not feel convinced. Perhaps this might have been different if there had been no Buddhist statues in the room—but we were in the context of a Buddhist monastery. If she came from an Orthodox Jewish background, depending on the strictness of interpretation, she would not even have been allowed to enter a room in which statues of the Buddha were present. One half of the other participants were Ladakhi Buddhists, who devotedly made their prostrations to the Buddhas on the altar. The rest were Europeans, either secular or practicing Buddhists, who readily joined everything. Although I told the young Jewish woman that it was perfectly fine not to bow and not to join the prostrations, she chose to continue, uneasily, not wanting to be the only one "sticking out".

In the first Zen retreat I helped coordinate in Israel in 2012, in consultation with the Jewish co-organizers of the retreat and out of respect for their sensibilities, we decided not to do any prostrations at all, but nevertheless to bow when entering the Zen hall. It had been agreed not to place any figure of the Buddha on the altar, only flowers and a candle. At the end of the retreat, one participant said in the final sharing that his initial resistance to the bowing had melted away when he saw the Japanese teacher bow to his food. This was the moment when he understood bowing as a deep and beautiful expression of gratefulness. With this new understanding he had no more problems with the bowing. In the following retreat in Israel, in the fall of that year, four young Palestinian men from Yata participated. They bowed when entering the Zen hall, but, as they explained and showed to me, they did it in their own way. They briefly raised their palms to their forehead when entering the Zen Hall, but they did not bend their body, because, as they said, "we will only bow before Allah".

Buddhist sensitivities regarding what comprises appropriate behavior in a Zen hall or temple in the presence of an image or statue of a Buddha or bodhisattva can also be quite different from those of Western practitioners who are not culturally Buddhist. At one time we had Buddhist nuns from Master Hsin Tao's monastery in Taiwan staying at the Maria Kannon Zen Center in Dallas. When some of the Western members of the Center stretched their legs in the Zen hall after a sit, the nuns pointed out that this was not appropriate, because, as they said, "you never point your feet in direction of the Buddha". In Taiwan, one of the nuns got very upset when she found a Jewish participant of a conference of the Elijah Interfaith Institute sitting inside the temple on a cushion with his legs stretched out in the direction of the altar. Her displeasure had to do with the fact that this participant, who was a regular meditator, had requested special permission to meditate in the small temple-hall. To the nun, it seemed that a meditator would know how to behave properly in a temple and not offend "Lord Buddha" by pointing his feet at him in a seemingly disrespectful way.

But her being upset had to do with more than just this. This interfaith conference, which included Orthodox rabbis among the participants, had required great flexibility and effort from the Buddhist hosts. For example, the conference hall of the monastery, which was sometimes also used for Buddhist ceremonies, had to be completely devoid of any Buddhist statues or images, since most Orthodox rabbis would not enter a non-Jewish religious space that is used for worship. The altar in the conference hall was therefore removed (as were the statues) in order to accommodate everyone. While the monastery is accustomed to hosting interreligious events in conjunction with the Museum of World Religions in Taipei (which was also founded by Dharma Master Hsin Tao), and in spite of the fact that there is great sensitivity to the dynamics of interreligious dialogue, removing the statues from the conference hall was not readily understood by, nor emotionally easy for, the monastery personnel who carried out the orders. What and how much can be achieved in interreligious dialogue in a case like this, where it is not possible for some participants to even enter the sacred space of the religious other?

The closing ceremony of the conference was not held in the Buddha hall of the monastery, as would usually be the case. However, the Buddhist hosts did not want to send everyone off without a prayer for the peace of the world, and thus the prayer was offered in a neutral space, a hall inside the Museum, where dinner was served. The hall was adorned by a statue of the Buddha, which could be considered a cultural artifact, since this was a museum, not a place of worship. The Buddhist hosts thus thought that inviting all participants to place a lighted candle in front of this Buddha as an expression of the prayer for peace would not offend any sensitivities—in this however they were mistaken. Taken by surprise, some of the Orthodox rabbis stood up and demonstratively turned their backs to the Buddha and the procession of candle bearers, to signal that they were no part of this, as the other participants bowed down to put their candles in front of the Buddha.

This situation obviously caused misgivings on all sides. These examples are not given in order to criticize or blame the rabbis, however. They were not as free to step beyond the boundaries of their prescribed religious observances as some of the participants from the other religions. Or, one could even go as far as to say that they took putting a candle in front of the Buddha seriously, seeing it as an expression of religious devotion that they had to eschew if they wanted to uphold their own religious tenets. In this they were not different from our Muslim participants in the Zen retreat who would only bow before Allah, or the young Jewish woman who had qualms about making the prostrations. Not joining the candle ceremony was not meant as a show of disrespect to their Buddhist hosts, but as a signal to the other Jewish participants who had joined the candle offering that they had crossed a boundary.

The dilemma here is the following: for cultural Buddhists, bowing before the Buddha or making prostrations is a religious act of devotion, not different from a Christian making the sign of the cross. For Western Buddhists, or secular people practicing meditation, this is not necessarily the case, since Buddhism has, for better or worse, become so embedded in secular culture in the West that a statue of a Buddha may be found about anywhere, from a pizza parlor to a massage center. In such a context, bowing does not necessarily express any religious adherence or devotion at all. Those participants in a retreat or interfaith setting who do not wish to bow may actually be the ones who understand the religious significance of the act better than those who have the more liberal interpretation. In other words, to make the bowing or prostration acceptable to non-Buddhists, it needs to be emptied of its distinctive religious content. But are rituals that are emptied of a distinctive religious content desirable as a lowest common denominator in an interfaith setting? Are they transformative? Do they create a greater sense of community than a heart-to-heart dialogue or a shared meal between practitioners of different religions?

Since I took refuge in 1983, I am no longer a "non-Buddhist", but a practitioner of both traditions. This means in practical and ritual terms that when I attend Catholic Mass (which I do almost every week), I fully join every movement of the body, spirit, and mind culminating in the Eucharist, for me the most intimate moment of receiving the body and blood of Christ, both on the personal and on the communal level, which are completely one—the body of Christ. When I come home to my Buddhist monastery in Taiwan, I bow when entering the main hall, participate in the chanting of sutras and the prostrations that start and end the prayer service, and join in the meditation. For me, bowing, and especially the prostrations before the altar, regardless of whether there is a Buddhist statue present on it or not, are expressions of boundless gratitude, of humility, and of the prayer that all may realize their true Self and be free from suffering. Do I address this prayer to God or to Buddha? This question makes sense on a level where God and Buddha point to different conceptual realities. I do not claim that they are the same. But on the level where I enter prayer, embody it, and offer myself up with my whole heart to the universe, my only answer to the question would be: "I truly don't know. I am before a Mystery beyond human words and concepts."

3 Bowing before Allah

In his book *At the Entrance to the Garden of Eden*, Yossi Klein Halevi describes in fascinating detail his experiences of joining a religious prayer line and dance with Sufis in the Holy Land. The book itself is an inspiring account of his spiritual journey as a practicing Jew among Christians and Muslims in the Holy Land in search for a common language. In the course of this search, Halevi befriended the Sufi Sheikh Ibrahim in the West Bank village of Karawa, who brought him and his friend Elijahu McLean, a well-known interfaith activist, along to Sheikh Saud's community in Ramla, near Tel Aviv, during an evening close to Eid al-Adha, the festival commemorating Abraham's sacrifice of Ishmael. Entering the crowded prayer room, Halevi was filled with a sense of foreboding when an elderly man bluntly asked him whether they were Jews, then harshly remonstrating Sheikh Ibrahim for bringing them there. With the young men in the room keenly staring at them from a distance and the older men simply pretending they were not there, Halevi wondered if his coming here had not been a great mistake: "We had come to a place where we did not belong. Maybe the premise of my journey was flawed. What was the point of imposing myself on a faith that wanted to be left alone?" (Halevi 2002: 102).

But it was time for evening prayers, and the men arranged themselves in a straight prayer line, which expresses the equality of the Muslim believers before God. Halevi and his friend stepped into the prayer line, nobody stopped them, and Sheikh Ibrahim, who led the prayers, adjusted his shoulders so that he would be in full alignment with the others:

> 'Allahu akbar,' he called out, God is great, his voice deep and commanding. 'Allaaa-hu' he repeated, like a long exhalation, then quickly expelled 'akbar,' as if any human description of His grandeur was superfluous. Israelis dreaded that call to prayer as incitement to murder: the terrorist's cry before pressing the detonator on a crowded bus. But Ibrahim restored to those words their benign intensity. I entered the flow of Muslim surrender, so caught in the rapid

hypnotic movement that I forgot my self-consciousness, even forgot to feel elated for having broken the barrier of Islamic prayer. *Allahu akbar*: bow and stand. *Allahu akbar*: kneel and prostrate and kneel. *Allahu akbar*: prostrate and kneel. *Allahu akbar*: stand. And again and again, over and over, disorienting and reorienting, aligning the self with the prayer line and offering the body to God. *Allahu akbar*: prostrate and kneel. I wanted to remain prostrate, embraced by surrender, but the will of the line pulled me up to my knees. My body lost solidity, as if its bones had been extracted; turning to water, a particle in the wave of prayer. (Halevi 2002: 102)

The prayer was followed by the *zikr* dance, led by Sheikh Saud, which lasted for about an hour. Participating in the prayer and the dance had not only completely changed Halevi's feelings toward the place and the other participants, but theirs toward him as well:

I felt charged, cleansed, as if I'd been submerged underwater and had learned to breathe in a new way. To my surprise, I felt purged of my unease in this place, at home among its lovers of God. They obviously felt the same way toward me. For the first time, we made eye contact and exchanged smiles. We were at once too exhausted, too energized, and to exposed to hide behind wariness. Even though we didn't know each other's names, we had together inhaled the name of God, joined in the brotherhood of the *zikr*. (Halevi 2002: 104)

By the time Halevi and his friend departed after conversations and tea, Mahmoud, the old man who had initially asked them if they were Jews, had completely warmed up to them, expressing his regret that he had never been to any services at the synagogue across the street, and that members of the synagogue had never come to their place either. "Come back soon," Mahmoud urged as they took their leave, "and bring back more Jews like you" (Halevi 2002: 106).

For the feast of Lailat al Miraj, commemorating the Prophet Muhammad's night journey from Mecca to Jerusalem and from this world to the other world, Sheikh Ibrahim invited Halevi and the late Rabbi Menachem Froman to join a *zikr* dance held in the Nuseirat refugee camp in Gaza. Rabbi Froman was the founder of the Gush Enumin, a messianic movement that led settlers into the territory captured by Israel in the 1967 war. But he was a passionate advocate of befriending and working with Muslims for peace, based on his conviction that peace with the Palestinians was only possible in sensibility and appeal to religious ideals.[7]

Halevi describes how he had to overcome his own deep fears in accepting this invitation, since he had once been an occupation soldier conducting house-to-house searches in Nuseirat. What would be the attitude of Sheikh Abdul Rahimin and his followers to a Kippa-wearing Jew towing along a settler rabbi? But they were received with warmth, and invited to a meal with the Sheikh and his followers. Halevi was struck by the fact that he knew the faces of the men "with bad teeth and grey skin"—that they were "our gardeners and waiters. But I'd never seen them in their white holiday robes and green caps, drinking tea from delicate cups and reclining like royalty." This led to his realization that "one of the sins of the occupation … was that it kept us from respecting the dignity of Islam" (Halevi 2002: 303).

Finally, the *zikr* dance began with cymbals and drums, and Halevi and Rabbi Froman entered the circle, coordinating their movements with the words of prayer: *La illaha ill'Allah*. There is no God but Allah, repeating the words "slowly, then faster, until the word merge[d] into one word, one breath. We sway[ed] in unison, a dance of controlled ecstasy balancing effusiveness and restraint, stripping way inhibitions but avoiding hysteria, gradually losing ourselves in heightened ground" (Halevi 2002: 305). In the course of the movements, bowing and exhaling, rising and inhaling, Halevi forgot "to worry about being observed, the outsider trying to keep in step. I [was] no longer an Israeli with a kipah in a Gaza mosque but part of the great human wave of surrender." Rabbi Froman broke from the circle in ecstasy and cried out "Allah! Allah!",[8] drawing Halevi's comment that "after all these years of lonely search for peace with Islam, he [was] finally embraced by Muslim prayer" (Halevi 2002: 305).

Here is a striking example of crossing religious boundaries in a situation that is both religiously and politically challenging. Halevi and Rabbi Froman were not spiritual seekers who had left their own religion behind in search for new grounds, but were practicing Jews, deeply committed to their own tradition but likewise open to receiving and being received by their Muslim brothers in a very intimate way—by taking a risk and fully joining their devotions. The shared experience of prayer was a deeply transformative religious experience for both sides. It allowed the Muslim hosts, despite the situation of political occupation, to extend their traditional hospitality, grace, and friendship to their Jewish brothers, a former soldier and a settler rabbi at that, dispelling mutual distrust. Even more, the Muslim hosts admitted outsiders into their most intimate devotions—prayer and a *zikr* dance on the night celebrating the Prophet's ascent. For Halevi and Rabbi Froman, the experience of being "part of the great human wave of surrender" confirmed their intuition that peace in the Holy Land will be achievable, but only when Jews and Muslims learn to love each other and respect each other's religion. Rabbi Froman was a person unfazed by the fact that few of the 3,000 residents of the Tekoa settlement agreed with his outreach to Muslims, which included meetings with many Sheikhs—even with Yasir Arafat and Hamas chieftains— and threatened to expel him.[9] Joining a *zikr* dance for him was possible precisely because of his deep commitments—to his own religious roots and community as well as to his endeavor of creating peace with his Muslim brothers whose religion he deeply respected and loved.

4 Conclusion

In this chapter I started from a personal experience of crossing boundaries, as a Catholic Christian, in taking refuge with my Buddhist master, understanding this act as not contrary to but in accordance with the will of God. My experience of spiritual peace and joy, in spite of initial apprehension and reluctance, is mirrored in the account of Yossi Klein Halevi in his experiences of crossing the barriers of Islamic prayer by joining the Muslim *zikr* dance, dissolving his ego and all of its fears in "the great human wave of surrender". One could argue that these acts of breaking ritual boundaries were strictly personal, and that they do not have any significance for the vast majority of other Christians or Jews. This is true to a certain extent. While I am happy to share my own experiences, I would not think of decreeing that all other Christians also need to take refuge with a Buddhist Master, unless they were already specifically considering this step and asking for my advice on the matter. In much the same way, Halevi would not specifically ask other Jews to join a Muslim prayer line. And yet these acts have borne fruit, in his life and in mine, that go beyond the strictly personal in several ways, and have influenced our respective spiritual paths. What I have experienced in my turn to Buddhist practice as a Christian, and what Halevi experienced in his explorations across the Abrahamic traditions, are deeply personal events intertwined with our own individual spiritual journeys, for which we can only be truly grateful, as they have been transformative in my life and in his, in differing ways.

In my case, taking refuge strengthened my bond with Shih-fu and the Buddhist community, as well as shedding light on my own quest for a spiritual path that completely integrates my Christian identity with my Buddhist studies and the practice of meditation. Taking refuge also deepened my commitment to work for interfaith understanding and peace. As such, it benefits the wider human community. For example, through a series of ongoing dialogues between Buddhists and Muslims initiated by Shih-fu right after the events of 9/11,[10] we have been able to forge stronger bonds of understanding and friendship between these two communities. In a similar way, Halevi's ongoing commitment to working for understanding, friendship, and peace between Jews and Muslims, now as member of the Shalom Hartman Institute, was strengthened by his spiritual experience of "bowing to Allah" in a line of surrender, together with his Muslim brothers.

During my most recent stay in Israel in May 2013, I discovered some fruit borne of the willingness of Rabbi Froman's free spirit to break religious boundaries. At that time, I gave a one-day contemplative retreat in the Old City that brought together a group of Palestinians from south of Hebron and Yeshiva students from the settlement of Otniel, located in the West Bank close to Hebron. The retreat was organized through the Interfaith Encounter Organization and involved an introduction to meditation and conversations on contemplative practices in both traditions. When I asked the Yeshiva students what had motivated them to pursue interfaith encounters with Palestinians, they said they had been inspired by Rabbi Froman's example. In this retreat, needless to say, the meditation involved no prostration, no bowing and no chanting. But participants from both sides spoke in their sharing about the powerful experience of simply sitting face-to-face in silence, mindfully breathing in and out together. For the Palestinian participants, the crossing of boundaries was perhaps even more challenging than for the religious students from the settlements. While the Palestinians had to literally cross the political boundaries to enter into Israel on one hand, they also had to cross the boundaries of their own fears, not only of the always unpredictable reaction of Israeli soldiers at the checkpoints, but more importantly of being "discovered" by other Palestinians and treated as collaborators and traitors because they met with Israeli settlers.

While breaking a religious boundary is always an act of courage, necessary for spiritual growth, this act obviously is more easily "committed" on an individual rather than a communal basis. When my first Zen teacher, Father Enomiya-Lassalle, after two years of study with the Japanese Zen Master Harada Sogaku, published his book *Zen, A Way to Enlightenment*, he was ordered by the Vatican to stop publishing on the subject. Enomiya-Lassalle continued his own practice and started teaching, and eventually the ban on publishing on this topic was lifted after the Second Vatican Council. His last and most important Zen teacher, Yamada Koun Roshi, also broke the boundaries of his tradition by expressly stating that Christians do not have to give up their own beliefs in order to become enlightened, in contrast to what his own teacher Yasutani Hakuun and the majority of Buddhists at the time would have thought on the topic.

Different communities obviously have different boundaries and ranges of flexibility within those boundaries. As I attempted to show in the first part of the chapter, even such a simple act as putting one's palms together and bowing in a gesture of respect is not so simple if investigated more deeply. The implications of this act vary from person to person, and differences of understanding need to be respected. A gray area surrounds the question of who can pray together with whom and how; who can share the religious devotions of others and how. No general rules can be deduced from individual examples.

During the Elijah Interfaith Institute conference mentioned above, which involved the Board of World Religious Leaders of the Institute, we did have joint prayer times every day for all of the participants—Buddhist, Hindus, Sikhs, Jews, Christians, and Muslims—in a format that we keep in all of those biannual meetings: the groups pray in proximity to each other, in adjacent rooms or a shared space in a great conference hall, within hearing distance from one another, but keeping to their own traditional prayers. Participants are free to choose whether they want to join their own religious group or participate in the prayers or meditations of others. I personally find this format the most satisfying, since it creates a sense of being together while respecting differences, and without changing the texts of the prayers in a way that would make them generic for all religions, thereby losing the distinct spirituality and heritage of a tradition.

A similar approach to prayers was devised by Pope Benedict XVI in the prayer meeting held in Assisi in 2011. There was no joint prayer in public, but participants prayed in their own rooms at the same time and then came together for a shared pledge of peace. If we can allow each other space in this way, being together in times of prayer, but not necessarily in the same room or saying the same words of prayer or making the same movements, then we can feel at home and flourish in our differences, until we find the next step for the communal crossing of boundaries in a creative and meaningful way.

Chapter 4

ENLIGHTENED PRESUPPOSITIONS OF (SPIRITUALLY MOTIVATED) CROSS-RITUAL PARTICIPATION

Walter Van Herck

1 Introduction

This chapter is a philosophical approach to the question at hand, namely: What happens when people participate in prayers, ceremonies, and rituals of a religious tradition which is not their own? Perhaps we can term the phenomenon *cross participation*, and the person who becomes involved in this type of activity, a participating outsider. The position I will try to defend is critical of this phenomenon. My criticism does not aim at stopping people from doing what they are doing. Contrary to some ideologies, I am not of the opinion that philosophers should try to change people or the world we are living in. Others are more qualified. But understanding what is happening is a philosophical task. In a number of cases, the cross participation practices do rest on specific presuppositions concerning the nature of ritual. Because of these specific views on the nature of ritual presupposed in these practices, it cannot be excluded that such views—if given broad dissemination—will ultimately transform our concepts of ritual and religion. This transformation will probably be welcomed by some and rejected by others.

Among the reasons given for this behavior, the following are named: (i) curiosity; (ii) the search for understanding; (iii) an educational opportunity; (iv) a powerful token of interreligious hospitality raising the spirit of dialogue to a new level; (v) a religious expression of "being on the way to the ineffable"; and (vi) a compliance with social pressure, as in the case of religiously mixed marriages. The first three motivations all come down to wanting to learn more about an unknown religion and its rituals. The fourth motivation is perhaps more important. By cross participation, or by allowing and inviting cross participation, one hopes to send a message of recognition and hospitality. Formal recognition of the rights and freedoms of a religious group is often guaranteed by law, but a more subjective form of recognition of people is never given in a direct way, but only indirectly, by appreciating what they appreciate. Since religion is of the highest value to immigrant and minority populations, a recognition of their religious customs and traditions is a way of welcoming these groups. This can be done by (partially) participating in their rituals or by inviting them and their dignitaries to attend religious services of the majority religion on specific occasions. Obviously, religion is here used to attain political goals. The cross participation is aimed at signaling this recognition. The sixth motivation is the most obvious and perhaps the most ubiquitous.

In this chapter I will focus on the fifth motivation. The fifth motivation is also intended to communicate a message, but its character is more individualist. In this case cross participation is indicative of one's (individual) spiritual journey which will lead one—it is hoped—beyond words and rituals. This attitude is typical of a mystical-experiential view of religion. Religion is thought to be a quest that detaches people from all materiality (Van Herck 2007). In the end it also disengages from and surpasses specific religions, institutions, traditions, symbols, and rituals. By cross participating one signals one has reached a stage which goes beyond the demarcations of traditional religious groups.

2 The enlightened view of ritual

One could term the view of ritual which is presupposed in this type of motivation for cross participation, an enlightened view of ritual. An illustration of this view can be found in Diderot's *Encyclopédie*, the warehouse *par excellence* of Enlightenment concepts. Under the heading *cérémonies* a reflection on political and religious ceremonies or rituals is offered. The article ends with the following thought.

> When it comes to the question of the necessity of ceremonies for a cult, its answer depends on the answer to another question, namely whether religion is made for the philosopher alone or for philosopher and people? In the first case, one could perhaps hold that ceremonies are superfluous, because they have no other goal than to remind us of the objects of our faith and of our duties of which the philosopher reminds himself very well without the aid of sensible signs. But religion is made for all men without distinction. ... As the prodigies of nature bring the philosopher continuously to the existence of a creating God, so in Christianity for example ceremonies bring the Christian continuously to the law of a crucified God. Sensible representations, of whatever nature they may be, have a prodigious power over the imagination of the common people: never could the eloquence of Anthony do what the robes of Caesar did. *Quod litteratis est scripture, hoc idiotis proestat picture* (Images are to the illiterate what writing is to the literate), says Saint Gregory the Great, lib. IX, let. ix. (Diderot and d'Alembert 2011: vol. 2, 829)[1]

The author of this article—Diderot himself—hopes to save ritual from superfluity by assigning it a function, namely, to bring the truths and laws of a religion to the common people. In fact, rather than saving ritual from redundancy, this claim attests to the exchangeability of ritual. Everything which ritual attempts to attain can be reached by another, shorter route: the philosophical exercise of the mind. Philosophy is the shortcut that brings you everything that ritual can offer, but without the sensible representations and signs. Ritual has a function, but its function is not unique. Ritual is irreplaceable for the common people, but not for philosophers.

Here and elsewhere in the *Encyclopédie* it is clear that rituals are disdained. They have nothing specific to offer and they are instrumental to higher (mostly moral) truths. Rituals are means to more important ends. In this way a specific ritual is completely arbitrary—it can be replaced by anything, for example, another ritual which attains the same goals. This idea is not specific to the *Encyclopédie*, but can be found in many modern authors from the Reformation[2] onward, from Spinoza (Lemmens 2010) to Kant and beyond. It testifies to a modern misunderstanding of ritual, which sees it not as an end in itself—not as a category *sui generis*—but as a mere expression of a concept which can be apprehended prior to the ritual or independently of it. This last element refers to a distinctive intellectualist trend in Western culture.

3 Intellectualist presuppositions

The enlightened presupposition is related to a much greater intellectualist prejudice in Western civilization. It consists in giving theory and knowledge an absolute priority over practice.[3] Since intelligent practices always comprise the application of some rule or insight, the idea is commonly held that to perform a practice is really to do two things. It is to do a bit of theory and then a bit of practice, as Ryle (Ryle 1980: 30) remarks. Theorizing is an autonomous activity; practice is not. It involves, next to its evidently active phase, a preceding theoretical phase. Practice depends on theory, but not the other way around. It is—again in the words of Ryle—a "stepchild" of theory. There is also a more sentimental variant of this in which the anterior element is not insight or knowledge, but emotion. Art, for example, is often regarded as the expression of an earlier emotion. Of course, art also requires the mastery of mediums like paint or clay, and as such it is a combination of an intelligent practice and an emotional practice. In both cases, the practice expresses an anterior mental act, be it rational or emotional. Ryle has posed serious questions regarding this intellectualist model. As he makes clear, theorizing is itself a practice that can be done well or poorly. If this means that theorizing must itself involve the application of theory, we end up in an infinite regress. That is why at the beginning of a practice stand imitation and trust (Wittgenstein 1979: §§ 139, 160, 493). Gilbert Ryle's famous analysis of "knowing that" and "knowing how" is directed at pointing out that—contrary to the dominating opinion—knowing *how* has priority over knowing *that* (Ryle 1971). In the same way, Michael Polanyi's work (1967) on personal and tacit knowledge wants to correct the intellectualist and objectivist self-image we seem to have.

Granted of course that some of our practices do involve the application of theory—which should not lead us into thinking that theory is primary—we must make a second distinction between intelligent and traditional practices. Building a bridge would be an example of an intelligent practice. It would involve a theoretical phase followed by a practical phase. First, theoretical insight in the physical properties of the building materials is necessary, coupled with the physics of power vectors and so on. The design that follows is a theoretical and conceptual exercise. Only when this intellectual work is complete can the building process— the practical phase—begin.

Traditional practices, on the other hand, have a totally different structure because they do not result from a prior intellectual investigation. Speaking your mother tongue for example is not the result of linguistic research or design. Though grammatical insight into your native language is of course possible, the practice of speaking a native language is not the product of theoretical insights.

Now we can understand Ryle's antiintellectualist position as saying that of these two practices, the traditional practices are the most fundamental. Intelligent practices depend upon the unreflective mastery of our mother tongue, of elementary ways of dealing with material objects and other people. But given the success of science and technology, intelligent practice has become in the minds of many the prototypical model to think about human action and behavior. In consequence, one tends to understand traditional practices according to the model of intelligent practice. Ritual is a good case in point. Although a traditional practice, one tends to seek the prior opinions and insights upon which the ritual practice is based. One wants to know which thoughts, feelings, insights, and opinions the ritual "expresses." Ritual is thought of as an expression of the prior beliefs concerning supernatural beings shared by its celebrants. Ludwig Wittgenstein (1971: 29) reproaches James Frazer for this intellectualist style of interpreting ritual: "When he explains to us, for example, that the king must be killed in his prime because, according to the notions of the savages, his soul would not be kept fresh otherwise, we can only say: where that practice and these views go together, the practice does not spring from the view, but both of them are there." Wittgenstein's intuitions go in the opposite direction: "A religious symbol does not rest on any *opinion*" (Wittgenstein 1971: 30).

4 The myth-ritual debate

In religion, the theoretical factor is represented by myths, creeds, and dogmas. The practical element is found mainly in rituals, observances, and ethical behavior. In philosophy and anthropology there are—next to theories which give separate explanations for myths and rituals—theories which maintain that myth and ritual necessarily operate together. The origins of the idea that myths arose in connection with rituals are found in the introductory pages of William Robertson Smith's *Lectures on the Religion of the Semites* (1889). Smith calls the modern habit of looking at ancient religion from the side of belief "anachronistic" (Smith

1998: 1). The modern scholar looks first for the "creed" which he thinks will provide the key to rituals and practices. Instead, one should according to Smith look from the side of practice. Most ancient religions will not even have a "creed" or anything that resembles it. What comes closest to a theoretical component is myth. Myth, according to Smith, is secondary. It provides an explanation of "the circumstances under which the rite first came to be established, by the command or by the direct example of the god" (Smith 1998: 28). In so doing, myths attach meanings to rites—meanings which are often rather vague and diverse. In Smith's words:

> So far as myths consist of explanations of ritual their value is altogether secondary, and it may be affirmed with confidence that in almost every case the myth was derived from the ritual, and not the ritual from the myth; for the ritual was fixed and the myth was variable, the ritual was obligatory and faith in the myth was at the discretion of the worshipper. (Smith 1998: 28)

The modern, intellectualist approach turns things the other way around: ritual is the enactment or application of myth. According to the anthropologist Edward Tylor (1871) for example, myth is a form of primitive science. In his perspective, myth is primary and ritual is nothing more than its magical-technological application in order to control the universe.

The fact that the myth-ritual debate is still ongoing can only mean that the way in which myth and ritual operate together is crucial for our understanding of ritual. Nor is it without consequence for our understanding of what happens when an outsider joins a ritual. Does the participating outsider want to express an opinion through the use of ritual? If so, he is in the grips of an Enlightened, intellectualist view of ritual. The problem seems to be that ritual action and other types of action are treated in the same way. The specificity of ritual action is ignored.

5 The specificity of ritual action

The anthropologists Humphrey and Laidlaw have devoted a book, *The Archetypal Actions of Ritual. A Theory of Ritual Illustrated by the Jain Rite of Worship* (1994) to the question of how ritual action differs from other types of action. They too start by noticing that contemporary Western people seem unappreciative of the unique character of ritual action, which is regarded as a means to communicate or express specific beliefs and meanings. Because this is the prime purpose, alterations and adaptations which can convey their intentions and beliefs are allowed.

> Different again in their attitudes to ritual are post-Reformation Protestant contexts where faith in the efficacy of ritual has been terminally undermined. In this case, churches conduct their own service with the degree of ritualization they wish. Thus the service may be changed from time to time, with a view to engaging the religious participation of different congregations. With this has

come the triumph of the idea that this changeable ritual is, or should be, only a way of communicating or expressing the religious beliefs and moral ideas of the participants. So pervasive is this idea that ritual on its own, without subjective convictions, comes, for many, to seem mere mumbo-jumbo. (Humphrey and Laidlaw 1994: 8)

The idea that ritual is essentially communicative and expressive has almost become a dogma in anthropology according to them. The reason why anthropologists begin to follow this wrong track is obvious. As anthropologists they question people about their ritual practices and in this way they learn certain ideas. They then fallaciously think that the purpose of the ritual is to communicate or express these ideas. This however is not the purpose of the ritual, as the people already know these ideas (Humphrey and Laidlaw 1994: 73). Humphrey and Laidlaw see the same intellectualist danger cropping up: "This attempt to interpret ritual as functioning to communicate what the anthropologist has learned or surmised, can lead to a contrived intellectualisation of ritual" (Humphrey and Laidlaw 1994: 74).

What they want to do is to question the anthropological orthodoxy that rituals are essentially systems of meaning (Humphrey and Laidlaw 1994: 36). Two ways in which ritual has been seen by anthropologists are: "a distinct category of events; and as an ever-present aspect of all actions. ... Both these approaches are mistaken" (Humphrey and Laidlaw 1994: 64). The first possibility is untrue because the activities which are performed in rituals—like eating, washing, offering, greeting, and so on—can also be done in nonritualized ways (Humphrey and Laidlaw 1994: 72). Not *what* one does, but *how* one acts is essential to ritual. The second possibility is obviously a definition that is far too broad. There are completely secular modes of acting. So, more positively formulated, ritual is "a quality which action can come to have—a special way in which acts may be performed" (Humphrey and Laidlaw 1994: 64). What they call "ritualization" is a particular, occasional modification of an intrinsic feature of all action, namely its intentionality (Humphrey and Laidlaw 1994: 73). The definition they give of ritualization is as follows: "Action may be said to be ritualized when the actor has taken up what we shall call the 'ritual commitment', a particular stance with respect to his or her own action" (Humphrey and Laidlaw 1994: 88).

Humphrey and Laidlaw describe four characteristics of ritual commitment: non-intentional, stipulated, elemental or archetypal, and apprehensible. With "non-intentional" they mean that although people have intentions and accord meanings to their ritual acts, these intentions are not constitutive of the ritual act as ritual. The identity of the act does not depend on the agent's intentions. Normal, daily actions have intentional meaning. When we grasp their point, we grasp the intention one has when doing it (and not before doing it). The paperboy leaves the newspaper on my doorstep. This act is called delivery because it was his intention to deliver a newspaper. It was not a case of donating and not a case of losing. Actions are not movements precisely because of this inherent intentionality. Someone stretches his arm away from his body. Is he waving to a friend? Is he beginning a yoga pose? Or is he trying to feel whether there is a draft in the room? (Humphrey and Laidlaw 1994: 94). What this person did in stretching his arm depends on his intentions. But in a ritual, intentions have no such constitutive role. This also means that corrections which could be made to normal actions, like saying "that's not what I meant," are irrelevant in ritual (Humphrey and Laidlaw 1994: 98).

This is related to the second feature, namely the stipulated character of ritual action. Not intentions, but constitutive rules make up the ontology of ritual. The actor acts in a way in which his intentions are no longer constitutive. His actions are not chosen; rather, he executes a fixed, predetermined, preexisting act. In ritual the sort of amendments which elucidate daily actions are no longer relevant. You cannot perform a ritual and say: "sorry, I intended a different meaning." The reason is obvious. In ritual, intentions no longer determine the identity of the performed act. The ritual act is there, like an object. "You have still done it, whatever you were dreaming of" (Humphrey and Laidlaw 1994: 5). For the same reason, the celebrant has no duty to an observer to clarify what he is doing, as is the case in normal action. Ritual acts are, so to speak, ready-made (Humphrey and Laidlaw 1994: 96).

The third feature is ritual's elemental or archetypal (no reference to the Jungian concept) quality. Ritual acts are like entities. "Celebrants' acts appear, even to themselves, as 'external', as not of their own making" (Humphrey and Laidlaw 1994: 89).

The fourth feature, ritual's apprehensibility, concerns its openness for interpretation. Because ritual acts are "external," they can be interpreted in a variety of ways.[4] In daily actions the actor has a privileged position in determining what he did, because his intentions are constitutive of the identity of the act. In ritual everyone can give an interpretation. If we post ourselves on the steps of a temple or a cathedral, asking all the "believers" coming out exactly what it was that they did in there, we will be confronted with a variety of opinions: learned or childish, moral or spiritual, progressive or conservative. Sometimes these interpretations are institutionalized: "the institutional imposition of meaning is a reaction religion can have to ritualization, not part of it" (Humphrey and Laidlaw 1994: 81). In sum:

> Action is ritualized if the acts of which it is composed are constituted not by the intentions which the actor has in performing them, but by prior stipulation. We thus have a class of acts in which the intentions which normally serve to identify acts, that is to say, intentions in action, are discounted. By "ritual commitment" we do not mean that the actor holds any particular beliefs, such as that the ritual is sacred or really will cure an illness, only that he or she is now committed to a particular attitude or stance, and that this is different from stances taken towards everyday actions. ... A set of constitutive rules is accepted as determining the kinds of acts which he or she will perform. In adopting the ritual stance one accepts, that is, that in a very important sense, one will not be the author of one's acts. (Humphrey and Laidlaw 1994: 97–8)

6 Why rituals are appealing or moving

Ritual produces a special kind of attentiveness, namely in becoming aware of the relation between one's own act and the stipulated archetype. This is one dimension of ritualization

> which can provide for an inner debate, or a feeling of freedom, in the very context of prescriptive rules. ... It [this freedom] includes in fact the possibility of non-reflection, of not having any religious thoughts or beliefs at all, and this results in the ritual act as a mere copy. This is what seems to have caused most anxiety for religious leaders. (Humphrey and Laidlaw 1994: 103)

In the historical development of most religions, there are oscillations between appreciation and depreciation of ritual. In this line we also find theological currents approving or disapproving of ritual. David Hume observes these contrary tendencies in his essay *Of Superstition and Enthusiasm,* in which superstition mainly refers to Roman Catholicism and enthusiasm to some trends in the Protestant tradition. Superstition is defined as consisting "in ceremonies, observances, mortifications, sacrifices, presents, or in any practice," while its counterpart enthusiasm receives the following descriptions: "raptures, transports, and surprising flights of fancy; and confidence and presumption still increasing" (Hume 1985: 74).

Notwithstanding the triumphs of enthusiasm in modern history, ritual survives. Its capacity to become a void copy is nothing but the flip side of its capacity to be filled with meaning and to lift up those participating. Because rituals are ontologically constituted beyond individual intentions, the participant feels a part of something larger than life.[5] As such rituals are a rest/break in the daily sequence of intention-laden activity. As Humphrey and Laidlaw (Humphrey and Laidlaw 1994: 99) note: "It is this gap—a potential freedom from the everyday and inexorable suffusion of action with personal intentions—that provides a space which may suggest a reason why people perform ritual." Rituals free me of myself, of my ever-present ego, of ever-present wishes, beliefs, and intentions.

What then is the difference between a ritual and a secular festivity? A festive gathering has no binding rules. A good example is a farewell meeting for a colleague who retires. His colleagues can decide whether or not they want to organize such an occasion, and what it will consist in if they do. They can have speeches, songs, cakes, gifts, sketches, toasts, meals, practical jokes, and so on, in an order and with the content they can select themselves. As such a festive meeting is the subject of human invention and construction. Its purpose is to express emotions and to evoke emotions: emotions of thankfulness, of friendship, of wishing well. Such an occasion has an impact on people because of this emotional expression and evocation. It appeals in a very personal way. Some lose their voice when formulating their warm thanks and hopeful wishes. From time to time a tear has to be swept away.

Rituals seem to have a rather different, if not opposite, nature. Celebrants cannot decide what the ritual will look like or in what order actions have to be performed.

The ritual consists of prefixed action sequences. Its origin is, in the eyes of the believers, divine: God, or a god, or a saintly person under divine inspiration has established it in a mythical past. And instead of expressing and eliciting emotions, ritual seems to imply stepping into something bigger that goes beyond our petty little emotions, wishes, and intentions. Ritual appeals to people not because it evokes emotions but because it frees us of the ever-presence of emotions. It appeals in a de-personalized way. Although ritual and festive meeting are quite different, if not contrary, the prominent impression is that ritual is no longer understood. People have a tendency to reduce ritual to—or to treat ritual as if it was—a festive event as described above. They want to construct a ritual themselves (a contradiction?) and have it in a personalized form.

What is the difference between being an outsider in the first case of a secular meeting and in the second case, a ritual? In the first case, among those invited to the party, the difference between outsider and insider does not necessarily apply. Only because of the institutionalized character of rituals is it possible to be an outsider.

7 Concluding remarks

In Section 12 of his *Natural History of Religion* David Hume describes a strange meeting that he witnessed in Paris:

> I lodged once at Paris in the same hotel with an ambassador from Tunis, who, having passed some years at London, was returning home that way. One day I observed his Moorish excellency diverting himself under the porch, with surveying the splendid equipages that drove along; when there chanced to pass that way some Capuchin friars, who had never seen a Turk; as he, on his part, accustomed to the European dresses, had never seen the grotesque figure of a Capuchin: And there is no expressing the mutual admiration, with which they inspired each other. (Hume 2007: 68)

Hume's story makes it clear that to a certain degree there have always been encounters and, in that line, forms of cross participation between religions. Being present at a strange ritual—however passive—is a way of participating. Being present is a way of acknowledging the existence of a specific, differing religion and its rituals. By turning one's back to it or by going about one's own business one may try to ignore it, but in most cases this is not what happens. One is present as a bystander and, in many cases, one has also inadvertently or intentionally fulfilled "entrance conditions" like removing one's shoes, washing one's hands and feet, or adhering to dress codes—some of which are part of the ritual itself. This type of passive, acknowledging participation involves agreeing to a low-intensity involvement. One's status is not that of a full celebrant. This brings us to a first conclusion: ritual involvement does not have to be seen as binary, as a question of being in or out, but can be seen as gradual, allowing degrees of involvement. The question at hand is—so it seems—about the wish to be a full participant. This wish is mostly motivated by an individualist approach. It uses cross-ritual participation to signal one's advancements on the road to complete spiritual detachment, leaving behind all institutional or traditional adherence (cf. the fifth motivation in the introduction of this chapter).

Whoever is led by these spiritual motives falls victim to an intellectualist presupposition that sees the ritual actions as nothing more than the expression of thoughts and feelings. Next, ritual is distorted and reduced to an instrument of communication signaling spiritual progress. All this fits in the wider picture of our culture, which tends to lose sight of the specificity of ritual.

Those who are led by the fourth motivation for cross-ritual participation, namely the urge to communicate deep recognition to other faith groups using ritual as the mode of communication, testify to laudable intentions. They should be conscious of the fact however that their participation is nothing but a symbolic presence which does not really involve them in this ritual. The specific ritual performed is indifferent to them as long as they get the chance to show their symbolic recognition.

A participating outsider behaves in the way in which a student or an apprentice would behave in a religion. The outsider signals that this strange religion is valuable to him by wanting to learn from the insiders and from their religion. But in many cases the insider will sense an insincerity: the participating outsider is not a real pupil, and his participation is not a first step toward conversion. Rather than a step toward conversion it is sometimes a confused way of signaling spiritual openness and superiority.

Chapter 5

RELIGION IS AS RELIGION DOES: INTERFAITH PRAYER AS A FORM OF RITUAL PARTICIPATION

Douglas Pratt

1 Introduction

This chapter discusses interfaith prayer, sometimes referred to as interfaith worship, as a specific form of ritual participation; one which is perhaps not so obvious in terms of "ritual" as are other forms. For prayer *per se*, even public prayer, is arguably not usually identified as ritual as such—rather as a component of some rituals, including of course worship and other liturgical acts. Interfaith prayer is today an arena of cross-religious participation. This discussion of it will include a specific case study of interreligious prayer and an exploration of some theological rationales for Christian engagement in such prayer. An examination of different modes of language is also relevant, for language is a key component of prayer. While the following makes reference to literature and examples of what has been called interfaith "worship," I suggest that for the most part what has been meant, and what has been happening, may be better thought of and understood as interfaith prayer *per se*. Participation in worship or liturgical acts of another religion may well fall within the scope of the consideration of ritual participation; but the very concept of "interfaith worship" is highly problematic and fraught with difficulties. "Interfaith prayer"—for the most part—is both a phenomenon in its own right and encompasses what has occurred under the banner of interfaith worship. This prayer is our focus here.

Peoples of different faiths have occasion, from time to time, to join together in some form of prayer act, such as prayers for world peace or community prayer in response to a shared event—usually a trauma such as an earthquake, tsunami, or war, for example—that can range across more than one religion so far as the input or content of the prayer act is concerned. To this extent, interfaith prayer is something that religious people do, or at least have the capacity and opportunity to do. And scholars of religion have long recognized that the starting point for any understanding of religion, or religious phenomenon, is observing and inquiring about what religious people actually do (Harvey 2013). To be sure, coming together from diverse religions to plan or reflect upon a common action of a shared spiritual experience—such as doing interreligious or interfaith prayer—is something that is still, for many, comparatively novel and relatively rare. Yet the impetus for various acts of interfaith prayer is increasing as more and more experiences of cross-religious engagement and dialogical encounter occur, and as religiously diverse communities address common issues or respond to local crises (Wingate 2005: 82–114).

So far as ritual participation is concerned, the example of interfaith prayer is less about ritual *per se* as it is about a cross-religious participatory sharing in a dimension of religion that is, or can be, an individual and so personal or relatively private phenomenon. On the other hand, prayer can also be a public performance, albeit, by its very nature, a performance that may follow discernible patterns, so thereby including an *element* of ritual; but prayer is of necessity a highly verbal, indeed cerebral, form of religious behavior. The sense of "participation" may thus be less overt than in other examples of ritual participation. Furthermore, I suggest that for the most part rituals are preeminently for the initiated. They make sense and are replete with meaning for the insider. They may intrigue and attract an outsider; they may be equally puzzling, meaningless, and even off-putting. This is no less the case when it comes to prayer, and in particular public expressions or performances of it. And with prayer it is language, as mentioned, that is at the heart. Language is the bearer of symbol and meaning for the one who is making the prayer. To what extent can another be said to be able to participate? What are the sorts of problems and issues of language that arise? Such issues will be addressed below.

The opportunity for sharing in multireligious acts such as interfaith prayer is likely to increase. In some corners of the globe this is already the case; for others it is only just emerging into the horizon of possibility. For example, the 2012 National Interfaith Forum in New Zealand included a multifaith Sunday "service," in fact a form of arranged interfaith prayer, that involved a number of different faith traditions—Jewish, Muslim, Hindu, Baha'i, Christian (Anglican, Methodist, Catholic), Mormon—all of whom contributed up to five minutes of reflection, reading, meditation, music, and so on. Prayer centers on language, but its forms may go beyond language—as in the silence of contemplative meditation, or the evocative impact of music accompanying reflection. This multifaith example was the kind of event that can be easily critiqued and dismissed as a superficial smorgasbord; in fact it proved the most appreciated element of the entire weekend's program, and many found the experience to be very moving. It was, *qua* worship or "service," a devotional type of prayer act; something that within Christianity would fall more naturally within the realm of Protestant Evangelical liturgical formats. Nevertheless it was, without doubt, quite a highlight for all who participated, both from a spectrum of Christian denominations and also with respect to participants from other religions. So what can we make of such events? And what can we say of the development trajectory of interfaith prayer and, indeed, of the issues, questions, and opportunities it might present?

2 Interfaith prayer: The development of a "Dialogue of Experience"

From an interfaith perspective, participation in the religious rituals of others, or in some form of multireligious "worship" event such as interfaith prayer, arguably falls within the realm of the "dialogue of experience" (indeed, some might refer to interfaith prayer as a form of spiritual dialogue). There is now a reasonable and diverse history of multifaith worship and other interfaith prayer events that have either accompanied, or been the focus of, interreligious dialogical engagement— the regular and global World Day of Prayers for Peace, for example, and the well-publicized Assisi "Day of Prayer for Peace" interfaith prayer events (Pratt 2010: 214–16), as well as community multifaith acts of commemoration or prayer following such disasters as September 11, 2001; the 2004 Christmas (Boxing Day) tsunami; the 2011 earthquake that destroyed the city of Christchurch, New Zealand; among many others. In the United Kingdom, for instance, the modern phenomenon of multifaith events taking place especially in cathedrals is cited as going far back as the 1942 memorial service for Sir Francis Younghusband, founder of the World Congress of Faiths. In 1953 a multifaith service was held to mark the coronation of Queen Elizabeth II, and from the mid-1960s there have been annual multi-faith "Observance for Commonwealth Day" services held at Westminster Abbey, London (IFCG 1992).

The experience of the development of such multifaith observances and services of "worship"—for the most part variants of interfaith prayer—within Great Britain over the past half-century or so find echoes elsewhere, as well as offer some useful points to consider. In 1968 the British Council of Churches (BCC), noting the concerns and opposition raised to multifaith services as tending to syncretism and threatening, in this case, the integrity of Christian mission and witness, nevertheless endorsed:

1. exchanges of visits for sympathetic and instructed observation of one another's worship; and
2. occasions on which those of different faiths do in turn what is characteristic of their own religion, enabling the others present to share to the extent to which they conscientiously can. (see the BCC's *Statement on Inter-Faith Services* [1968], as cited in IFCG 1992: 11–12).

The BCC formally encouraged member churches "to engage in common action" of a community-affirming sort; to arrange, carefully, occasions of mutual inter-change, both of dialogue and "unambiguous testimony to their beliefs"; where possible to undertake "sympathetic observation of the worship of other faiths" for the purposes of enhanced understanding"; and "to accept gladly whatever experience of communion with God arises in such relationships" (IFCG 1992: 12). The concern for faithful integrity of all parties was uppermost.

In 1974 the World Congress of Faiths made an attempt to understand Christian resistance to multifaith worship and ameliorate objections, concluding by advocating "the attendance of people of one religion at the worship of another," but also recognizing "a need for 'specially designed acts of common worship' which, however, 'should not replace the normal worship of any religious tradition'" (IFCG 1992: 13). Around the same time, the increase in religious plurality fed the growth of multifaith worship occasions, prompting the critical question "whether people of different faiths 'are doing intrinsically the same thing when they worship, or whether it is a case of separate and different things being done side by side'" (Akehurst and Wootton 1977, cited in IFCG 1992: 13). Because the distinctiveness of worship in different religions was such that "it cannot easily be engaged in together," it was advised that, if and when held, multifaith worship should have limited aims, be based on mutual respect, emerge out of prior relationships, and above all ought to avoid any theological inconsistency and "situational dishonesty" (IFCG 1992: 14).

By 1979 the UK Archbishops' Consultants on Interfaith Relations had identified three forms of multifaith services:

1. Christian services with guest participation from other faiths;
2. Interfaith services of the serial multifaith type;
3. Interfaith services with an agreed common order of service.

These three were regarded as complements to, not replacements of, the regular liturgical life of the Church. "Interfaith is not a new religion," the Consultants note; "equality is of believers and not of beliefs" (IFCG 1992: 15). Such caveats notwithstanding, the third quarter or so of the twentieth century can be roughly seen to have been a period of relative explosion of interest and engagement in varying sorts of multifaith ritual participation including, in particular, interfaith prayer. And today there are many examples of everyday life-situations wherein people of one faith can find themselves encountering, at some depth, people of other faiths. This might be in respect to interfaith marriage, for example, or corporate cooperation in a common cause of social concern. In many such cases there can be opportunity for interfaith prayer to occur. But what of sustained examination and reflection on this phenomenon—what has been engaged and by whom?

3 Interreligious prayer: A case study

During the closing decade of the twentieth century, the World Council of Churches (WCC) and the Vatican engaged in a joint study of interreligious prayer (Pratt 1997). The project involved the then Office for Inter-Religious Relations (OIRR) of the WCC, and the Pontifical Council for Interreligious Dialogue (PCID) of the Vatican (Ucko 1993, 1995). The questions which lay behind this venture remain relevant today, of course, and require continual reflection and fresh thinking. When the natural human response in any given situation is to pray, and the context of that response is multireligious, what can we do together? How can we do it?

Indeed, ought we to do it? And if we do, on what basis may we proceed? It is not my purpose to rehearse or summarize the outcomes of the project; such can be found elsewhere.[1] However, it is important to delineate just what might be meant by the term "interreligious" (or interfaith) as applied to the context of prayer, or some other such experiential event—by which is meant a multireligious occasion that may embrace more than just elements of prayer, but that includes prayer and/ or meditation as part of an overall act of interreligious liturgical engagement. And, indeed, an exploration is also needed of what is meant by the term "prayer" in a multireligious context.

Arising out of the combined WCC and Vatican project, four possible modes of meaning and usage of the term "interreligious" may be discerned. First, and most simply, a so-called interreligious event can in fact be a *shared multireligious* act wherein there is a presentation, in some sort of serial or simultaneous fashion, from a number of religious traditions or groups, without necessarily presupposing any depth of coordination, nor implying any particular level of mutual acceptance or agreement. The diverse offerings are simply allowed to be; they are passively "observed" rather than actively apprehended or responded to by others participating in, or at least attending, the event. While there may be a common theme or occasion to which the various contributions are oriented, no attempt would be made to coordinate thematically, critically, and intentionally the contributions to cohere them into a recognizable, and acceptable-to-all, whole. It is a matter, simply, of spiritual or liturgical potluck as the smorgasbord-like spread of differently sourced religious items contribute to the worship or prayer or liturgical event. This was more or less the style of the event that took place at the New Zealand National Interfaith Forum mentioned above. And, as noted, it worked well enough, attracting very appreciative responses from those who participated in the faith presentations and from the majority who simply respectfully observed.

Second, there is the possibility—amply demonstrated, for example, in the two World Days of Prayer for Peace held in Assisi in 1986 and 2002 at the invitation of Pope John Paul II, and the 2011 event hosted by Pope Benedict XVI—of a *contiguous multireligious* act. Here the principal event is constructed along the lines of having different religious traditions engage in their own prayer act, each in their allocated "space"—whether a different location for the purpose, as in the Assisi events, or some other form of spatio-temporal demarcation. There is no intermingling of principal prayer actions; the full integrity of religious identity and the authenticity of specific actions are maintained. But, importantly, this spatio-temporal demarcation is also bounded: the diversity of the prayers offered is held together by the virtue of some manifest contiguity. As at Assisi, it might be by way of being held within a unifying time and place: the same town on the same day, and including an opening and closing shared action. The essential focus and meaning of the event is found through the fact of being conjoined by virtue of shared temporal and geographic situation. The theological context is clear: coming together, in order to pray; but doing that separately such that no one is compromised, and no reductionism or relativism can be imputed.

This form of multireligious prayer is not uncommon in many pastoral situations like those experienced by hospitals and other chaplains, where two or more people from different faiths may find occasion to pray with and for each other, but to do so "independently" as it were, even if in the same room and at the same time. There is no suggestion of an overt corporate act of multireligious sharing. But there is a context of multireligious contiguity enacted: people are together, praying, but they are not engaged in praying together. With respect to the Assisi occasions, while each religious group performed its own ritual independently of the others in accord with the contiguity model, there was also a dimension of the shared multireligious act. Typically the day concluded with an act of coming together to share, each with the other, some suitable meditative, reflective, or otherwise prayer item, and to bear common witness to the world of a shared concern, at least, with the theme of peace. So these Assisi events, in their totality, embraced both multireligious contiguity and a measure of shared multi-religious action.

Third, and potentially the most problematic, interreligious prayer can be taken as the occasion to have an *intentional-combined multireligious* act. In this case, the aim is to create, out of the resources of a multiplicity of religions involved, a prayer event that produces a "blended" or otherwise "combined" content which may be effectively "owned" in its entirety by each of the participating groups or their religious representatives. Inevitably the only way this can be achieved is by taking the approach of the lowest common denominator. The distinctive and particular is shorn in order that a baseline of harmony and acceptability may prevail. In some cases, negotiations—in dialogue—to achieve such an outcome may themselves be quite considerable, as well as beneficial to those involved, even if, from the perspective of any one participating tradition, the combined outcome seems rather banal and overly simplified. Further, if this was the only mode of interreligious prayer, such prayer and allied liturgical activity could be justly criticized as a reductionist and necessarily relativistic, even syncretistic, enterprise: all the fearful concerns mounted against the cause of interreligious dialogue would come home to roost (see Ratzinger 2004: 108–9). Indeed, I suspect that this is often the assumption of many people when they hear the term "interreligious prayer," and this concern becomes a reason cited for avoiding it.

Fourth—and seemingly reflecting the best of the reported experiences of interreligious or interfaith prayer—is the occasion that has been carefully planned, but not as a syncretistic blending as such. This is what I term *coherent-integrated interreligious* prayer wherein, from the contributing religions, there comes a thematic and critical interlinking of prayers and/or co-coordinating of allied liturgical items. These are selected and rendered mutually congruent around a particular theme, event, need, or some other appropriate communal point of reference. The intention is of bolstering a sense of underlying unity or internal coherence in the outcome, while permitting the real differences, unique dimensions, and contexts, as well as the different content of the contributions and the religions from which they are drawn, to be mutually respected and upheld. There is no intention, through the event, of presupposing or enacting some form of syncretistic union of the participating religions, nor of subsuming them under some inclusive umbrella. There is no attempt to blend the rich diversity of contributions into a kind of spiritual porridge; nor is the outcome marked by the happy randomness of a smorgasbord. No religious tradition is compromised, no reduction of essence or denial of religious self-identity of the participating traditions occurs. Yet, some sense of greater wholeness may emerge nonetheless; an intuition of a larger context, a wider or deeper sphere wherein a unifying spirit is at work, may be discerned. Again, this is without prejudice to the particular sensibilities of any of the contributing religions, permitting an acknowledgment and affirmation of the result as authentic to the occasion.

To summarize, the four possibilities are *shared* multireligious; *contiguous* multireligious; *intentional-combined* multireligious; and *coherent-integrated* inter-religious events. The first three are clearly activities whereby the multiplicity of religions involved are brought together, in varying degrees, in a more or less loose or serendipitous way. But with the fourth, the level of cooperation, and with it the depth of dialogical consultation that is necessarily implied, means that a two-fold shift occurs. The interfaith prayer event is planned and executed as coherent and integrated; at the same time, the "coming-together" of participants suggests a level of interaction beyond what is possible to experience in terms of the other possibilities or types. Thus, hopefully, a genuinely interreligious outcome is the result: and it is *inter*-religious as opposed to *multi*-religious. Something takes place between (inter) the participants, and between their religious systems, in regard to the prayer event. Yet this involves no synthesizing of identities, beliefs, and so on. I do not claim that these four options exhaust all possibilities. However it is only as we can identify and refine such options that progress with understanding and engaging in interfaith prayer as an example of interreligious ritual participation can be made. However, identifying and reflecting on prospects for such participation is one thing; enabling potential up-take by religious communities and their peoples so they may participate is something else. This is the task of preliminary theological or other ideological reflection. I cannot speak for religions other than my own, so let me offer some ideas concerning the propriety of Christian participation in interfaith prayer and allied events.

4 Interfaith prayer: Christian justification

A Christian theological perspective on prayer may reveal other undergirding dimensions which provide further criteria for the guiding of interreligious practice. Such discernment and discussion also helps to elucidate the theology of dialogue as it applies to interfaith prayer. Prayer, the language of love, is the communion of heart and mind in the context of spirit. In prayer there may be discerned the affirmation of diversity in unity, the promotion of acceptance through active forgiveness and reconciliation. From a Christian perspective, prayer can be a means to a deeper communion with the mystery of the Divine Other. It can also be a moment in which there is a deepening of self-understanding. Thus prayer serves both the cause of interreligious relations as well as self-reflective spiritual growth: in both, prayer embraces a dimension of self-encounter and the transcending of self in order to go beyond self. If prayer can be thought of as a moment of "dwelling-*in*"—or "indwelling"—one's faith, then interfaith prayer may be viewed as an occasion of "dwelling-*with*" the religiously other in their own indwelling of faith. Thus interfaith prayer can constitute a relational bridge, as it were, interconnecting peoples and faith communities. It can provide the opportunity to acknowledge the sacredness that is presented in and by the other. In affirming and honoring that sacredness, it may even evoke and manifest—that is, bring-into-present-being—an overarching sense of sacredness in which the particular moment of interreligious prayer is situated, and which is not inappropriate to the participating traditions.

Interfaith prayer may occur with theological legitimacy because of the two dimensions—responsiveness and hospitality—of interaction that it involves. The *responsive* dimension has to do with the "outward-facing" orientation of humanly reacting to an external situation or event. On the one hand there is clearly an anthropological ground. It is in the nature of human being to respond, to react as appropriate to the event in question: to provide succor and aid, to respond with sympathetic grieving or whatever the occasion evokes. On the other hand, the responsive dimension may provide the occasion for discerning a pneumatological impulse, sensing the Spirit at work in and through the human reaction, with the response itself giving evidence of more than the merely anthropological at play. Broadly speaking, the two modes of prayer as response are, first, occasions of communal crisis or other such significant events and, second, appropriate occasions of civic celebration offering opportunity for a religious contribution. Christians may participate in the religious response dimension—as in an act of interfaith prayer—by virtue of the gospel imperative to love the neighbor, and the call to serve others with compassionate empathy. Compassion is the enacting of a being—or standing—with the other in their time of need; it constitutes the legitimate context for the expression of Christian values of cooperative praxis and sympathetic spirituality.

By contrast, the *hospitality* dimension signifies events that are "inner-facing" in the sense of hospitable communal ingathering of persons of different religions on occasions wherein the reciprocal roles of host and guest set the parameters for interaction. This provides the context for mutual respect. As host, a Christian community, for example, may invite members of another community to join with it in a specific event wherein the intention is simply that of offering hospitality as such, whether materially, spiritually, or both. The structure of the commonplace act of hosting a guest is the practical guide to the event: invitation, reception, welcome, attending to need, offering reassurance and comfort; sharing and interacting; closure. The motif of God being found in the Christ who both goes before us among our neighbors and comes to us in the guise of the stranger in our midst, provides, in part, a theological rationale for Christian engagement in interfaith prayer as a responsive event. And there are many biblical examples of the exercise of hospitality to stranger and neighbor, with the clear message that in so doing an appropriate response and relationship to the Divine is being enacted. In the life of the Church there may be moments of Eucharistic hospitality, for instance, when the Christian companion of another tradition is admitted to the intimate and tradition-specific enactment of the ritual because, in the prevailing context, for whatever reason, they have no other avenue of accessing this means of grace. The discharge of hospitality is not just a duty; it is also itself a moment of grace infused with deeper spiritual significance.

As guest, the Christian individual and community, in humility, receives and experiences what the host offers, and in return shares the gift of the *euangelion*, the "good news," which, most simply put, states: "God loves you." The life of discipleship, the witness of Christian grace, may be seen as a contribution to be added to that which the host presents. Here the biblical reference to disciples being sent to seek and respond to the invitation to enter the house of the other (cf. Mk 6:7-10), to offer good news and receive hospitality (or not) and so experience the mutuality of receiving in gratitude and with thanksgiving that which is offered, provides a scriptural example to place alongside the examples of hosting. And there is risk and vulnerability: the prospect of an appreciation gained on the one hand or, on the other, the possibility of resultant indigestion, are equally potential outcomes for which there are spiritual equivalents to the physical. Hospitality, given and received, offers an opportunity to learn something of, to get to understand better, to sample the cuisine of another. And just as with cuisine, where the act of appreciation of the other implies no necessary or profound change to one's own culinary customs, so with other aspects of hospitable engagement: the interchange and sampling is for the purposes of mutual enrichment, not conversion.

Of course, culinary openness may well lead—indeed often does—to an expansion of cuisine: modifications of eating patterns, or the acquiring of new tastes. Generally, however, this is in the context of retaining one's fundamental eating preferences: remaining with the foods that are known to nourish, which are palatable in consumption. But, adding to that, there can be an increased range of options, an expansion of flavors, a wider appreciation of a diversity of nourishment and enrichment. We are broadly familiar with this culinary experience as a cultural phenomenon: the realm of the spiritual or religious may be viewed as analogous. Interfaith prayer provides an opportunity, on the basis of offering hospitality, to enhance our own spiritual life through exposure to a wider diversity of spiritual enrichment. There is no need to treat persons of other faiths as proffering an inherently threatening cuisine. The notion of a host forcing the guest to eat that which is clearly unpalatable vitiates the principles of good hospitality, as does the idea that when someone brings their contribution to a shared meal they would expect the table to be cleared of all other offerings. Such exclusivisms would be unacceptable in the gustatory realm: they are no less so in the realm of interreligious engagement. From this discussion of theological justification for interreligious prayer, we turn to the question of language as earlier indicated. What does an exploration of forms and types of religious language contribute to our understanding of interfaith and its dialogical implications?

5 The question of language

Language is arguably our primary mode of communication and meaning-making. It plays a vital role in religion; it is the *sine qua non* of prayer, especially in the public realm. But there are some critical problems. The words and sentences that comprise language can function at multiple levels and in myriad ways. Confusion and misunderstanding can quickly arise if the context and nature of the language used is not fully appreciated. While language can function as a bridge, enabling communication to happen, it likewise can form a boundary, as in sloganistic phrases or utterances that immediately signal a position or mark an identity, so indicating who belongs and who does not. Clearly interfaith prayer involves language; religion, as prayer, is "done" in and through words—especially as "performative utterances"—as much as in behavioral gesture and action. And not just "ordinary" language, but often a highly nuanced and religiously charged language—ordinary words, maybe, but replete with complex layers of usage and meaning. To attempt any critical understanding of interfaith prayer requires at least some measure of thinking about and reflecting upon the nature of religious language used in it.

I suggest that a clue is given by way of understanding the religious utterances involved in prayer as *evocative* (e.g. biddings and responses, such as "Hear us Lord") in distinction from utterances that are *definitive* (e.g. dogmatic teachings and explanations about the meaning of "Lordship") or *stative* (as in creedal or belief statements such as "Jesus is Lord"). Let's look a little closer at these three modes of religious language. A religious utterance or locution may function as an evocation of faith or identity—that is, it draws forth a response of identity affirmation, commitment to action, reinforcement of judgment, and so forth. But religious utterances may equally convey a statement of belief as such, or be a philosophical-type definition. In some cases, utterances or statements can belong to one mode but not to another. On the other hand, statements can be verbally or literally identical, but may range across all three modes. Thus, for example, the Christian utterance "God is Love" may be made *evocatively*, as in the context of prayer or worship, as well as in debate and discussion, wherein the effect of the utterance is primarily to evoke a matrix of religious empathy; where it is a shorthand formula used to stimulate or excite the sense of the divine in the context of a particular (in this case, for example, Christian) apprehension of deity as such. Alternatively, it may be made *statively* as, for example, when quoting the scriptural passage that contains it—thus stating or asserting an item of Christian belief or understanding. But also the utterance "God is Love" may be made *definitively*, that is, the purpose of the utterance is to declare the predicate "love" as a defining attribute of God. The definitive sense is most typically philosophical, while the stative is most typically theological, and the evocative is most typically liturgical.

The contrasts can be further demonstrated by considering Christian Trinitarian language. The Trinitarian concept of God is a uniquely Christian construct. It juxtaposes three "names"—Father, Son, Spirit—with three aspects or elements of the operation or essence of God as understood theologically—viz., creation, redemption, ongoing sustainment—and it associates the names and aspects with the three "personae" of deity that appear in the drama of the New Testament—the One God referred to as "Father"; the man Jesus as "the Son of God"; and the Holy Spirit identified as the continuing enlivening "presence" of God. So the appropriate and accurate expression is not so much the naming of three different "realities" (which can appear to be the case) but in ascribing a threefold name to the one complex reality: God the Father; God the Son; God the Holy Spirit. One God; three named "aspects" indicative of the nature of the reality, or "being," of God. We can examine three ways in which the Christian idea of Trinity is actually used, and note how these ways illustrate the distinction of evocative, stative, and definitive modes of religious language. Thus the Christian concept of God as Trinity finds expression in the following statements:

1. "In the name of the Father, Son, and Holy Spirit;"
2. "The Son is begotten by the Father, and the Spirit proceeds from the Father and the Son;"
3. "God exists as one substance in three persons."

These are all sentences that equally refer to the same subject—God. But they are all saying different things, and are typically used in different contexts such that transposition of statement and context is not normally possible.

The phrase "In the name of the Father, Son, and Holy Spirit" is an *evocative* utterance typically associated with Christian liturgical activity, including prayer, as well as other forms of language-performative events such as funerals, weddings, blessings, etc. The context here could also be thought of as one of association: the force of the statement is to reinforce, forge, or assert the link between the Divine Reality—God—and the person or persons involved in whatever liturgical activity is taking place wherein the formulaic utterance is used. The sentence—"The Son is begotten by the Father; and the Spirit proceeds from the Father and the Son"—is a *stative* utterance: it simply asserts or states an item of Christian metaphysical belief despite its superficial appearance as an explanation, which is another form of utterance. The sentence describes a relational pattern that certainly derives from a metaphysical consideration of the Trinitarian concept of God, but as a statement it begs explanation rather than provides it. The most typical context for the utterance of this proposition is one of belief-assertion or belief-affirmation, for the sentence itself is found within a creedal statement. Finally, the sentence—"God exists as one substance in three persons"—is a *definitive* utterance that derives directly from philosophical consideration upon the metaphysical meaning of theological statements, which then frame the language of the faithful at worship. The sentence itself is not typically used within Christian worship—the most normal context wherein Christian religious language is utilized—either as a liturgically evocative statement, or a stative belief-assertion. But any theological student enquiring after the meaning or definition lying behind the liturgical and creedal language will find this as the summary statement of the tradition of Christian reflection.

So, in this case there are three modes of utterance—evocative, stative, and definitive—around the one subject matter, the Trinitarian concept of God. They are interlinked, but it is a matter of considerable confusion when the modalities are transposed, which they sometimes are in an uncritical environment. If the evocative utterance "In the name of ..." is taken as a stative, for example, then it is likely to be received—and will certainly appear so in the act of utterance—as a statement about three different entities, one called Father, a second called Son, and a third called Spirit. If the utterance is made with definitive effect, it may well indeed infer (albeit unintendedly) a tri-theistic conceptuality. So Muslims (and others), for example, have traditionally accused Christians of crypto-polytheism, for Christianity appears to be advocating a belief in a divine "threesome" when the meaning of "trinity" is confused with "triumvirate." It is worth noting that creedal utterances, which are constructed and construed as theological statements, thus as statives, are actually used in a liturgical context for the most part. That is, their setting is primarily evocative, although their usage is ostensibly stative. Hence Christians may find themselves apparently saying things they do not really believe (namely a stative), or using language that has no contemporary meaning, if they are not tuned in to the appropriate mode of their utterance. A creedal utterance used evocatively means that what is being asserted is not so much the belief statement as such, but the historical tradition which binds the community of Christians through time as the religious entity called "Church," the identity of which is symbolized by or asserted via the communal recitation of its historic creedal formulae.

On the other hand, Christians can be accused of hypocrisy or double standards if, for example, a creedal formula spoken in good faith as an evocative utterance is presumed by an outside "listener" to be a stative or, more particularly, a definitive utterance. But, arguably, this is precisely not what is intended. Liturgical evocative language is about the encouragement and reinforcement of faith-identity and faith-commitment. Despite appearances to the contrary, liturgical language is not primarily about belief-assertion (which, arguably, belongs more appropriately in an educational or discursive context than in the context of worship). It is certainly not about metaphysical explanation.

If we consider for a moment the two key words for deity in the Christian and Islamic traditions—"God" and "Allah"—it is worth noting that, in the evocative context of Christian usage, the term "God" is most usually prefaced with a preposition of address. Thus, "*Oh* God," "*Dear* God," "*Father* God," "*Almighty* God," and so on, the import of which is to evoke the degree of familiarity or distance appropriate to the context of address. By way of comparison, the term "Allah" in its very locution seems adequately evocative as it stands. Yet it would appear that the oft-used *al-Rahman, al-Rahim* (the merciful, the compassionate) phrase as a standard corollary of address, wherein the name of Allah is invoked, functions to extend the evocative utterance. These Arabic words are terms of primary identification and reference for the divine, at least in the evocative mood. However, depending on context, they may be perceived as stative or as definitive utterances. It is a matter of Islamic belief that there are ninety-nine "names" of God, for example—yet there is no suggestion of believing that there is more than one God. To the extent the nature of God can be defined in an Islamic sense, these "names" constitute the attributes of deity. Hence, as with the Christian expression "God is Love," Islam also has religious utterances that are context-dependent so far as appropriate mode is concerned. Religious language, of whatever religion, is susceptible to modal analysis as evocative, stative, or definitive, among others.

6 Dialogical implications of interfaith prayer

Clearly the issue of language—its function, use, nuances of meaning, and context—plays a considerable role in respect to interfaith interactions of all sorts, and especially so in interfaith prayer. Any linguistic misunderstanding can have profound consequences for interfaith dialogue, as also for the meaning and relevance of any multifaith worship event such as interfaith prayer. Some forms of multifaith ritual participation, such as one of the modes of multireligious or interreligious prayer outlined above, may offer a better—more accessible—way than others, for, in general, prayer is both ubiquitous and relatively innocuous in that there is not the same range of physicality involved as, for example, participating, even passively, in various temple or other "high" rituals across many religions where necessary concomitant actions (e.g. bowing, prostrating, genuflecting) tend to increase the sense of physicality of the participation, thereby potentially compromising both the outsider who cannot properly engage and the insider who may feel that the intimacy and sensitivity of the ritual is compromised.

The nature of the dialogue required for interfaith prayer to occur involves accessing the language of the religions concerned in the context of mutual allowability. Such mutual and reciprocal participation may be engaged as a route to interfaith dialogical and relational development, provided there is both a sense of respectful presence as well as empathetic, engaged participation. The inherent tendency to preserve self-identity needs to be acknowledged, requiring each participant to employ an applied epoché that, indeed, facilitates genuinely mutual acceptance, openness, and empathy. That is say, to the extent we might participate in an interfaith prayer that is not our prayer as such, then we need to set aside—to cognitively bracket-out for the moment—the normal expectations and assumptions of meaning and propriety we typically take into prayer. We do this in the first instance so that we may be enabled to accept, at face-value and without prejudice, the prayer event in question, appreciating it for what it is and nothing more; at a second level, to be open to it as indeed a prayer of value and meaning that is consonant with our religious identity even as it may extend and challenge that identity; and at a third level, to engage in it empathetically, so finding within it the sort of meaningful depth, insight, and experiential moment that is not at all unlike that which is normally, or at least often, the case with the prayer events or occasions in which we normally participate.

As with any interreligious dialogical encounter, reflecting on the process of dialogue involves discerning the threefold interplay of justifying rationales—what might be called the theology *for* dialogue; the reasons and cognitions involved in the doing of it: theology *in* dialogue; and the reflective moment of discerning the worth, value and cognitive and other impacts: theology *after*, or from, dialogue (Pratt, 2010). This last is also the arena of post-dialogue self-understanding: are we experientially and cognitively in the same "space" or "place" after the dialogical engagement as before it? Can we participate in interfaith prayer, as an interreligious dialogical event, without experiencing some form of impact or change to our preconceived perceptions and understandings?

7 Conclusion

In this chapter I have explored interfaith prayer and discussed theological rationales for Christian engagement in such prayer, the different modes of language involved, and noted some of the dialogical implications of such interfaith participation. Participation in interfaith prayer may take one of two forms. Either a host religion allows for, or varyingly incorporates, the participation of guests from other faiths; or an interfaith prayer event is cooperatively planned and enacted as a genuine multifaith event. In the former, participants from other faiths are in effect passive observers; in the latter the intention is to achieve mutuality of active participation. An example of the former might be a Sikh community welcoming a multifaith group to its Gurdwara to respectfully yet passively observe the ritual performance of prayers, and then actively partake of the *langar* (meal) that follows, which is regarded as nevertheless part of the overall ritual of their prayer event. An example of the latter might be where an interfaith council organizes a multireligious prayer for peace ceremony wherein diverse communities each contribute an element to make up the whole. While such events are increasingly advocated, and often experienced as moving and perhaps even insightful, a number of attendant critical issues and problems invite careful and considered reflection, which, when mutually engaged, can likewise provide the opportunity for interfaith communion and relational development.

Chapter 6

INTERRELIGIOUS RITUAL PARTICIPATION: INSIGHTS FROM INTER-CHRISTIAN RITUAL PARTICIPATION

Martha Moore-Keish

1 Introduction

For the majority of its brief history, the theology of interreligious dialogue has taken the approach of most of the wider field of theology: conceptual reasoning based on critical engagement with texts, on topics such as God/the divine/the Real, the human condition, the world, and the relationships among these. While this is a fruitful approach, many theological scholars over the past few decades have challenged its limitations, calling attention to sources from the lives of ordinary religious practitioners and attending to lived, embodied ritual traditions. In particular, liturgical theologians have made significant contributions to Christian and Jewish theological work, showing how worship is not only a source for theological reflection, but is itself a site of theology in action.

Theology of interreligious dialogue will benefit from such attention to ritual activity, and particularly to the phenomenon of actual interreligious ritual participation. In this chapter, I will examine one instance of "interreligious" ritual participation from within the realm of Christianity: that is, the fraught question of whether Protestants and Catholics may "share" the Eucharist. Though this may seem initially odd, I am convinced that many of the issues that arise at the boundaries between religions arise with equal force, though in a different key, at the boundaries within one religious tradition. I will explore how this case, which has been interpreted primarily through a systematic doctrinal lens, has recently benefited from liturgical analysis. From this ecumenical inter-Christian interaction, I will then propose five insights on the general question of crossing boundaries to engage in the rituals of religious others.

2 Can we break bread together? The question of Protestant-Catholic Eucharistic sharing

The specific issue I will consider here is how, whether, and when Protestants and Catholics share the sacrament of the Eucharist. This is distinct from, though related to, the currently popular question about how, whether, and when it is appropriate for nonbaptized persons to participate in the Christian Eucharist, which Kearney discusses in this volume. I use the phrase "Eucharistic sharing" because of its specific inter-Christian implications. As Roman Catholic liturgical theologian Jeffrey VanderWilt has indicated (VanderWilt 2003: 2–3), Eucharistic sharing refers to "the practice of receiving Holy Communion by baptized Christians," and is regularly used in Roman Catholic ecumenical literature, including the 1993 Ecumenical Directory.

The term "Protestant" may include a wide variety of Christian churches, from nondenominational free churches to the Anglican Communion. I write as a Reformed Protestant, an ordained minister of the Presbyterian Church (USA), and thus as one shaped by a specific tradition that emerged from the sixteenth-century Eucharistic debates. I also write as one who has engaged in ecumenical dialogue with Catholic Christians for the past ten years, which has deepened my appreciation for the issues that divide and unite us when it comes to the Lord's Supper.

3 Doctrinal stances on Eucharistic sharing

Protestant churches differ widely in their interpretation and practice of the Eucharist (often called Holy Communion or the Lord's Supper in Protestant settings). They also vary in their official stance with regard to persons outside of their own church (such as Catholics) receiving communion in their worship services. For much of Reformed, Baptist, and Anabaptist history, for instance, members have been permitted to receive communion only after self-examination, and after having been judged by themselves and their church leaders to be worthy to partake of the Supper (see 1 Cor. 11:27-9).[1] In many cases, this has meant that communion in a local congregation is restricted to certain members of that congregation. Such "close communion" or "closed communion" upholds the sanctity of Holy Communion, and means that not only Catholics, but also many Protestants, are not invited to receive communion in such congregations.

In recent years, however, many Protestant churches have articulated more open invitations to all Christians present in a worship service to receive communion when it is offered, regardless of specific church affiliation. Churches may specify that communicants should be baptized, and/or in good standing with their own church, and/or trust in the Lord Jesus Christ and seek to follow him. However, I know of no Protestant church that bars its ministers from administering communion to Catholic Christians *because they are Catholic*. This practice is based on the strong conviction that the Lord's Supper embodies God's gift of grace in Jesus Christ to repentant sinners, not to the worthy. For instance, the current Directory for Worship of the Presbyterian Church (USA) states, "The invitation to the Lord's Supper is extended to all who have been baptized, remembering that access to the Table is not a right conferred upon the worthy, but a privilege given to the undeserving who come in faith, repentance, and love" (Directory for

Worship, *Book of Order 2011–13*, W–2.4011). The Lord's Supper is a meal for all who understand themselves to be followers of Christ, not only those who belong to a particular Christian family. From the Protestant side, then, Catholic Christians are frequently welcomed to participate fully in the Eucharist, including receiving the elements of bread and wine.

The official position of the Catholic Church is quite different. According to current canon law, "Catholic ministers administer the sacraments licitly to Catholic members of the Christian faithful alone, who likewise receive them licitly from Catholic ministers alone" (CCL, c. 844 §1; see Beal et al. 2000: 1024). Catholics may never lawfully receive sacraments from a minister who is not "in valid apostolic succession," which (according to canon law) includes all Protestant ministers, even Anglicans. In certain carefully specified cases, however, Christians not in full communion with the Catholic Church may *receive* sacraments from Catholic ministers. The requirements for such exceptions are these:

1. It must be a time of "grave and pressing need," such as danger of death.
2. The person must be unable to approach a minister of his or her own community.
3. The person must spontaneously ask for the Eucharist (a requirement which also applies to the sacraments of penance and the anointing of the sick).
4. The person must "demonstrate the Catholic faith in respect of these sacraments and [be] properly disposed." (CCL, C 844 §4)

Why such restrictions? From a Catholic point of view, participation in the Eucharistic ritual depends on one's understanding of and assent to certain specific theological claims about the nature of Christ's real presence in the Eucharist, the Eucharistic sacrifice, the ordained priesthood, and the Church. In the Catholic Church alone "subsists the fullness of Christ's body united with its head" (CCC, no. 830), which implies the leadership of ordered ministry in apostolic succession, under the primacy of the successor to Peter, the bishop of Rome.[2] It is the Church that celebrates the Eucharist, which is "the efficacious sign and sublime cause of that communion in the divine life and that unity of the People of God by which the Church is kept in being" (CCC, no. 1325). Receiving the elements of bread and wine at the Eucharist, then, is never simply an act of eating and drinking, but an act of conscious participation in the unity of the Church.

Recent years have seen important progress in mutual doctrinal affirmations regarding the Eucharist, mitigating some of the polemical divides of the sixteenth century. The landmark 1982 ecumenical document *Baptism, Eucharist, and Ministry*, the fruit of fifty years of ecumenical dialogue, outlined five major "meanings" of the Eucharist: thanksgiving, memorial/anamnesis, invocation of the Spirit, communion of the faithful, and meal of the kingdom (BEM 1982: §§3–26). These common affirmations were explicitly developed as part of the ecumenical desire for full visible unity of Christian churches. "If the divided churches are to achieve the visible unity they seek, one of the essential prerequisites is that they should be in basic agreement on baptism, eucharist, and ministry" (BEM, preface). Since

1982, ecumenical dialogues between Catholics and Protestants have continued to deepen their mutual affirmations in the area of Eucharistic theology. For instance, the seventh round of the United States Reformed-Roman Catholic Dialogue (2003–10) produced a final report entitled *This Bread of Life*, which identified significant convergences as well as continuing points of divergence in Eucharistic theology in the areas of epiclesis, anamnesis, presence, sacrifice, and discipleship.[3] In addition to ecumenical dialogue, some systematic theologians have made significant contributions to ecumenical understanding in Eucharistic theology in recent years. Notably, American Reformed theologian George Hunsinger offered careful, substantive proposals toward resolving the long-standing issues of real presence and sacrifice in his 2008 book *The Eucharist and Ecumenism: Let Us Keep the Feast*.

Despite these recent theological developments, it remains the case that Protestants and Catholics are not officially able to share in Eucharistic celebrations, and that this is rooted in continuing doctrinal differences regarding the meaning of this ritual. What difference might it make to shift attention to the "doing" of this ritual rather than focusing on the "meaning" alone?

4 A liturgical and ritual approach to Eucharistic sharing

In recent decades, the field of liturgical theology has emphasized the ways in which liturgy itself produces meaning, or is "epiphanic," according to David Fagerberg (1992: 180). Christian theologians such as Alexander Schmemann, Aidan Kavanagh, Kevin Irwin, and Gordon Lathrop, as well as Jewish scholars such as Lawrence Hoffman, have insisted that liturgy/ritual action does not merely enact meaning already evident in texts prior to performance. Certainly liturgical scholars attend to texts and official guidelines on liturgical action, both as readers and as authors of such texts. Yet increasingly, liturgical theology has taken seriously the performance itself as primary. I will briefly describe two major emphases in liturgical theology since the 1970s and suggest how these have influenced the question of Protestant-Catholic Eucharistic sharing.

4.1 Lex orandi, lex credendi

One significant focus of liturgical theological discussion has been an ancient phrase from patristic theologian Prosper of Aquitaine, who around 435 CE recorded the line *ut legem credendi lex statuat supplicandi*, usually translated "the law of praying establishes the law of believing," and now often quoted in shorthand form as *lex orandi, lex credendi* ("law of praying, law of believing"). In its original context, this was part of Prosper's larger Augustinian argument that divine grace precedes human believing. Prosper employs this motto to point out that the church regularly prays (*supplicandi*) for faith (*credendi*), which demonstrates that our faith depends on the prior grace of God (see De Clerck 1978, 1994). In its practice of prayer, the church voices and establishes its faith in the God of grace.

This motto has prompted much debate among scholars regarding the relationship between the Church's prayer (or more broadly, its liturgical practice) and its articulated theology (often called belief or faith). Orthodox theologian Alexander Schmemann and Roman Catholic Aidan Kavanagh both argued strongly that the Church's liturgical experience, as an encounter with the living God, precedes and establishes the Church's articulated faith (Schmemann 1972: 89f; Kavanagh 1984: 91–2). The Church has drifted dangerously from this understanding, they argue, so that "faith" is too often conceived as a series of doctrinal propositions, divorced from the life-giving relationship with the triune God embodied in worship. Instead, we need to recover the priority of liturgical action, where we actually meet the God who is described in official theological statements. We should understand "belief" or "faith" (*lex credendi*) as subordinate to the Church's prayer (*lex supplicandi*).

Geoffrey Wainwright and Kevin Irwin offer more modest interpretations of Prosper, suggesting that liturgical practice is not the only source for belief, but that "liturgy manifests the church's faith" and that it is "a theological source to the degree that it is founded on scripture and is the expression of a praying Church" (Irwin 2002: 59; cf. Wainwright 1980: 224–7). Wainwright, an American Methodist liturgical scholar, traces the interplay of *lex orandi* and *lex credendi* throughout the history of the Church's theologizing, showing how the appeal to liturgical practice has at times been helpful, and how at other times an appeal to "faith" has helped to correct malformed liturgical practices. The law of praying and the law of believing, according to this view, are not unidirectional, but mutually formative.[4]

4.2 Liturgy *as* theologia prima

Many liturgical theologians since the 1980s have gone on to say that not only does liturgy establish faith, but that liturgical action itself *is* theology. Liturgy is not simply raw data that theologians must organize to produce meaning; liturgical action itself produces meaning. It may thus be called "primary theology" (*theologia prima*). As Lutheran liturgical theologian Gordon Lathrop puts it, "Primary liturgical theology is the communal meaning of the liturgy exercised by the gathering itself. The assembly uses combinations of words and signs to speak of God" (Lathrop 1993: 5). Or, as Aidan Kavanagh famously described it, in liturgy the assembly is brought to the edge of chaos in a holy encounter with God, which changes them deeply. Such change prompts a subtle "adjustment" in their next liturgical act. The adjustment, says Kavanagh, is "theology being born, theology in the first instance. It is what tradition has called *theologia prima*" (Kavanagh 1984: 73–4). Secondary theology, then, is the reflective act that occurs outside of worship, which organizes and critically assesses the knowledge of God that emerges in the liturgy and equips people to participate more fully in the act of worship.[5]

Of course, this intentional turn to ritual cannot ignore interpretations of ritual action. A concern about "meaning" has too often eclipsed "doing"; this is the valuable point that ritual theorists and liturgical theologians alike have raised, and which scholars of interreligious ritual participation need to hear. It is possible, however, to overstate this, portraying ritual participants as initially blank slates, performing actions without any prior notion of what they are doing or why they are doing it. Humans rarely engage in action without some sense of what and why.[6] Michael Aune, professor of liturgical and historical studies at Pacific Lutheran Theological Seminary, has made this point in a recent critique of forms of liturgical theology that make liturgical action prior to any interpretive categories. Aune argues that the relationship of act and interpretation is interwoven: "the particularity of worship and faith rests upon categories and structures with which worshippers make sense of a liturgical event." He thus challenges any simple distinction between primary and secondary theology, saying, "this so-called 'secondary theological reflection' is actually a primary theology... because it is born of and rooted in a particular way of knowing, a participatory knowing, in which a person of faith knows both *that* and *how*" (Aune 2007: 155).

This is not to say that "secondary" theological interpretation trumps the "primary theology" of Eucharistic practice. It is simply to point out that secondary reflection is inseparable from particular kinds of liturgical participation, and conversely, that the primary theology enacted in any Eucharistic celebration is already shaped by interpretive categories that participants bring with them. As Graham Hughes points out in his insightful work *Worship as Meaning* (Hughes 2003: 7), people in a liturgical event of any kind will at least in part shape the meanings of those events out of stocks of meaning available to them.[7] "Primary theology" itself, therefore, includes not only the unreflective action of participants, but their own present and evolving interpretive work as a constitutive part of the liturgical action.

4.3 Ecumenical convergence in liturgical practice enables "interreligious" participation

Though these discussions of *lex orandi*, *lex credendi* and primary and secondary theology are complex and contested, liturgical theologians share the basic conviction that embodied liturgical performance is a fundamental site for human encounter with God and thus gives rise to faith. Human ritual performance (at least in this Christian setting), therefore, is never merely human ritual performance; it is a meeting place of humanity and the divine. Through liturgical actions, persons and communities are shaped in basic habits of gratitude and praise, lament and beseeching. Don Saliers and Gordon Lathrop have paid particular attention to the ways in which liturgical action both expresses and shapes worshippers in fundamental affective patterns, which in turn shapes their interaction with the wider world (Saliers 1994, esp. the chapters on "liturgy as prayer"; Lathrop 1993: 54ff).

Over the past fifty years, increased attention to the power of liturgical action to shape belief, and to liturgical action itself as theological activity, has benefited from significant biblical and patristic scholarship on worship by both Protestants and Catholics. The fierce debate over interpretation of Prosper's motto *ut legem credendi lex statuat supplicandi* is one vibrant example of this. Such ecumenical attention to biblical and patristic sources, coupled with recovery of attention to liturgical action itself, has led to some remarkable convergences in liturgical practice, as Protestants and Catholics alike have returned to shared sources for reform of their liturgies. In particular, this has led to increasing similarities in Eucharistic practice. Since the 1960s, for instance, many Protestants have rediscovered a greater attention to the Lord's Supper as central to Christian worship, which has led to increased frequency of communion; at the same time, Catholics have increased attention to the importance of proclamation of the Word as a vital part of the Mass. This has led both of these Christian traditions to greater balance of Word and Table in ordinary Sunday worship services. Also, during this period many Protestants as well as Catholics have developed Eucharistic prayers that are deeply influenced (though not bound) by fourth-century patterns of praying at table.[8]

Ecumenical scholarship has contributed to these developments, and formal ecumenical dialogue is paying attention to its results. As Protestants and Catholics increasingly share similar Eucharistic practices, people are being formed in increasingly similar ways. This in turn affects theological interpretations of the Eucharist, so that liturgical practice is in fact shaping statements of faith. Further, this means that much Eucharistic participation is actually enabled, even though full "Eucharistic sharing" remains elusive.

I offer a few examples to illustrate. Since at least the 1970s, many Protestants, including Lutherans, Presbyterians, and Methodists, have been offering Eucharistic prayers in which congregational members share in the opening dialogue as well as a sung or spoken Sanctus.[9] These congregational responses are very similar, if not identical, to responses offered in the Roman Catholic Mass.[10] As a result, Catholics and Protestants who find themselves at one another's worship services are actually able to offer the congregational responses together without script or prompting, as apparently full members of one worshiping community.

In addition to shared texts, many Protestants and Catholics now share common embodied gestures during the celebration of the Eucharist. For instance, whereas a generation ago most Presbyterians would have celebrated communion only by passing trays of bread and individual glasses of grape juice down the pews, today very many Presbyterians also celebrate by coming forward to receive bread and cup from ministers, as do most Roman Catholic Christians (see Moore-Keish 2008: 127–30). As a result, Presbyterians and other Protestants accustomed to this method of distribution of the elements feel profoundly at home in Catholic services in which people move forward to receive communion—even if they are not officially permitted to receive those communion elements themselves.

Another way in which American Protestants and Catholics already engage in Eucharistic participation concerns shared congregational music. During this same era of liturgical renewal, there has been a surge of new congregational music composed by both Catholics and Protestants, and much of it has come to be shared across denominational boundaries. Specifically Eucharistic hymns and songs such as "Eat This Bread," "One Bread, One Body," and "You Satisfy the Hungry Heart,"[11] are sung by both Catholic and Protestant congregations, so that worshippers who find themselves at one another's Eucharistic services can sing together with ease and gusto, rather than the tentativeness born of unfamiliarity.

These instances of actual Eucharistic practice demonstrate that, despite official boundaries to full "Eucharistic sharing" between Protestants and Catholics, there is real liturgical sharing going on, thanks to common structures of prayer, common gestures, and common song. Common prayer, gesture, and song, in turn, contribute to shared theological reflection on the nature of the Eucharist.[12] By thus looking at the "doing" of the Eucharist in addition to the official doctrinal statements, we realize that the boundaries between these different Christian families are not impermeable. Liturgical theology enables us to see that this case of interreligious ritual participation is more complex than it first appeared.

5 Protestant-Catholic Eucharistic sharing and interreligious ritual participation

What can this intra-Christian case contribute to the larger question of interreligious ritual participation? I suggest five preliminary insights:

1. Ritual action, not only doctrinal teaching, shapes faith.
2. Different religious rituals have different thresholds of participation.
3. Participants often approach the same ritual with different interpretive frameworks.
4. Religious communities are not clearly separated from one another, which blurs the boundaries implied in the question of engaging in "someone else's ritual."
5. "Ritual participation" is a complex term, and often the question is not *whether* one can participate in the religious rituals of others, but *how*.

First, liturgical theology, with its keen attention to liturgical practice, focuses on how ritual participation shapes people in their fundamental attitudes and relations to each other, the world and God. Whether we take a strong or a more moderate interpretation of the motto *lex orandi, lex credendi*, the insight that the way we pray deeply affects what we believe is surely true for religious traditions other than Christianity. It is not enough to ask how belief affects practice; it is necessary also to observe how ritual practices shape and complicate belief. This basic point deserves attention among those engaged in interreligious dialogue, because it earnestly regards embodied practices—in addition to textual sources—as sources of wisdom.

Second, when we begin by taking embodied practices seriously, adhering to clean general principles about who participates in which religious rituals, and when and where, quickly becomes complicated by specificity. The question of how, whether, and when to participate in other people's rituals cannot be resolved in the abstract, but must be addressed with attention to each particular case. This is partly because different ritual actions have different "thresholds" of participation. For instance, singing together is often more permissible than breaking bread together. At least in the case of Protestant-Catholic relations, joining voices in song requires no special dispensation, while receiving bread and wine from the hand of another has a much higher threshold, requiring that certain criteria be met for full ritual participation. Scholars of interreligious ritual participation would be wise to consider the particularities of each ritual action, guarding against generalization about whether a given community is more open or "closed" to the participation of outsiders.

Furthermore, and thirdly, participants often approach the "same" ritual with different interpretive frameworks. When it comes to the Eucharist, many Protestants welcome Catholics to participate fully in a Protestant celebration, including receiving the elements of bread and wine, based on a theological commitment to baptismal unity, and a conviction that Christ (rather than a specific institutional church) is the host at the table. Catholic teaching, however, stipulates that Catholic faithful may lawfully receive sacraments (including Eucharist) only from Catholic ministers, for reasons detailed above. There are thus two theological interpretations at work here: that of the tradition hosting the ritual, and that of the one(s) seeking to participate. In any instance of interreligious ritual participation, both need to be taken into account. Both the variety of ritual actions and the variety of theological frameworks used to interpret them, therefore, mean that the question of ritual participation is always messy and *ad hoc*, not something that can be settled according to general principles.

Fourth, the boundaries between religious communities are themselves not always clear. The Protestant-Catholic Eucharistic puzzle, for instance, challenges any simple categorization of people into discrete, separable religious communities. In this case, both Protestants and Catholics understand themselves to belong to the broad category "Christian," though they debate all that is entailed by that term. Furthermore, the boundary between these communities is quite porous in practice; many Christians move easily from one to the other, or even understand themselves to be both Protestant and Catholic at the same time.[13] Even for those who identify clearly with one confessional community, Protestants and Catholics share many ritual elements, and thus the Eucharist simultaneously draws the worshiping community together and draws boundaries within a gathered group of Protestants and Catholics. Something similar is true when Christians and Jews participate in one another's rituals; because of some shared scriptures as well as shared ancient history, we are neither one community nor absolutely separate communities. We can and do sing the psalms together. We can and do hear the stories of Abraham, Moses, and David with the sense that they are "our" stories. There may well be analogous instances with regard to other religious traditions, such as Hinduism and Buddhism, which have shared ancient history and symbolism. As a result, "crossing over" to participate in the religious ritual of "another" may not require leaving behind one's own community. The traditions themselves overlap with and borrow from one another. Consideration of interreligious ritual participation, then, will benefit from recognizing that boundaries between and within religions are not neat and clear. At least in some cases, participation in another's religious ritual is simultaneously participating in one's own.

Finally, this turn to embodied practices reveals that participation in a religious ritual is a complex notion. What does it mean to "participate" in a ritual, either in one's "home" tradition or another one? Douglas Pratt, in another chapter in this volume, suggests that there are two forms of participation in interfaith rituals: either one religion enacts its ritual and invites others to attend, or a ritual is cooperatively planned and enacted as a multifaith event. I suggest, however, that the first kind of participation is more complex than Pratt suggests. The case of Protestant-Catholic Eucharistic sharing shows that "participation" is not a binary term, but one which admits of multiple modes. That is, one does not simply "participate" or "not participate" in a ritual; one participates in a particular way. For instance, Protestants who attend a Catholic Mass may not be invited to receive the elements of bread and wine, but because of common patterns of prayer and shared congregational songs, Protestant worshippers can and do participate in real ways in the ritual celebration. The reverse is also true: Catholics attending a Protestant Lord's Supper may be prohibited by their own canon law from receiving the elements (and therefore it may seem that they are "not participating"), but they may easily sing and pray with their neighbors as full participants in the majority of the worship service.

Having said this, of course, I do not mean to obscure the real power dynamics that specify who may licitly come to any specific Eucharistic table. Other scholars have raised important and troubling questions about who has the power to decide the boundaries of the table, and whether such power is exercised in keeping with the Christian gospel of liberation (Carvalhaes 2013). My point here is that ironically, the recovery of attention to the centrality of the Eucharist in recent decades may have contributed to a narrow focus on "reception" in a way that obscures other dimensions of genuine Eucharistic participation. Such genuine participation may constitute subversion of another kind. Consideration of interreligious ritual participation, then, will benefit from recognizing that the answer to the question "may members of one religion participate in the ritual of another religion?" is often not "yes" or "no," but "how"?

6 Conclusion

What finally does this case study have to offer scholars of interreligious ritual participation? In brief, rituals, like bodies, are mobile, particular, and hard to constrain within general principles. The lesson from the Catholic-Protestant Eucharistic question is that in fact, interreligious ritual participation is already happening in a variety of ways, in spite of the fact that official reception of the Eucharistic elements is in most cases forbidden. Because of common praying and singing, because of common history and symbolism, because of multiple Christian belonging, because of the varying thresholds of liturgical participation, these "two" religious communities are not simply two. The path ahead for those who investigate the boundary-crossings of different religious rituals is to attend to the messy particularity of those rituals themselves and refrain from assuming a clear unbroken divide where there is in practice a fluid and porous frontier.

Part II

MUSLIM AND CHRISTIAN-MUSLIM PERSPECTIVES

Chapter 7

RECEIVING THE STRANGER:
A MUSLIM THEOLOGY OF SHARED WORSHIP

Tim Winter

1 Introduction

In April 1874 the Hungarian Orientalist Ignaz Goldziher attended Friday prayers at the mosque of Imam al-Shafiʿi in Cairo. Persuaded through his studies that Islam was a model of antisuperstitious, rational monotheism, and deeply sympathetic to Egyptian nationalist causes, he seems to have felt no qualms of conscience in doing so; indeed, he experienced a kind of mystical epiphany. "In the midst of the thousands of the pious," he recalled, "I rubbed my forehead against the floor of the mosque. Never in my life was I more devout, more truly devout, then on that exalted Friday" (Patai 1987: 28).

In an age of empire and Orientalist reductionism, such openness of heart was unusual. Rather more typical was the mindset of Goldziher's teacher Arminius Vámbéry (1832–1913), a polyglot traveler and spy who had also participated in Muslim worship. Disguised as a dervish, Vámbéry had made the hazardous—for non-Muslims—journey to Bukhara, where he made a point of praying in the city's mosques. But his devotion seems to have been opportunistic and spurious, and he immediately shook it off on his return to public adulation in Budapest, where he published a sensational account of his travels (Vámbéry 1973).

The two men had attended the *salat*, the normative Muslim worship, with different hearts. Goldziher was evidently entranced by Islam, while Vámbéry treated it with a kind of affectionate contempt. Although today's moral judgment is likely to be in favor of Goldziher, Vámbéry in practice presents fewer difficulties for Shariʿa assessment: his public *shahada*, his self-affirmation of his Islamic belonging, was enough to open the mosques to him in the eyes of the revealed law; his private conviction was a matter between him and God. But Goldziher, despite his evidently purer heart, was, canonically speaking, trespassing: he was unconverted, a Jew at the Friday prayers.

The present chapter, relying on an Islamic insider's paradigm, will ask whether this paradox, mirrored in the paucity of Islamic legal and liturgical guidance on such interreligious intrusions, might be remedied. The treatment begins with an investigation of the potential challenges to the internal religious integrity of non-Muslims which any invitation to mosque worship might entail. Next we consider the resources available to majoritarian Sunni Islamic discourse in supplying genuinely informed and thoughtful guidance for mosques where non-Muslims wish to join congregations for formal worship. As we shall see, a raft of difficulties, shaped by anxieties over purity, transgression, and identity, immediately present themselves, and have provided a major influence in shaping the canonists' verdicts. Yet they do not appear to be entirely insuperable, and we conclude with some larger reflections on the significance of prayer as an indicant of Islam's self-understanding as an "Abrahamic" religion in a global and inclusive mode. Our focus will be directed primarily to the question of Christian participation, given the more extensive literature which exists on the subject, but the treatment and conclusion may apply in a significant measure to the question of Jewish attendance as well.

2   The modern context

In the age of Goldziher and Vámbéry, this question arose but seldom. In contemporary multireligious societies, however, it presents itself with increasing frequency. One commonly reported case is the situation of mixed-faith married couples. The inability of such couples to pray together has been shown to add a significant strain on relationships already made challenging by other cultural and ethnic differences (Elison et al. 2010: 963–75). Further distress and alienation may be generated when a non-Muslim spouse, children, or other relations are excluded by mosque personnel from joining the funeral prayer (*salat al-janaza*), and this underlining of the spouses' religious difference is reported as a significant addition to the pain at a time of bereavement.[1] Although these and other relevant pastoral issues appear pressing, and are likely to recur with increasing frequency, the literature on Muslim chaplaincy and ministry in a contemporary multifaith context seems reluctant to address the issue.

The premodern jurisprudential manuals, generated in cultures in which it was assumed that non-Muslims would not wish to join Muslim worship, are of little help. More recent *fatwas* may recognize that non-Muslim friends and relatives may wish to watch the ceremony, and often offer instructions on modest dress or comportment; however the assumption remains that they will be excluded from actual participation.[2] In mid-twentieth-century Bosnia, for instance, in a society marked by an unusually rich and extensive social interaction between religions, official *fatwas* supported the presence of non-Muslims at funerals, and provided guidance for their reverent attendance, but assumed that they would not be joining the prayer itself (Đozo 2006: 226–7, 340, 349).[3] Even in the modern multifaith West's radical "context of otherness," groups that encourage the practice of informal interfaith prayer, often using generic and inclusive "Abrahamic" liturgies, will normally draw the line at supporting Christians and Jews who wish to join the worshippers in the mosques. Perhaps signaled by the purity laws, which are often received as signs of exclusive belonging and acceptability to God, the Muslim *salat* prayer continues to be understood by many as the symbol of an Islamic sacral identity constructed in difference.

3 The integrity of the unbeliever

Shari'a provisions concerning Christians and Jews were historically far from egalitarian, but they did seek to respect the "People of the Book" in their desire to maintain the integrity of their own doctrines and rituals. In a Shari'a jurisdiction a non-Muslim woman who marries a Muslim man retains her creed and practices intact, even where the jurists regard them, as they usually do, as abrogated or otherwise unacceptable to God. A theology which seeks to welcome non-Muslims to mosque worship will therefore need to ensure that this basic right to internal Christian or Jewish fidelity is not compromised. Hospitality is only authentic if it respects rather than compromises the rights of the guest.

The discussion must therefore start with the recognition that there are People of the Book who for a range of reasons may themselves seek inclusion. At the cynical end of the spectrum we note Vámbéry's dissimulation; this, however, may be set aside for our purposes as an adventurer's subterfuge, emulated today only by some Christian missionaries who adopt a Muslim disguise to work in difficult or risky outreach situations.[4] At the other end of our spectrum stands Goldziher, who appears to have believed in the *salat*'s beauty and even efficacy while retaining his lifelong Jewish identity. Between these extremes there stretches a great diversity of degrees of belief, sincerity, and commitment. Common, however, is a general view that Muslim prayer is worthy of respect and should be seen as a disciplined, dignified enactment of a proper humility before God (Valkenberg 2006: 149). Christian scholars have compiled anthologies of Muslim petitionary prayers (*du'a'*) to emphasize the close commonalties that they believe they have identified with the prayer life of their own faith (Padwick 1961; Cragg 1999). It was out of respect that Pope John Paul II asked Christians to pray and fast, in their own way, during Ramadan (Valkenberg 2006: 150); he seems to have expressed a broad theology of this after the 1986 "peace summit" at Assisi, when he proclaimed, in the spirit of *Nostra Aetate*, that "every genuine prayer is inspired by the Holy Spirit, who in a mysterious way is present in the heart of every human being" (*Redemptoris Missio* 29).

Older claims that Muslim prayer is not addressed to the God worshipped by Christians, while maintained by some, appear to be increasingly subject to challenge. In a significant departure from older practice, Vatican II asserted that "the plan of salvation also includes those who acknowledge the Creator, in the first place among whom are the Muslims: these profess to hold the faith of Abraham, and together with us they adore the one, merciful God, mankind's judge on the last day" (*Lumen Gentium* 16).[5] Among evangelicals, Miroslav Volf has recently made a forceful case that Muslims and Christians "worship the same true God" (Volf 2012: 123), which allows him to add that the example of Muslim prayer might help Western Christians "to rediscover 'submission to God' as a key dimension of spirituality" (Volf 2012: 197). For Christian Troll, "the two images of God share such essential elements that under certain circumstances Christians and Muslims can and should jointly pray to God" (Troll 2008). While Muslims must not seek to arbitrate between alternate Christian convictions, the presence of such informed opinions (which may turn out to be even more widespread among parishioners than among church leaders and theologians) appears to permit the Shari'a to rule that Christians are not automatically being invited to compromise their own integrity by praying in a Muslim way, or with Muslims who are worshipping a "Muslim God."

The Shari'a manuals affirm the *salat*'s purposes as generically Abrahamic, as an enactment of pure thankfulness and praise. Typical is the assessment of al-Kasani (d. 1191), who identifies seven purposes to the ritual: (1) an expression of gratitude to God for His excellent creation of humanity; (2) gratitude for bodily well-being; (3) the integration of all the members and faculties (*jawarih*); (4) gratitude for the softness of the body's joints; (5) manifesting one's servitude ('*ubudiyya*) to God; (6) a protection from sin; and (7) an atonement for sin (al-Kasani 1421 AH: I 225–6).[6] In this Hanafi jurist's list of the prayer's functions we find nothing with which a non-Muslim monotheist is likely to disagree.

The form, also, of the Muslim *salat* rites, while popularly construed as paradigmatically Muslim, does not appear to be intrinsically anti-Christian or non-Christian. The similarity of the Muslim daily prayer schedule to the daily rhythm of many monastic traditions is frequently noted (Wright 2013: 302–5). Prostration, bowing, and kneeling were common devotional postures in the Near East at the time of Islam's emergence, while "prayer mats, still one of the most familiar features of the mosque today, were extensively used by Christian monks as far apart as Syria and Northumbria or Ireland before the coming of Islam" (MacCulloch 2010: 258). One modern Anglican nun who works in dialogue with Muslims in Oxford has adopted the practice of the *salat* as a gesture of solidarity and respect, "to the extent of learning of God from another tradition." She begins with the *takbir* and the Arabic *Fatiha*, with its "similarity" to the Lord's Prayer, and follows the various canonical formulas, noting the Christian value of each. "A threefold declaration of 'Glory be to God' with my body was a real blessing, giving the whole of my body a chance to express itself prayerfully and with movement" (Judith 2012: 132–43). The final words of the prayer, said to fellow congregants to right and left, are "Peace and the mercy of God be with you," which closely parallels a widespread Christian liturgical usage in which words of peace close the ceremony as an affirmation of reconciliation and fellowship. Islam's cultic forms did not emerge in isolation, but evince clear parallels with Christian and other ritual customs which interacted in and grew from the complex "culture compost" of late antiquity,[7] and the nun asks whether a particular blessing might not inhere in exposure to Muslim worship as a means whereby Christians could be "reunited with their roots" (Judith 2012: 135). There is some evidence that in the Prophet's city Muslims and Jews were able to worship together (Friedman 2003: 31), which again suggests a confessional universe in which ritual forms and boundaries were not seen as absolute. While linear influences are difficult if not impossible to demonstrate, forms of worship in the Near East at the time of the rise of Islam may very easily be interpreted as variations operating within a single ecumenical culture of monotheism.

Such a recognition that the current boundaries between Islam and Christianity are the result of historically complex reifications of originally blurred frontiers amid varied appropriations of a shared Near Eastern patrimony, might even allow the informal revival of ancient Christian views of Islam as one form of a hugely diverse Christianity. If Trinitarian Christians can attend Unitarian services, it is far from clear why attending the *salat* ritual should be thought less acceptable. For Ian Markham, a prominent theorist of this venturesome type of ecumenism: "If I manage to sit alongside a fundamentalist Christian and trust that God is receiving our worship equally, then there should be no problem about sitting alongside a Muslim or a Jew. The diversity is no greater" (Markham 2009: 34).

Hybridized and interactive religious origins gave way to more reified boundaries; but these were in many cases never absolute. At Islam's "edges" much later in its history we observe a historic proliferation of interactive religious forms which again threaten reified Same/Other dichotomies. The phenomenon of syncretism and multiple religious belonging is particularly well-attested in India, where in many communities the devout simultaneously engaged in Muslim and Hindu practices, despite the ostensive gulf which divided the two thought-worlds.[8] This also appears in numerous contexts of Muslim-Christian coexistence, where hybridization or even the simultaneous observance of two religions could yield sustainable forms which endured sometimes for hundreds of years. During centuries of Ottoman rule in the Balkans, Muslims regularly had their infants christened, considering the procedure to be a form of talismanic protection, while Christians frequently adopted key aspects of Islamic practice. Both would celebrate the feast of St George, to which they attached somewhat different meanings. In many Albanian communities Christians would externally practice Islam, often to overcome the social and legal disadvantages inherent in the *dhimmi* condition, while privately continuing with a version of Christian identity. In some cases these were crypto-Christians practicing a straightforward dissimulation; but the faith of these "dappled" (*laramane*) believers could also be experienced as what might be dubbed "bifideism": the concurrent and believing performance of two religions (Deringil 2011: 111–55). As an English traveler commented in 1717:

> These people, living between Christians and Mahometans and not being skill'd in controversie, declare that they are utterly unable to judge which Religion is best; but to be certain of not entirely rejecting the Truth, they very prudently follow both, and go to the Mosque on Fridays and the Church on Sundays. (cited in Reinkowski 2007: 422)

Such premodern patterns of double or multiple belonging are in many contexts under threat from modern highly reified definitions of adhesion. However in a Western context they seem likely to proliferate, thanks to conditions of liberal individualism, doubt concerning creeds, and globalized access to a vast range of religious options. Volf notes the case of Ann Redding, an Episcopalian priest who has declared herself simultaneously Muslim and Christian (Volf 2012: 195–6). Another American, the distinguished translator of Arabic texts Nancy Roberts, self-identifies as Muslim, but in addition to praying the *salat* three times a day, adds a Christian prayer twice daily, observing "I coexist peacefully with the intellectual incongruities" (Roberts 2013: 328). To this mix one might add the Christians who have found a particular value in Islam, such as Louis Massignon, "a Muslim-Christian," a "Christian in a Muslim way," who had no doubt about the divine inspiration of the Qu'ran, and sought, through his informal *badaliyya* confraternity, to live as a Christian "inside" Islam, acknowledging, if not replicating, its canonical "pillars" (Massignon 2011: 345). This *badaliyya* principle is currently enjoying a modest renaissance among devout Catholics convinced of the efficacy and grace found in Muslim worship; a senior advocate has been Paolo Dall'Oglio SJ, who described his first experience of the *salat* in these terms:

> The beauty, the universality, the gentleness, the truth of the Muslim prayer unveiled itself to me in all its power! I was there, with these villagers, and at the same time I was in every mosque in the world. The Muslims say that to be at prayer is to be held between the two hands of the Merciful, as God, in the Bible, kneads man out of the potter's clay. It was in that manner, in that mosque in Bosra, in the midst of the believers, that the mystery of the Muslim prayer entered my own life of prayer. (Dall'Oglio 2009: 32)[9]

The heart of the *salat* is the transformation of the believer through the resonant reception of God's Word. Massignon's Franciscan disciple Giulio Basetti-Sani insisted that on Christian criteria he was convinced that the Prophet was inspired by God, and that the entirety of the Qu'ran ought to be seen as divine revelation (albeit not literally, but by inspiration). Christians, however, possess the true Christological key which allows them to understand this revealed scripture more correctly than Muslims do themselves (Basetti-Sani 1977). Such insights into the Qu'ran's status as divine speech surely enable a real Christian enactment of the *salat*, whose living heart is the Word.[10]

Very many other examples of Christians creatively interrogating or overstepping our boundaries could be adduced (Aydın 2002: 135–99).[11] These forms of generous Christian affirmation of the spiritual efficacy of *salat* and the scripture which lies at its heart suggest not that Muslim thinkers and jurists ought to regard Christians as in some sense obligated by the practice, or that their participation is in any way expected where Muslims and Christians gather together. Neither should Christian participation be considered tantamount to an affirmation of the full religious validity of Islam.[12] Our conclusion is simply that they need not regard Christian attendance at such congregations as always inimical to the autonomy which the revealed law of Islam allows to the People of the Book.

4 Muslim integrity

As noted earlier, premodern *fiqh* seldom imagined the possibility that a *dhimmi* neighbor might be inclined to join Muslim worship. Discussions in the juristic canon preferred to focus on the question of whether *dhimmis* may enter mosques at all. For the Hanafi school (the most numerous) this was thought to be permissible, so that they may even enter the Great Sanctuary in Mecca; while Shafi'is and some Hanbalis held that Christians and Jews may enter other mosques but not that of Mecca itself; and only the Malikis forbade the mosques to them absolutely (a prohibition which is still maintained in Morocco and certain other Maliki jurisdictions). In his study of Islam's practices toward non-Muslims, Antoine Fattal holds that the practice of the earliest Muslims supports the Hanafi view (Fattal 1958: 91–3), and the evidence is not hard to seek. The *sira* literature preserves the memory of the Prophet's decision to lodge non-Muslims on various occasions in his mosque in Medina. We learn that on one such occasion a delegation from the pagan tribe of Thaqif was admitted to the mosque, where the Prophet erected a tent or booth for their comfort during his negotiations with them (ibn Hisham 1936: IV 184). The Christian clergy of Najran were accommodated in a more significant way: the *sira* accounts report that the Prophet allowed them to pray in his mosque and that they wore magnificent silk and gold clothes as they stood praying to the East. The Prophet then refused to speak with them until they had changed into monk's habits, as "before that the devil was with them," after which he greeted them and opened a long disputation over the nature of Christ (ibn Sa'd 1985: 357; al-Bayhaqi 1405/1985: 386).

Prophetic practice, partly enshrined in the Shari'a provisions, thus supplies considerable justification not only for non-Muslim entry into Muslim sanctuaries but also for active hospitality, to the extent of permitting Christians to conduct their ceremonies within a mosque's precincts. Here a logical question becomes difficult to avoid: if the Shari'a knows that the *salat* is more pleasing to God than the Mass, and is more appropriate in a house of God, then would the Bishop of Najran's participation in the *salat* ritual not have been preferable in the perspective of the final Abrahamic dispensation than his celebration of a Christian rite? Was the Eucharist not, in Shari'a jargon, *tark al-awla*, the failure to choose what was more appropriate and right?

The response would seem to be that non-Muslim participation in *salat* is impossible because the presence of individuals who have failed to accept the fullness of Abrahamic monotheism in its Qu'ranic consummation would detract from the full fellowship of communing Muslim souls. The prayer line (*saff*) of God's true lovers must be continuous, and just as it is disliked that it be interrupted by a gap, or by some obstruction such as a column, so also it would be unacceptably interrupted by the presence of a heart which is not spiritually attuned. Attachment to an older, partial, or abrogated version of the Abrahamic religion (*millat Ibrahim*) is so willful and wicked as to contaminate the Muslim congregation.[13]

Such an objection, which at least seems implicit in the vague Shari'a prohibitions, appears difficult to measure on purely juridical grounds. Even the usual reliance on analogy does not help the case for prohibition. On the contrary, if a Muslim man may be the head of a household in which a Christian is his wife, then is it persuasive to argue that a Muslim imam cannot or should not lead a Christian in prayer? To argue that marriage is a more practical and social institution is implicitly to desacralize it, suggesting that the marital act itself is alien to the saints. In a fully monotheistic perspective which denies the reality of the "secular," and in which God's grace and power are acknowledged as the unimpeded active principle which sanctifies every movement and meaning in creation, it seems theologically subversive to suggest that certain Shari'a assumptions determine a "profane" realm and cannot guide jurists in discerning norms in a "ritual" sphere. God is "closer to man than his jugular vein" (Qu'ran 50:16); He is *al-qarib*, the Near; the great prophetic insight of revelation is His absolute presence and accessibility. In the environment of intimacy with the Divine which Islam seeks to foster, the project of the "secular" appears simply as an ideology of divine insignificance or absence.

The objection to non-Muslim participation just cited is rooted ultimately in the techniques of *maqasid* (the purposes of God's command) and of *'illa* (*ratio legis*). No scriptural evidence exists for it: a revealed text (*nass*) which expressly forbade interreligious prayer would decisively settle the case; but this is nowhere forthcoming. Neither can one identify a decisive analogy (*qiyas*) with an evidently commensurate practice for which a proof-text has been transmitted. Hence the resort to a pragmatic argument based on a purported reasoned opinion (*ra'y*), which has carried the day in those infrequent instances where the *fiqh* literature considers the matter.

One need spend little time pointing to the context in which the developed Shari'a was adumbrated. The earliest period of Islam had been a time of provisionality, flux, and accommodation in which Christians readily entered mosques and were even permitted to act as scribes of the Qu'ranic text (George 2011: 377–429). By contrast, the Shari'a manuals of the high medieval period reflect a settled and triumphalist thought-world which was also notably fearful: the Other within (the *dhimmi*) lived as an ongoing reproach to Islam's capacity to attract souls and as a potential fifth-columnist for invaders; while the Other *ante portas* was lethal when in militant mode (frequently we find that the manuals are more favorable to Jews, who had no external allies, than to Christians (Fattal 1958: 92)). The notion that the Christian Other represented a radical failure not only to conceive of God in properly monotheistic terms, but also a totalitarian political threat rooted in the *cuius regio eius religio* principle (the Crusades and the Inquisition sprang too readily to Muslim minds), cast a long shadow over the Muslim sense of the depth of Christian belonging to their societies. To allow Christians into mosques to pray (on the rare occasions when that might be sought) might bring to the surface insecurities about the Christian "dark other" as harbinger of violence, driven by a false and deleterious understanding of God (Malouf 1984: 266). The widespread belief that Christians were unconcerned with personal hygiene and were unfamiliar with the institution of the *hammam*

(Hillenbrand 1999: 274–82) further exacerbated this blurred but major identification of the Other with impurity.

While Muslim congregations are likely to wish contemporary practice to be demonstrably rooted in tradition, it is hardly controversial to argue that *ra'y*-based verdicts inherited from earlier ages are open to revision or abolition on the grounds that the circumstances of the world have changed. Although the Shari'a has, overall, maintained its vision for a society focused on divine service, repudiating the claims of a reductive secular sovereignty over human fulfillment, it has been obliged to adapt very drastically over the past two centuries in its attempts to preserve this vision. Its substantial contingency and historicity are well known to the jurists. Even on issues where the manuals found a superabundance of proof-texts in the revealed sources, Qu'ranically faithful strategies have been found which have amended or even overturned earlier norms of thinking and judgments in areas as diverse as rulings on financial practices, land tenure, contract law, and many others (Zaman 2002). For a contemporary mufti to disallow, for instance, a contract of slavery, while enforcing a premodern prohibition on interfaith worship, might be to commit a serious inconsistency of jurisprudential method.

The contemporary multicultural context in the West, in which non-Muslim believers in the One God occasionally seek inclusion in the *salat*, is very remote from the polarized universe which the medieval jurists, with their dichotomy between the Abode of Peace and the Abode of War, believed that they inhabited. As we have seen, ours is a context of hybridization and a widespread and seemingly unstoppable desire for experiment, entanglement, and intersubjectivity. At times this is shaped by relativism and theological insouciance, but it is also, on occasion, driven by a sincere human need to cross boundaries for the sake of solidarity and in the belief that the Other offers the soul something of genuine worth. The Other cannot be automatically dismissed as adversarial. While it is true that some Muslims maintain older views of the Christian world as susceptible to moods of religiously informed aggression (Winter 2011: 394–411), theologians and jurists need to be firmly reminded that established Christian leaders do not sanction those moods, and indeed, campaign actively to overcome them. Christians who respect Islam, particularly those who have found ways of accepting the Qu'ran as "a word of God," are important allies in the struggle against the type of "warrior Christianity" which in the eyes of many Muslims was a key driver in recent Western military interventions in Muslim countries. Excluding them from worship is likely to appear as a significant failure of courtesy and perception.

5 An Ishmaelite theology of hospitality

Louis Massignon's complex understanding of Islam was rooted in his own experience of Muslim hospitality (*qira*); he saw Islam as paradigmatically Abrahamic in its emphasis on this virtue. In his agonized reflections on the Palestinian tragedy he identified the exiled, maltreated Ishmaelite as the true repository and sign of the Abrahamic principle, the victim of a mistaken, exclusionary reading of the

Jewish heritage. The Arabs are to be the models and exemplars of the principle of hospitality, who suffer at the hands either of what he believed was an earlier, more exclusionary dispensation, or of a self-absorbed Europe whose cold Enlightenment paradigm shunned heteronomy (Derrida 2002: 356–419).

More recently Jon Levenson has offered an extensive meditation on Abraham's significance for the Self-Other constructions of the three monotheisms. His approach is reminiscent of the Scriptural Reasoning project in that it is pragmatic (in Peirce's sense) and reparative. While learning all we can from the Higher Criticism, and maintaining a reluctance to impose single interpretations on scripture, we must reread the texts for new exegetic outcomes, typically in the quest to overcome polarities which an older hermeneutic believed it had found in God's word. Levenson's work seems particularly interesting to Muslim theologians as it seeks to undermine the dichotomy between chosen and unchosen as the scriptural trope which figures the Same and the Other. For Paul and Augustine, the opposition Ishmael/Isaac (or Hagar/Sarah) supplied the Bible's great figure of the carnal against the spiritual, and hence the impure against the elect (Robbins 1991: 4–5). For Levenson, however, such total readings fail to do justice to the biblical text, for there is not one but several Abrahams: Genesis 15 gives us the Abraham of conquest, chosenness, and exclusion, but in Genesis 17 we are shown the patriarch "as a kind of international figure," "the father of a multitude of nations" (Levenson 2012: 49). A careful and pragmatic reading may conclude that "identity need not be forged in opposition, [and] outsiders need not be identified with impurity" (Levenson 2012: 34).

This capacity to find a second reading of Genesis is of critical importance for Muslims, who have been historically immune to the practice of constructing an alleged rivalry between Isaac and Ishmael as the original paradigm of the Same-Other division. Levenson is aware that "the notion that one of the brothers takes precedence over the other is as alien to that scripture [the Qu'ran] as it is natural to its Jewish and Christian antecedents" (Levenson 2012: 196). The Qu'ran is itself reasoning scripturally in its reparative and harmonizing second reading of the Genesis text. Under this reading, for Levenson as for the Qu'ran, the patriarch is not to be associated with communal particularity but with a theology of reconciliation: he does not represent election but inclusion. The "Abrahamic" is not a canon of judgment signaled by an eternal and hopeless sibling rivalry, but is the ultimate archetype of tacit or explicit hospitality, denoting membership of a "family of mutual influence."

The *salat*, including the *salat al-janaza*, indispensably incorporates and culminates with the Abrahamic Blessing (*as-salat al-ibrahimiyya*), and is offered while physically facing Abraham's "Ancient House," which abuts the "grave of Ishmael" (al-Jaziri 2009: 690). Everything which Muslims understand to be Muhammadan is by the same token Ishmaelite and hence authentically Abrahamic—although the "charism of Ishmael" always implies the universal hope expressed in God's promise to Abraham, represented in the gathering of nations to the Hajj and in Hagar's Gentile blood. All these axioms of the final major monotheism are signs of inclusivity and of God's wide embrace: by being "in Ishmael" the worshippers accept God's own astonishing acceptance of the one who is externally designated the outcast and rejected, who, in the person of the "gentile Prophet," shows God's final dismissal of narratives of privilege and exclusion. In a modern context in which Ishmael and his faith find themselves distressed and despised, the *salat* becomes a genuinely Abrahamic sign of comfort, a token of God's ongoing commitment to those who will not compromise for the sake of the approval of a materialistic and instrumental global culture.

This reading of the Islamic modality of being Abrahamic underlines the larger significance of the *salat* as the ritual of all who self-identify with Ishmael. To be "in Ishmael," in this form of practice, is to accept God's will that His servants are to be the "Ishmaelite" refugees in an age when privilege and power despise Ishmael more than they despise anything else. To turn toward the Ishmaelite sanctuary in a ghetto mosque in Moscow, Beijing, or Washington is more than a simple act of love for the One God enacted in "religious ritual," it is a symbolic act of solidarity not only with those whose beliefs and laws are anathema to the global elites, but to all others who are that elite's victims. Turning one's face to God with the words "God is Greater" is the paradigm of turning one's back on an implacable Nimrod, and of living in "serenity and coolness" (21:69) in his fire, which is kindled from desire and a vehement worldliness.

The *salat* might be viewed, from this interpretive perspective, as the most symbolically freighted of all acts performed against global materialism. On the streets of Paris it is considered so shocking that it has been criminalized.[14] The same Massignon who risked his life leading protests against the French occupation of Algeria would probably in our time have participated in the *salat*, symbol of resistance to a totalizing republican principle which he regarded as anticlerical, antireligious, and the antithesis of everything Abrahamic. For Massignon, Abraham is the source of an entire theology of liberation.

Any exclusion of willing worshippers from the *salat* runs the risk of breathing life into the "other Abraham," the patriarch of exclusion, rather than the Abraham of radical inclusion and promise affirmed by Islam's founder, the prophet who, according to the hadith, led the earlier prophets in a single congregational prayer (Ibn Saʿd, I 214; Bayhaqi, II 362). Ishmael, with his full affirmation of his brother's lineage, indicates that Abraham's bosom is not the site of a zero-sum game. Only Nimrod and his present-day simulacra are excluded.

The prayerful presence of welcomed adherents of the covenant through Isaac would demonstrate a further dimension of the *salat*'s broader significance. Directed toward the Kaʿba, whose history predates "Islam-as-religion" and even the promise of the specifically Ishmaelite universalism, it is a recollection and reenactment of the primordial covenant (*mithaq*) which included all humanity before the moment when God differentiated them into the various "laws and ways" (Q 5:48). To join the *salat* is thus symbolically to recall and participate in the cosmic worship of all human souls as they testified to the presence and lordship of the One who created the world out of gratuitous love and mercy. This day of

"Am I not your Lord?," the primal congregational prayer elaborately theorized by the most significant strands of Sufism, is attested in revelation itself:

> When thy Lord drew forth from the children of Adam—from their loins—their descendants, and made them testify concerning themselves: "Am I not your Lord?" They replied: "Yes, we testify!" [This,] lest you should say on the Day of Judgment, "Of this we were unaware." (Q 7:172)

The people of the *qibla* cannot, therefore, be exclusively the people of "Islam" as a specifically evolved version of Abrahamic monotheism; they are, finally, the entirety of "Adam's seed." It is by virtue of *adamiyya*, "Adamness," that all human beings are innately vested with rights, notably the five rights which are the irreducible axioms of the Shari'a: the right to life, property, religion, reason, and family (Şentürk 2002: 39–69). From this perspective the Shari'a cannot deny non-Muslims, who are irreducibly Adamic and thus still in God's image (*fi suratihi*),[15] the right to turn their faces to the "Ancient House" with its primordial, "pre-religious," and universal significance. With Muslims, other Abrahamic believers may, if they choose, testify to God's lordship as symbolized by the Great Sanctuary, the "first house appointed for mankind" (Q 3:96). For Muslims, this should be the final and truest form of what Massignon called "sacred hospitality."

This "Great Covenant" perspective, which neither syncretizes nor overlooks difference, but merely refuses to exclude those attracted to the blessings of Ishmaelite devotion, can only be scripturally faithful if, in the spirit of true hospitality, it resists the danger of assimilating the Other to the Same. No judgment ought to be made on the basis of the internal creedal life of non-Muslim participants; recalling the insight of Josef van Ess, who proposes that Muslim diversity was historically facilitated by the fact that the *salat* does not incorporate a detailed creed (van Ess 2006: 13), the prayer supplies a framework within which worshippers may conceive of God in distinct ways while remaining faithful to the delineations of a broad Abrahamic affiliation. As Ernest McClain concludes from his study of the Qu'ranic Abraham's profession of God's unity: "there is no cultural lobotomy of other peoples' viewpoints, for this statement is left undefined ... it is free from the slightest taint of Islamic parochialism. The Unicity of God embraces an infinity of reasons" (McClain 1981: 11). The Abrahamic Other is affirmed as a lawful participant and witness to *No God but God*, insofar as his or her distinctiveness is honored and welcomed as a potential source of enrichment of our own understanding of the prayer's meaning.

Chapter 8

INTERRELIGIOUS PRAYER BETWEEN
ROMAN CATHOLIC CHRISTIANS AND MUSLIMS

Gavin D'Costa

1 Introduction

In this chapter I will carry out a three-stage investigation into whether Roman Catholic Christians and Muslims might pray together. In parts of the world this already happens, but this is not an empirical investigation or an anthropological study; rather it is an attempt to examine the *theological* justification of such ventures. I specify "Roman Catholic Christians" because each Christian denomination is bounded by differing views on these matters, and to give a "Christian answer" is not yet possible. First, I will distinguish the various ways in which the term "pray together" might be understood. I will focus on what I call interreligious prayer, rather than multireligious prayer. By interreligious prayer I mean praying together using the same words, with the two groups united in heart and mind; multireligious prayer is praying one's own prayers in the presence of another religious group, where they are silent and respectful, and possibly may be joining in silently and internally. I argue that in the early literature on the matter there is a danger of conflating the two different types. In the second section, I will show that some Catholic communities, following the initiatives of Pope John Paul II, have reached a consensus that interreligious prayer is problematic while multi-religious prayer is not. In the third section, I will consider an essay by Joseph Ratzinger in which he discusses the preconditions for interreligious prayer and argues that they could almost never exist, except perhaps for Catholics and Jews. I argue that the first precondition specified by Ratzinger, that prayer must be addressed to the one true God, allows us to analogically examine the possible grounds for interreligious prayer between Catholics and Muslims. This focuses on the most basic theological question underlying discussion of interreligious prayer: do Christians and Muslims believe in and worship the same God? Here I employ the help of a prophetic Anglican bishop, Kenneth Cragg, who supports interreligious prayer, to further the discussion. I come to a tentative conclusion that interreligious prayer would be very difficult to justify, but cannot be ruled out of court given the state of debate on the question: do Christians and Muslims believe in and worship the same God? There are marginal grounds for answering this question with a "yes, but." I believe this is a significant conclusion, although it admittedly is tentative, and the discussion on this matter is in its infancy.

2 Defining terms and avoiding confusion

It is important to clarify some conceptual terms so that we can get to the heart of the question to be explored: can Catholics and Muslims pray together? Conceptual clarity can easily suffocate the complexity of the human realities, and actual practices do not, thankfully, respect conceptual spaces. It will nevertheless be helpful to propose a distinction between two basic forms of prayer when Muslims and Catholics come together. I use the term "multi-religious prayer," following the definition already given, to refer to prayer in which Muslims and Catholics pray together, but each using their own prayers, and each explicitly not joining in with the other's prayers. This may take place in a structurally organized and public fashion or in a private spontaneous or preplanned manner. Within multireligious prayer, there are further distinctions, such as serial multireligious prayer (when each religious group prays in turn, while the others listen and perhaps participate silently in whatever manner they choose), or simultaneous multireligious prayer (when each religion is allocated a different space in the same building, where they pray separately, but at the same time, for the same cause or concern—for example, world peace). I use the term "interreligious prayer" to refer to Muslims and Catholics praying together, using each other's prayers or hybrid versions of each other's prayers. This may happen in a structurally organized and public fashion or privately.

I exclude from this entire discussion cultic liturgical prayer, understood as prayer that is defining of the *cultus*, such as the Eucharist. These cultic acts are often central for the self-definition and most sacred practices of a religion. Currently, even Trinitarian Christians of different denominations are not yet able to share the Eucharist, let alone share it with non-Christians. This is the case with Roman Catholics, although the rules of hospitality at Eucharist vary with different denominations. Some cultic liturgies do have participants from other religions, as, for example, in a service of marriage between a Catholic and Muslim in a Catholic Church, or a mixed congregation at a Catholic funeral. However, these liturgical forms do not constitute interreligious prayer or multireligious prayer as defined above. They represent fixed liturgies for followers of one religion, and according to circumstances, those not part of that religion can participate in varying ways. For example, I took a Muslim friend to a Catholic Mass, and he sat and watched with reverence and remained in his seat during the Eucharist. This is neither interreligious nor multireligious prayer, but more akin to respectful presence. No one knew he was present. I have prayed in a mosque in Cairo as a Muslim friend assumed I would join him for prayers and took me along. It was a complex situation where I did not have time to consider the matter, although

I have no regrets. I followed what everyone was doing and learned much from it and was grateful for the experience. I did not verbally join in the prayers but prayed to "God" during the process. I knew my friend knew I was a Catholic, and I hoped that I was not appearing to do something which would give false witness. Again, that situation was neither interreligious nor multireligious prayer. Clearly, the unity of heart, will, and mind is required for genuine interfaith prayer. There may also be some analogy between the distinction drawn by Catholics between cultic prayer (such as the Eucharist) and private prayer (such as praying with a friend who is ill) and the Muslim distinction between *salat* (ritual prayer) and *du'ā* (intercession). In what follows I am not referring to cultic prayer and *salat*, but other forms of gathering for prayer. I cannot of course speak for Muslims on this matter, which has not received enough detailed contemporary Muslim consideration—although Tim Winter's piece in this collection marks an important step forward in this matter. Admittedly, not all Catholics are agreed regarding the boundaries of cultic exclusivism and some compassionately and movingly argue for interfaith Eucharistic communion, based on pioneering heroes like Abhishiktananda. Richard Kearney's chapter in this volume is an eloquent voice testifying to this. However, I am dealing with Roman Catholicism as it is in terms of canon law and sacramental theology to address the question, not with how it could or might be. Whether the theology and law can change on these matters would have to be addressed in a more systematic manner, but since this is such a new area of concern and questioning, one cannot rule out options for the future. What follows is an examination of precisely such future possibilities given the current state of affairs.

I am primarily investigating interreligious rather than multireligious prayer between Muslims and Catholics, because the theological case for the latter is reasonably strong, although not without pragmatic problems. However, the distinction between the two has not always been made, possibly because this is a new area of research and reflection. Roman Catholics in England have accepted multireligious prayer, with varying degrees of qualification. Anglicans support multireligious prayer and have tentatively affirmed interreligious prayer (ICG 1992), while Catholics currently think it out of the question (CBEW 2010).[1] In Germany and the United States, a similar pattern can be found among Catholics.[2] Further, three working parties on this issue, from the Office on Inter-Religious Relations of the World Council of Churches and the Pontifical Council for Interreligious Dialogue, have concluded there was a case for multireligious prayer and thus a case for interreligious prayer.[3] As with the Anglican document in England (ICG 1992), there was an assumption that if one justifies multireligious prayer, interreligious prayer is thereby justified too. However, I believe this is a simple category mistake. Inclusivist arguments are often offered to justify multireligious prayer along the lines of: Islam can be interpreted, from the Christian point of view, as related to the triune God, even if Muslims explicitly reject this claim. Thus when Muslims pray, they pray to the one God to whom Christians pray. Multireligious prayer is therefore justified, and interreligious prayer is therefore also justified. But this argument does not work, for interreligious prayer involves a key feature that is not present or required in multireligious prayer, and which stops us moving from the latter to the former without further justification. This feature is co-intentionality. Intentionality signifies the meaning and purpose behind say, Jane praying a particular prayer, the "Our Father." In multireligious prayer there is no necessity for co-intentionality, for one is respectfully listening to Jane and praying in one's own way. Co-intentionality may exist, but it is not a necessary precondition. In interreligious prayer, in order for it to be other than multireligious prayer, the intentionality must be shared; it is a necessary precondition. Both Jane and Mustafa must believe that the "Our Father," as understood currently by both communities, satisfactorily becomes words by which they both might pray to the triune God and "Allah" respectively. In the literature reviewed above, the argument for multireligious prayer amounts to one or more of four claims: (i) God is present in the world religions; (ii) this is the same God that Christians recognize in the Trinity, even if Muslims do not agree with this; (iii) Christians therefore may pray with people from world religions; and (iv) praying together serves common needs and binds people together. Co-intentionality is not logically required for multireligious prayer. Point (ii) means that it is only necessary for one of the parties involved to believe that their God is present in the other religion; there is no need for the other person to accept this claim in any of its various possible formulations.

The same category mistake can be found in the Islam in Europe Committee (IEC)[4] Study Paper: *Christians and Muslims: praying together? Reflections and texts* (2003), which registers objections from Evangelicals and the Lausanne Movement. These critics argue that Muslims pray to a human perception of God and that many of the documents justifying multireligious and interreligious prayer draw no distinction between God's grace in creation and God's grace in salvation. The study paper counters such objections by responding: "the possibility of praying together does not depend on theoretical agreement about a common perception of God. God's reality goes far beyond our human understanding" (IEC 2003: 7). While it is true to say that God's reality goes beyond human understanding, the justification for interreligious and even multireligious prayer can hardly be based on adducing a common understanding of a reality that is beyond human understanding; such a reality could not be the basis for co-intentionality as normally understood, for the only predicate is that it is beyond human understanding, which does not allow us to conclude that the same reality is predicated by both parties. It may well be that it is, but that which is within human understanding seems to suggest otherwise and, while that is not determinative of the matter, if arguments are going to convince communities, they have to be robust and contain conceptually defensible positions.[5]

One more qualification before addressing the question: I am approaching interreligious prayer as a Roman Catholic theologian and will limit myself to appropriate literature, although in a fuller study it would be wise to look at the vast documentation from other churches, nationally, and internationally. This exercise is not meant un-ecumenically, but recognizes the varying constraints that are placed upon different ecclesial communities. Any ecumenical consensus will first require each community to reach agreement with regard to its own authoritative texts. Second, our attitude to interreligious prayer will partially depend upon our situation: in war-torn Palestine, in Washington at high-level meetings between Muslim and Christian intellectuals, living in a monastic community in the Algerian mountains among Muslims, or being (like myself) a middle-class Christian Asian in Bristol committed to interreligious dialogue. One can only begin to articulate principles that might "normally" cover most situations. Delightfully, life never behaves itself, and novel situations constantly emerge and will particularly do so given the forces of modernity and communications that bring different religions together all the time. In due course, there may be a need for the universal magisterium of the Catholic Church to pronounce on this issue if serious disputes develop between Catholic theologians and communities. For the moment, there are very tentative steps of practice taken by the magisterium. The practices of Pope Francis with Jews and Muslims in his calling for a prayer meeting with the Presidents of Israel and Palestine continue to show the now nearly fully established practice of multireligious prayer. Pope Benedict's widening of the Assisi meetings to include atheists also indicates that the limits of that meeting are within the context of multireligious, not interreligious, prayer.[6]

3 Multireligious prayer—Some clarifications in Catholic approaches

It would be fair to say that the official Catholic Church was catapulted into multireligious prayer by the actions of Pope John Paul II in calling the Assisi prayer meetings, first in 1986 and then again at other occasions. The practice was taken over and slightly modified by his successor, Pope Benedict XVI, and Pope Francis has shown a particular Abrahamic penchant, as indicated above. The first meeting, which included a number of important Muslim leaders, caused deep controversy among Catholics. This controversy resulted in John Paul II providing a theological commentary on the matter, which was delivered as a Christmas address to the Curia in December 1986 (see John Paul II 1987). He gave two basic reasons for calling the Assisi meeting and a clear definition of what it was (multireligious prayer), and what it was not (interreligious prayer). The two reasons given were: (i) the event was unitive of religious life—it was important that there be a witness by the world religions that they are committed to peace in a world torn by war and strife, and this witness was aptly provided by their coming together in prayer; and (ii) the event signified the workings of the Holy Spirit—the Holy Spirit is present in these prayers, for

> every authentic prayer is called forth by the Holy Spirit, who is mysteriously present in the heart of every person. This too was seen at Assisi: the unity that comes from the fact that every man and woman is capable of praying, that is, of submitting oneself totally to God and of recognising oneself to be poor in front of him. (John Paul II 1987: 60)

This argument was repeated four years later in the encyclical *Redemptoris missio* (29), where it was given a broader context. And here, John Paul II helpfully elaborates: (iii) all people are created in God's image, which means there is a fundamental unity between all peoples; (iv) in so much as God's presence is acknowledged in differing and manifold ways as preparing the adherents of world religions, at their best, for their fulfillment in Christ and the Catholic Church, then Catholics should attentively and respectively listen to this Spirit in any "authentic prayer" that might take place in multireligious prayer. This basic theological argument is then supplemented by an addendum: (v) in as much as the human spirit seeks for peace and prays for peace, as only God brings a peace beyond understanding (the world's own resources), such prayers are "authentic." One might have a variant on the addendum: "peace" could be replaced by "justice," "love," "consolation of those who suffer," "strength in times of hardship"—as all these virtues stem from the grace of the true God. I take point (iv) to imply that, with this teaching, John Paul II is not moving beyond seeing the Spirit in terms of prevenient grace or in some way actually sanctifying structures within other religions *de jure*, as *Dominus Iesus* (21) clearly rejected this type of theological view.

It should be underlined that multireligious prayer is substantiated by a Christian theological evaluation of the significance of the non-Christian religion in question, which would not require any assent from the other religion to establish the validity of the argument. In so much as there is no mingling of the cultus, there is no question about the integrity of Christian prayer being called into question, but there is no justification from the argument so far to support a move to interreligious prayer.

This "magisterial" argument is the basis for advocating multireligious prayer that is found in the English and Welsh Bishops Conference teaching document, *Meeting God in friend and stranger* (CBEW 2010: 57–65). This document was not specifically directed toward Christians and Muslims, but it is helpful in moving us further along in understanding what is at stake. Multireligious prayer is applauded and clearly distinguished from interreligious prayer, building on the Assisi principle:

> We don't come to pray together, but we come together to pray. As each religion prays, thus expressing its own faith, the others do not join in: they respect and silently give encouragement to those who are praying, and are in quiet solidarity with them on the basis of their own belief, and of the inner prayer that flows from it. (CBEW 59)

Finally, the chain that collapsed together multi-religious and interreligious prayer has been severed, and there is a clear Catholic case for multi-religious but not as yet for interreligious prayer. The bishops urge Catholics to be wholeheartedly involved in multi-religious prayer: "Catholics should thus feel confident, and be encouraged to 'come together to pray' with those of other religions" (John Paul II 1987: 59). Why such encouragement? Because it serves the unity of all people and their unity with God, and it is thus part of the mission of the Church and an "expression of love for our neighbour, and of respect for the integrity of the religions involved, and shows attentiveness to the universal presence of the Holy Spirit" (John Paul II 1987: 59). All this is held without denying the importance of mission, the truth of the Catholic faith, and the *praeparatio* status of the world religions (meaning that all religions at their best are a preparation for the fullness of truth found in Christ and his Church).

What of interreligious prayer? According to the Catholic Bishops, it is not possible: "There is an old Latin saying, *lex orandi, lex credendi* (our prayer is an expression and ratification of our belief). For that reason we cannot literally pray together, because prayer is an expression of faith, and we do not share one faith" (John Paul II 1987: 58).[7] The document does not differentiate between cultic/public interreligious prayer and *ad hoc* private interreligious prayer as I have done in this chapter, and the point is presented in such a way that it would seem to be excluding only cultic interreligious prayer. Admittedly, this public-private distinction is artificial because the Catholic catechism recognizes all prayer to be the prayer of the Church (*Catechism of the Catholic Church* 1994: § 2767), but it is still an important heuristic distinction. For example, there is a helpful distinction to be drawn between a public interreligious prayer event open to all and advertised in the press and an event where two brothers from different religions pray together: "May God keep us together now, and after death" as one dies of cancer in a hospital ward. Nevertheless, CBEW (2010) clearly distinguishes between interreligious and multi-religious prayer, and the door to the former is closed. Some years earlier the German Catholic bishops also criticized interreligious prayer, not on cultic grounds, but because there was a clear "danger of monopolizing the other" and covering up "existing differences" (German Bishops Conference 2003: 20). The German bishops did not want to engage in an action in which Christians affirmed that a Muslim's prayer must be true (i.e. that its referent is a true objective referent and contains no error). They wished to avoid the difficult questions regarding whether the two religions pray and worship the "same God." They clearly realized that interreligious prayer requires co-intentionality. If this is the general position slowly being taken by Catholic bishops in different parts of the world, is the door thus closed to multi-religious prayer?

4 Interreligious prayer—A possible Catholic step forward?

The then Joseph Cardinal Ratzinger throws some interesting light on the closed door.[8] His text has no formal authority, as he was not writing in his official capacity (as Prefect for the Congregation for the Doctrine of the Faith), but as a private theologian. Ratzinger, an objector to the Assisi meeting in 1986, writing in 1992, discusses multireligious and interreligious prayer. He declined an invitation to be present at Assisi 1986—a multireligious prayer event—concerning which he says critically that there were "undeniable dangers" and that it was easily open to being "misinterpreted by many people" (Ratzinger 2004: 107). Further: "Those who meet also know that their understandings of the divine, and hence their way of turning to him, are so varied that shared prayer would be a fiction, far from the truth" (Ratzinger 2004: 106). Positively, Ratzinger says, Assisi expressed what these groups had in common: "an acute concern for the needs of the world and its lack of peace; they share a longing for help from above against the powers of evil, that peace and justice might enter into the world" (Ratzinger 2004: 106). Notice his stress on the anthropological and unitive dimensions, rather than the divine reality and the theological reasons given by John Paul II. There is no mention of the Holy Spirit—and none of God.

Ratzinger concludes that multireligious prayer, while permissible, must fulfill two basic conditions. First, it "can only exist as a sign in unusual situations, in which, as it were, a common cry for help rises up, stirring the hearts of men, to stir also the heart of God" (Ratzinger 2004: 107). As Pope in 2011, Ratzinger/Benedict changed the character of the Assisi meeting to emphasize the social working together between the religions and the nonreligions so that there could be no "danger" of the meeting underwriting the view that all the religions present were ways to the same God. He also included atheists in these meetings, perhaps to send a clear signal that the groups were not meeting on a common belief platform. However, Ratzinger's position in this article is in interesting contrast to the CBEW (2010) document, which positively encourages Catholics to be involved in multireligious prayer. Is this a difference of prudential judgment, rather than evidence that the bishops are not working from the same principles as Ratzinger? I think this is likely, except that Ratzinger is more acutely aware of the likely long-term significance of multireligious prayer than are the Catholic bishops. He is aware that even multireligious prayer may lead to indifference and syncretism.

This leads us to Ratzinger's second condition for multireligious prayer: "[Because] it almost inevitably leads to false interpretations, to indifference as to the content of what is believed or not believed, and thus to the dissolution of real faith ... that is why [multi-religious prayer requires] a careful explanation, of what happens here and what does not happen" (Ratzinger 2004: 107). Ratzinger has deep reservations about the dangers involved in multireligious prayer. However, unlike CBEW (2010), Ratzinger surprisingly does not rule out interreligious prayer and actually considers three conditions under which it might in principle take place—although he believes it most unlikely, if not nearly impossible that they will be met (Ratzinger 2004: 108). However, it is worth specifying these three conditions, as they take us to the heart of the problem of interreligious prayer.

The first condition relates to the "object" of prayer: the true God. One might say this implies co-intentionality in both parties; Ratzinger does not mention this point, but I shall be taking it for granted. The German bishops realized that, if there is no co-intentionality, interreligious prayer can turn into a monopolization of the "Other," that is one party, X, is confident that the other party, Y, are praying to X's God. This was specifically a danger in meetings of Muslims and Christians. Interreligious prayer, Ratzinger argues, would require that both partners had the same object of prayer: "We can pray with each other only if we are agreed who or what God is and if there is therefore *basic agreement* as to what praying is: a process of dialogue in which I talk to a God who is able to hear and take notice" (Ratzinger

2004: 108, my emphasis). Strangely, Ratzinger does not specify a Trinitarian God, and the context might suggest he is speaking about Judaism, although what he says could in principle be applied to a form of theism that accepted Judaism, which is what Muslims believe the Qu'ran does. Ratzinger writes regarding Israel's God: "As in the case of Abraham and Melchizedek, of Job, of Jonah, it must be clear that we are talking with a God above all gods, with the Creator of the heaven and the earth— with my Creator. ... The First Commandment is true, particularly in any possible interreligious prayer" (Ratzinger 2004: 108). Using this criterion, might Ratzinger be open to interreligious prayer? This seems to be clearly possible in relation to Jews (prescinding from the question of whether contemporary Jews believe as did Jews before the time of Christ). I want to tentatively speculate whether this can be extended to Muslims, while fully recognizing the *sui generis* status of Judaism.

Fourteen years later, as Pope in 2006, Ratzinger/Benedict would pause in the Blue Mosque in Turkey, standing alongside an imam in silent prayer. Days later, back in the Vatican, Benedict said it was "a gesture initially unforeseen," but one which turned out to be "truly significant" (Wooden 2011). In Jerusalem in 2009, Benedict prayed at the Temple Mount/Wailing Wall and said afterward that faith demands love of God and love of neighbor:

> It is to this that Jews, Christians and Muslims are called to bear witness in order to honour with acts that God to whom they pray with their lips. And it is exactly this that I carried in my heart, in my prayers, as I visited in Jerusalem the Western or Wailing Wall and the Dome of the Rock, symbolic places respectively of Judaism and of Islam. (Wooden 2011)

Here, the common theism of Judaism and Christianity is extended to Islam. Neither gesture by Benedict amounts to interreligious prayer, but the first is a form of multireligious prayer. The informal commentary Benedict provided on the Jerusalem event suggests the possibility that the object of worship for Muslims is the same: "that God to whom they pray," and thus could fulfill one condition for interreligious prayer. Ratzinger is clear that nontheistic traditions cannot pray to a personal God (Ratzinger 2004: 106). But in the case of Islam, my sole concern here, are we reaching an opening in the forest?

An important text related to this question that does have dogmatic authority is *Lumen Gentium* (16), propounded at Vatican II, which tactfully says of Muslims: "they profess to hold the faith of Abraham" (*qui fidem Abrahae se tenere profitentes*) (Tanner 1990)—reporting a self-description by Muslims, with no Catholic assent or judgment. It is clear that there are serious differences between the two religions. But the sentence continues with a remarkable phrase: "and along with us they worship the one merciful God who will judge humanity on the last day" (*nobiscum Deum adorant unicum, misericordem, homines die novissimo iudicaturum*).[9] What we find here is that, despite serious differences of belief (including the Catholic Church's claim to be the true Church, founded on the Incarnation, and the source of salvation to the world), nevertheless, it is simultaneously affirmed that Muslims worship the one merciful God who is judge, and Catholics worship that God too.

This is a phenomenological statement with a normative theological judgment underpinning it.

This breakthrough is reiterated in *Nostra Aetate*, which has no dogmatic status but is nevertheless important in identifying what the Church has "in common" (*mutuum consortium*) with others. This does not call into question the fact that there are deep differences between the religions, nor the claim of the Catholic Church about God's definitive activity in Christ and the Church, and that other religions are *praeparatio evangelica* at best.[10] Rather, the claim about Muslims seeks to identify true features (that a Muslim would assent to) and affirm them from a Catholic perspective:

> The Church also looks upon Muslims with respect. They worship the one God living and subsistent, merciful and almighty, creator of heaven and earth, who has spoken to humanity and to whose decrees, even the hidden ones, they seek to submit themselves whole-heartedly, just as Abraham, to whom the Islamic faith readily relates itself, submitted to God. (NA §3)

There is no concession to Islam's claim to belong to *this* same covenant tradition via Abraham and Ishmael, although Abraham—with his unquestioning faith and concern to do God's will—is a model held in common by Islam and Christianity. Nevertheless, these further predicates help identify the one true God in whom belief is shared. Are these shared beliefs in the one God (living and subsistent, and so on) sufficient for a basic agreement on the God who is prayed to?

Before addressing this question, what of Ratzinger's two other stipulations regarding interreligious prayer? Ratzinger's second stipulation is that apart from the shared doctrine of God, "there must also be fundamental agreement ... about what is worth praying about and what might be the content of prayer"—and the Lord's Prayer is "the measure" (Ratzinger 2004, 108). Anything that is in conformity with the Lord's Prayer would in principle be worth "praying about" in interreligious prayer. Presumably the supplications for peace and justice, two characteristics of the Kingdom of God, and forgiveness and the strength to resist evil, would all qualify. While this needs much unpacking, we can see ways in which this condition might be met in conjunction with the first stipulation. Kenneth Cragg provides examples of Muslim and Christian prayers that are united in these concerns (Cragg 1970: 108–56).

The third stipulation is that any interreligious prayer event "must be so arranged that the relativist misinterpretation of faith and prayer can find no foothold in it" (Ratzinger 2004: 109). This is ultimately a pragmatic requirement. For instance, participants could wear T-shirts (emblazoned: "We are not relativists; X is the true religion"), or they could publish a press release stipulating this claim clearly. This requirement is not an impossible one, but nevertheless calls for tact and prudence, although T-shirts such as I have suggested may not be the most tactful way forward.

So let us return finally to the central problem for interreligious prayer: do Christians worship the same God as Muslims? This is the fundamental question isolated in Ratzinger's reflections that take us to the heart of the matter. If the answer is yes, then interreligious prayer might well be possible in theory.

5 Do Catholics and Muslims believe in the "same God"?

How can we speak of Islam having the "same God" as Catholics, knowing there are profound differences between the two communities' conceptualization of God? To investigate this possibility further, I will turn to a very important non-Catholic theologian who addresses this matter head on. The Anglican bishop Kenneth Cragg is a scholar of Islam with rich experience of the Arab Muslim world. The Jesuit Islamicist Christian Troll is similar in instinct to Cragg, although Troll actually formally concludes, as Ratzinger does about multireligious prayer, that interreligious prayer should "remain exceptional" (Troll 2008: 374). Cragg strongly affirms interreligious prayer and recognizes the difficulty of justifying it, which is what makes his work so challenging and helpful.

In answer to the question, do Muslims and Christians worship the same God, Cragg's answer is: "Yes! And No!" (Cragg 1970: 18). He argues that we cannot really claim there are any differences if there is no underlying commonality, basing this argument on an analogy between subject and predicate: "But such inconsistencies of predicate are only significant as *differences* if the theme is acknowledged as identical. With the unity of the subject we cannot change, correct, or even employ, the diverse terms or affirm that some of them are inconsistent" (Cragg 1970: 17). From the Catholic point of view, the statements of Vatican II could be read in this manner, while the critics in the Lausanne Movement call into question Cragg's assumption that the subject is the same, saying the Muslim "god" is a human concept, and, although its predicates bear a resemblance to the Christian God, it is in fact a matter of different subjects. Indeed, those Catholics who think Vatican II is heretical on this point about Islam would agree with the Lausanne critics, but I discount this view, accepting instead the authority of the Vatican Council.[11]

Why does Cragg accept interreligious prayer despite recognizing serious differences of predicates, even if there is a common underlying subject, God? He gives the following reasons. First, in nations where many religions are represented in shared schools, hospitals and workplaces, there are "needs and occasions calling for inter-religious action and, therefore, for inter-religious prayer" (Cragg 1970: 13). One might credibly respond to this that multireligious prayer satisfies this need; this is hardly an argument for interreligious prayer. Second, Cragg argues that, while risky, the deepest impulse to prayer calls us to consider the possibility of interreligious prayer. This seems to be the type of argument used by John Paul II in affirming that the Spirit moves every genuine prayer, and clearly Christians would feel the impulse to join with the Spirit if it is the same Spirit. But John Paul II endorsed multireligious, not interreligious, prayer. Third, at every turn, Cragg accepts those who say no to interreligious prayer with integrity. Their refusal must be honored. This is generous, but perhaps fails to take the question of scandal seriously enough. Until the Church everywhere accepts interreligious prayer, it might be argued that it should not take place anywhere. But it could also be argued that until interreligious prayer is explored in practice and theorized rigorously, the natural inertia and antipathy to it should be set aside to allow potentially prophetic individuals and communities to "experiment," while always avoiding syncretism and indifference.[12] As Kearney argues in this volume, these prophetic individuals are most important, although their testimony has to be balanced with many other factors as well. Fourth, Cragg asks concerning multireligious prayer (my term): "Is it not more safe and prudent to bring our presence into the others' prayers, with sympathy and silence, rather than venture into the difficult world of somehow 'neutralized' language and form?" (Cragg 1970: 35). He responds that for those who seek to pray to God together, such responses will finally be the "participation … of 'passengers' being 'conveyed', at worst merely physically present for the sake of a unity they do not seek, at best spiritually inarticulate in a unity they do not find. And prayer is never physically achieved and never spiritually dormant" (Cragg 1970: 36). The argument from the experience of a longing for interreligious prayer by those involved in Muslim–Christian engagement would seem decisive for Cragg. This type of point is repeated in much of the literature. It should be considered seriously, but it should also be balanced by regard for the individuals' and groups' accountability to the universal Church. Finding the balance is vital but difficult, but representative communal acts cannot find their sole justification in individual desires, even when prompted by love.

But let me return to the question of the forms of similarity and dissimilarity, for Cragg helps us in seeing the case for possible interreligious prayer, but under very strict conditions. Are the factors for agreeing with interreligious prayer finally ecclesial (as in Cragg's reasons above) rather than rigorously doctrinal, or can the resolution of the tension between similarities and dissimilarities be resolved in a way that is internal to the doctrinal question itself? The latter is surely required if we can advance the case of interreligious prayer. Too often the resolution is pragmatic, which suffices to justify a particular case at a particular time, but fails to offer a theological rationale that might be more enduring.

There are a number of levels to this question: Is the God to whom Muslims and Christians pray the same God? I point here to three levels: (a) the narrative accounts of this God's actions; (b) philosophical-theological reflection upon this God's characteristics, partially based upon these narrative accounts; and (c) philosophical reflection not based upon this God's characteristics in the narrative accounts (a form of natural theology perhaps). Many would want to stress a fourth level—the God beyond all these three levels, beyond human understanding—but I have already indicated that agreement on that level alone is not sufficient to answer the question either positively or negatively, and securing agreement on that level is problematic for philosophical reasons. It would seem that Vatican II's teaching would indicate that the first two levels could deliver a "yes." Vatican I would allow us to explore the question on the third level in its teaching that belief in the existence of God can be attained through the use of human reason alone (not unassisted by grace).[13] But Vatican II moves us up the levels, so in what follows I will consider only the first two levels.

On the narrative level, the Qu'ran actually provides grounds for seeing that the same God is operative in Christianity and Islam. Of course, Christians do not recognize this narrative as authoritative or true in all its parts. The Christian narrative account might accept some of the Muslim narrative at a chronological level up to the time of Abraham, and from then on only accept an attenuated version of the Muslim narrative. With Abraham, we come to points of deep similarity (a model for faith) and deep dissimilarity—that he built the Ka'ba in Mecca with Ishmael and is the founder of Islam (Troll 2009: 97–108, 145–7).[14] Muslims perhaps go further than Jews in accepting Jesus as a great prophet who was born of the Virgin Mary, but for Muslims, as for Jews, Jesus's divinity is unacceptable (see Robinson 1990). While there is a shared narrative regarding Adam, Noah, Abraham, Moses, and Jesus, there are also differences at every point of that narrative, for Christianity sees the narrative as unfolding a progressive relationship between God and humankind, entailing various covenants, whereas Islam sees the narrative as referring to one primal revelation, given first to Adam and then invoked by this series of prophets, of whom Muhammad is the greatest and the last (see Madigan 2004). Do these partially shared histories of God's creating of the world and speaking to his people express a "shared" spiritual heritage and narrative history? Yes and no; but, tentatively, I would argue that the no has more weight simply because, on the narrative level, the whole story must be told to make sense of the parts. And the whole story, when told, is ultimately a different story, even if it uses the same narrative materials. In one, the cross and resurrection interpret the world, both before and after Jesus; and in the other, the Qu'ran and Muhammad interpret the world, both before and after these events. Both renderings can positively account for the elements of the other and even positively absorb elements of the other narrative, but finally, not on the terms of the original narrative. Hence, this rendering can deliver a positive reading of the other tradition, but not in its own terms, and thus cannot affirm interreligious prayer. It does amounts to a type of inclusivism, however, and can certainly help in multireligious prayer.

Interestingly, the narrative approach can go in different directions. For example, George Lindbeck, the narrative theologian and founding father of postliberalism, emphasizes difference, because for him the Bible is the primary narrative and interprets all other narratives. In his view, the Bible reads the world and thus everything is located within Christological and ecclesiological contexts. Alternatively, "scriptural reasoning" groups, founded on Lindbeck's and Hans Frei's narrative theologies, have instead tended to affirm that which might be held in common, but without denying difference (see Lindbeck 1984; Ford and Pecknold 2006). The latter may be in danger of lapsing from postliberalism.

But this problem of commonality/difference runs deep, and is already present in the Christian–Jewish context, where, despite the fact that Christians and Jews share the same scripture (calling it the "Old Testament" and the "Hebrew Bible," respectively), Christians read the Old Testament as inspired only insofar as it points to Christ: typologically, allegorically, and morally. Thus the story is read, as it were, from a different "conclusion." Apart from sharing the same text, one might honestly ask whether Jews and Christians share the same narrative, for it is like reading a dramatic story with two incompatible endings. Imagine a Hamlet in which the prince marries Ophelia, and she does not drown! Would it really be *Hamlet*? Interestingly, this has not meant that Christians claim they have a different God from Jews, despite the Christian development of a narrative with a Trinitarian twist with the founding of the Church as the beginning of a new chapter in the story. And Christians make this claim despite the fact that post-second-temple Jews have not accepted the Christian Trinitarian account of God. If this level of dissonance with regard to "God" is allowed in the Jewish–Christian encounter, then surely there is some analogical similarity regarding the differences with Islam that might act as a trope for a possible similarity? The fact of the *sui generis* relationship with Judaism may call this analogical trope into question; or rather, strong arguments are needed before the analogical trope might actually be employed.[15]

However, to my relief, the Vatican II passages do not rest the claim of commonality on the narrative account, at least insofar as the Qu'ran and Muhammad are not mentioned in either of the two Vatican documents. This may well indicate from the Catholic side that to accept that God is worshipped by Muslims would not require accepting the authority of the Qu'ran and Muhammad, for that would entail self-contradiction. Thus, the problem cannot be resolved at the narrative level. It would seem that, for Vatican II, the commonality is based on predicates of God that can be found in the philosophical-theological traditions that draw upon the Qu'ran and Muhammad for their basics, but can be specified without asserting the truth of these narrative histories wholesale. A creator God who is just and who rewards the good and punishes evil is what is being identified. This may well be related to the tradition in Acts that "any one who fears him and does what is right is acceptable to him" (Acts 10:35). This does not mean, in the context of Acts, that they should not convert to Christ, but that their hearts are already turned toward God, whom they know in a limited manner. The crucial question then becomes: can this "limited manner" be all that is required to cover co-intentionality?

The *shahāda*, the Islamic confession of faith, runs as follows: "I bear witness that there is no God but Allah, and I bear witness that Muhammad is Allah's messenger." This statement makes two sets of claims: first about the oneness of God, which is a metaphysical statement, and second about Muhammad, which is a historical statement. Can the first clause be true, without the second clause being true? Is the first part logically dependent on the second part? The first part bears analogy to the first paragraph of the Christian creed, although "Father" is an understandably problematic term for Muslims. But the similarities here are significant. Even so, at level two (Christian belief that God is Trinitarian and that God has become incarnate in Jesus Christ) there is a range of deep dissimilarities. As long as Muslims reject these two claims (incarnation and Trinity), we have a serious problem. Admittedly, there are strong arguments that, as they are expressed in the Qu'ran, these two claims have never been properly encountered by Muslims, let alone rejected. But at the historical ecclesial level, this difference remains an obstacle. Might there be a case here for arguing that, on the basis of the unity of the one God, the first section of the traditional dogmatic schema, there might be unity between Christianity and Islam, as there is between Judaism and Christianity, while the differences only become fully clear in the second part of the dogmatic schema, the acknowledgment of the Triune God? (see Ott 1955). I personally think this is a promising avenue of enquiry. Then, the question from the Christian side would be: could the metaphysical doctrine of God held in Islam "open up" toward recognizing the reality of the Trinity, just as traditional Jewish monotheism "opened up" toward the Trinitarian reality? David Burrell and others show that this path is both promising and precarious (see e.g. Burrell et al. 2010; Burrell 2004).

6 Conclusion

Do Christians and Muslim worship the same God? I have shown that this is difficult to straightforwardly affirm or deny. Each religion gives a yes/no type answer to this question and I have only looked at the dynamic from the side of Christians. Each religion can give a "yes" "inclusively," on its own terms, which justifies multireligious prayer, but that strategy will not suffice for interreligious prayer. If the commonality is affirmed by a Christian, with the expectation that a Muslim will say, "Yes, I can agree with both your self-description and your description of my God (in Islam)," then co-intentionality might just be possible and the door is open for interreligious prayer to be tentatively justified. Given the current state of discussion on this matter, a theological conclusion is difficult, but circumstances require practical decision to be made by churches. Hence, this becomes a matter for ecclesial decision based on the experience of those Christians who feel that interreligious prayer is a deep calling and that their practices will not lead to syncretism, indifference, or a dulling of the missionary zeal that is inherent to the faith, nor infringe the cultic communal aspect of prayer. Whether, as Ratzinger predicts, such occasions will be extremely rare, if they occur at all, or more frequent, and meeting with greater communal assent, remains to be seen. But it would be impossible to rule interreligious prayer out of court even if it is difficult to see solid grounds on the basis of which the Catholic Church will take this step with regard to Islam.

7 Acknowledgments

I am grateful to the group supported by Georgetown University, Washington DC, convened by Dr David Marshall at Campion Hall, Oxford, where this chapter first saw the light. In particular, I am grateful to the following for their further comments on the first draft of this chapter: Rev. Dr Damian Howard, Rev. Dr Canon Michael Ipgrave, Rev. Dr Catriona Laing, Rev. Dr David Marshall, Dr Anthony O'Mahony, and Rev. Richard Sudworth. I am also grateful to the journal of *Islam and Christian–Muslim Relations*, 24:1, 2012, 1–14, DOI: 10.1080/09596410.2013.731728 which published an earlier version of this article and have granted permission to use that earlier material. Further, I am grateful to Professor Marianne Moyaert for her helpful comments on how to further develop that paper into the present chapter.

Chapter 9

BACK-AND-FORTH RITING: THE DYNAMICS OF CHRISTIAN-MUSLIM ENCOUNTERS IN SHRINE RITUALS

Albertus Bagus Laksana, SJ

1 A space of encounter

Father Johannes Prennthaler was a Jesuit missionary from Tirol, Austria, who labored for many years in south central Java near the Sendangsono Marian Grotto (often dubbed "The Lourdes of Java"), which he founded in 1929. The saga of this grotto colored the inner life of this great missionary. In particular, his anxiety was related to the difficult and complicated relationship with the modernist Muslim communities around the shrine. In fact, he envisioned this special place partly as a tangible sign of a Catholic existence in a rather hostile Muslim environment. He was very intentional about the formation of the local Javanese Catholic community around the shrine, largely by emphasizing the inward and outward dimension of a robust Catholic identity, promoting both public rituals and festivals as well as the more inward formation of faith. The angelus bells that he brought from Europe are one example of his attempt to strengthen a Catholic outpost in a Muslim stronghold. He understood the need for the bells as a counter to the Muslim mosque drum and call to prayer (Prennthaler 1935: 171). Father Prennthaler thus expressed to his Dutch benefactors his effort to counter the boisterous, provocative, and triumphant sound of the Javanese traditional music and Muslim songs: "Definitely we must display our own music and songs against them and our music got to be so much louder, more provoking, intimidating, and triumphant!" (Prennthaler 1930: 228).

Despite this early problem with the Muslim other, it is curious that the grotto has become a place of hospitality where the religious other is welcome. Now, not only Catholic but also Muslim pilgrims have begun to attend the shrine as well. More particularly in the realm of music and rituals, there has been some close cooperation between Muslim and Catholic groups around the shrine, based on the similar music genre that they share. This genre, the *slawatan*, comes originally from the Muslim prayers of praise for the Prophet Muhammad (*salawāt* in Arabic) that have been quite popular in Java. Over the years, this genre was adopted by the Catholics and augmented with lyrics from the Bible. However, during the cooperative services, Muslim singers also join in singing the Christian lyrics (Courtens 2009: 112).

Shrines across Java have become places of hospitality. In my view, it is very important to point this out since the openness of these shrines serves as the background for the particularity of this chapter, which looks at the propriety and structures of back-and-forth ritual participation. In general, my argument here stems largely from the dynamics of the rather widespread practice of "shared" pilgrimage and spiritual encounters between people of different religious communities and traditions in sacred places that involves a certain degree of shared rituals as well. At the shrine of Our Lady of Seidnaya, Syria, Muslim and Christian pilgrims participate in a common culture of devotion to Mary and share a common shrine ritual as well. As various scholars have shown, this phenomenon is quite widespread in the Eastern Mediterranean and might signal a complex situation where genuine respect for others was mixed with a certain dose of rivalry.[1] In other settings, for example in India among Christians, Muslims, and Hindus, similar cases also abound.[2] In Java, Muslims, Hindus, Buddhists, and Protestants visit Catholic pilgrimage centers and participate, to a certain degree, in the rituals of the shrine, seeking tangible and spiritual blessings.

At this point, three crucial elements of this cross-ritual participation at shrines need to be noted. First, since the decision to participate in the ritual of the other is a highly complex one, involving personal discernment in particular situations, the practice of cross-ritual participation can vary in terms of mode and intensity. Second, for the most part, the motivation to participate in shrine rituals is couched in a larger context of seeking God's blessing, and not for experimentation, for 'interfaith dialogue', and the like. Third, this cross-ritual participation happens in shrines (instead of mosques or churches) where the rituals do not normally belong to the most defining aspects of the religious tradition in question. In most cases, shrines and their rituals are located rather in the in-between space between self and other, and they are open to the public in general, beyond the formal or institutional boundaries of the religious communities. It is in this constellation that the question of the appropriateness of this particular cross-ritual participation should be understood.

2 Back-and-Forth riting in comparative theology

In this chapter, my more particular interest lies in illustrating how back-and-forth riting plays a role in the new comparative theology (Clooney 2010). Elsewhere I call this "double visiting" (Laksana 2010: 1–20, 2014: 191–218). In general, this dynamic of double visiting is related to the basic element of the new comparative theology, namely visiting the religious other, which in my view consists of both the study of the other and immersion in the complexity of the other beyond the textual, including ritual life and other quotidian aspects of other religious tradition. All of this is done with the view of the comparativist's transformation as theologian that might include theological, spiritual, affective transformations, to such a degree that his loyalty to his own tradition is intensified and enriched through this complex comparative engagement (Clooney 2010: 58–9).[3]

In this regard, my own comparative focus so far has been on the lived practice of religious tradition, whose historical and concrete dynamics can then be grounded in and expanded through textual and doctrinal engagement aided by a thematized comparative theological method. To facilitate this dynamic, the comparative immersion—in the sense of entering the world of the other—should be made as rich as possible. More concretely, in my view, the sensory and affective dimensions of this immersion should be particularly emphasized as well. For the experience of entering into the sensory world of the religious other might be likened to the process of comparative reading where one is inundated by the images of the world of the other (Clooney 2009: 154). On this point, Clooney writes:

> This double reading remains unsettling. ... It unsettles us by its sheer abundance; such a reading dramatically *expands intellectual and affective possibilities*, as the reasons, images, and affective states proposed and promoted in each text enter into a most agile interplay with those of the other text; there are always more options available to us than we can manage to appropriate and reflect upon. (Clooney 2009: 186)

In the dynamic of the comparative theology that Clooney envisions, this double reading leads to the affective expansion of one's religious sensibility as a result of the visit to the other. So what is at stake is the transfiguration of one's intellectual and spiritual situation and commitment, where one becomes vulnerable to the force and beauty of the religious other, becoming more open to give deeper and more inclusive meaning to religious ideals and practices (Clooney 2009: 26, 2010: 5). Clooney writes further:

> Through this disciplined reading, extended over a longer period of time, the comparative theologian can acquire something at least of the psychological and spiritual freedom needed to accept what she is learning, and *to grow spiritually* in accord with it. ... The endless, intensifying spiral of reading is clearly more than the reader can master; the reality of surrender becomes *all the more vivid* as the theologian herself loses control of her own project. (Clooney 2010: 126)

In this respect, my visiting the religious other through participation in the life of the Muslims at their shrines (including their rituals) is significant in part because of the rich sensorial dimension of the encounter. For the sensory experience of being near the other has the power to make us not only open but also vulnerable to their world, not primarily at the level of religious concepts, but rather at the deeper affective, emotional, and experiential level (Clooney 2009: 2). In my view, this exposure to the sensory world of the other constitutes a very distinctive and concrete step in this dynamic movement of comparative theology, since it is the stage when one actually "senses" the other. The power of sensory experience in the context of liturgy and worship in forging a distinctive religious identity has been very real (cf. Myamoto 2010: 56–70). In late antiquity, for instance, the Church prohibited mixed marriage between Christian woman and pagan man for similar reason, that is, to ensure that the Christian wife's religious identity was not diluted by the exposure to her husband's pagan religion through sensory experiences in daily life through rituals (Harvey 2005: 140–62).

The practice of double reading/visiting in comparative theology, as Clooney states, complicates simple religious identity and loyalties, thus apparently confirming this earlier concern for maintaining religious boundaries through prohibition of cross-ritual participation. Typically, textual comparison is already a complex endeavor, as Clooney's works have shown. And, I suspect, things are even more complicated in the realm of cross-ritual participation. Again, the sensory aspect of this participation can be overwhelming or simply too much for any believer to face; while reading the texts of religious others can appear to be an objective and religiously neutral scholarly activity, or just a sign of intellectual or spiritual curiosity where a distance might be easier to maintain, cross-ritual participation seems to assume a further, deeper, and more serious "consent" to both the theological understanding and the "divine reality and presence" of the religious other. Cross-ritual participants are putting themselves in a distinctive religious mode that is quite different from that of the readers of texts, largely because they are now addressing the Divine in his very presence. This creates a rather intense situation where distance is much harder to maintain, as the mind, the heart, and the body of the believer are involved. As one can imagine, the personal discernment and negotiation in this particular setting can be very complicated and overwhelming. Indeed, cross-ritual participation poses a distinctive challenge that can be harder for some to take, especially those who lack a solid theological grounding (wisdom) and spiritual maturity (experience) in their own tradition or enough exposure to the theological and textual world of the other. In the context of comparative theology, we are talking about the cross-religious participation of a faithful scholar, not the participation of a neutral outsider.

Surely this acknowledgment of the complexity of cross-ritual participation should not deter comparativists from attempting it. A healthy dose of cross-ritual participation, if done properly within a clear theological framework, can also lead to the deepening of one's religious identity as well as the broadening and transformation of one's religious sensibility and horizon, as Clooney noted. In my own practice of double visiting and back-and-forth riting, the fundamental dynamics is captured by the very Catholic notion of "communion" with God through different means, including the saintly paradigmatic figures and other sacred realities of the other, as conveyed by the doctrine of *communio sanctorum*. And I understand "communion" as a very concrete, integral (tangible, sensory, affective, and spiritual), and positive encounter with the religious other (more on the renewed understanding of *communio sanctorum* later). To a certain degree, this process is nothing other than the expansion of my religious, spiritual, and theological sensibility as a fruit of my visit to the richness of the religious world of the other.

3 My back-and-forth riting

My experience of back-and-forth riting or visiting goes back to my research and fieldwork in south central Java (the Greater Yogyakarta area) a few years ago.[4] Back then I was embarking on a comparative theological analysis of pilgrimage practices among Javanese Muslims and Catholics. I designed my research by first choosing three different sites or shrines on each side (Muslim and Catholic) in the same geographical and cultural area. The Muslim sites are mostly holy shrines or graves of local Muslim saints (*wali*) who have played a crucial role in the creation of local Javano-Muslim communities in south central Java with its distinctive and hybrid religio-cultural practices. The shrine of Tembayat, for example, houses the grave of Sunan Pandanarang (sixteenth century), a prominent student of Sunan Kalijaga. Kalijaga is the most important Muslim *wali* in south central Java and has been considered to be the iconic and paradigmatic embodiment of hybrid Javano-Muslim identity, that is, an authentically Muslim identity that takes important facets of local Javanese culture very seriously. On the Catholic side, the choice of sites includes a Marian shrine, a Sacred Heart shrine and a mission mausoleum of the community's martyr and founders. Over the years, all these sites have accumulated meanings that are quite foundational for the local Catholic community's understanding of self, as they are connected intimately to the foundational moments as well as the founding figures of the community. The Marian Shrine of Sendangsono that I mentioned earlier is located on the site where the first massive baptism of local Javanese by the Jesuit missionary Father Franciscus van Lith in 1904 marked the real beginning of the local Javanese Catholic community. The Sacred Heart Shrine in the outskirt of Yogyakarta has become the icon of the inculturation of the faith in Javanese culture, while the mission mausoleum in the small town of Muntilan preserves the memory of the founder of the community, Fr Franciscus van Lith, as well as the community's protomartyr, Fr Richardus Sanjaya. These men, along with some other prominent missionaries and early leaders of the community, are buried in this mausoleum.

It must be noted that the physical proximity among those various shrines is highly crucial in the local Javanese cosmology. Due to the influence of the religio-cultural tradition of the Javano-Muslim court of Mataram (represented by the current sultanates of Yogyakarta and Surakarta), the area is understood as a supernaturally charged area, serving as a cosmological *mandala* (Woodward 1989: 199). This framework connects the shrines or sites with one another on a supernatural plane whose physical expression requires negotiation on the experiential or personal level, as the pilgrims who flock to these sites can attest. Furthermore, this proximity also signals some complex historical interactions between the various communities of the shrines. Though these groups may differ in terms of formal religious affiliation, they nonetheless share some common history and religio-cultural sensibilities that facilitate further fruitful interactions.

This point reveals a deeper interaction between a given religio-cultural framework and one's personal participation. This means, among other things, that back-and-forth riting or visiting does not occur in a vacuum, free from preexisting individual and communal assumptions, worldviews, and histories. Rather, my argument is that this dynamic flows from the underlying and wider and deeper patterns of communion and sharing that have marked the religio-cultural interaction between the local Muslim and Catholic pilgrims and their communities over a longer historical continuum. In fact, one of my major findings is that this wider connection and encounter has been aided and made very fruitful by the Javanese culture that they share. In this framework, cross-ritual participation is also facilitated in some concrete and subtle ways by Javanese religio-cultural tradition, as I will illustrate later. Beyond Java, this pattern might be true in other cases as well, in locations such as South Asia, Central Asia, the Mediterranean basin, and East Asia.[5]

This research design allowed me to visit these different sets of shrines on a regular basis and in a rather smooth process, again due to their spatial and cultural proximity. On a typical day, I would visit two shrines: one shrine of the religious other and another of my own tradition. This double-visit becomes the main methodological element of my research. But during the course of this research, this method led me into a deeper and more personal engagement and participation, surpassing mere method. For, over a period of time, Muslim saints gradually became part of my Catholic identity and experience as a Javanese Catholic. Very often during these visits I found myself rather intensely immersed in meditative prayers, and to my surprise, I felt as though I could connect to these Muslim saints and holy figures in deeply ineffable ways. Without doubt, my religious world has been inundated by these figures. To a certain degree, I experience the spiritual presence of these saints, but not separately from the deeper presence of God and His Spirit, as I understand it within my own Catholic theological framework.

This experience of spiritual presence leads me to a "limited" and selective participation in the ritual etiquette of tomb or shrine visitation where I happened to be visiting during a particular moment. It should be noted here that typically I would not fully and consistently recite the prayer formulas with the Muslim pilgrims. However, through this limited participation, I feel that I can enter into the spiritual presence and effect that the prayers create in the shrine during that moment. Driven by this spiritual connection, at times I can utter parts of their prayers as well. This way of praying is one of the possible ways of praying with Muslims suggested by Christian Troll, although I went a bit farther.[6] However, in my experience, this participation is made possible by the Catholic theological framework of *communio sanctorum* (understood more fundamentally as inclusive ways of communing with the saints and the Holy), but it has been concretely facilitated by some religio-cultural categories of the Javanese.

In terms of the ritual setting, my cross participation has also been made possible largely because there is no fixed ritual for all pilgrims in all these Muslim shrines.[7] This allows for a personal space of ritual freedom. At these shrines, both hybrid (Javanese and Muslim) and more standardized Islamic ritual etiquette of tomb visitation (Ar. *adab al-ziyāra*) are welcome. It is in this ritual space that pilgrims of different religious orientations can encounter one another. However, I would argue that as a Catholic, I can "connect" to even the standardized Muslim ritual etiquette of tomb visitation, precisely because of the Catholic framework of *communio sanctorum*, as I will explain more fully later.

The basic structures of the standardized Muslim ritual etiquette of tomb visitation consist of: the recitation of the formula "no god but God" (*tahlīl*), other short prayer formulas like the *tasbīḥ* (prayer for the glory of God) and the *istighfār* (request for God's forgiveness); the recitation of Qurʾ ānic chapters, typically the *Sūra Yā Sīn* or the *Sūra al-Ikhlāṣ*, or at least the Throne Verse (Ar. *āyāt al-kursī*) from the second chapter of the Qurʾān; the prayer for blessings on the prophet Muḥammad (*ṣalāḥ*); and the intercessory invocations of prophets, saints, and other righteous persons (*tawassul*) (Labib 2000: 8–13).

As we can see, this ritual is in fact a combination of prayers of supplications and intercessions (Ar. *tawassul*) to God and His spiritual company, particularly the prophets and saints, and rather inclusive prayers for the dead, something that is not foreign to Catholic ritual practice. Here, it is crucial to note that in this Muslim framework, the invocations of the prophets and saints are always done in the framework of praise and prayers to God. The underlying logic at work here is that of a prayerful remembrance of the prophets and saints in the form of offering prayers and blessings to them. In this respect, visitation of the dead is conceived as no different from visiting living persons. The pilgrims greet the dead, both the pious and the ordinary, in direct speech because the dead are present or aware of their visits. It is for the same reason that pilgrims have to bring a gift (of prayers) as a sign of love, respect, and connection.

Only within this framework of prayerful remembrance of God and His spiritual company could one understand the intercessory part of the prayer. Sometimes in very general terms, pilgrims request the intercessions of the prophet(s) and saints before God. In this connection, the dynamic of inclusivity of the list of the holy and paradigmatic figures being invoked in the prayer is worth noting. It starts with the Prophet Muḥammad and his family; then proceeds to other prophets, angels, saints, and martyrs, and all the righteous (Ar. *ṣaliḥūn*), before mentioning particular saints, typically ʿAbd al-Qādir al-Jīlānī and the local saint whose tomb is being visited. The list then continues with all the inhabitants of the graves (Ar. *ahl al-qubr*), both the *muslimūn* (literally those who submit to God) and the *muʿminūn* (those who have true faith, not mere belief), before it concludes with the immediate ancestors, teachers, and parents of the pilgrims. The universal and inclusive tone of this concept is made rather clear in the prayer, for it specifies further that these figures are both men and women, from East and West, those in the sea and on the land (Labib 2000: 57).[8] Very interestingly, a specific mention is made about all those persons who have been instrumental in the lives of the pilgrims. Again, the inclusive scope of this list is striking, and the sense of lively and overwhelming communion with all these figures is remarkable.[9]

This sense of communion with the entire community that includes not only the living and the dead members (ancestors) but also the future members is similarly expressed in the ritual etiquette of tomb visitation, especially in the greeting to the dead: "May God bless our predecessors as well as those who come after us; and God willing, we will join you in the intermediate world (*barzakh*)." Thus, there is the sense that the living members of the Muslim community are not only praying for the dead, but also for the future generation of Muslims. Furthermore, the communion between the living and the dead is greatly enhanced by the realization that the pilgrims will eventually be joining the community of the dead as well. In all this, the intergenerational aspect of communion is quite remarkable, as well as its universalism or inclusivity. For while special categories of the dead are acknowledged, such as particular saints and one's parents, all the dead are also addressed (Anies 2009: 96–7).

Many Javanese Muslim pilgrims to this shrine also understand their pilgrimage to shrines of saints as a respectful visit to their own ancestors (Javanese: *nyekar, sowan*). During this visit, they combine the traditional Javanese etiquette of tomb visitation—such as putting certain kinds of flowers on the gravestone and holding a communal ritual meal (Javanese: *slametan*)—with the Islamic etiquette of visiting sacred tombs that includes specific prayers and vows related to the saint.

Among traditionalist Muslims in Java, prayers for the dead in general (*tahlīl* prayer) is normally part of the pan-Javanese communal meal (the *slametan*) where food is shared after being blessed. In fact, this Islamicized ritual communal meal is also popularly called *tahlilan,* and the sharing of food is also considered a sharing of God's blessings. Muslims consider the food shared during this communal meal to be voluntary alms (*ṣadaqa*), a means of fostering brotherhood and solidarity (Anies 2009: 5). This ritual communal meal—which has always been a hybrid ritual where the spirits of pre-Islamic ancestors are invoked—is also appropriated by local Javanese Catholics to express their communal religiosity, including their respect for ancestors. In Java, this ritual meal is always open to participation by all members of the community regardless of their religious affiliation. Javanese Catholics regularly participate in this Muslim ritual meal. The Catholic shrine of the Sacred Heart of Jesus at Ganjuran, in the outskirt of Yogyakarta, even held this ritual meal where the prayers of thanksgiving are offered consecutively by officiants of other faiths, including a Muslim officiant (praying in Arabic), something that is rather unusual in Java. To a certain degree, my participation in the shrine rituals of Muslims should also be understood within this larger religio-cultural practice of cross-ritual participation.

In this regard, in general my religio-cultural sensibility as a Javanese has helped me considerably in the back-and-forth movement between Muslim and Catholic shrines. It minimized the sense of alterity when I visit Muslim shrines. Because of this sensibility, I could relate rather easily and naturally to the overall religio-cultural framework of meanings in these shrines, represented in their spatial and architectural arrangements as well as in their rituals and festivals. Not surprisingly, I was never asked about my formal religious identity while spending time at Muslim shrines.[10] Javanese pilgrims know that communing with the Divine is at the very heart of what it means to be human; it thus can occur in many different ways and contexts that somehow intersect on deeper levels. In their profound openness, these Javanese pilgrims recognize the overwhelming energy for communion of all sorts. Ultimately, this recognition might be related to centrality of the ideal of harmony, understood precisely as the fruit of the right relationships with the

Divine, self, other people across religious boundaries, society at large, and the entire cosmic reality.

For this reason, it was natural for me as a member of this culture to participate in the pilgrims' conversations on the deeper meanings of life. As a Javanese, it is natural for me to join their practice of pilgrimage as *tirakat*—that is staying with them all night while doing various spiritual and ascetic practices in the shrine— or to participate in ritual communal meal (Javanese: *kenduri*) and other rituals and festivals. My earlier study of Islam, which included both academic study of foundational texts and history as well as immersion into the wider Islamicate culture outside of Java or Indonesia (including Turkey, Syria, and Egypt), definitely contributed to this personal dynamic. However, the overwhelming presence of a shared spiritual epistemology and cosmology creates a much more significant ambience of intimacy and familiarity that can lead to a deeper engagement like cross-ritual participation. Within the Javanese spiritual epistemology and cosmology, the macrocosm and microcosm are always in interaction with each other in search for harmony. In the Javanese sensibility—shared by Muslims and Catholics alike—communion with the Divine is always understood in the relation to a wider and deeper web of interrelationships, including paradigmatic figures in the context of sacred places.

Since I grew up in this atmosphere of communion, my participation at Muslim shrines both in the realm of the rituals and beyond became quite effortless. Javanese pilgrims in general tend to employ the same basic spiritual and cultural vocabularies when talking about their experience. For example, pilgrimage is understood as a *tirakat*, an intensive and intentional journey of self-purification, and the blessing of pilgrimage is understood as profound and lasting peace (Javanese: *tentrem, slamet*). When Javanese pilgrims, both Muslims and Catholics, employ the category of *tentrem* or *slamet* to talk to one another, there is no need for further clarification or argument. They readily understand not only the truth of it as an experience, but also the existential bond implicated in this common search for the underlying peacefulness of human existence. In this regard, the role of the fundamentally inclusive language of *rasa* (deepest inner sensing) is also remarkably real in this context, precisely because it makes possible this kind of deeper communication among pilgrims. Due to this religio-cultural framework, I essentially was already living in a comparative theological context, so to speak, where a common language is in place, and where encounters and conversations between peoples of different religions can occur using a common third language that does not obliterate the specificities of these traditions but rather enriches them on many different levels, including the level of affective connections.

To come back to my moments of comparative insight, it is important to note that my visit to Muslim shrines was typically followed by a heartfelt longing to commune with God and His spiritual company of saints in the familiar Catholic universe. This is why I readily returned to my habitual spiritual world: I would visit a nearby Catholic shrine after my visit to a Muslim one. However, this homecoming was never simply a return to the familiar, for I brought with me my spiritual experience with God through multifaceted and complex encounters with

Muslim saints and paradigmatic figures; my familiarity with and immersion into their shrines and rituals, including the prayers to which I have adjusted my spiritual sensibility; my quite personal encounters with the Muslim pilgrims, and so forth. This manifold realization often led me to a profound sense of gratitude to God for sending to the world these Muslim saints. As a Javanese, it is rather natural for me to see Javano-Muslim saints, such as Sunan Kalijaga, as paradigmatic ancestors whose religio-cultural legacy has become in many ways, both subtle and obvious, part and parcel of my own identity; their legacy is something that I consciously cherish, together with the legacy of the European Jesuit missionaries and other foundational figures of my local Catholic community.

Definitely, visits to Muslim shrines, which sometimes involve a certain degree of ritual participation, would evoke an aspect of spiritual presence of these saints and a personal connection to them. I still pray as a Catholic, because I could not do otherwise; however, particularly at these moments, my spiritual world ceased to be the earlier familiar "Catholic" one. Instead, while maintaining all traditional "Catholic" spiritual practices and sensibility, it is becoming more "Catholic" in the original sense of the word: that is, more universal, inclusive, and expansive, without being necessarily fuzzy or indiscriminately porous.

4 *The theological framework of* communio sanctorum

As mentioned earlier, I can enter more deeply into the ritual and spiritual world of Muslim pilgrimage tradition due to my own Catholic framework of *communio sanctorum*. In general this framework corresponds to the overwhelming reality of communion involved in both the Muslim and Catholic pilgrimage traditions in which I participated (described above). More specifically, this framework also enables me to see and personally appropriate some meeting points between Catholic practice and the Muslim ritual etiquette of tomb visitation.

In the context of Catholic theology, the doctrine of *communio sanctorum* offers one of the richest and most comprehensive theological frameworks of communion. This theology also originally stems from the common experience of being graced by God, a spiritual reality that lies at the very foundation of the pilgrimage tradition as well. For what is meant by the doctrine of *communio sanctorum*, as the Catholic theologian Elizabeth Johnson puts it, is a multifaceted communion with God in all His diverse manifestations. It includes communion with paradigmatic figures or "saints" (Latin, *sanctus*), with all the members of the community graced by the Spirit of God, including the deceased and those outside the boundaries of our religious tradition who have also been touched by the same Spirit of God. Furthermore, *communio sanctorum* also refers to communion with the holy things (Latin, *sanctum*) such as things used in liturgy, holy places, religious arts, sacred time, and so forth (Johnson 2005: 220).

According to Johnson, paramount in the doctrine of *communio sanctorum* is the fundamental idea of wholeness and comprehensiveness, both spatial and temporal, of the communion under the guidance of the Spirit. Johnson takes seriously the fact that the Catholic doctrine of *communio sanctorum* belongs to the third article of the Apostles' Creed that specifically professes belief in the Holy Spirit. In this creedal and pneumatological framework, the doctrine of *communio sanctorum* refers to a comprehensive web of relationships and communions that include individual human beings (both living and dead); communities of humankind here on earth and in heaven, including the paradigmatic figures and saints; the past and the future human family; and cosmic and earthly realities, as well as the richness of human life in general (Johnson 2006: 102). As one can see, the temporal and spatial scope involved in this doctrine refers to the very milieu where the Spirit of God is at work.

Furthermore, as Johnson understands it, the category of *communio sanctorum* also points to the heartfelt relationship of friendship with saints (canonized or otherwise) or other spiritually significant figures of the community. However, much more than just "veneration of saints," it indicates inclusive networks of friends and friendships, as well as a community built by solidarity under the principle of the work of the grace of God in all. In this respect, the reality that the doctrine of *communio sanctorum* points to is a community of grace-filled friends of God, thus echoing the Islamic notion of *walāya* (sainthood) as friendship and proximity. In particular Johnson grounds this communion on the idea of inclusive solidarity that is built among people in the common struggle for life and in the face of human suffering.[11] She highlights the view of the grace-filled nature of ordinary human life and struggle as the ordinary milieu for *communio sanctorum*. In this framework, *communio sanctorum* is concerned with the struggle in this life while extending beyond to the past and the future. The past generation is crucial for the present community because "they struggled to be faithful, leaving an imprint in the heritage of life in the Spirit that we inhabit" (Johnson 2006: 313). So, to summarize, the theologian Elizabeth Johnson understands the doctrine of *communio sanctorum* as a rich tapestry of communion in the framework of the Spirit of God. This communion is integral, interpersonal, intergenerational, cosmic, and supra-temporal.

In my case, I have actually come to learn the richness of this Catholic doctrine via my extensive engagements with the Muslim other. As a comparative theologian, I was naturally looking for the right theology for this engagement. In a way, my exposure to the richness of the Muslim practice of saint veneration leads me deeper to my own tradition. Then, armed with this enriched and renewed theological framework, I became more and more receptive to the many similar dynamics in the Islamic tradition of pilgrimage and saint veneration. I was more easily drawn to appreciate these similarities and deeper connections. For example, from a theological point of view, I could see that these Muslim saints are also persons who have been touched by the Spirit of God in many different ways. They are archetypal figures whose struggle I have personally benefited from, a crucial point raised by Johnson mentioned above. It is becoming so much clearer that the cosmic blessings of the Spirit are also manifested through these saints and their communities. This expressed the Islamic idea of cosmic blessings (*raḥmatan lil-'ālamin*), and this cosmic vision could not be undermined, for it brought me to a deeper realization of the fundamental fact that Muslims and Christians live in the same cosmos, the same *mandala*, that comes to be blessed with our prayers and common devotion to God through His saints. To a large extent, we draw our lives from the same sources. This vision also belongs to the Muslim notion of *raḥma*, that is, of God's absolute creative and salvific Love for the whole cosmos (Morris 2005: 296–8). All of this allows me to commune more easily with Muslim saints, their spiritual presences as well as cultural legacy.

This pneumatological understanding of *communio sanctorum* likewise helped me understand the words of John Paul II:

> The Church's relationship with other religions is dictated by a twofold respect: "Respect for man in his quest for answers to the deepest questions of his life, and respect for the action of the Spirit in man." Excluding any mistaken interpretation, the interreligious meeting held in Assisi was meant to confirm my conviction that "every authentic prayer is prompted by the Holy Spirit, who is mysteriously present in every human heart." (*Redemptoris Missio* 29)

Reading this passage, I was also reminded of John Paul II's own visit to the Western Wall (March 2000) where he prayed according to Jewish custom by placing a written prayer in the cracks of the Wall. That he was moved by the Spirit to pray that way confirms the spiritual intuition that led me to cross-ritual participation in Muslim shrines.[12]

5 Concluding remarks

At the end of this chapter, let me return to the anguish of Father Prennthaler that I mentioned at the very beginning of this chapter. During my countless visits to the Sendangsono Grotto (the shrine that he founded), I was often shocked by a realization that his anguish over the threat of the ritual features of the Muslim other was not mine, nor was it the other pilgrims' that I encountered there, it seems. The sounds of the neighboring mosque's call to prayer, for example, did not disturb me, but rather put me into a deeper and wider praying mode, since it called me to carry my Muslim saints, ancestors, and neighbors in my own prayer. My experience with the Muslim other turned out to be rather different from his, due to the deeper dynamics of back-and-forth visit made more fruitful theologically through the renewed framework of *communio sanctorum*.

So, is it "inappropriate" for a Catholic to participate in the rituals at Muslim shrines? In his reflections on common prayer with Muslims, Christian Troll argues that there is no single and no unambiguous answer to this question, due to the variety of times and places, forms and particular situations, as well as the sensitive question of theology involved. He then writes that this situation should not prevent Christians "from finding themselves together—wherever there are meaningful opportunities—for common supplication of God, for praise of the one whom both faith-communities confess as their Creator, Preserver and Judge, by whom they know themselves to be called in common responsibility" (Troll 2011: 70). In this chapter, I have attempted to offer an example that should be understood in its very particularity, including its theology, for it occurs within the context of a very modest exercise in comparative theology, done in a particular religio-cultural practice of shared pilgrimage culture and informed by the Catholic theology of *communio sanctorum*.

As I have mentioned, my back-and-forth riting has been made possible by a favorable constellation of different elements: the reality of hybrid and shared practice of saints veneration among Javanese Muslims and Catholics, my religio-cultural identity as a Javanese, and my role as a Catholic comparative theologian. As a result, my back-and-forth riting is very particular. This constellation has allowed me to be a Catholic believer and theologian (instead of an ethnographer) who can participate more deeply in, and learn many properly religious and theological things from, the ritual practice of the local Muslim communities. As Francis Clooney has shown, comparative theologians will do better by doing small and very particular practices of comparison. In the process, the "theological" and "comparative" aspects should be maintained. In my case, the theological framework of *communio sanctorum* helps me understand the theological import of the realities of encounters between Islamic and Catholic practices of saint veneration. Of course cross participation in other ritual settings (such as canonical prayers, scriptural recitation, and informal meditation) needs to be placed within a particular theological framework deemed proper by comparativists. It is unlikely that my case can readily be applied in different cross-ritual settings.

Having said this, however, I do think that in general, similar dynamics might be found within different religio-cultural contexts where religious communities have come to share some common religious practices due to the role of the underlying common cultural framework. Again, in my view, the role of comparative theology is to help us enter more deeply into the properly "theological" and "comparative" dimensions of these shared practices or mutual encounters between different religious traditions, including cross-ritual participation.

Part III

CHRISTIAN AND EAST ASIAN RELIGIOUS PERSPECTIVES

Chapter 10

OFFERING AND RECEIVING HOSPITALITY: THE MEANING OF RITUAL PARTICIPATION IN THE HINDU TEMPLE

Anantanand Rambachan

1 Introduction: A new Hindu temple (Mandir*) in Minnesota, USA*

During the weekend of June 29 to July 2, 2006, the Hindu community in the US state of Minnesota celebrated the opening of a new temple in the city of Maple Grove. The central icon (*mūrti*) of the temple is God as Viṣṇu. He is represented iconically as Śrī Varadarāja Swāmī (Lord of Blessings) and is accompanied by his feminine counterparts Śrī Lakṣmī (Goddess of Wealth) and Śrī Bhūdevī (Goddess of the Earth). The Varadarāja icon of Viṣṇu is modeled after a temple and *mūrti* (icon) by the same name in the south Indian city of Kanchipuram. A traditional verse (*kṣetram gītam*) was composed, celebrating Viṣṇu's new abode in the city of Maple Grove.

> I bow in respect and offer worship to:
> Śrī Varadarāja Swāmī who is Lord of Śrī Bhūdevī and Śrī Lakṣmī;
> Who has the city of Maple Grove as His auspicious abode and liberates us
>   from sins, as He is kind and compassionate;
> Who resides in the divine Minnesota Temple, bestows bliss in both worlds
>   and is realized by His devotees;
> Who is the refuge to many kinds of seekers and fosters tolerance and peace;
> Who shines with splendor along with deities such as Śiva, Durga, Gaṇeśa,
>   Skanda; and who is worshipped in a thousand names such as Rāma,
>   Kṛṣṇa and Govinda.[1]

This composition, celebrating Viṣṇu as dwelling in the Hindu temple in Maple Grove, Minnesota, highlights richly some of the significant assumptions about orthodox Hindu worship involving icons (*mūrtis*) and the meaning of the temple itself. As will become clearer in the course of this discussion, the *mūrti* is viewed not merely as a symbol of God as Viṣṇu, but as God's living embodiment in this world.[2]

This theological understanding of the nature of the *mūrti* is quite prominent in the tradition and community of Śrīvaiṣṇavas who look to the religious poetry of the *ālvārs* (500–800 CE), centered on the love of Viṣṇu, as authoritative. The most influential and famous systematizer and exponent of the theology of Vaiṣṇavism is Rāmānuja (ca. 1000 CE), whose interpretation is referred to as a qualified nondualism (*viśiṣṭādvaita*) to distinguish it from the nondual (*advaita*) theology of Śaṅkara (ca. 700 CE).[3] Although sharing with Śaṅkara the view that the infinite *brahman* is the only reality, Rāmānuja contends that *brahman* is internally complex and diverse. The all-inclusive *brahman* contains within itself a real diversity consisting of unconscious matter (*acit*) and conscious selves (*cit*). For Śaṅkara, on the other hand, *brahman* is the single ontological reality, and all differences express the variety of forms and names, but not ultimate being. In spite of such significant theological differences, Rāmānuja's theological understanding of the nature of the *mūrti* has exerted profound influence on Hindu traditions and has been widely adopted, even within the tradition of Śaṅkara.

There are also reformist Hindu traditions that reject the doctrine of the *mūrti* as a living embodiment of God. Prominent among these is the Arya Samaj, founded by Swami Dayananda Saraswati (1824–83). Dayananda Saraswati equated the use of *mūrtis* with idolatry, viewing this practice as a symptom of the degeneration of the Hindu tradition from its pristine teachings in the Vedas. Hindu temples affiliated with this group do not have altars with *mūrtis* for ceremonial worship. Dayananda Saraswati also rejected the teaching of divine incarnation (*avatāra*) and affirmed the formless nature of God. There are other traditions in which the *mūrtis* are used but are seen as symbols that are helpful for focusing the mind in meditation or prayer (Jordens 1978).

My focus in this discussion, however, is with (1) clarifying the orthodox Hindu understanding of the meaning of the *mūrti*, especially as articulated in the Vaiṣṇava tradition. This clarification is the necessary prelude for (2) describing the nature of Hindu temple and domestic worship and for considering the requirements of participation. This analysis enables us to (3) reflect on the implications for outsider participation.

2 Mūrti *as the embodiment of God*

According to Rāmānuja the *mūrti* or *arcā* embodiment of God is one of the five forms of divine manifestation (Vasudha Narayanan 1985: 54). In His supreme (*para*) form (1), God eternally abides in the heavenly world. The emanations (2) (*vyūhas*) of God preside over the functions of creation, preservation, and destruction. At periodic intervals, God incarnates and persons such as Rama and Krishna are believed to be earthly incarnations (3) (*avatāras/vibhavas*) of God. God resides in the heart of all beings as the inner controller (4) (*antaryāmin*). Finally, and most importantly for Vaiṣṇavas, is the presence of God in the icon (5) (*arcāvatāra*). This form is wholly God, and is not understood as contradicting the all-pervasive presence of God in the universe. This view of the *mūrti* must be distinguished from perceptions of *mūrtis* as just useful forms for focusing the mind during periods of worship or meditation or as visual theologies that symbolically communicate insights about the nature of God. *Mūrtis* may certainly facilitate concentration at the time of worship and serve didactic purposes but these are secondary purposes for the devout Hindu. The understanding of the *mūrti* as a living incarnation (*avatāra*) is a radically different theological claim. It is this understanding that makes worshipful interaction (*puja*), especially in the temple, possible and meaningful. It also explains the faith, expressed in the composition at the beginning of this chapter, that God resides in the temple in a form that is real and tangible. This is the specific theological context in which we may consider appropriate and inappropriate behavior in relation to worship in the Hindu tradition.

3 From material object to living embodiment

How does an inanimate object become a living embodiment of God, a proper recipient of ritual worship in the Hindu temple? Every step in the making of a *mūrti* for ritual worship is governed by ritual prescriptions and guidelines. As Diana Eck notes, traditional texts (*śilpaśāstras*) "specify the proper proportion of the parts of the body, the appropriate number of arms, the gestures of the hands (*mudrās*), the emblems and weapons to be held in the hands, and the appropriate animal mount (*vāhana*)" (Ecks 1981: 51). Religious artists (*śilpins*) follow these instructions closely. There are ritual instructions even for the selection of the materials to be used.[4]

Once the *mūrti* is prayerfully and properly fashioned, it undergoes a series of consecratory rituals culminating in what is referred to as *prāṇapratiṣṭhā*, or the establishment of the breath of life in the *mūrti—prāṇa* (life breath), *pratiṣṭhā* (establishment). The final step in this elaborate ritual occurs when the artist completes his work by opening the eyes of the *mūrti*. One of the prayers (*mantras*) during the ceremony articulates well the worshipper's awareness of the paradox, mystery, and grace of inviting God to be present in the *mūrti*.

> Lord, you are omnipresent, yet I am inviting you to be present in this form as one would use a fan to the air. Just as the divine fire, lying hidden in the wood comes out to be experienced and savored, let your presence be felt by your devotees.[5]

The point of both analogies in this verse is the same. God, who is present everywhere and pervades everything, like the air or like heat in a piece of wood, graciously becomes manifest and receives worship in response to the devotee's longing.

The consecrated *mūrti* is housed in the innermost shrine of the temple referred to in Sanskrit as the *garbhagṛha*, the womb-room. Located at the center of the temple, the womb-room is identified externally by the tallest (*śikhara*) of a series of pyramidal or peak-like spires rising progressively from the entrance of the temple. The *śikhara* denotes honor and eminence. The womb-room is usually a dimly lit, cube-shaped enclosure, with minimal decoration, regarded as the dwelling place of God (Daniélou 2001). The priest (*pūjārī*) or priests serving and caring for the *mūrti* are alone permitted to enter the innermost shrine. While still not typical for most temples, in some of the newer temples constructed in North America, devotees are able to approach the *mūrtis* directly. The Vishnu Mandir and the Devi Mandir in Toronto, Canada, for example, have open altars that enable worshippers to have direct access to the *mūrtis*.[6] This is a deviation from the tradition that only the priests have the requisite purity to interact directly with the *mūrti*.

4 Pūja: *Hospitality and honor to God*

Once the *mūrti* is properly consecrated and is a living embodiment of God, the temple becomes a special dwelling place of God. It is now a sacred environment where everything is centered and focused on God, who is honored through a series of hospitality offerings (*upacāras*) spoken of generally as *pūjā*. These are about sixteen in number and include the invitation to receive worship (*āvāhana*), the invitation to a seat (*āsana*), the washing of the feet (*pādya*), acts of adoration through the offering of flowers (*puṣpa*), the burning of incense (*dhūpa*), the waving of lights (*dīpa*), and food (*naivedya*). Worship always concludes with the offering of *prasada*—that is, food which has been ritually offered to God.

Within the Hindu temple, the *mūrti* is regarded as the king of kings, or the queen of queens in the case of a feminine form of God. Although regional traditions in India differ, worship generally starts in the quiet dawn when the deity is roused from sleep with soft, solemn music and the recitation of sacred verses. The awakening ceremony is followed by the ceremonial bath, after which the deity is anointed with sandal paste, dressed in royal robes and decked with ornaments and flowers. These ceremonies are usually done with the *mūrti* screened from public viewing, since such viewing would be considered inappropriate and intrusive. The public is invited to see God only after these rituals are completed and the *mūrti* is properly adorned. Hymns (*stuti*) are sung and offerings are made at regular intervals during the day. Worship ends with an elaborate evening light (*āratī*) offering, after which the deity enjoys a nightly rest.

In explaining the meaning of such worship, Diana Eck cites appropriately the well-known Vaiṣṇava theologian, Pillai Lokācārya, who speaks of God entrusting Godself to the care of human devotees:

> This is the greatest grace of the Lord, that being free He becomes bound, being independent He becomes dependent for all His service on his devotee. ... In other forms the man belonged to God but behold the supreme sacrifice of Īśvara, here the Almighty becomes the property of the devotee. ... He carries Him about, fans Him, plays with Him—yea, the Infinite has become finite, that the child soul may actually grasp, understand and love Him. (cited in Eck 1981: 46)

The priest caring for the *mūrti* and the worshipper reverently observing the ritual share a profound sense that God is the immediate recipient of this loving honor and hospitality.

As in the case of the Hindu temple, the presence of a consecrated *mūrti* transforms the family home into an abode of God and most Hindu homes have a room or a corner of a room set aside for the purpose of *puja*. Great care is taken to maintain its purity and sanctity. Here is kept the *mūrti* of the family's chosen form of God (*iṣṭadevata*). The *murti* is a potent reminder of God's presence and the home becomes a sacred space in which all aspects of life are centered on God. In the *mūrti*-form, God is the beloved household guest around whom all activities revolve and to whom everything is dedicated. Daily worship in the Hindu home is not as elaborate as the temple and consists usually of selected *puja* procedures. Common is the offering of light (*āratī*), waved in a clockwise direction before the *mūrti* and then passed on to family members who receive the blessings of God by placing their hands near the flame and touching their eyes and forehead. Food, a portion of which may be offered first to God, is distributed and sandal paste applied to the forehead of family members present.

5 A Hindu experience of Darśana (seeing God) and Prasāda (receiving blessings)

Although included in the *puja* ritual, it is revealing to highlight and comment on two elements that are especially important for participation in Hindu rituals. These are *darśana* and *prasāda*. We begin with *darśana*.

Darśana is a central practice of Hindu worship. We do not usually speak of visiting a Hindu temple for the purpose of worship, but we do speak often of going for *darśana*. The same term is employed often to describe the purpose for visiting a saintly person, a religious teacher (*guru*), or a site of pilgrimage such as a sacred river, mountain, or even a holy city.

There is no easy English equivalent for translating *darśana*. Eck speaks of it as "auspicious sight" (Eck 1981: 4). *Darśana* comes from the Sanskrit root "*dṛs*", meaning "to see". Although literally meaning "sight", it is not employed to describe all acts of seeing. It is reserved for describing the seeing of that which is imbued with religious meaning and may be rendered as "sacred seeing". It is most commonly used to describe the seeing of the *mūrti* in the Hindu temple. Hindus visit temples to stand before and look at the consecrated *mūrti*, fixed in the consciousness of seeing and standing in God's presence. The theology of the *arcāvatāra* or *mūrti*-embodiment of God makes *darśana* possible and meaningful. God graciously makes Godself accessible and available for the devotee's seeing, and this act alone satisfies, for many Hindus, the purpose of visiting a temple. It is an intimate and immediate experience of God.

For the devout Hindu, *darśana* is a dual mode of experience. It is a profound sense of seeing God and, at the same time, a consciousness of being "seen" by God or standing in God's presence. In *darśana*, I see and know that I am seen.

I am aware that God's eyes are upon me. To enhance this experience, the eyes of the *mūrti* are usually prominent and conspicuous and, as noted above, the final act in the ritual installation of a *mūrti* involves the opening of the eyes. An icon with eyes closed does not engender the sense of being seen by God. *Darśana* is a special communion between the devotee and God. To know that the eyes of God are upon me is to overcome feelings of anonymity and insignificance. Much of what transpires when Hindus visit temples and stand before a *mūrti* become inaccessible to the outsider without an understanding of the experience of *darśana*.

The second prominent element of Hindu worship is *prasāda*. *Prāsada* is derived from the Sanskrit root "*prasad*," meaning to be satisfied, pleased, or happy. As a noun, *prasāda* refers to a gift or favor, especially one that is received from God. It is a gift that fills with joy. In the specific context of Hindu worship, *prasāda* describes that which is given to the worshipper at the end of worship and received as a special gift of God. Although *prasāda* is usually something edible, such as fruit, sugar crystals, or even a complete meal, it may be a flower or even drops of water. The distinctive feature of *prasāda* is that the gift is received as coming from God. One of the hospitality acts in the performance of *puja* in the temple or Hindu home is the offering of food (*naivedya*). Some of this is distributed at the end of worship as *prasāda*. Hindu devotees visiting a temple usually take an edible offering which the priest places before the *mūrti* on behalf of the worshipper. After God receives it, a portion of it is returned to the worshipper as *prasāda*. The manner in which an ordinary edible item gets transformed into *prasāda* is a revealing insight into Hindu worship and the significance of the *mūrti* as an embodiment of God.

Let us imagine that before visiting my favorite temple, I stop by a vendor on the road leading to the temple to select a few bananas for purchase. I pay the vendor, place the bananas in my bag, and continue my journey to the temple. During this process, I do not think of the bananas as being different from the rows of bananas on the vendor's cart. After arriving at the temple, I make my way to the sanctum with my bananas, give these to the priest, and wait patiently as he takes my banana to *mūrti* and offers it with appropriate *mantras*. When he returns the bananas to me, a profound transformation occurs in my perception of the fruit. I immediately lift these to my head with reverence and joy. I receive the bananas with a heart full of gratitude. These are now no longer ordinary bananas from a vendor's cart, but *prasāda*—and there is a world of difference between the two. In fact, I will no longer use the word banana to describe the fruits but speak of these only as *prasāda*.

It is evident that the bananas have not changed; they are no different in appearance and content. When, however, I receive the banana after the temple priest offers it to the *mūrti*, the living embodiment of God, I see it as *prasāda*, as a gift and blessing from God. This understanding brings about a corresponding change in my state of mind that may be best described as one of cheerful serenity and joy. *Prasāda* refers both to the tangible object received as the gift of God of as well as the state of mind which this gift awakens.

An object becomes *prasāda* when it is seen as coming from God and when that perception results in a mental and emotional state of joyful gratitude. The value of the banana can no longer be measured by its purchase price. It has now become priceless. The worth of the gift comes from the gift-giver, who, in this case, happens to be God. If I offer this banana to a friend or family member, after my return from the temple, with the explanation that it is *prasāda*, his or her response will be one of joyful reverence and acceptance. *Prasāda* reminds us of God's generosity and loving grace. One never refuses *prasāda*, and it is sacrilegious, in Hinduism, to offer *prasāda* for sale or to commercialize it in any way.

6 The outsider and the Hindu temple

With rare exceptions, there are no restrictions on non-Hindus entering Hindu temples. One exception is the temple of Jagannath (Lord of the Universe) in Puri, Orissa, where a sign on the temple-gate announces, "Only Orthodox Hindus are allowed."[7] The reasons for the prohibition are not clear. Some speculate that it may be connected with attacks on the temple during the Mughal rule. The Puri King, Gajapati King Dibya Singha Deb, offered the explanation that since "Puri is the original seat of the Lord, there is restriction on the entry of non-Hindus. However they can have *darshan* of the Lord in other Jagannath temples elsewhere."[8] Stephen Huyler speculates that the reason is connected with the Hindu understanding of the doctrine of *karma*, and the belief that negative mental states generate undesirable outcomes.

> Those not trained in the customs of approaching and honoring a sacred image might consciously or unconsciously pollute it. In the same way that the power of images and sacred spaces is believed to be enhanced by prayers and positive actions, it may also be damaged by careless or malevolent gestures, thoughts, or actions. (Huyler 1999: 255)

Quite recently, in a most interesting decision, the Tirumala Tirupati Devasthanamas, the group managing India's richest and perhaps most famous temple, the Tirupati Temple in Andhra Pradesh, prohibited the entry of all non-Hindus into the temple unless they signed a register affirming their faith in the deity, Lord Venkateshwara.[9] The signing of the register was a voluntary act in the past and the recent enforcement was triggered by the refusal of a devout Christian political leader to comply. The temple body is concerned also about Christian proselytization in the precincts of the temple. It will be very helpful if temples like the Jagannath in Puri, Orissa, and the Tirupati in Andhra Pradesh clarified their reasons for excluding non-Hindus. Who, for example, is an orthodox Hindu? What does it mean to have faith in Lord Venkateshwara? Such theological clarification will help us to understand how these temples conceive of Hindu worship and the corresponding requirements for participation.

Barring these prominent exceptions, most Hindu temples warmly welcome guests of other faiths, providing that the visitors observe temple norms. These include the removal of shoes before entering the worship space and modesty in dress. All temples have designated areas for the storage of shoes. Visitors should also avoid pointing their feet toward the *mūrti* if they choose to sit on the floor.

The Hindu temple, as described above, is a sacred space where God makes Godself accessible and present in a special *mūrti* form. A temple is referred to as a *devālaya* or abode of God—*deva* (God), *ālaya* (house). One enters a Hindu temple as God's guest and the Hindu priest (*pūjāri*), the servant of God, happily welcomes the guest with a hospitality that is ancient and deep-rooted, both cultural and religious. The practice of a non-Hindu going to a Hindu temple as an observer who does not wish to participate in rituals is a relatively recent one. Most Hindu temple priests assume that the visitor has come to see God (*darśana*) and to receive the blessings (*prasāda*) of God. This assumption is easier also since Hindu traditions are decentralized and do not require membership for participation.

The priest expresses his hospitality in a gracious and spontaneous inclusion of the visitor in the temple worship, assuming that the non-Hindu will be happy to be included. If the non-Hindu visitor happens to be present at the shrine during worship (*puja* or *arcana*), she will be offered the same expressions of welcome and blessing as the Hindu visitor. These generally include *tilaka, āratī, caraṇāmṛta, sātari*, and *prasāda*. *Tilaka* is sandal paste, vermillion, or ash applied to the forehead as a mark of welcome and blessing. *Āratī* is the offering of light that is waved in a clockwise direction before the *mūrti* and then brought to the worshippers. A devout Hindu will lift her hands toward the flame and then over her head and face. *Caraṇāmṛta* is the water used to wash the feet of the *mūrti*. The priest gives drops of this to the worshippers for sipping. The *sātari* is a gold or silver crown, with the imprint of the *mūrti's* feet. It is placed on the head of the worshipper as a mark of blessing. Bowing one's head at the feet of God or a religious teacher (*guru*) is an expression of respect and humility. *Prasāda* is an offering brought to the temple, usually edible, that is then distributed to the worshipper. All of these offerings to the worshipper by the Hindu priest reinforce the understanding of the *mūrti* as a living embodiment of God interacting with the visitor. Non-Hindus who wish to participate in Hindu temple rituals should not be fearful that errors might cause offense. Hindu priests understand well their lack of familiarity and give more value to intent and attitude than ritual correctness.

The Hindu temple priest feels a deep obligation to include the non-Hindu visitor in his ritual routines since he is God's agent and God's hospitality and blessings are available to all who come to the temple. The choice in not on the part of the priest; it is with the visitor who must decide to accept or decline. No Hindu priest, however, will insist on the ritual participation of the non-Hindu visitor to the temple. A respectful gesture of declining (bringing the palms together and a bow of the head) will suffice, and the priest will move on to the next person. Hindus should see that such a gesture of refusal could be born from a deep respect for the tradition and its special theological claims.

7 Idolatry, polytheism, and Hindu worship

The reluctance to participate in Hindu temple worship on the part of some Jews, Christians, and Muslims is sometimes caused by concerns and fears about idolatry. Many believers from these religions perceive the *mūrti* as an idol and condemn Hindu traditions as being idolatrous. The choice about participating in Hindu rituals is one that must be exercised on the basis of one's own theological commitments and one's understanding of the meaning of these in relation to the teachings and practices of other religions. It is important, however, that our understanding is true and faithful to the other's self-understanding. The clarifications that I offer here are not for the purpose of persuading others to participate in Hindu worship. I do so only to enhance the interreligious understanding. At the same time, I believe that participation in the rituals of another tradition should be done with clarity about the theological and other assumptions underlying these.

If idolatry is construed as a simplistic equation of the uncreated and infinite God with a created and finite object, this is certainly not the understanding of the Hindu worshipper. Hindu theological traditions, dualistic and nondualistic, exemplify an appreciation of God as both immanent and transcendent, near and far, beyond name and form and with name and form. The language of paradox, as in this verse from the Īśa Upaniṣad (5), is familiar to Hindus when speaking of God:

> It moves, it does not move;
> It is far and near likewise.
> It is inside all of this:
> It is outside all of this. (The Upaniṣads 2003: 8)

Hindu texts like the Bhagavadgītā invite us continuously to see God as present in every form and to see every form as existing in God.

> I am the taste in water, the brilliance in the moon and sun, the sacred syllable
> (Om) in all the Vedas, the sound in air and virility in men.
> I am the pure fragrance in the earth, the radiance in fire, life in all beings and
> austerity in ascetics. (Bhagavadgītā 7:8-9)

This vision, as the verse above makes clear, is not an anthropomorphic one. Hindus journey from afar for *darśana* of the Himalayan peaks and the rushing waters of the River Ganges. Nature is a vast theater in which the divine is known and experienced. Reflecting on her Christian fears about worshipping nature and not God and on looking only to history as the medium for God's revelation, Diana Eck invites us to enlarge our understanding of these as opposites:

> But "nature" and "history" are not true opposites. Do we really need to choose
> one and not the other? ... Both nature and history are revelatory. Both are

infused with the energy and breath of God. If I can attest to the life of the Spirit in the daring history of the modern Christian ecumenical movement, I can also insist upon the presence of the Spirit in the cyclical renewal of nature. (Eck 1993: 141)

The general Hindu theological orientation is to see the omnipresent God as present in and pervading the universe and all forms within it, and also beyond it. God is not limited to any particular form. A traditional Hindu prayer for forgiveness movingly expresses the Hindu sense of the paradox of all worship:

> In my meditations, I have attributed forms to You who transcend all forms.
> In my songs of praise, I have contradicted that you are indescribable.
> In my pilgrimage, I have denied your omnipresence.
> O Lord of the universe, forgive me these limitations.[10]

The nature of Hindu worship and the issue of idolatry was one of the topics of discussion at a historic Hindu-Jewish Leadership Summit Meeting in Jerusalem (February 17–20, 2008).[11] Perhaps the most significant affirmation of the joint declaration reads as follows:

> It is recognized that the One Supreme Being, both in its formless and manifest aspects, has been worshipped by Hindus over the millennia. This does not mean that Hindus worship "gods" and "idols". The Hindu relates to only the One Supreme Being when he/she prays to a particular manifestation.

This does not imply that Jews will or should now feel comfortable about participating in Hindu worship, but it certainly marks a significant step in Jewish understanding of the theology of the *mūrti* and its use in Hindu worship.

Another issue of concern about Hindu worship for Jews, Christians, and Muslims, members of what is now commonly referred to as the Abrahamic religions, is the multiplicity of images and names for the divine in the Hindu tradition. This phenomenon is widely regarded as polytheistic and is denounced. Most Hindu temples, while having a central *mūrti*, will have also many other forms of God. In "monotheistic consciousness", notes Diana Eck (Eck 1993: 59), "this singular is the proper number for questions of Truth: There is one God, one Only-Begotten Son of the Father, one Seal of the Prophets, One Holy Book, one Holy Catholic and Apostolic Church."

Here again, it is important for people of other faiths to engage the Hindu understanding of the oneness and manyness of God. Although it is true that the multiplicity of the forms in which God is represented in the Hindu tradition reflect the religious and cultural diversity of the Indian sub-continent, each region having its own favorite representation of God, there is an ancient theological interpretation of this diversity that is pervasive. This understanding is expressed earliest in a famous Ṛg Veda hymn (I.164.45–6).[12]

Speech hath been measured out in four divisions.
The Wise who have understanding know them.
Three kept in close concealment cause no motion;
of speech men only speak the fourth division (45).
They call him Indra, Mitra, Varuna, Agni, and he is
the noble-winged Garutman.
The One Being, the wise call by many names:
they call it Agni, Yama, Matarisvan (46).

Verse I.164.45 provides the context with an insight about the nature of human speech. It does so by presenting the totality of speech as consisting of four quarters. Human speech comprises only a quarter of the total speech potential. In describing the three quarters of speech as "kept in close concealment" and causing "no motion", the verse suggests powerfully the language of silence and the ultimate inexpressibility of the One Being (*ekam sat*) referred to in the verse following.

Hindu sacred texts and tradition remind us constantly that, in relation to God, our language is always limited and inadequate. God is always more than we can define, describe, or understand with our finite minds and fragmented language. No representation of the divine in image or words can ever be complete. When we employ our limited language, a fraction of the total potentiality of language, to speak of the limitless One, our language will be diverse. We use many names (Indra, Mitra, Varuna, Agni, Yama, Matarisvan, Garutman) not because the gods are many, but because of the limits of human language and experience. The different names are not just names. Each name also points to a different way of imagining and understanding the nature of the One Being, and each name and way of understanding implies its own peculiar limitation.

Acknowledging the diversity of human names and ways of understanding God, the Ṛg Veda text is unambiguous in its assertion that God is one (*ekam*). It is the one God that is called and imagined differently. Those who name and worship God as Indra, Agni, or Varuna are not, in reality, addressing themselves to different beings but to the One True Being. One name alone is not true and all others false, and one name does not include or represent all others. Each is a name for the One. The text rejects the existence of many gods and proclaims the truth of the One. As Maitrī Upaniṣad (5:1) states this teaching:

You are Brahma, you are Vishnu too;
You are Rudra, you are Prajapati;
You are Agni, Varuna, Vayu:
You are Indra, you are the Moon.

Hindus usually think about God in other traditions through the lens of this verse. Extended to other traditions, we may say that the text does not allow for a Jewish, Christian, Muslim, or Hindu God. It does recognize multiple understandings, while denying multiple divinities. The oneness of God is not compromised by the manyness of names and forms or ways of speaking. This insight enables us to think of persons in other traditions, not as strangers with alien, false, or rival deities, but as fellow beings whose God is our God. This outlook explains the ease with which some Hindus enter other places of worship and participate in alien rituals.

8 Theology and crossing religious boundaries

The Christian theologian Thomas Thangaraj noted and reflected on this while observing the ease with which his Hindu friend, Ganga, a visiting scholar at an American University, "attended a nearby Methodist church every Sunday, participating in all the elements of the liturgy, including the Eucharist" (Thangaraj 1997: 8). Upon inquiry, Ganga explained that in the absence of Hindu temples, the Methodist church was a sacred space where he could worship God. Ganga was undoubtedly expressing the perspective of the Ṛg Veda text above. Thangaraj contrasted his own religious inhibitions with Ganga's freedom:

> How can my Hindu friend worship God easily in a Christian setting, while I have so much difficulty doing the same in a Hindu temple? When I consider this problem carefully, it becomes clear that the ideas and practices that shaped my religious devotion are very different from those that shape Ganga's. My religious experience has produced an approach to other traditions that makes it difficult for me to pray with my Hindu friend and in a Hindu setting of worship.

Although there are Hindus who problematically minimize religious difference on the basis of this Ṛg Veda text, the text itself does not suggest this. Instead of underplaying differences, we may infer from the text the necessity for attentiveness to diverse ways of speaking about God. It is the wise, after all, who speak differently. Theological diversity is not dismissed here as the consequence of ignorance. By attributing differences to the speech of the wise, the text invites a respectful and inquiring response to religious diversity. We must not hastily and arrogantly denounce the sacred speech of the other as undeserving of sincere and serious contemplation.

The value of this text is to be found particularly in the articulation of an overlooked implication of God's oneness—the fact that my neighbor of another faith, who speaks a different religious language, and I are addressing and relating ourselves to the same God. Through differences of name, symbols, cultures, and theologies, we comfortably clothe God with an identity that is similar to our own and fail to recognize the one God in other theological and symbolic dresses. Discerning the truth of the "One Being the wise call by many names" is profoundly transformative. It explains, in part, the ease of Ganga, the Hindu, in crossing physical and theological boundaries and discovering God in a Methodist church.

The Hindu tradition, with rare exceptions, has not developed conversion ceremonies for those who wish to become Hindus.[13] This makes it easier for people of other traditions to participate in Hindu worship if they desire to do so. Hindus will not generally see it as problematic for a Christian, for example, to remain Christian while practicing Hindu rituals. This is also possible because Hindu temple worship is not usually congregational in structure and offers a great measure of freedom to the worshipper. The choice, however, is always with the worshipper to accept or reject the hospitality of God offered in the Hindu temple.

Chapter 11

TOWARD AN OPEN EUCHARIST

Richard Kearney

"A restricted Eucharist is false. ... Whoever 'loves' his brother has a right to the Eucharist."[1]

— Abhishiktananda, 1998

In this chapter I wish to make a case for an open Eucharist. I will be speaking as a philosopher of Catholic formation paying special attention to two pioneering priests who struggled to share the Body of Christ with people of other faiths. In revisiting their testimonies, I hope to show how such figures—and others after them—helped pave the way for a less restrictive, and in my view more deeply Christian, approach to the Eucharist. But first, let me offer some remarks from a more personal narrative perspective.

1 D'où parlez-vous?

My Paris teacher and mentor, philosopher Paul Ricoeur, used to greet students entering his seminar with the question: "*d'où parlez-vous*?" Where do you speak from? So let me begin with some stories of Eucharistic sharing and nonsharing which I experienced as a young citizen of "Catholic Ireland" in the second half of the twentieth century.

First, the sharing. I had a very devout and beautiful mother who took me to Mass every morning, where I served in a local Cork convent as altar boy from the age of seven to eleven. These were magical moments and I will never forget the experience of daily Eucharist received from a kindly priest (and a keen rugby player), Father Buckley, to the sounds of an angelic choir and the perfume of sweet incense, beeswax candles, washed nuns, and altar wine. The wafer first thing every morning was heavenly food indeed. On Sundays, our large family (seven children) would attend public Mass in the city where we trooped up to the communion rails of a packed church with every class and character of Cork citizenry—"rich, poor, and indifferent"—an inclusiveness I have always cherished in my Catholic religion. Later, at a Benedictine boarding school in Limerick, I continued to participate in daily Mass, singing and playing music in the choir. The plain Gregorian chant of the robed monks added to the sense of sacred presence.

My monastic education was sufficiently broadminded to encourage us adolescent students to receive the host daily rather than agonize over endless inventories of sins (like so many of my parents' generation). In short, the Eucharist was Word made flesh every day of my life from the age of seven to seventeen: the divine made present in the most simple material ingredients of edible bread and heartwarming wine. I felt blessed to receive such an extraordinary sacramental gift—the daily host—and as I became increasingly familiar with those of other faiths, I wished to share it with them.

But not all in my Church agreed. My first rude awakening occurred during an ordination at my monastic school. The sacrament was performed by the local Bishop and while the Abbot and monks were extremely open—hosting annual ecumenical meetings for the different denominations in our conflicted island—the Bishop in question was decidedly less so. When the widow of a local Protestant Dean, who had a close relationship with the Abbey, came to receive Holy Communion at the conclusion of the ceremony, the Bishop turned his back. As she stood there in front of him, at the top of a long queue with hundreds in attendance, he declined to share the Eucharist with her. A holy monk participating in the Mass, said to me afterward: "That was one of the most unchristian acts I ever witnessed." I could not but recall the foreign Phoenician woman saying to Jesus, "even dogs receive the crumbs from your table ..." (cf. Mk 7:28).

I was deeply shocked by how the Body of Christ—offered for *all* the "hungry" of this world: Jew or Gentile, Pharisee, Samaritan, or Syrian—could be used in this way as a mark of exclusion and exclusivity. If not for my largehearted monastic friends, I think I might have left the Church that day. And, God knows, with the multiple scandals of child abuse, paternalism, Vatican banking, condemnation of gay love and contraception (even to prevent AIDS, venereal disease, and unwanted pregnancies) as "morally evil," there were other reasons to abandon my religion at that time. But there was, I must confess, something particularly chilling about the Eucharist—the sharing of the presence of Christ with those most in need: the wounded, the lost, the searching, the sick, the hopeless, the faithless, the hungry—being refused to a woman clearly wishing to participate in one of the most sacred Christian rites of love and hospitality. If Christ identified himself as the stranger (*hospes*) five times in Matthew 25, who had the right to refuse his body to other strangers? Was it not with hungry, thirsting strangers *above all* that we should share this blessed food? Was not interconfessional communion a Christian imperative? These were some of the questions which buffeted my young soul as I was faced with the public humiliation of an Anglican widow genuinely desiring to be in communion with the Church I knew and loved.

My second story is of more public proportions. Mary McAleese, as President of Ireland, received Communion at the Protestant Christ Church Cathedral in Dublin in 1997. The then Catholic Archbishop of Dublin, Desmond Connell, denounced her participation as a "sham." He not only rebuked President McAleese as a Catholic receiving a Protestant Eucharist, but also later chastised the Protestant Bishop of Ireland, Walton Empey, for offering the Eucharist to Catholics in the first place. Archbishop Connell claimed that Anglican ministers who welcomed all baptized Christians to celebrate the Eucharist were failing "to respect the faith and obligations of our members." He said: "For Roman Catholics, when we receive Holy Communion, it is a statement that we are in full communion with those people with whom we are taking Communion. But our Communion with the Church of Ireland and other Protestants is incomplete; because we and they do not have the same faith about, for example, the Eucharist." Reverend Empey responded by saying: "At times like this, I feel that Jesus is weeping and the Devil is doing a dance." He said the Church of Ireland "welcomed to Holy Communion all those baptized in the name of the Holy Trinity." I too felt I could hear Jesus weeping that day, unable to comprehend how one of the highest representatives of the Catholic Church in Ireland (my church) could not acknowledge the healing power of intercommunion between our religiously divided peoples.[2] That the Eucharist could be the occasion of ongoing acrimony in our war-torn land was a matter of deep sadness and shame.

Ironically, shortly after the election of Pope Francis, fifteen years later, there were reports in *The Irish Times* that Mary McAleese might be elected the first woman cardinal of the Catholic Church! And it was a source of great relief for many Irish Catholics to hear Francis bravely declare that the Eucharist should be considered food for the "hungry" rather than a toll-house reward for rule-keepers.

Witnessing such ungenerous experiences—and others where the consecrated host was denied to remarried divorcees or practicing gays—I asked myself how the Eucharist, of all sacraments, rituals, and gestures, could be the cause of such egregious hurt? "One Bread, One Body," my fellow Catholics chanted as they knelt to receive Holy Communion—but, according to official Church doctrine for centuries, that was *only* if you were members of the "True Church": Roman Catholicism, as dogmatically defined by the Congregation for the Doctrine of the Faith. The rest—non-baptized in the one true holy and apostolic Church—were "not" part of the One Body. And even if Vatican II put an end to the injurious notion that there was "no salvation outside the church" (*extra ecclesiam nulla salus*—a doctrine that ran from the Lateran Council in 1215 to 1964) (Sullivan 1992; Sesboüé 2004; D'Costa 2011), the rule still pertained that the most holy of sacraments was *not* to be shared with "strangers"!

Given these dispiriting examples, it was with relief and joy that I later discovered not only the generous sacramental ecumenism of many monks and nuns within my church, but also the exemplary witness of two pioneering priests of an inclusive Eucharist, Abhishiktananda and Teilhard de Chardin.

2 Passing East: Abhishiktananda and Teilhard de Chardin

2.1 Abhishiktananda (Henri le Saux)[3]

"The discovery of Christ's I AM is the ruin of any Christian theology, for all notions are burnt within the fire of experience."[4]

In 1948 the Benedictine monk Henri le Saux left his monastery in Brittany, France, and sailed to Pondicherry in India. Like several missionaries before and after him, Henri le Saux (renamed Abhishiktananda in India) felt compelled to revise some of his Catholic dogmas when confronted with "strangers." It seems to be no accident that, after his encounter with a spiritual culture deeply foreign to his own, his approach to the Christian Eucharist underwent radical questioning and finally resulted in a real opening to other faiths.[5]

One such opening occurred in 1972, during an Easter Saturday Vigil in Pune (north-west India). His friend and disciple, Sara Grant, a Sacred Heart sister from Scotland and a fine theologian, described the ceremony as a major "breakthrough" in interreligious communion. She writes of how her CPS ashram at Pune—a "multi-religious household" functioning as a center of liturgical "experimentation"— hosted a particularly meaningful Eucharist with Abhi and a Hindu Panditji, as well as other Hindu and Jewish guests during that Easter weekend. The ritual was performed out of conviction that "liturgical celebration is the setting par excellence for reflection on the mystery of Christ in the light of both biblical and non-biblical scripture" (Grant 2002: 72).[6]

Though Abhishiktananda was the chief celebrant, he himself seems to have written little about this event—yet there are some telling hints in diary entries which I shall consider below. It was the host, Sara Grant, who provided the best account, describing the Vigil as a genuinely "trans-cultural celebration" which was much more than a "preparatory para-liturgy." And while the sharing of scriptures from different biblical and Vedic sources was central, what was most striking for her personally was the "*bodily* aspect of the being and the fact that we experienced it *as community*." She explains: "suddenly we realized that until his death, Jesus was bound by history and its limitations, but through his death and resurrection he had burst the bonds of space and time and could be recognized as not only Lord and Christ but as *Sat purusha*, the archetypal Man of Vedic tradition in whom every member of the human race can recognize the truth of his or her being" (Grant 2002: 72).

While I have not been able to locate any explicit reference to this "breakthrough" event in Abhishiktananda's published works, I did discover a number of journal entries which provide some revealing context for what transpired.[7] On Good Friday (March 31, 1972), the eve of the sharing between Abhi, Grant, and their Hindu guests, Abhi writes: "The disciple of Jesus does not 'boast' that in the Cross he knows some higher secret of wisdom. He lives in conformity with his experience of the Cross and in all humility he gives an account of it to anyone who asks him." On Easter Sunday (April 2, 1972), the day after the Vigil, Abhi adds this note on the importance of interreligious insight: "Grace is the answer of both the Christian and the *bhakta* (seeker of God) … Jesus is still only understood by Christians as the guru who is other—*anya iva*—as the Purusha, Creator, Sacrificer, Savior. Only too rarely has the flash of 'Thou art Thou' (*tat tvam asi*) shone forth and the I am! (*aham asmi*) sprung up simultaneously."

Six days later, still reflecting back and forth across Christian and Hindu scriptures, Abhi expands on this idea that Christianity discovers its true self by journeying out through the other, the stranger, the outsider. He describes this pilgrimage from self to other as a revolution of the Spirit: "Truth cannot be formulated. … Christianity is neither knowledge, nor devotion, nor ethics and ritual—nor is it duty, religion (formulas, institutions). It is an explosion of the Spirit. It accepts any religious basis (*jnana/bhakti/karma*) to the extent necessary in each case." And he adds, quizzically: "But what makes the Christian inspiration distinct? Why this search for distinction, for identity? ... Christianity is the *discovery of myself in the other*" (April 8, 1972).

On October 25 of the same year, just one year before his death (October 6, 1973), Abhi's interreligious hospitality stretches to more explicit formulations: "Do I call him Christ? Yes, within one tradition, but his name is just as much Emmanuel—Purusha. Can he be Krishna? Rama? Shiva? Why not, if Shiva is in Tamilnadu the form of that archetype which seeks to become explicit at the greatest depth of the human heart?" (October 25, 1972). And while Abhi normally refrains from mentioning the actual role of the Mass as such (silence being his preferred voice), on November 1 he explicitly addresses the question of the Eucharist, making the bold claim that "when you pass beyond the *namarupa* (external forms), the mystery takes all forms (*sarvarupam*). The clash is not with a particular *namarupa* but with those who absolutize it. The Church is so immense a mystery that the apologists water it down in trying to make it fit into their narrow historical views!" And then, at this crucial point of critical reflection, he poses the question: "The liturgy, the Mass—is it not a necessary compensation for the drastic *neti*, negation of *advaita*?," suggesting that "psychic health spontaneously (unconsciously) calls for this complement ... to keep one's balance! However liturgy, Mass, should never be forced. Read the breviary, celebrate the Mass, never out of duty, but as if by instinct, spontaneously" (November 1, 1972). The Mass is conceived here, in other words, as a kataphatic corporeal counterpart to the apophatic emptiness of "beyond God." It is the affirmation which accompanies negation, the resurrection after the kenosis of the Cross, food and wine after hunger and thirst, the sharing of Emmaus after the solitude of Gethsemane. Advent after Advaita. But if participation in the Mass requires dismissal of his closest Hindu brothers in Spirit, it is a price too high to pay. Abhi would never renounce the deepest spiritual epiphanies of his life, experienced in a cave on the holy Hindu mountain of Arunachala in close proximity to the ashram of his beloved Sri Ramana. Rarely is Abhi's profound commitment to double belonging—as Christian and Hindu—so pronounced:

> If to become Christian again I had to give you up, O Arunachala, to abandon you, O Ramana, then I would never be able to become Christian again, for they have entered into my flesh, they are woven into the fibers of my heart. How could I become Christian again if I had to forget Ramana and the people of the mountain... all those who were my companions on the way, and were each in his own way my helper or my guide toward the great enlightenment. If to say Mass I had to give them the slip, then I could never again say Mass. (Abhishiktananda 1998: 175)

But there is more. As death approaches, Abhi's interreligious convictions become even clearer. He has moved from being a Christian guest to his Hindu host to becoming a host in his own right. In the Spirit, guest and host become interchangeable. The timeless I AM of Christ and Purusha traverse historical divisions. On February 17, 1973, he claims that:

> The mythos of the Purusha (Spirit) is wider than that of Christos; not only does it include the cosmic and metacosmic aspect of the mystery, but it is also free from the attachment to time entailed by the mythos of Christ. Rather it recognizes all the symbolic value contained in the mystery of Time, but refuses to compress the absolute separately into a particular point of time.

"The Purusha," Abhi insists, "is simply there, like the Atman, Sat, Brahman, once the human being awakes to himself. 'Before Abraham was, *I am*.'" In short, the mystery of the divine is greater than any particular confessional mythos in time, place, and history. It is transconfessional and transhistorical, without denying the indispensable need for symbolic, ritual instantiations. In the same entry, Abhi goes on to see the "symbols of Christ" as "bearers of universality" and offers this explanation: "They radiate their Catholicity (ecumenism = universality). They exist *ad* (toward) the totality, *pros* (toward) the totality = *sarvam prati!*" And he follows this immediately with one of his most radical claims for interreligious communion—a key statement for my case: "A restricted Eucharist is false. 'Leave your offering before the altar!'... Whoever 'loves' his brother has a right to the Eucharist." To host the stranger from other religions has now become the ultimate meaning of the Communion Host.

These end-of-life insights into interconfessional hospitality were accompanied by some of Abhi's most acute theological reflections. Several weeks later, struggling with illness as he prepared a series of lectures for the Jesuit faculty at Delhi (Vidyajyoti) on Christology, Abhi penned some extremely subtle journal entries on the question of the "unicity" and "uniqueness" of Christ. The singularity of Christ becomes the very basis of his university. In one particular entry, he suggests that the most elective "only one" contains the most expansive "only one." The ostensible paradox, he insists, contains a sacred mystery, calling for a delicate balance between unique election and inclusive embrace. He offers the following articulation of this astonishing insight:

> If Christ is the "only one" for me … may I discover in him the glory of the Only One. And what does it matter if I discover the glory of the Only One in *whatever created form there may be*! For the glory of the Only One is in all one. This alone is important: that Christ should be Everything for me. … *Let every human being be the only one for me,* my everything to whom I give myself totally. In this alone I will have the experience of the Only One. (March 22, 1973)

In other words, the point of most ostensible exclusivity (Christ is the only one) becomes in truth the most intimate point of inclusivity (Christ is each "only one," that is everyone I welcome in their singular uniqueness and "thisness"). It is not stretching things, I think, to hear echoes here of Christ's identification with each stranger (*hospes*) in Matthew 25. The singular and universal in one. And perhaps even an echo of the beautiful Scotist notion of divinity being incarnate in each person's irreducible "thisness" (*haecceitas*) (Osborne 1999: 68, 106–7, 150–65, 185–9), an idea so central to Gerard Manley Hopkins' entire religious poetics.

On April 21, 1973, one year after the interreligious Easter Vigil with Sara Grant at Pune, Abhi returns to the idea of intercommunion. Perhaps it was the lapse of time, offering a certain interval of reflection, which enabled him to return to the "breakthrough" experience after the event, *après coup, nachträglich*. The repetition of the Paschal ritual, one year later, seems to have triggered a revisiting of the original event—an event as ineffable as it is profound: "Easter night, night of the awakening to being (*sambodhi*). The vigils of *Sakyamuni* which culminate in the Awakening… Neither Jesus nor Buddha *described* their Awakening." And it seems Abhi is following suit. Yet on April 28, he breaks his silence and strives to say the unsayable in the following terms:

> People are converted. … They become Christian, Muslim, Sufi, Vedantin, etc. All those are superimposed forms. Whereas the essential thing is to strip oneself of all that is superfluously added. … The *advaita* formulation is just as much a superimposition as are the Koranic or the Trinitarian formulations. And people fight to defend their own formulations and to condemn those of others!

Two days later, brushing the limits of "negative theology," he touches on the ana-theist notion of a God who is reborn "after" (*ana*) the death of God. Citing John of the Cross's notion of the Night in which we witness the "disappearance of God," Abhi observes that "the God that I project, the God of superimposition is surely dead …;" and, consequently, he claims, it is out of this demise that emerges—paradoxically and mysteriously—the "dazzling light of the true 'I'." From this flows a refusal of all dogmatic apologetics and a revolutionary embrace of interreligious pluralism: "One who knows several mental (or religious and spiritual languages) is incapable of absolutizing any formulation whatever—of the Gospel, of the Upanishads, of Buddhism, etc. He can only bear witness to an experience—about which he can only stammer…" But out of this apophatic stammering may arise, Abhi insists, the Awakened person who "rides upon the Spirit. His place is 'open space'" (May 4, 1973). This proclamation of an open space of the Spirit—underlying Abhi's plea for an open (i.e. "unrestricted") Eucharist—was made less than six months before he finally passed away.

These ruminations in the year leading up to his death can, I believe, be read retrospectively as a radicalization not only of Abhishiktananda's Pune liturgy but also of his first insight when setting up an interreligious ashram in Shantivanam in 1958. This is how he formulated his original founding vision:

> Should we say that the Revelation of Christ has absolutized Semito-Greek "ideology"? (That is the point of view of *Humani Generis*.) Or else should we say that this Revelation, although providentially poured into Judeo-Greek culture, so transcends it that there will be new, deeper, purer, more real expressions of

this Revelation that will develop providentially in other cultures, and above all in this far-eastern world of *atman-nirvana-Tao*. (June 4, 1958)

What an extraordinary act of trust in interreligious communion made by a young Benedictine from Brittany arriving in India for the first time! It was an act which was to blaze trails for many Christian interreligious pioneers who followed in his Indian footsteps—from Bede Griffiths (his immediate successor at Shantivanam) to Sara Grant, Sister Vandana, Murray Rogers, Raimon Panikkar, and Bettina Baumer, not to mention the countless Hindu swamis (Ramana, Chidananda, Shivananda) and Buddhist lamas who engaged with him on his interreligious journeys from Pondicherry and Shantivanam to Rishikesh and Gongotri. By the end of his interreligious journey, Abhishiktananda had embraced the idea of an "unrestricted" Eucharist involving the sharing of Spirit and food. In his life and testimony, the Eucharist expanded outward and upward from a specific Catholic rite, which he always cherished, to a more inclusive act of hospitality to strangers—a missionary expansion which he believed was one of the most fundamental messages of Christianity: namely, "the discovery of oneself in another. ... For whoever loves his brother has the right to the Eucharist."

2.2 *Teilhard de Chardin: Mass of the world*

Teilhard de Chardin was another prophetic missionary of the Eucharist. Also traveling east—in his case to China rather than India—he too discovered a passion to share an open Eucharist with the world.

In an early essay entitled "Cosmic Life" (1915), the young French priest spoke of a cosmic communion with the earth leading to a communion with God. Echoing Paul's Eucharistic notion that "because there is one bread, we who are many are one body, because we partake of the one bread" (1 Cor. 10), Teilhard envisaged forms of "sacramental communion" which bring unity to the Mystical Body of Christ. The earth itself, matter in its lowliest forms (and what is more simple and alimentary than bread!), is part of a 'sanctifying moment'. "Since first, Lord, you said, '*Hoc est corpus meum*,' not only the bread of the altar, but ... everything in the universe that nourishes the soul for the life of Spirit and Grace, has become *yours* and has become *divine*—it is divinized, divinizing, and divinizable" (King 2005: 9).[8]

In a timely and engaging commentary, entitled *Teilhard's Mass*, Thomas King SJ details Teilhard's various efforts to formulate a "Mass on the World" (King 2005). From early in his life, as both priest and expeditionary, Teilhard envisioned the flesh of God extending outward into the universe from the tiny Host in the monstrance. "It was as though a milky brightness were illuminating the universe from within, and everything were fashioned of the same kind of translucent flesh," he wrote, "through the mysterious expansion of the host the whole world had become incandescent, had itself become like a single giant host" (King 2005: 10). Teilhard spoke accordingly—and I think this is one of his most signature insights— of "*extensions* of the Eucharist," each amplifying out from the consecrated host to the "infinite circle of creatures (which) is the total Host to consecrate." And by the same token, the "crucible of their activities is the chalice to sanctify" (King 2005: 10). The *bread,* for Teilhard, was conceived as the element of nourishment and growth, the *chalice* that of suffering and pain—both elements needing to be blessed.

It seems there were few limits to the range of this sanctifying Eucharistics, embracing all forms of organic matter. Indeed, Teilhard recorded how as a child he first recognized God in stones! "The Sacramental consecration," as he later put it, "is haloed by a universal, analogical consecration" (King 2005: 11). Nothing is alien to this sacramentalizing of the universe, and the role of the celebrant is to "Christianize the organic and spiritual currents from which come forth the Body of Christ" (King 2005: 11). No one is excluded from the cosmic Eucharistic body, which is why Teilhard saw his vocation as a call to become "more widely spiritual in my sympathies and more nobly terrestrial in my ambitions than any of the world's servants" (King 2005: 11). No small mission! The operative words here are *sympathy* and *terrestrial.* Teilhard's ontology of sacred flesh defied the dualisms of both Platonic metaphysics and Cartesian rationalism which split the human being into body and soul and cast matter as an impediment to spiritual ascension. With Teilhard's host, as with Jacob's ladder, there is no way up that is not also a way down. Word and flesh beat with the same heart, the systole and diastole of matter.

On his first trip to China in the 1920s, to conduct anthropological and archeological field work, Teilhard started making notes for what would become his path-breaking *Mass on the World.* As he discovered and documented various ancient fossils and bones, he saw parallels between the development of the human body and the divine body. The Eucharist was increasingly revealed as an exemplary emblem of this evolving theo-genesis, the prolongation of God's love through creation. "Each communion," he wrote, "each consecration is a notch further in our incorporation into Christ" (King 2005: 11). As the Word becomes flesh in humanity, humans become God through the same process of mutual embodiment, echoing the patristic teaching that God became man so that man could become God. This understanding likewise provides a powerful rebuttal of docetism and other Gnostic attempts to deny the full carnality of Christ.[9] The cosmos itself is deemed a sacred body.

In 1924 Teilhard wrote a personal, passionate essay entitled, *Mon Univers,* where he articulated one of his most powerful accounts of the "extensions of the Eucharistic Presence." Given its importance for my thesis, I cite at some length:

> We must say that the initial Body of Christ, his *primary body,* is confined to the species of bread and wine. Can Christ, however, remain contained in this primary Body? Clearly, he cannot. Since he is above all omega, that is, the universal "form" of the world, he can obtain his organic balance and plenitude only by mystically assimilating all that surrounds him. The Host is like a blazing hearth from which flames spread their radiance. Just as the spark that falls into the heather is soon surrounded by a wide circle of fire,

so, in the courses of centuries ... the sacramental host of bread is continually being encircled more closely by another, infinitely larger Host, which is nothing but the universe itself—the universe gradually being absorbed by the universal element. Thus when the Phrase "*Hoc est Corpus meum*" is being pronounced, "*hoc*" means "*primario*" the bread; but "*secondario*," in a second phase occurring in nature, the matter of the sacrament is the world, through which there spreads, so to complete itself, the superhuman presence of the universal Christ. (King 2005: 16–17)

Teilhard leaves the reader in no doubt as to which "host" has ultimate priority, from both an historical and eschatological perspective. He insists:

The world is the final and the real Host into which Christ gradually descends, until his time is fulfilled. Since all time a single word and a single act have been filling the universality of things: "*Hoc est Corpus meum.*" Nothing is at work in creation except in order to assist, from near at hand or from afar, in the consecration of the universe. (King 2005: 17)[10]

When word reached Teilhard in 1926 of the 28th International Eucharistic Congress to be held in Chicago, he wondered if there would be one voice in all the thousands of theologians, priests, and scholars present who would dare explain the "true extensions of the Eucharist and its animating place in human work," and he prayed to be given just ten minutes in the giant Chicago stadium to shout aloud what it means to "sympathize" (King 2005: 17)! A rhetorical prayer, perhaps, but not a sentimental one. For Teilhard, such *sympathy* was no devotional piety; it was a radically transformative pathos extending from fellow humans—acting and suffering—to all living, organic, sentient beings in the universe. Though Teilhard was no partisan of Buddhism (he remained somewhat critical of its acosmic tendencies), his capacious understanding of Christian *caritas* sometimes seems coextensive with Buddhist *karuna*.

It was during a visit to China in the same year—1926—that Teilhard began to practice and write about what he called a "Mass upon the altar of the world." The purpose of such a Mass was to divinize each new day in a "sacrament of life animated by God" (King 2005: 20). The original Eucharistic offering and gift was, he insists here, that of Jesus of Nazareth, but extending and expanding outward from that is an evolving "sacrament of the World" (the title for a major work he planned but never completed). He explains, "as our humanity assimilates the material world and as the Host assimilates our humanity, the Eucharistic transformation goes beyond and completes the transubstantiation of the bread on the altar" (King 2005: 21). From 1926 on Teilhard worked ceaselessly on what came to be called the "Mass on the World." But it was on New Year's Day 1932 that he first wrote explicitly of celebrating this Mass with non-Christians on an expedition to the Gobi desert. He was the only Christian, but every member of the scientific trip attended. His sermon on that day contained the following prayer of universal sacred presence, embracing not only those present but also absent friends and fellows. Again we witness the expanding circles of incorporation: "What we ask of that universal presence which envelops us all, is first to reunite us, as in a shared living center with those whom we love, those who are so far away from us here, and themselves beginning this same new year ... I offer to [God] this Mass, the highest form of Christian prayer" (King 2005: 23). Teilhard does not offer details here of consecrating and distributing hosts, but it is clear from the context, and from his ongoing thinking about cosmic Eucharistics, that the Host is the real presence that includes all those attending the desert Mass and those remembered or imagined during its celebration.

Teilhard did not see Eucharistic communions as discrete isolated performances but as successive "contacts" and "assimilations" to the power of the Incarnate Word—a whole developmental theo-genesis ultimately coextensive with the duration of a life. "All the communions of our life are," he explains, "only successive instants or episodes of one single communion—in one and the same process of Christification" (King 2005: 28): a process he describes elsewhere as the "innumerable prolongation of [God's] incarnate being" (King 2005: 138). Well into the 1950s—during further work expeditions and travels to Africa and America—Teilhard recorded several new versions of his "Mass." And in the weeks leading up to his death in 1955, he entered a final account of his belief that "the words of the Consecration appl[y] not only to the sacrificial bread and wine but, mark you, to the whole Mass of joys and sufferings produced by the Convergence of the World as it progresses" (King 2005: 32). On April 7, Holy Thursday, Teilhard cited three verses of Paul that ended with the prayer "that God may be all in all" (I Cor. 15). At Easter Sunday dinner, celebrated with his close friends Rhoda de Terra and her daughter in their New York apartment, Teilhard finally passed away. His Paschal passing may be interpreted as a true fulfillment of his prayer, expressed in *The Divine Milieu*—"Teach me to treat my death as an act of communion" (King 2005: 33). His life in the Eucharist included death itself.

Teilhard's view of the Eucharist informed several of his other theological views. First, it vindicated his childhood conviction that God exists already in rocks: the certitude that it is through tasting, touching, seeing, and sensing matter that the divine enters our world, and only secondly through knowing. Hence Teilhard's alertness to the material findings of the sciences, especially anthropology, archeology, and the forensic research which discovers the universe in a grain of sand or curve of bone.[11] Teilhard fully endorsed Tertullian's view that Christ must be present in the full carnal particularity of "shaped bones and cross-veined hands." For if we can *believe* without seeing and sensing, we cannot *adore*. Teilhard was with Thomas and Mary Magdalene: he wanted to touch the body of God. He believed that matter would achieve its "definitive salvation" in the words of the Mass: "This is my Body." Christ had claimed the cosmos as his corpus, and it is for humans to eucharistically respond, one way or another. Even if for Teilhard there was only one Christ, there were many ways to Christ—for Christ was the one of many ways (King 2005: 181). His own Church's "Roman theologies" had, he felt, sometimes reduced the Christ of universal and multiple "adoration" to an increasingly restrictive code, "too small to be adored" (King 2005: 133); they had placed doctrinal belief over seeing, touching, tasting—the deeply corporeal idioms of the Eucharist itself. Christ, after all, spent his last hours sharing food, washing feet and undergoing passion—and the first hours after he arose, he fed his disciples with fish on Lake Galilee and with bread in the inn at Emmaus!

The problem with contemporary Christian society was that it separated the world of belief and the world of work, the extraordinary world of faith, and the ordinary world of sensible experience. Teilhard believed the Eucharist was the crossing of these worlds. And he firmly believed that his everyday work on fossils and bones was part of the work of God. "Adoration's real name," he once claimed, "is research" (King 2005: 133)! Indeed he claimed that, in his own case, without scientific research and experiment there would be no possibility of "real mystical life" (King 2005: 134). It was in this light that he understood the appeal of Marxism and vitalism as a recall to the things themselves, the working of the Word through the material world of acting and suffering flesh; here too Christ needed to be rediscovered and revered. This is what the cosmic Christ of St Paul was originally about: discovering the transcendent in the immanent and the immanent in the transcendent. He highlighted a paradox central to the transformative power of the Eucharist: the conversion of that which appears absurd and incoherent into something "adorable" (King 2005: 134). Eucharistic adoration and sharing, he continued to profess, involve all the complex, conflicting fibers of the "unifying universe" (King 2005: 134–5). The world serves as the altar of matter becoming "Christifiable" (King 2005: 135). But this cannot occur without us, each one of us, becoming its poets, mystics, servants, researchers, and priests. The goal for each Christian was to be present eucharistically, where "Christ may inform the very growth, through man, of the universe in movement" (King 2005: 136). Or as he put it later in life, "the communion with time," understood as the communication with the *becoming of things*, is the supreme form of adoration. In the wake of Eucharistic communion, both sensing and believing become one. And we may say, with Thomas after touching the wound of Christ: "My lord and my God" (King 2005: 137).

Equally radical was Teilhard's reinterpretation of the priesthood. All of humanity—"believer and unbeliever alike"—is, he held, possessed of a single desire and hunger: the longing for a great communion. And those who work as scientists, scholars, and in other activities that serve the growing unification of humanity, may thus be viewed as priests of a kind, for "every work of discovery is in the service of Christ, which thus hastens the growth of his mystical body, shares in his universal priesthood" (King 2005: 103–4). Considering things in light of the sacred work of communion, Teilhard, toward the end of his career, went so far as to claim that "everything becomes the business for consecration—the business of the priesthood" (King 2005: 104). He did not hesitate to declare that lay people may also be "true priests" who can offer his spiritual Mass on the World. Or more exactly, all Christians may be spoken of as "lay quasi-priests" in keeping with I Peter 2:5 which talks of believers forming a "holy priesthood." When God is seen present everywhere, continually embodied in the flesh of the world, all of life becomes a communion (King 2005: 104). Flesh is matter animated by the Word, and Christ is the soul of the cosmos. Everything that happens is adorable in so far as it is part of God's love. Or, more emphatically, the universe may be conceived as an "immense host made flesh by the touch of the Word" (King 2005: 108). Accordingly, genuine prayer enables us to contemplate—and touch—the world not as a "veil but as flesh." Even the red earth of China appeared to Teilhard like the "wounded flesh" of Christ. The entire world, he insisted, becomes the "flesh of Christ" for those who believe, and this belief is incarnational. Anticipating the claims of fellow French thinkers, Maurice Merleau-Ponty and Gabriel Marcel, Teilhard argued that we do not see the spirit of anyone or anything except through their flesh (voices, gestures, movements, hesitations, glances). When we recognize Christ as the spirit within people and things, matter becomes animated as "flesh."

In short, for Teilhard flesh is the "divine milieu" of the world, a carnal Eucharist indeed. We are all involved in the "mystery of the flesh of God," as he puts it amorously at the end of his *Mass*: "I can preach only the mystery of your Flesh, your soul shining forth through all that surrounds me. ... Like the Flesh, [the universe] attracts by the charm which floats in the mystery of its curves and folds and in the depths of its eyes" (King 2005: 108). Teilhard inscribes himself here in a long tradition of religious poetics from the Shulammite's *Song of Songs* to the theo-erotic musings of John of the Cross, Teresa of Avila, and the Beguines, right down to the mystical poetics of George Herbert or fellow Jesuit, Gerard Manley Hopkins—not to mention the "cosmotheoandric" tradition running from Saint Francis to Raimon Panikkar. "Sun and moon bless the Lord:" that is what the sun and moon, in adoration, are doing (King 2005: 121).

And yet Teilhard was not naïve. He was keenly aware of the dangers of "indifferentiation." He warned against the "destructive fusion of which pantheism dreams," preferring instead a unity that differentiates. "Within us without being us" (*in nobis sine nobis*), was his catchcry that reflected transcendence within immanence without ever abandoning transcendence. Life for Teilhard was a divine milieu, increasingly differentiating even as it simultaneously transmuted—in joy and pain—toward unification. There is no denying darkness, death, or depression (from which Teilhard himself greatly suffered at key periods in his life). Wrestling with both *thanatos* and *eros,* one struggles toward communion. "To bring Christ by virtue of a specific organic connection, to the heart of realities that are esteemed the most dangerous, the most unspiritual, the most pagan—in that you have my Gospel and my mission" (King 2005: 123). For Teilhard, nothing human was alien to the Eucharist's transfiguring power. Flesh, the focus of the divine milieu and signal of transubstantiation, is what animates life as singular life, in each particular instance, and resists the temptation of indefiniteness. Even the tension of remaining within a specific, historically and hierarchically determined Church—one which limited, confined, and sometimes even censored him—was for Teilhard part of the work of differentiation and dialogue. If everything is declared materially one in premature fusion, there is no room for sacred *eros*, love, desire, hunger. There is only the boredom of sameness. Genuine Eucharistic communion is anything but that. "Unity differentiates" is Teilhard's final word.

3 Lonely roads

Abhisktananda and Teilhard could only go so far. These Christian pioneers of an open Eucharist were prophets, not gods. Their brave searching for ways to amplify the Eucharist as a gift for all hungering beings—and who does not hunger?—was not without its hazards, obstacles, and omissions. When Abhi and Teilhard were reprimanded for their experiments and writings, they acquiesced and remained silent. They did not leave the Church or resign the priesthood, as certain others did, out of protest or indignation. They did not publicly defy the Vatican authorities. Indeed their obedience, while consistent, might even appear to some as compromising or complicit (though hindsight is easy after Vatican II). The Eucharistic masses and liturgies which they carried out with friends and colleagues—for Abhi, fellow travelers on the path of Christian-Hindu dialogue like Sara Grant, Murray Rogers, and Bettina Baumer; for Teilhard, mainly fellow researchers in China and Africa—were not performed as public acts of ecclesiastical revolution: they rather took the form of quiet quotidian rites made in the name of love and hospitality. And that hospitality had its limits and conditions.

In Teilhard's case, for example, one does not find formal interreligious invitations to concelebrate communion in a reciprocal way. Non-Catholics were invited to become guests, rather than hosts, at the Mass on the World; and he rarely if ever spoke of what he as a Catholic priest learned from the Taoists or Buddhists of Asia which might have altered his own Christian understanding of the Eucharist. Indeed Teilhard was, as noted, quite critical of what he saw as the nonincarnational character of much Asian spirituality. Nor did Teilhard or Abhi, to my knowledge, ever contemplate inviting women (fifty percent of the human race) to concelebrate at the Eucharistic altar, although they had deep spiritual friendships with women (Lucile Swan and Rhoda de Terra in the case of Teilhard; the Baumers, mother and daughter, Sara Grant, Sister Vandana, and Shirley du Boulay in the case of Abhi). The question of women's ordination did not seem to preoccupy them as it does so many in the Catholic Church today. Nor, at a more theoretical level, did they reflect critically on questions of the incommensurability of religious "language games," on how the hermeneutic diversity of faiths and the attendant sense of Eucharistic hospitality, requires that each "host" respects the strangeness of each stranger, the otherness of each guest—in order to avoid the temptation of totalizing inclusivism.[12] Indeed, there are even moments when Abhi and Teilhard seem to embrace a sense of Catholic supersessionism: though for the most part they prefigure the more open Vatican II acknowledgments of the legitimacy of non-Catholic and non-Christian faiths (see council documents like *Nostra Aetate*, albeit as anticipations of the "full truth" which the Church alone possesses).

Teilhard and Abhi were more fieldworkers than theologians; they were practicing rather than preaching, experimenting and improvising in far flung lands rather than strategizing, and networking in Vatican congregations. And while their voices certainly influenced some of the most visionary reformers of Vatican II— Yves Congar, Henri de Lubac, Hans Küng among others—they themselves did not, alas, live to see the new awakening (*Aggiormomento/ressourcement*). They traveled a lonely road, with the Eucharist as companion, guide, and sustenance. They paved paths for others to follow.

4 Extending Eucharistic circles

Just as Jesus engaged with Samaritans and Paul with Gentiles, it was among strangers that both Abhishiktananda and Teilhard de Chardin worked to extend the Eucharist to those beyond the fold. In order to develop their idea of extending circles of Eucharistic communion, it may be timely to reconsider a number of basic issues. By way of conclusion, I offer the following four points.

First, let us consider the doctrinal relationship between baptism and Eucharist, where the former is seen as prerequisite for the latter. Christ, after all, did not ask for baptismal certificates when converting water to wine at Cana or communing over bread and water with Phoenician and Samaritan women. At the Last Supper he did not ask for professions of faith, but shared food and washed feet; and when he finally offered his body on the Cross, it was to *all* people—Jews and Gentiles, Romans and Samaritans. If one wishes to preserve the link between baptism and Eucharist, might it not be as simultaneous rather than successive sacraments? See, for instance, the precedent of young catechumens cited by Saint Timothy of Alexandria in his fourth-century canons.[13] Here the notion of baptism of desire was as important as baptism by water—the Eucharist was given to those who genuinely desired to commune.

Second, we might do well to reexamine the connotations of blood sacrifice. Here we rejoin thinkers like René Girard, Rudolf Bultmann, and Paul Ricoeur, who call for the demythologizing of the fetish of the crucified Savior as filial expiatory victim, with its ancillary cults of periodic bloodletting and ritual purification. To avoid misconstruing the Eucharist as a rite of scapegoating or payment of ransoms and debts—rightly denounced by Nietzsche—we ought to observe its original meaning as thanksgiving for the Gift of new life. This means the conversion of old rites of violent blood sacrifice into new rites of hospitality through the celebratory sharing of bread and wine. When the Eucharist becomes a feast of love rather than an expiation of guilt, Christ's offer of new life is replicated with each new offering of consecrated food with neighbors and strangers, allowing carnal healing rather than purgative reparation. In the life of Jesus of Nazareth, this nonexpiatory narrative reached its apogee in the breaking of bread at Emmaus and the cooking of fish for the disciples at Galilee. Both Eucharistic events reprise the narrative of Abraham and Sarah's meal with the three divine strangers at Mamre.[14]

Third, it might be wise to conceive the Eucharist less as changeless dogma than as a subtle and transforming "art." And in this regard perhaps it is no accident that some of the most imaginative experiments in interreligious communion have been conducted by nondiocesan religious like Jesuits, Benedictines, Franciscans, and Sacred Heart missionaries—pioneering spirits inspired by a special charisma of creative adventure and empathy. There is a long and venerable tradition of voices from the mystical and monastic margins inspiring the ecclesiastical center, keeping it open and attuned to ever-new acoustics of the Spirit. The great scholar of Christian-Buddhist dialogue, Fr Joseph O'Leary, formulates the notion of Eucharistic "art," reminding us that "from the start the Church has been creatively interpreting the Eucharist" (O'Leary 2008a: 171).[15] In this spirit, Vatican II sought "not to impose 'rigid uniformity' in the liturgy but to 'respect and foster the qualities and talents of the various races and nations' (*Sacrosanctum Concilium* 37)" (O'Leary 2008b: 95). And this meant that "the art of our own times from every race and country shall also be given free scope in the Church" (SC 123). Like all works of art, the universality of the Eucharist is, O'Leary argues, embedded in particular times and places, rooted in the specificities of distinct historical cultures. So if we are invited to see the Eucharist as Christ's gift to the world, we cannot receive this art-work without "re-imagining" it anew. Christ's "instituting" the Eucharist should be interpreted accordingly as "the opening up of a creative space of celebration and community, as the initiation of a living tradition" (O'Leary 2008a: 172). The work of inculturation has to play a vibrant role in this ongoing rethinking of the Eucharist, from the most local liturgical experimentations to such artistic innovations as Leonard Bernstein's *Mass* of 1971 (performed in the Vatican in 1973 and 1983) and Stravinsky's *Mass* of 1948. And one might add the long history of artistic representations of the Last Supper and Emmaus, from Leonardo and Rembrandt to Andy Warhol and Sheila Gallagher. As O'Leary concludes:

> Like every work of art, the Eucharist lives only by dying to former modes of its existence. It is doubly fitting that the Eucharist, as a meal of sacrifice and self-abandonment, itself undergoes death and resurrection. ... If the great modern works of art are among the "signs of the times" that the Gospel must engage ... the Eucharist itself as a work of art must be refashioned as a sign for the times, becoming an historical happening of truth. (O'Leary 2008a: 173–4)

Fourth, we might be well advised to amplify the *hermeneutics* of the Eucharist in tune with the prophetic breakthroughs of figures like Abhishiktananda and Teilhard. The Eucharist, as I hope our testimonies show, has multiple layers of meaning. Mono-eucharistics should increasingly give way to poly-eucharistics, understood as centrifugal expansions in ever-widening circles from the consecrated host on the altar to the multiple carnal hosts of the world. For, as Gerard Manley Hopkins reminds us, "Christ plays in ten thousand places/ lovely in eyes, lovely in limbs not his/ to the Father, through the features of men's faces" ("When Kingfishers Catch Fire"), I suggest that we might begin with the following extending circles, moving from the most circumscribed to the most open:

1) *Canonical Eucharist.* In the strictest Catholic sense, this refers to the consecration and distribution of Holy Communion in a liturgical Mass, celebrated by an ordained male priest and exclusively available to those baptized in the Catholic faith in a condition of absolution and "full communion

with the Church." The latter includes a doctrinal belief in the "real presence" of God in transubstantiated bread and wine. Since Vatican II there are certain "exceptions" permitted regarding reception of the consecrated host—for example, some cases of inter-Christian marriage and the last rites to non-Catholic Christians without pastors. Several recent theological discussions engage the question of whether receiving the Eucharist presupposes Catholic baptism and confession of the Holy Catholic and Apostolic Church (as currently defined by the Congregation for the Doctrine of the Faith) or whether it is open to non-Catholics who "desire to be in communion with the Church." These genuine conversations about the importance of Church order regarding the sacraments—baptism before Eucharist, ordination before consecration—offer real grounds for hope.

2) *Interreligious Eucharist.* This involves a special Eucharistic sharing with non-Catholic Christians—and, more controversially, with Jews and other non-Christians. One thinks of the special meetings at Assisi or Taizé or other interconfessional ceremonies conducted in eschatological anticipation of Communion between all Christian Churches, and by ultimate extension, all non-Christian religions. The Catholic Church has not yet officially espoused such moves, but Pope Benedict gave the consecrated host to the Protestant Frère Roger in Taizé, and there are hopes for further openings under the papacy of Francis. Such interconfessional Eucharistics might eventually allow for female concelebration, as more women become ordained in non-Catholic denominations.

3) *Fraternal Eucharist.* This third extension of the circle is based on the original Christian principle of "two or three gathered in my name" (Mt. 18:20). It involves informal groups of Christians gathering to celebrate the Last Supper/Emmaus sharing of bread and wine among "brothers and sisters in Christ." This may include readings of scripture and a variety of prayers and reflections. But it is not confined to the sacramental liturgy of any one church. Here the interreligious sharing with non-Christian religious seekers (willing to participate in spiritual communion with Christians) is easier to accommodate and encourage. This third category of poly-eucharistics could be said to take its cue from Francis and Claire of Assisi who celebrated Christ's choice of bread as the most common alimentary material (not silver, gold, caviar, or filet mignon). And perhaps, as noted, Pope Francis is gesturing in such a direction when he recalls that the Eucharist is for "the hungry" rather than as a reward for those who follow rules.[16] The story of the prodigal father and son is clearly relevant in this regard, as is the dedication of a fraternal meal to the Giver of Gifts (in commemoration of Christ's inclusive sharing with all guests at table—the empty place for Elijah and hospitality to the stranger). The most common prayer here is the standard "grace before meals," with its personal and poetic variations. No one is excluded—of whatever faith—who wishes to share in the blessing of food in simple thanksgiving (Greek *eucharistia*). Many of a humanist or open-atheist persuasion can feel

welcome in such ceremonies of gratitude—moments which acknowledge, as in the Eastern practice of *puja*, a special "sacred" quality in the sharing of food with strangers.

4) *Carnal Eucharist.* This is the widest and most embracing circle, referring to the translation of Word into Flesh in quotidian acts of incarnate love; it reflects an open-heart Eucharistics. Here the sacred becomes embodied in everyday forms of touch and taste. Incarnation goes all the way down, from head to foot, from agape to eros. Such Poly-eucharistics can be seen as polymorphism, where nothing and nobody is in principle excluded from the sacramentalizing of the profane. It echoes from the Shulammite's cry to Molly Bloom's Yes. Even the simplest carnal acts of "sensing" may serve as sacraments of communion.[17] At this omega point of extension, there is no end to the Eucharist.

Chapter 12

THE PRACTICE OF ZAZEN AS RITUAL PERFORMANCE

André van der Braak

1 Introduction

As the transmission of Buddhism to the West matures, it becomes possible both to differentiate more clearly between the various Buddhist traditions in their historical development, and to come to a cross-cultural hermeneutical understanding of them that takes into account local and historical conditions and contexts. Such an understanding is sensitive not only to the differences between past historical manifestations of Asian Buddhist traditions but also to the differences between Asian and Western connotations of certain key terms within those traditions. In an earlier publication I investigated such different connotations of the term "enlightenment" in its Asian and Western contexts (van der Braak 2008: 87–97). Now, I want to extend this investigation to the notions of meditation and ritual in the Buddhist Zen tradition, as it is practiced in both Asia and in the West.[1]

The Zen Buddhist practice of sitting meditation (*zazen*) is widely practiced in the West. From a Western perspective, such meditation practice is often seen as aimed at the improvement of several mental skills, such as the capacity for attention and concentration. Moreover, in Protestant and romantic circles of Anglo-American culture, Zen iconoclasm is associated with a forceful critique of "ritualized religion." Religious ritual is seen as inauthentic, formulaic, and repetitive. As Steven Heine and Dale Wright argue in a recent collection of essays, however, such an "anti-ritual" variety of Zen has, however, been constructed by modern Japanese Zen scholars in order to make Zen more relevant to the modern age (Heine and Wright 2008: 16).

From a Japanese Buddhist perspective, the practice of zazen meditation should properly be understood as a ritual performance, in which the Buddha's enlightenment is enacted within the practitioner. Zen Master Eihei Dōgen (1200–53) calls zazen "the practice-realization of totally culminated awakening." Rather than being a technique aimed at spiritual acquisition, zazen is the expression of Buddhahood itself.

This chapter explores this discrepancy between Western antiritual perspectives on zazen and the Japanese perspective on zazen as ritual performance. It will argue, with Robert Sharf (2005), that there is no precise Asian Buddhist analogue to the Western distinction between ritual and meditation, and that this very distinction needs to be deconstructed.

2 Zen as an antiritual meditation tradition

Whereas nineteenth-century Western thinkers were fascinated with early Buddhism and considered Mahāyāna Buddhism to be a later degeneration and vulgarization of the Buddhist teachings, in the beginning of the twentieth century the Zen Buddhist tradition was presented to the West, especially through the writings of the Japanese scholar D. T. Suzuki (1870–1966). Suzuki did much to rehabilitate Mahāyāna Buddhism and especially Zen; in his writings, he cast Zen as an East Asian and particularly Japanese form of philosophy, psychology, aesthetics, or direct mystical experience—anything but a religion encumbered by unscientific beliefs and nonsensical rituals.

Suzuki claimed that Zen was, more than any other form of Buddhism, all about meditation rather than ritual, and therefore perfectly relevant to the modern age.[2] Zen meditation offered direct access to the mystical kernel of all religions, without the detour of culture-specific ritual. Suzuki and other Zen apologists to the West, such as the philosopher Nishida Kitaro (1870–1945) and other members of the Japanese so-called Kyoto School, appropriated William James's notion of "pure experience" and sided with the Western phenomenological tradition in its critique of Cartesianism. Zen became popular in the West as a way to let go of dualistic thinking and to realize a direct, nondual insight into reality: *satori* or enlightenment.

However, scholars now appreciate that this view of Zen is historically misleading. In a critical article, the American Zen scholar Griffith Foulk notes how such a description of an "idealized" Zen is at odds with what has always been practiced, and still is being practiced, in Japan and China. Westerners interested in Zen are often attracted to meditation practice in order to realize enlightenment, but are uncomfortable with the "rituals" of offerings, prayers, and prostrations made before images on altars. In Japan, however, serious meditation practice is not that common; it mainly occurs in the special Zen training monasteries (*sōdō*). And what is often overlooked, Foulk notes (Foulk 2008: 38), is that the primary function of such training monasteries is to prepare the monks for careers as specialists in mortuary rituals. Moreover, there are only about sixty Zen training monasteries in Japan, and more than twenty-one thousand ordinary temples.

The reason that Zen has been presented to the West as an antiritual meditation tradition was that it was mediated through sectarian Japanese (Rinzai) Zen scholars.[3] As Foulk points out, when Japan opened up to Western influences early in the Meiji era (1868–1912), Buddhism came under attack for its superstitious beliefs and unscientific views of the world, and was even in danger of being entirely eradicated. This led to the need for modernization, i.e. bringing Buddhism into accord with Western science and philosophy. Leaders of the Zen tradition attempted to rationalize their faith and practice, and dissociate it from merely popular Buddhist beliefs.

Japanese Zen historians (often the sons of Zen parish priests) conceived the idea that the spiritual geniuses of the "golden age" of Zen in the Chinese Tang dynasty (618–907) had been iconoclastic reformers who rejected all forms of ritual. They claimed that Zen had deteriorated in China afterward, and had disappeared altogether in the Qing dynasty (1644–1912). Only in Japan had the true spirit of Zen, with its emphasis on meditation, managed to survive. In order to be in line with Western sensibilities, meditation practice was presented as leading up to the inner subjective experience of enlightenment, conceived as going beyond a limited Cartesian subject-object relationship.

But if the notion of Zen as an antiritual tradition is highly misleading, then what exactly is the place of ritual in Zen as it has traditionally been practiced in China and Japan? In order to answer this question, we should take a brief detour to the doctrinal foundations of Mahāyāna Buddhism.

3 The ritual enactment of buddhahood

Mahāyāna Buddhism follows the *trikaya* doctrine of the three bodies of the Buddha. According to this theory, the Buddha manifests himself in three bodies, modes, or dimensions. First, in his historical manifestation as Shākyamuni, the Buddha has a *nirmanakaya*, a created body which manifests in time and space. Second, as an archetypical manifestation, the Buddha can manifest himself as a sublime celestial form in splendid paradises, where he teaches surrounded by bodhisattvas, using a *sambhogakaya* or body of mutual enjoyment. Third, as the very principle of enlightenment, the Buddha manifests himself as a *dharmakaya*, the reality body or truth body, also interpreted as ultimate reality (Keown 2004).

According to the Mahāyāna Buddhist worldview, reality (the *dharmakaya*) should be seen not as a collection of lifeless objects but as a vital agent of awareness and healing. Reality itself is continually coactive in bringing all beings to universal liberation. The sacred is immanent in space and time. Such a worldview has great soteriological consequences for spiritual practice. Rather than aiming at achieving higher states of personal consciousness, or therapeutic calm, the point of spiritual practice comes to embody, or appreciate, or participate in, or achieve a liberating intimacy with reality itself.

In early Buddhist soteriology, the way to liberation was conceived as a path (*marga*) from bondage (*samsāra*) to liberation (*nirvāna*). The aim of spiritual practice is for the individual practitioner to dispel ignorance, greed, and aversion. In Mahāyāna Buddhism, however, liberation is realized through the ultimate insight (*prajñāpāramitā*; literally: the wisdom beyond all wisdom) that nirvāna is not a goal to be attained. As the famous Mahāyāna philosopher Nāgārjuna (ca. 150–250 C.E.) expressed it: there is not the slightest difference between samsāra and nirvāna (Garfield 1995: 331).

Indologist Karl Potter (1963) has made a useful distinction between "path philosophies," which consider liberation to be the result of continued spiritual practice, and "leap philosophies," which stress liberation as an immediate realization. Early Buddhist and some Mahāyāna Buddhist schools can be characterized as path philosophies, whereas some other branches of Mahāyāna Buddhism, including the Zen school, can be characterized as leap philosophies. They view all path-like approaches to liberation as preliminary teachings that ultimately have to be superseded by *prajñāpāramitā*. The point is therefore not so much to attain enlightenment, but to realize it.

Especially in the esoteric Vajrayāna tradition (popular in Tibet and Japan), and its tantric practices, such a worldview has led to the development of practices of transcendent faith and ritual enactment of Buddhahood that are dependent not on lifetimes of arduous practice, but rather on immediate, unmediated, and intuitional realization of the fundamental ground of awakening (Leighton 2007: 7). The replacement of spiritual cultivation by a leap is expressed in the Zen tradition by "sudden enlightenment," and in more devotional Buddhist traditions by a "leap of faith."

In the context of medieval Japanese Buddhism, this "leap paradigm" was represented by the immensely influential Tendai Buddhist discourse of "original enlightenment" (*hongaku*), the assertion that all beings are already inherently enlightened Buddhas.[4] This discourse was very important to the thirteenth-century Japanese Zen Master Eihei Dōgen. Since Dōgen grew up in the Tendai school, this *hongaku* discourse also functioned as the intellectual matrix out of which his thought emerged (even though he was also critical of it).[5]

According to Dōgen, all of existence is grounded or embedded in the ultimate reality of the *dharmakaya*. The *dharmakaya* should not be interpreted ontologically as a transcendent cosmic Being that contains or projects the world, but should be seen as the fundamental activity of the world itself. In this sense, all of existence is itself Buddhahood, and therefore lacks any value beyond itself. What is ultimately valuable is built into existence itself, whether this is recognized and appreciated or not. It is constituted by what Dōgen calls "the rightly transmitted teachings of the Buddha" (*shōden no buppō*), which refers neither to a body of creeds, the content of certain experiences, any Absolute, nor a return to the letter of the teachings of the historical Shākyamuni Buddha: it is the symbolic expression (*dōtoku*) or activity (*gyōji*)[6] of Buddha's spirit (not only the historical Shākyamuni Buddha but also the cosmic *dharmakaya*). In different historical and cultural circumstances this spirit needs to be continually reexpressed and reenacted.

For Dōgen, such a rightly transmitted teaching of the Buddha consists in "the samādhi of self-fulfilling activity" (*jijuyū-zammai*), which is concerned with the self-enjoyment of the *dharmakaya*. The notion of samādhi usually refers to a concentrated state of awareness, but Dōgen uses it to refer to a state of mind that at once negates and subsumes self and other; a total freedom of self-realization without any dualism or antitheses. This does not mean that oppositions or dualities are obliterated or transcended, but that they are realized. Such a freedom realizes itself in duality, not apart from it (Kim 2004: 55).

"For playing joyfully in such a samādhi," Dōgen writes, "the upright sitting position in meditation is the right gate" (quoted in Kim 2004: 55). He refers here to the sitting practice of zazen. For Dōgen, zazen is not so much a psychological training aiming at particular states or experiences, but the ritual expression, embodiment, and enactment of Buddhahood. In his *Fukanzazengi* (Universally Recommended Instructions for Zazen), Dōgen stresses that the zazen that he speaks of is not meditation practice, and he admonishes the practitioner to not try to become a Buddha (Dōgen 2008: 532–5). The purpose of zazen is not to attain a mental state of liberation, but to pursue an ongoing transformation that is as much physiological as it is psychological, in which one "realizes" one's own Buddhahood, in the sense of fully participating in it. It is not a state but an activity.

From this perspective, zazen can be seen as a communal ritual—a ceremonial performance that expresses ultimate reality (the *dharmakaya*). Dōgen stresses that all practitioners should practice zazen together: "standing out has no benefit; being different from others is not our conduct" (Leighton 2007: 170). In such a way, he radically deconstructs standard Buddhist views on meditation and reinterprets it as a liberating expression and activity of Buddha nature. Zazen does not *lead* to enlightenment, zazen itself *is* enlightenment. Dōgen uses the term practice-realization (*shūshō*) in order to indicate how the two notions are mutually interwoven. For Dōgen, practice-realization is seen not as a psychological state, but as a liberating activity, a liberating intimacy. The enactment of the sacred in ritual takes prime importance.

Since zazen is seen as a ritual enactment of the enlightenment of the Buddha, it should not be practiced in order to gain therapeutic or religious benefits. Rather, for Dōgen, zazen is the prototype of ultimate meaninglessness. According to the twentieth-century Sōtō teacher Kōdō Sawaki (1880–1965), the practice of zazen requires leaving behind a means-end rationality: "Zazen is an activity that comes to nothing. There is nothing more admirable than this activity that comes to nothing. To do something with a goal is really worthless. ... Because it takes you out of the world of loss and gain, it should be practiced" (Braverman 2003: 58).[7]

For Dōgen, the practice of zazen is a somatic practice in which enlightened reality is embodied. Zazen is not so much a discipline of the mind, aimed at attaining spiritual insight, but a discipline of the body, in the larger context of ritual embodiment. Zazen can be learned by putting one's body into the meditation posture and sitting. The body learns what zazen is, and the mind follows the body. In this way, an embodied understanding becomes possible.

In the practice of zazen, the Buddha's enlightenment plays itself out in the practitioner—or better: between the practitioners. A Buddha field arises between the practitioners. By practicing zazen, a kind of cosmic resonance arises that Dōgen calls *bodaishin* (the mind of awakening): a mind that is aimed at awakening, that longs for awakening. In zazen, the longing for awakening grows. But for Dōgen this is not a personal longing, but a resonance with the entire "Buddha-naturing" cosmos. Dōgen rereads the standard Mahāyāna claim that "all sentient beings have the Buddha nature" to mean that "entire being/all beings is/are the Buddha nature."

All of reality is a "Buddha-naturing" process. The practitioner of zazen resonates with that process.

For Dōgen, therefore, zazen is an enactment ritual, a ritual enactment, and expression of awakened awareness (Leighton 2007: 168). The physical posture of zazen is an expression of ultimate reality, and by engaging in it, meditation practitioners are led to realization of that reality. The ritual performance of zazen leads to an expressive and embodied realization that is not merely cognitive or intellectual.[8]

4 The reevaluation of Zen ritual

The realization that the presentation of Zen as an antiritual meditation tradition has little to do with the actual situation "on the ground" in Japan and China, now and in the past, has led to an impasse in Zen studies, and has called for a reevaluation of the place in Zen of such notions as meditation, ritual, and enlightenment.

Buddhist scholar Steven Heine has distinguished two factions within the contemporary scholarly debate on Zen. One the one hand, there are traditionalists who continue to articulate and reinforce a view of Zen that Heine calls "the traditional Zen narrative." They argue that the essence of Zen is an ineffable enlightenment experience that transcends contingent institutional and ritual forms. Such an experience can only be realized by means of a "special transmission outside the teachings" (*jiaowai biechuan*), undertaken "without relying on words and letters" (*buli wenzi*). On the other hand, Zen scholars who engage in historical and cultural criticism claim that the iconoclastic notion of Zen enlightenment has traditionally functioned as a rhetorical tool, used by religious factions in order to maintain institutional legitimacy and power (Heine 2008).

The recently published collection of essays *Zen Ritual* makes a start in correcting the neglect of the study of ritual in the Zen tradition (Heine and Wright 2008). But the problem lies even deeper. Even to state that Zen attaches great importance not only to meditation practice but also to ritual can be a misleading way of framing it. The very distinction between meditation and ritual is a Western one, and fundamentally alien to the East Asian tradition. As Foulk notes:

> The East Asian Buddhist tradition itself has no words for discriminating what Westerners are apt to call "ritual" as opposed to "practice." The Japanese term that comes closest in semantic range to "ritual" is gyōji, which I translate as "observances," but that term encompasses a very broad range of activities that Zen clergy engage in, some of which we might prefer to call "ceremonies," "procedures," "etiquette," "training," "study," "meditation," "work," or the "ritual sacralization of everyday activities" (such as eating, sleeping and bathing). (Foulk 2008: 23)

Both the supporters of the traditional Zen narrative, with its emphasis on meditation and enlightenment, and the supporters of historical and cultural criticism, with their emphasis on ritual and power politics, still operate within the very Western distinction of meditation and ritual. According to Zen scholar Robert Sharf, "both positions remain wedded to the very distinctions they attempt to resolve—the dichotomies of inner versus outer, subjective versus objective, form versus content" (Sharf 2005: 261). Both strands of Zen thought are still caught in Western oppositions. The traditional Zen narrative privileges inner meditative experience over outer ritual. Historical and cultural criticism reduces accounts of inner experience to historical, cultural, and political factors.[9] A third approach is therefore necessary that reexamines our notions not only of Zen but also of meditation, ritual, and enlightenment.

5 *The dichotomy between meditation and ritual*

The Western dichotomy between meditation and ritual is related to other Cartesian dichotomies: inner and outer; subjective and objective; mind and body; transcendent and immanent. In the West, meditation is seen as a spiritual practice aimed at an inner spiritual transformation, culminating in a religious experience of enlightenment that allows the individual to transcend the prevailing social norms and attitudes. As Sharf points out, such a view of meditation makes it appear to be the very antithesis of ritual, which is often seen as precisely instilling those very same prevailing social norms and attitudes by means of outward scripted and stylized activity (Sharf 2005: 260). As Sharf puts it:

> Some scholars have argued that ritual is inherently conservative; it serves to maintain legitimize, and reproduce the dominant social and political order by reference to an unchanging and/or transcendent source. ... In other words, ritual legitimizes local norms and values by casting them as an integral part of the natural order of things. (Sharf 2005: 248)

In the West, ritual has long been seen as a research topic of not much interest, but since the 1970s, the field of ritual studies has greatly developed (see Bell 1997). Although one usually recognizes a ritual when one sees it, it is hard to define what counts as a ritual and what does not. According to sociologist Emile Durkheim, a ritual is the communal means through which a culture's beliefs and ideals are communicated to individual members of the society. However, to some scholars, such an approach places too much emphasis on cognition. They argue that ritual does much more than communicate beliefs and ideals. It causes its participants to perceive the world and understand themselves through the patterns impressed upon them by the repeated action of ritual on their body and mind. A ritual effects a fundamental change in a person's perception of self and world, primarily through its capacity to mold not so much the mind but the body.

Some contemporary scholars have therefore advocated a performative approach to ritual: a ritual is a performance that has a transformative effect on those that practice it. The participants in the ritual are literally "attuned." According to this approach, the question to ask of a ritual is not so much "what does it mean?" but "how do the participants come to do what they do?" The communicative and cognitive approach looks for the meaning of a ritual, and in this way treats ritual as a text that is in need of interpretation. The performative approach treats ritual more like music. To approach ritual as a text is like reducing music to its score, or reducing a territory to its map. Whereas the communicative interpretation emphasizes the cognitive aspect of rituals, the performative interpretation focuses more on the aspect of action: the social institutions and practical training through which ritual mastery is acquired. Sharf notes however that, whereas the performative approach aims to overcome the limitations of Western enlightenment thought, it still remains mired in it:

> The so-called performative approaches to ritual offered to date, despite the avowed intentions of their proponents, turn out to be predicated on the very dichotomies they have tried to avoid: distinctions between thought and action, the subjective and the objective, private and public, and inner and outer. (Sharf 2005: 252)

In both approaches, ritual would still be strictly separated from meditation, maintaining the dichotomy between meditation (positively valued as an "inner" transformative activity) and ritual (negatively valued as an "outer" empty shell).

6 Meditation as ritual play

Another approach to ritual might be through the notion of play. Gregory Bateson concluded from observing the play of monkeys that their behavior must contain certain cues that allow others to interpret it as play (Bateson 1972: 177–93). Children that play learn to manipulate certain cues in order to construct an as-if world. The child that rides a broomstick turns it into a horse. As sociologist Erving Goffman (1959) notes, however, this as-if quality of play is to some degree an aspect of all socialized human interaction. We all play many social roles during our day-to-day interaction with others. Robert Sharf uses the work of Bateson and Goffman on play in order to approach ritual as a special form of adult play. Religious rituals, he claims, blur the distinction between the map and the territory. In ritual, as in play, the orientation to objects is altered. As Sharf puts it,

> One partakes of the wafer *as if* it were the flesh of Christ; one hears the voice of the shaman *as if* it were the voice of an ancestor; one worships the stone icon *as if* it were the body of a god; one enters the ritual sanctuary *as if* one were entering a buddha land; one sits in *zazen* (seated meditation) *as if* one were an enlightened Buddha. (Sharf 2005: 256)

According to such an interpretation, Zen practice makes effective use of the imagination in order to foster change in its practitioners. They proceed in the ritual as if things were different than they seemed before entering the ritual. Zazen practitioners engage in zazen *as if* they were enlightened Buddhas, and in that act of imagination, something really changes. Sharf points out that it does not matter whether one truly believes that the wafer is flesh, or that one is an enlightened Buddha: "belief has little to do with it; one simply proceeds as if it were the case" (Sharf 2005: 257). This is similar to the playing child for whom a broomstick turns into a play horse. In ritual, a transitional world is created that is neither inside the "mind" nor outside in the "objective world" (Sharf 2005: 257).

Sharf approaches enlightenment and meditation practice not as an inner experience, but as a form of ritual, understood as play. He adds that viewing enlightenment as constituted in and through Zen ritual is not tantamount to a behaviorist reduction. The goal of Zen monastic practice (whether meditation or otherwise), Sharf maintains, lies in "the practical mastery of Buddhahood—the ability to execute, day in and day out, a compelling rendition of liberated action and speech, and to pass that mastery on to one's disciples" (Sharf 2005: 256). This does not mean that Zen monastic practice is a sham, or a cheap imitation of "the real thing." Sharf argues that there is no such thing, whether conceived as some kind of subjective inner enlightenment experience or otherwise, that can be qualified as "the real thing." This interpretation, Sharf maintains, is

> consonant with the appreciation of the intrinsic emptiness of all dependently arisen things. There is, in the end, no fixed or final referent to which terms like ... *buddha* or *enlightenment* can obtain. ... Chan monastic life may be play, but without such play there would be no transmission of the dharma. (Sharf 2005: 267)

It seems like Sharf reduces Zen practice to empty posturing, but according to him, this is exactly the point. If everything is empty (*sūnyatā*), then the Buddha is also empty. He quotes Dōgen, who writes in his commentary on the Japanese saying "a painted rice cake does not satisfy hunger:"

> All Buddhas are painted Buddhas; all painted Buddhas are Buddhas... Unsurpassed enlightenment is a painting. The entire phenomenal universe and the empty sky are nothing but a painting. ... Since this is so, the only way to satisfy hunger is with a painted rice cake. (Sharf 2005: 259)

The Zen masters teach us to practice zazen not so much from an inner state called "right intention," but from an attitude of no-mind. This may seem ironic, as an often-heard complaint about rituals is that they are mindless or thoughtless, a pointless activity of "going through the motions." Becoming mindless seems exactly the point in practicing zazen! But no-mind does not refer to a zombie-like state of mind where no thoughts are present at all. According to Linji, "no-mind" is the condition of someone who has nothing to do, who has transcended all purposes, especially the purpose of enlightenment (Welter 2008).

7 Conclusion

The reinterpretation of zazen practice as ritual could have interesting repercussions for philosophical thought. It forces us to rethink the distinction between thought and action. Viewing zazen as a ritual brings together thought and action, and leaves behind the Western tendency to privilege thought over action. Philosophers such as Wittgenstein and Heidegger have stressed that our interaction with reality is always practical and embodied. Thought and action are always connected. Thought is not something that sets action in motion; thinking is itself a form of activity. And our actions contain knowledge, not knowing that something is the case ("knowing-that"), but embodied knowledge ("knowing-how"), knowledge of how to live in such a way that one is attuned to people and nature around oneself, based on an understanding of mutual interconnectedness. By seeing zazen as a ritual embodiment and enactment of Buddhahood itself (van der Braak 2009), new avenues of research are opened into Buddhist soteriology.

As for the practice of zazen in the West, we could ask: what is the appropriateness of participating in an East Asian Buddhist ritual tradition when it is turned into a therapeutic practice? Many Western zazen practitioners do not realize that zazen is conceived in Japan and China as the ritual embodiment of Buddhahood. They do not feel they are engaging in ritual play when they practice zazen. In terms of the Zen tradition: they do not sit as a Buddha, but in order to become a Buddha.

It is an open question whether this should be viewed as problematic or not. On the one hand, the Buddhist tradition has always adapted itself to the new cultures it encountered. One could argue that Zen currently adapts itself to the antiritual sentiments in Western culture. On the other hand, we have seen that an active distortion has taken place by Japanese Rinzai Zen scholars in their presentation of Zen to the West. This distortion was motivated by missionary intentions, both in the West and back at home in Japan.

As the Sōtō Zen view, and the work of Dōgen, becomes better known in the West, the ritual participation of Western practitioners of meditation is bound to undergo a transformation. The conceptual dichotomy between ritual and meditation might be superseded by a new way, allowing zazen to be viewed as an expression of Buddhahood. Such an expression can be simultaneously viewed as a ritual performance and as a meditation practice. Perhaps this is a good example of how interreligious dialogue is an ongoing process that stimulates the mutual investigation of Western and Asian religious traditions.[10]

Chapter 13

THEORIZING RITUAL FOR INTERRELIGIOUS PRACTICE

James W. Farwell

1 Introduction

An increasingly prevalent and intriguing form of interreligious practice in the West is that of persons who engage simultaneously in the rituals of more than one religious tradition as a spiritual practice. This intertraditional participation is unremarkable in some parts of the world, especially in East Asia; but in the West, ways of thinking about religion as bounded traditions—ways closely connected to the theisms that have predominated in that region—have meant that one does not typically understand oneself to be involved in more than one tradition at a time. At the least, such a practice is thought to be incoherent; at the most, it is thought to be idolatrous or heretical. In the Western context, then, the question of the coherence and legitimacy of interreligious ritual practice is a potent one. Can theorizing ritual help to make sense of this practice?

Drawing from two different approaches to the exposition of ritual, this chapter will deploy a theory of ritual as *soteriological enactment* to throw light on this question of the coherence of interreligious practice, considering the particular case of Christianity and Buddhism.[1] Along the way, we will have occasion to reflect on religions and religious difference as such, since a relatively strong notion of religious difference is implied by this ritual theory. To anticipate, we will find that a theory of ritual as soteriological enactment can fund a sympathetic account of Christian-Buddhist interreligious practice, yet it will also become clear that it cannot *necessarily* do so, nor can it *necessarily* ground a defense of interreligious practice in general. A defense of the legitimacy of any form of interreligious practice will depend finally on the dense particulars of each tradition being examined, including the way in which they understand religion and religious plurality; what traditions are under consideration; and what rituals are being compared. Although ritual theory alone cannot do the work of accounting for interreligious practice, its contribution is in sharpening our sense of what is happening in this phenomenon and providing another set of tools for its analysis.

2 Ritual theory and religions

What, in fact, are religious rituals understood to be, to do, or to accomplish? A large body of literature in ritual studies partially addresses this question (see Kreinath et al. 2006). Functionalist, psychoanalytic, structuralist, and symbolic theories of ritual abound. Often enough, within that field, what one finds are *etic* accounts of ritual—accounts that attempt to construct from a variety of rituals a general theory of the characteristics, patterns, and types of ritual across several or even all traditions by scholars who are not necessarily practitioners of the traditions under scrutiny. These etic accounts are helpful, preventing us from taking the rituals or theories of ritual of any single tradition as normative for all. Much is learned from the fact that most religions have initiation rituals, or food rituals, or healing rituals, and from the way that various religions engage in initiation, eating, and healing. The risk, however, of these etic accounts is that despite their apparent attention to tradition-specific details they can push the content of religious traditions into the background in favor of an analysis of ritual patterns or types, reducing the meaning of the rituals to something other than what practitioners understand themselves to be doing. Surely if one wishes to understand fully the nature of, for example, initiation rituals, one must pay significant attention to that into which practitioners understand themselves to be initiated. Or with respect to rituals of identity conferral: it is not of primary concern to practitioners of a tradition that rituals confer identity; what is significant is the identity conferred. Being Buddhist, Muslim, or Jewish means to address particular conditions of existence that are not addressed simply by being religious but by being, precisely, Buddhist, Muslim, or Jewish. Cultural and ethnic factors play a role in these identities as well, depending on the tradition. Because etic accounts sometimes subtly diminish the significance of the particulars for the sake of understanding the patterns, they work best if joined together with *emic* accounts—thick descriptions that echo, in theoretical form, the voice of practitioners. Emic accounts of ritual attempt to articulate systematically what practitioners of ritual understand themselves to be doing in their own terms. Rightly understood, etic accounts of ritual call for supplementation by the kind of emic accounts that this chapter will emphasize.

We model this supplementation here by first positing briefly an etic account of rituals as the evocation, through performance, of a universe to inhabit. Those who participate in this performance construct and enter into an "as if" world, a kind of "subjunctive" reality taken to be normative and true, in contrast to the fractured or misshapen world of everyday experience, though not completely discontinuous with it. The ritual world is the real world, the actual world that is or will be, and one in which are practiced in ritual shorthand the virtues concordant with that universe (Seligman et al. 2008: 17–42). These repetitive, structured exercises are not reducible to other forms of discourse, yet their meaning is only discernible within the holistic religious worldview in which they are situated. When Christians take Eucharist, when Hindus do *puja*, when Jews build a *sukkah*, they are inhabiting these subjunctive worlds. In fact, the rituals of a tradition do not just reflect the worldviews of a religion; they also play an important role in actually giving rise to and reinforcing the particular religious worldview in which they are enmeshed.[2]

This etic model carries within it an implied substantive model of religion. We might define religions accordingly as webs of flexibly normative ideas, events, experiences, or persons[3] on which the discursive, ritual, moral, and devotional practices of a community are centered, continuously contested, and reinterpreted by the members of that community, and taken to disclose the truly real in its soteriological significance for ordinary life.[4] The religious traditions in which rituals are embedded and which they perform involve worldviews and assumptions about reality—about what is most important to human or cosmic flourishing, also expressed and produced in texts, teachings, counsel, social behavior, moral codes, and music. Sometimes—even often—these religious worldviews conflict. Even in religious traditions where global truth claims and the discriminating intellect that produces them are paradoxically problematized—as in, for example, certain forms of Advaita Vedanta, or Buddhist-Taoist traditions of Zen, or the mystical traditions within theisms—they are problematized for a reason, one that reflects the view of ultimate reality they enact. Religious traditions have *content*, and their rituals are inextricably tied to the production and reinforcement of that content.

3 Christian and Buddhist renderings of soteriological enactment

We will return later to the issue of the conflict, or at least the difference, between religions. Now, within the constraints of space and given the need for tradition-specific details that mark emic accounts, we single out here two traditions—Christian and Buddhist—from which to add to our etic definition of ritual as performance, a theory of what is performed. Like most religions, the Christian and Buddhist worldviews enacted in ritual include, self-reflexively, particular ways in which ritual itself is understood. Those theories of ritual within all traditions do not necessarily agree, although we will suggest that there is an analogy between the emic theories of ritual in the two traditions we examine. Before proceeding, we should note that the comparison of emic accounts of ritual is always, necessarily, *ad hoc* and intuitive. After all, an emic account, by definition, will pick up on one of the concrete ways practitioners speak within specific religious traditions, aware that contestation around normative ideas and diversity of expression exist within each tradition, even regarding where the limits of diversity lie. In a manner similar to that described by Francis Clooney in dealing comparatively with religious texts, one deals comparatively with ritual practices (and theories of ritual practices) that appear analogous, on the basis of one's best judgment, working with the significant voices, traditions, and practices that the analyst knows, and maintaining the humble willingness to abandon a comparison if it appears on further examination to misconstrue either or both traditions.[5]

In the two traditions to which we attend—Christianity and Buddhism—there is a way of understanding ritual that seems closely analogous: significant Christian and Buddhist voices speak of practices central to those traditions as the enactment of the very ends of the two religious traditions in the practitioner's own performance. It is this notion of ritual we will refer to as *soteriological enactment*, where entering into specific practices is seen not simply as a means to prepare for the goal, or to illustrate, underline, remember, celebrate, or recommit to the goal, but *actually to enact the goal*—to enter into it or bring it to pass, at least proleptically if not finally. Furthermore, in the case of Christianity and Buddhism, this is often conveyed as a matter of taking on, or participating in, the identity of the significant figure who makes that goal possible: Christ and the Buddha (or Buddha nature), respectively. These rituals are aimed at the reconstruction of the practitioner's identity through the performance.

3.1 A Christian account of ritual

Consider this notion of soteriological enactment in the Christian tradition. In the gospel of John, organic language connecting the disciples to Christ is common. The *logos* prologue in John holds that all things that exist are made through the divine reason that also abides with paradoxically singular significance and presence in the incarnation that is Jesus, implying that the true nature and destiny of human persons is already within the *logos* that he is. A similar organic connection is made with metaphorical identifications of, for example, Jesus as Vine and his disciples as branches of the Vine; Vine and branches are not distinct, but the latter exists as the instantiation of the whole that is the Vine. Soteriology in John, then, contains a strong element of organic connection, where disciples come to recognize or embrace their wholeness by owning "the Way, the Truth, and the Life" that is embodied in Jesus as their own form of life before God.[6] In a passage explicitly linked to ritual, this organic connection between Jesus and disciples comes to the foreground in behavior when Jesus exhorts the disciples to wash each other's feet because they should do exactly as he has done—linking the form of Jesus's service to others to the disciples' form of life through *mimesis*. This foot-washing becomes a ritualized action in later Christian liturgical practice in connection with baptisms and with the celebration of Holy Week, among the most significant holy days of the Christian year.

 Paul, even more sharply, speaks of the Church as integrally related to Jesus, not simply as his followers, but as his very "Body." Elaborated use of this metaphor identifies particular members of the church as the various parts of his Body, and the integral relationship lives in other metaphors as well. For example, in I Corinthians 5, in a ritual allusion, Paul likens the community to the unleavened bread of the Pasch of which Christ is himself the lamb, thus making of Christ and Church two dimensions of the one Paschal reality while simultaneously maintaining Christ's significance as its foundation. In I Corinthians 10, in a section dealing with food practices and idolatry, Paul's language moves from ritual allusion to specific reflection on the ritual of the Eucharist: "The cup of blessing that we bless, is it not a sharing in the blood of Christ? The bread that we break, is it not a sharing in the Body of Christ? Because there is one bread, we who are many are one body, because we all partake of the one bread." He extends this reflection into the next chapter, where he scolds the Corinthian Christians for engaging in food practices that divide the community, because this violates the fundamental character of a practice in which the Church enacts unity with Christ through its own ritualized unity.[7]

The understanding of ritual that lives in the work of "John" and Paul is elaborated in later developments. For Augustine, the Eucharist is quite explicitly participation in Christ, seen not only in several doctrinal writings but in his sermons and teachings. Speaking of the Eucharist, he says: "so if it's you that are the Body of Christ and its members, it's the mystery meaning you that is placed on the Lord's Table. It is to what you are that you reply *Amen*... Be what you can see, and receive what you are" (Sermon 272). Aquinas follows this line later when he argues that the Eucharistic bread's singularity is in its dissimilarity from other food: unlike other bread, which is transformed into nourishment for our bodies, this bread transforms those who eat into *it* (ST III, 73.3 ad. 2). This notion of Eucharistic eating as becoming or participating deeply in Christ is present in most traditions of Christianity, regardless of debates about the precise way in which Christ is present in, to, or with the bread and wine. Thus, Robert Taft can say of the purpose of liturgy, building on the Pauline material:

> Its purpose... is to turn you and me into the same reality. The purpose of baptism is to make *us* cleansing waters and healing and strengthening oil; the purpose of Eucharist is not to change bread and wine, but to change you and me; through baptism and Eucharist it is *we* who are to become Christ to one another, and a sign to the world that is yet to hear his name. (Taft 1992: 201)

The notion of "becoming Christ"—or, in some classic Christian writings, "little Christs"—is language with which Roman Catholic, Orthodox, and Anglican exemplarist and contemporary Catholic traditions would be most comfortable. Protestant and evangelical traditions tend to stress the distinction between Jesus Christ and all other human beings and use different terminology, yet even in the Protestant traditions this idea of soteriological enactment lives in the notion of "sanctification" in dogmatic and moral theology, and a surge of Protestant interest in liturgical theology in the last thirty years shows a recognition that ritual practices are the location in which the virtues of Christ are sketched in performance. Is there an analogous emic account of ritual in Buddhism?

3.2 A Buddhist account of ritual

The answer is yes, although this is harder to see at first because the nondualist character of the Mahayana traditions deliberately complicates the relationship between religious activities, teachings, sutras, traditions, and rituals, on the one hand, and the goal of awakening on the other—complicating even the notion of awakening as a "goal," but precisely to minimize the distinction between the Buddha and the practitioner. In the teachings attributed to him, the Buddha Shakyamuni indicts traditional religious practices of his time as inadequate to address the problem of *dukkha*—the deep existential dissatisfaction that attends the awareness that "no one is free from aging and death" (Bodhi 2005: 26). Neither dogmas nor textual study nor hymn writing nor chanting will remediate *dukkha*. In an exchange with Kapathika, the Buddha describes the lineage of the ritualist Brahmins as being "like a file of blind men: the first one does not see, the middle one does not see, and the last one does not see. What do you think ... that being so, does not the faith of the Brahmins turn out to be groundless?" After the Buddha dismantles several other defenses of the ritualists' practice, Kapathika is persuaded that only the practice of the ascetics will lead to liberation (Bodhi 2005: 96–103).

That ascetic practice is the Eightfold Path, the only remedy for *dukkha*, whose source is clinging—clinging to rituals or teachings, to pleasures, or the avoidance of pains (a reverse form of clinging), or to anything at all in the world as a bulwark against the fact that all things are always passing away. This pattern of attachment and aversion that human beings take up as a strategy to protect against the impermanence of all things, including the self, turns out to be not the solution to the experience of *dukkha* but the source of it. Release is found in awakening to this and adopting a path by which attachment and aversion cease.[8]

This does not dismiss ritual practice, nor the study of Scriptures, nor teaching (this is, after all, a teaching), nor devotional acts, nor social outreach, nor any other common dimensions of religious life, since the radical rejections of these things would itself simply repeat the pattern of aversion, one of the two sides of the coin that funds *dukkha*. Rather, these practices when properly understood cultivate precisely the awareness that *anatta* (no Self) and *anicca* (impermanence) mark all existence. In both the Buddha's context and in subsequent Buddhist tradition, meditation is itself a ritualized practice, coming out of a tradition the Buddha inherited and adapted: structured and repetitive, it often occurs in a broader ritual context of sutra chanting and, in some of the more esoteric traditions of South and East Asia, visualization practices. Such practices are coupled with a Mahayana Buddhology in which Shakyamuni is distinctive precisely and paradoxically in that he exemplifies the realization of which all are capable and the impermanence that all share: iconography and ritual do not make the Buddha other, but serve as a mirror in which the practitioner sees his or her own Buddha nature. In fact, seeing the Buddha as other than oneself is simply another form of attachment. Dogen, representing the especially paradoxical and iconoclastic tradition of Soto Zen, puts it this way:

> This birth and death is the life of Buddha. If you try to exclude it you will lose the life of Buddha. If you cling to it, trying to remain in it, you will also lose the life of Buddha, and what remains will be the mere form of Buddha. Only when you don't dislike birth and death or long for them, do you enter Buddha's mind ... [and] just understand that birth and death is itself nirvana. There is nothing such as birth and death to be avoided; there is nothing such as nirvana to be sought. Only when you realize this are you free from birth and death. (Dogen 1985: 74–5)

And where does this realization occur, for Dogen? Supremely, in sitting meditation, which, in contract to occasional misunderstandings of the paradoxical quality of Zen, is certainly itself a ritualized practice, both by virtue of its being a repetitious, structured behavior that follows a certain sequence of steps, and by its being embedded in a larger ritualized pattern that involves chanting, prostration, veneration, structured encounters with the teacher, and more. These rituals, with meditation at their core, are themselves further embedded in the rhythms of monastic life, where even attending mindfully to the work of the kitchen can be a practice of enlightenment (Dogen 1985: 53–66; see especially section 9).

If ritual soteriological enactment has a place even in Zen, it certainly has a place in the more esoteric schools in which rituals of visualization, chanting, and mandala contemplation are even more elaborate and central to practice. Thus Kukai, the founder of the Shingon tradition, claims that "the various postures and mudras [depicted in the mandalas] are products of the great compassion of the Buddha; the sight of them may well enable one to attain Buddhahood" (Kukai 1972: 145–6). Robert Sharf sets this in the larger practice of Shingon Mikkyo: "In entering the sanctuary and undertaking the rites, the priest learns to behave as if he were dwelling in a sacred realm ... as if he had merged with Vairocana" (Sharf 2001: 196).[9] The earlier *Bodhicaryavatara*, a beloved text in Tibetan traditions devoted to the practice of being a bodhisattva, is itself structured as a ritual: near its beginning, after opening praise of the Buddhas and a confession of faults, its author Santideva praises again the Buddhas and bodhisattvas—"Holding my hands together in reverence, I beseech the perfect Buddhas in every direction, 'set up the light of the Dharma for those falling into suffering in the darkness of delusion'"—and then in mid-stream converts to first person—"I am the protector of the unprotected... I have become the boat, the causeway, and the bridge for those who long to reach the further shore" (Santideva 1996: 20–1). Thus, in the ritual, the practitioner himself becomes one with the enlightened beings that are the object of his praise. That identification unfolds over the remainder of the text in which the ritual steps correspond to various aspects of the Eightfold Path, including meditative mindfulness, concluding with his self-dedication as a bodhisattva. This ritual seems to be rooted in, or related to, earlier texts of Indian origin like the *Avatamsaka* sutra, whose purpose is not simply to orient the practitioner appreciatively toward something done by the Buddha for one's sake, but "to participate through all senses and movement of thought and body in the eternal work of universal salvation that flows from infinite buddhas and bodhisattvas to infinite living beings" (Makransky 2000: 55).

4 Soteriological enactment, religious difference, and interreligious practice

We have compactly related two emic accounts of ritual as soteriological enactment, meaning that at least in the ritual practices considered here one does not simply prepare to receive an external good from the Christ or the Buddha, or demonstrate thanksgiving for something revealed, but rather *becomes* the Christ or the Buddha, that is, participates directly in the goal that Christ and Buddha, respectively, embody. Profound differences as well as further similarities exist in the way each figure is handled in its own tradition, and there is no intention here to level them comparatively or internally. But given the specificity of the enacted goals of each tradition, it might seem on initial view that the dual practice of both Christian and Buddhist ritual would be incoherent.

This judgment calls for a closer look at the way in which religions are understood in relation to each other. The emic theory of ritual articulated here implies a rather robust and specific difference between being Christian and being Buddhist, yet the theory does not theorize difference itself. Also, the notion of the "interreligious" itself assumes *some* kind of difference among the religious traditions. Any apparent incoherence of interreligious practice can be minimized or eliminated by perennialist positions of various types that suggest religions are different only at their surface, clothed in cultural distinctives with a similar human orientation at their core. Another, newer approach to religions that makes interreligious practice less problematic is exemplified by John Thatamanil and Michelle Voss Roberts in theological studies, and Meredith McGuire in anthropology. Thatamanil argues for the inherent hybridity of religious traditions and for the importance of comparison in understanding them at all (Thatamanil 2011); Voss Roberts, for the hybridity of individual practices and sensibilities, calling "identity" a more cogent metaphor for religiousness than that of "belonging" to a tradition (Roberts 2010); and McGuire speaks against the idea that any individual is a microcosmic replication of the official orthodoxies of the religion to which they belong (McGuire 2008: 185–213). With much sympathy for this third approach, for the sake of argument we will assume here a kind of soft particularism that retains the idea of religions as bounded traditions. While recognizing that hybridities exist within and across religious traditions; that their boundaries are not impermeable; and that some of these hybridities live as points of overlapping concern shared by different traditions, in the end we proceed on the instinct that religions are experienced as finally different from one another *when taken as wholes*. A full case for this position is beyond our scope here. For our present purpose, we assume this position because it seems consistent with the emic accounts of ritual presented (the differences between the Buddha and Jesus, soteriologically, thematically, geographically, historically, and culturally are rather significant) and because it presents the hardest, and therefore most instructive and illuminating possible case for a sympathetic defense of interreligious practice.

So, granting the strong theory of ritual soteriological enactment and a real difference between Christianity and Buddhism, is interreligious practice incoherent? Not necessarily.

4.1 Formation by multiple sources

First of all, it seems hard to argue that a human being who practices one religious tradition alone is *only that one thing*. The identities of those who practice only one religion are, like those of all human beings, also formed by cultural, ethnic, national, vocational, and family histories, mediated through thick personal narratives of experience and encounter over the course of a life. Why would a practitioner of Christianity and Buddhism be incapable of formation by two traditions simultaneously any less than those formed to be, say, Christian and Chinese, or Hindu and modern? This might appear simply to return us to Voss Roberts' contention that approaching religiousness as a matter of "identity" rather than "belonging" would ease the pressure of accounting for interreligious practice, and we could end our reflection here. But Voss Roberts' proposal, albeit rich and provocative, addresses the problems of interreligious practice by redefining it, arguing that the idea of belonging obscures important aspects of self-agency in the development of personal religiousness. That approach in turn obscures those to which we are committed in these particular emic accounts that take ritual practices not to be the context for the self-construction of identity, but to involve the willing submission of the self *to practices that reshape the self*, granting the "agency" to the tradition as it enacts its vision of the human condition and remedy—even if, in the case of Buddhism, the very outcome is a sense of self as impermanent, insubstantial, and existing inherently in relation with all other such selves. Because this notion of formation lives by various terms in the emic accounts of ritual we are working with, it is important to honor it. We are doing so here and suggesting that, since persons are formed routinely by more than one influence, there is no reason to rule out in advance the coherence of this phenomenon with respect to interreligious practice.

4.2 *A provisional sketch of dual Christian-Buddhist formation*

Secondly, and in accordance with this respect for formation, it does seem possible to sketch the beginnings of a coherent description of the interreligiously formed practitioner of Christianity and Buddhism. One might plausibly characterize Christian-Buddhist practice as the cultivation of a kind of *nonattached faith*. Formed as a Christian, a practitioner adopts and practices the virtues and habits of Jesus, in whom she trusts as an embodiment of the coming kingdom of God, a vision in which those in travail are granted safety and those well-situated are shaken up to their benefit to recognize the wild mercy freely given to all. At the same time, formed as a Buddhist, she understands religious goals—for example, the kingdom—are not actually "somewhere" or "sometime" separate from the self, nor identical to it, nor finally "arrived" at, but are alive and moving and experienced through and as both the practitioner's own mindful activity and as that which arises in and through the activity of others. Taking up compassionate service oriented to the flourishing of others, especially the marginalized, she would sit lightly with her conceptions of God and kingdom among other things, knowing with Buddha-mind the inherent problems with the discriminating intellect and its capacity for deluding us. She would recognize, even in service to God and kingdom, that neither are fixed existents among other existents, and that they exceed even the most theologically astute grasp of the practitioner—as do all other phenomena, too, in their impermanent and deeply interrelational being—and that this is actually what makes an openhanded, compassionate life possible. A sense of the divine relationality of the Trinity as the creative source of the world, permeating all things, would be enriched by an appreciation of the dependently co-arisen quality of all phenomena, and vice versa, both funding the very open-handedness valorized by each tradition in different ways.

This sketch—just the first steps of a full description of the sort of faith without attachment that being both Christian and Buddhist might produce—is not implausible. Some genuine sense of "being" both the Buddha and the Christ would have to be present in order for the practice to be consistent with what Christians and Buddhists understand ritual to do—at least with regard to Eucharist, meditation, and visualization rituals. But the theory of soteriological enactment in no way rules out that that the two singular ways of life being enacted will be mutually transformative. The ritual theory clarifies what is involved in interreligious practice and in this very function frames the questions that must follow regarding the degree to which Christian and Buddhist worldviews, mutually transformed, remain present in practitioner sensibility and identity. The questions can only be judged by going deeper still with an emic account of each tradition, deploying its vocabulary and entering its conceptual universe in order to clarify how the two traditions simultaneously live in the formation of the practice.

Perhaps someone objects that in the sketch above the Christian God is simply reframed in Buddhist terms. In response, a deeper exploration of the Christian tradition might be called for, a tradition in which some voices challenge all conceptions of God for risking idolatry. Possible objections from the other side that this practice as described reconfigures Buddhism in unacceptably Christian theistic terms might be pointed toward evidence that, notwithstanding the rationalizing tendencies of some Western converted Buddhists, Shakyamuni actually takes no position on theism (e.g. Bodhi 2005: 230–3), and most forms of Buddhist cosmology are amply populated with gods and demi-gods who also embody the *dharma*. That said, Buddhists do not mean precisely by gods what Christians do, and the Christian view of the creator's everlastingness is not exactly the same as *sunyata* that makes all phenomena possible, so the end result of the dual formation would surely remain a consciousness constituted by ongoing internal dialogue between the analogous points of both traditions. What they *do* mean, and whether those differences survive in mutually transformative ways, could—again—only be adjudicated by extended emic analysis of the two traditions.

4.3 *Productive soteriological undecidability*

Given this similarity in difference, it may also be possible that an intrinsic feature of interreligious consciousness is a kind of *productive soteriological undecidability* in which the lively vitality of "being the Buddha" is constantly enriched and critiqued by also "being the Christ," and vice versa, sharpening and placing under creative question what is most at stake for the human condition according to one tradition by what is most at stake according to the other. But again, whether each of the traditions could judge this perpetual soteriological undecidability as "productive" further depends upon which strands of each tradition the practitioner draws upon to give an *apologia* for this dual practice—in other words, it depends upon a deeper and even more detailed emic account of each tradition in dialogue with the other.

5 Conclusion

What is learned, then? That strong emic theories of ritual taken together with strong accounts of religious difference can be provisionally coupled with a defense of the coherence of interreligious practice and, in fact, clarify what is happening there. But such theory cannot, alone, settle the question of the coherence of the practice. That can only be demonstrated by going more deeply still into the rich, complex, and diverse theological/philosophical expressions that exist within each tradition in their interaction, and this indicates the difficulty of coming to any final evaluation of interreligious practice or religious pluralism apart from the dense particulars of the traditions in question. This was precisely the point of drawing on ritual theories that are themselves part of those traditions, and which are not the only theories of ritual at work there either. Some strands of the historic Christian tradition may be more easily combined in the ritual formation of a practitioner with strands in historic Buddhism in ways that make for a dual enactment of ends that reduces neither to the other. Among the relevant strands of those traditions will be the manner in which each handles the possibility of truth claims and truthful practices outside its own tradition, and the way "truth" itself is framed. Another significant factor in a defense of the legitimacy of interreligious practice is the particular traditions in question: Judaism and Hinduism, say, or Jainism and Islam might not conceptualize ritual in the same ways as Christianity and Buddhism do, or be as patient of dual practice in the same way that others might. Different rituals, too, might be more plausible partners in dual formation than other rituals, as well as different classes of ritual. The pairing of an ongoing practice of both Eucharist and meditation or visualization rituals might call for a different evaluation than that of, say, the initiation rituals of baptism and refuge-taking—not to mention the necessity for determining whether these are truly analogous pairs or not, the judgment of which returns one yet again to the emic accounts of each ritual in its own tradition.

In the end, theories of ritual as soteriological enactment do accomplish several things: they express what is happening in the rituals of at least some traditions, allowing practitioners to speak for themselves about what their ritual activity is specifically understood to inculcate; they flesh out the performative function identified by etic accounts of ritual; and, by identifying the outcomes of the rituals as understood by the traditions, they clarify what would make a practice genuinely interreligious while generating the additional questions that must be asked in order to make sense of it. Those questions, as well as deeper investigation into the meaning of specific rituals as traditions figure them, constitute a rich opportunity for continued inquiry.

Part IV

JEWISH AND JEWISH-CHRISTIAN PERSPECTIVES

Chapter 14

TRANSGRESSING AND SETTING RITUAL BOUNDARIES: A PUZZLING PARADOX

Rachel Reedijk

1 Introduction

After having been involved in Jewish-Christian-Muslim dialogue for a long time, I became interested in the question of how interreligious dialogue affects the identities of its participants (Reedijk 2010). In the relevant literature it is often supposed that it is not possible to remain faithful to one's own religious identity while simultaneously being open to the alterity of another (Moyaert 2011). The underlying assumption seems to be that identity precludes change. But is that really the case? This question requires serious inquiry.

To further explore the construction of religious identity in the context of interreligious dialogue, I conducted forty-four in-depth interviews in four European countries and used the contents of those interviews as the basis of my theoretical and empirical research. My basic question is to what degree do my informants, Jews, Christians, and Muslims, begin to embrace new ideas and practices after participating in interreligious encounters. To what extent is their identity affected and changed by dialogue?

One of the remarkable findings of this research is that, when it comes to balancing identity and openness in a context of dialogue, rituals in particular seem to form the greatest stumbling blocks. Although theological and political subjects may be brought into play as well to sustain the demarcation lines between Judaism, Christianity, and Islam, rituals seem to be the outstanding boundary markers. Ritual encounters between Jewish, Christian, and Muslim dialogue participants are ushered in with objections and caveats. The question that I will try to answer in this chapter is twofold: Why do Jewish, Christian, and Muslim dialogue participants feel that religious rituals are so holy? Are the ritual boundaries between religious traditions final or are there occasions where, according to my interviewees, ritual participation and thus the transgression of ritual boundaries becomes possible?

2 A note on methodology

The theoretical aspect of my research is based on an interdisciplinary—anthropological, theological, philosophical, and psychological—approach. The backbone of the resultant theory of identity construction is constituted by an analysis of in-depth interviews with forty-four key figures of Jewish-Christian-Muslim dialogue in the United Kingdom, Germany, France, and the Netherlands. One search criterion was that they had to be able to reflect on dialogue, their ownership in the dialogue process and the effect of dialogue on their identity. The second search criterion was that they had to be part of a Jewish, Christian, or Muslim congregation. More or less equal numbers of informants from each religious tradition (Judaism, Christianity, and Islam) represented a rich variety of religious affiliations, ranging from Orthodox and progressive Jews, to Catholics and Protestants, evangelical and Orthodox Christians, one Buddhist-Christian, and one Humanist. Muslim respondents came from backgrounds as diverse as the Ahmadiyya Movement, Milli Görus, Süleymancilar, the Union of Moroccan Mosques in the Netherlands, the Grande Mosquée de Paris, and the Union des Organisations Islamiques de France.

The interviews were semi-structured, with the sub-questions functioning as beacons leading the interviewees through the key subjects of this study. To be able to analyze the transcripts, the questions were broken down into sixty codes.

3 Profiles and general observations

My interviewees demonstrated strong motivations for contributing to interreligious dialogue, based on their conviction that encountering the other generates genuine comprehension. From this perspective, they also rejected aggressive missions and otherwise deliberate attempts to convert the dialogue partner, and they agreed that creeds and practices of different traditions must be treated with care.

A recurrent subject among my informants was the scope, meaning, and goal of interreligious dialogue itself: What is the purpose of these encounters? When and where do we illegitimately cross borders? In other words, what are we at liberty to do? I found that, although my informants considered open-mindedness the key to a successful encounter, they were inclined to circumvent delicate issues, emphasizing the paramount importance of the relationship. An analysis of metaphors reveals that many interviewees expressed their basic attitude to the subject of dialogue in confrontational terms, for example, entering a battlefield; confronting gaps, rocks, and sandy paths; plowing rocks; building bridges; an arranged marriage. Apparently, a large majority of dialogue participants feared the risks and pitfalls of the interreligious endeavor.

My data also show a consistent variety in the comments of the interviewees, such that three dialogue profiles could be distinguished: the advocate, the ambassador, and the boundary-dweller. The advocate (1) is not really interested in interreligious exchange, mainly because of the menace of syncretism. He is concerned about the preservation of his own religion. The real endeavor, from his perspective, is to convince others that his prejudices are not appreciated, engaging others with a rhetorical style that is rather apologetic or even polemical. The ambassador (2), because of her frequent contact with representatives of other religions, may eventually become interested in and even charmed by these foreign religious traditions, their beliefs and practices. In due course she will start explaining the background of those foreign traditions to her co-religionists. The ambassador may be called the paragon of hermeneutical prudence. Nevertheless, in extraordinary circumstances she is prepared to cross the boundaries of her tradition and create new openings. Typical of the boundary-dweller (3) is that he emphasizes the exploration of hitherto unknown routes. To prevent himself from walking too far ahead of the troops, the boundary-dweller shares his experiences in a dialogue *communitas*. Strikingly, these three dialogue profiles cut across the boundaries between Judaism, Christianity, and Islam.

4 Identity construction

Dialogue participants construed their identities differently in three distinctive dialogue contexts. From the perspective of their personal life histories (1), a large majority of respondents testified that the encounter stimulated personal growth. They felt reconnected with their roots and were simultaneously challenged by the religious heritage of their new acquaintances. When interviewed about principles of faith (2), it appeared that a large majority of dialogue participants tried to cope with the dilemma of truth-claiming and truth-finding by ignoring the theological issues and seeking refuge in the building of interreligious relationships. Ritual practices (3) were thought to represent the bridges that are most difficult to cross. Religious rituals were understood as being holy, and the interviewees viewed them as definitive boundary markers. A large majority of dialogue participants testified that participating in each other's rituals, for example, through joint prayer, is theologically invalid and psychologically inconceivable. The sharing of rituals, more than anything else, was felt to be very problematic and actually prohibited. However, about one-third of the respondents testified of ritual practices during which the holiness could be suspended—placed between brackets—during extraordinary encounters like interreligious funerals. In transgressing boundaries for an indeterminate period of time, they created opportunities to *participate without participation*. It raises the question of whether holiness—literally: setting apart—inevitably creates a divide between insiders and outsiders. Who is "in" and who is "out" in a dialogue setting?

5 Ritual boundaries

In Eliade's (1957) definition, holiness means *a qualitative difference*. In its secular instantiation, holiness is imputed to mundane practices (going to the movies once a week, exercising), ideals (support for a soccer club or political figure), and principles (human rights, the equality of men and women), which the adherents are unwilling to negotiate. In its religious meaning, holiness evokes images of a portal to the transcendent, an *Axis Mundi*, a Gate of Heaven, beholding the heavenly throne. Religious rituals are felt to be holier than anything else, representing a threshold not to be crossed. In this respect, it may be illuminating to draw a parallel between interreligious dialogue and an ancient Egyptian or Hebrew temple, which displayed a threefold structure. The Egyptian temple complex represented to believers the primordial yet continually recreated Island of Creation—the first sphere. As a consequence, adherents saw the temple as imbued with great religious power. The Israelites experienced the presence of their God—*Kevod Adonai*—in the sanctuary of the *mishkan* (literally: house of God). In the Tenach, the Hebrew Bible, the divine presence is described as a consuming fire: "It was often accompanied by a cloud, which perhaps was to protect the people from its overwhelming brilliance, or from other destructive effects" (Plaut 1981: 798).

Mud-brick enclosure walls surrounded the Egyptian temple precinct. Access was gained through an impressive façade. The silhouette of the pylon symbolized the horizon with the rising, or reborn, sun. In contradistinction to synagogues, churches, and mosques, the Egyptian temple was not a gathering venue. It was a house of the god—*hoet netjer*. Lay persons were only allowed to enter the open court; the temple proper was sacred territory and closed to the public. A roofed and dark hypostyle hall with lotus- and papyrus-shaped columns—the second sphere—gave entry to the inner sanctuary. A gradually rising floor level and increasing obscurity, flickering flares and the smell of incense: one must have been aware of the literally awful character of the *naos*. Only special priests were allowed to enter the Holy of Holies—the third sphere. The question now is: Is contemporary ritual practice somehow similar to entering the holiest places in ancient temples? Does entering the "*naos*" of interreligious dialogue—ritual practice—require special terms and conditions?

6 Ritual roles

Whenever Jews, Christians, and Muslims take serious cognizance of one another's ritual practices, they are most likely confronted with questions of boundary preservation and boundary transgression. In view of this challenge, hypothetically, dialogue participants seem to have four different options at their disposal. Building

Table 1 Four ritual roles

Ritual Roles	Observing	Participating
Service	*Visitor*	*Guest*
Celebration	*Bystander*	*Partner*

on the distinction between a service with its fixed liturgy on the one hand and a celebration with its explorative character on the other, I have drawn an analytical distinction between four ritual roles.

First, congregations may decide to invite or allow nonmembers to attend a *service* in the role of a *visitor*. Second, they may be requested to participate in certain parts of the service as a *guest*. Third, groups and individuals may choose to attend an interreligious *celebration* and play the part of a *bystander*. Fourth, if and when representatives of different religions decide to organize an interreligious celebration together, they may become *partners*.

At first glance, the simplest solution to the dilemma of observation and participation, when attending the service of another religion, is to keep to the role of visitor. Some respondents found a solution to this problem through posture. One Jewish woman said: "sometimes I am required to attend a service as an active member of my dialogue group. I always take a seat in the back." Another Jewish woman divulged: "I am always sitting in the rear. To me it's like observing a theatre play. I get up when they get up because if I don't, everyone looks at me." "Once a year our imams meet a group of priests and ministers," a Muslim man revealed; being unfamiliar with the service, "we created our own ritual: if they stand up, we stand up." Upon further consideration, an apparently similar answer—finding a solution in posture—may have different meanings. Mimicking the movements in the service was felt by some to be an act of politeness; others experienced the ritual as observing what was nothing more than a performance.

7 Strong objections to ritual participation

To some of my interviewees, however, even taking up the role of visitor—for example, by taking a seat in the back—could be a dicey enterprise. One might be seduced into loving their music, and if one loves their music, one might be tempted to read and even appreciate the text, and so forth. The most vehement objections to an exchange of religious rituals, in whatever guise or form, were voiced by a group of seven respondents—three Jews, one Christian, three Muslims. To them, such involvement simply was not allowed. As one Jewish man argued, "Interreligious ritual is a slippery slope. Once you talk to a *goy* (non-Jew), you will eat with a *goy*, you will marry her and forget about *kashrut*." According to an Orthodox Christian, watching the other's rituals, if it is done with a curious mind, unavoidably opens the door to the relativization and hence corruption of the truth:

> I believe that Scripture does not provide us with authorization for multi-religious celebrations. As long as we are guided by God's spirit in Jesus, whom we hail, confess, and proclaim as *abba* (father), any form of mixture with or equation to other forms of religious celebration is prohibited. Multi-religious celebrations unavoidably induce the relativization of one's confession and open a discourse about truth. It will inevitably issue into the denial of the Gospel.

A variant of the slippery slope that reportedly frustrated interviewees was the attempt to annex the rituals of others for the use in an interreligious context. A couple of years ago, the dialogue committee of my own (progressive Jewish) congregation was confronted with a project by a local alderman, who had asked citizens from different religious and ideological backgrounds to describe their preferred rites. The best stories were going to be published. Among the essays awarded was the story of a family presenting the Passover *matzah* as a uniquely Christian symbol. The dialogue committee protested, and after a while the local authorities agreed to add an *erratum* to the brochure. One of the Christian comments on the Christian appropriation of a Jewish ritual was: "Christians organizing a *Seder* or building a *Sukkah*, it's not ours! It will unavoidably be interpreted in a Christian fashion; we will give it our own twist." As one British and one Dutch Christian respectively note:

> It's not helpful. We have demonstration *Seders*. Somebody demonstrates what it is, creating as much as possible the sphere and the explanation and the meaning. But it is not actually the same as being present at the *Seder*. Deliberately taking on board Jewishness, for its own sake, is definitely not something that I would recommend. For the simple reason that Judaism and Christianity. ... We have grown miles apart.

> The use of Hebrew words, Adonai instead of Lord, I'm sorry but that sounds ludicrous to me. This is rather innocent. I will tell you a real story. A fellow student of mine became a priest in the bulb-growing area; they are quite Catholic there. In one of the first services he had to conduct he said: "Oh, Adonai." And he did that for months. One day a bulb-grower's wife approached him after the Mass in all innocence and asked him: "Father, what does that mean, Adonai? Who is that man?" Therefore I think, please, do me a favour! This is dialogue hobbyism.

Other anxieties about the slippery slope are (a) the metaphor of contamination and (b) the never-again experience. One Muslim man admitted that the mosque members whom he had encouraged to visit a synagogue created their own threshold by using the house rules—the "contagious" yarmulke—as a pretext:

> Visiting the synagogue with a group of Muslims was in itself an experience of transgressing borders, effectively a rite of passage indeed. The very problem arose when they were asked to cover their heads. I said to them: "I won't force you to go in, but you have to know that without a yarmulke you cannot get in. It won't transform you into a Jew! Look at me, I have been there before, the mufti has been there; and it did not stick to our head, it is not contagious." You see, the border rises on the spot. From the positive side, it offers something to talk about.

Two Muslim respondents blamed the board of their mosque for the absence of any serious interreligious exchange. The first person admitted that his presence alone at a Christian service shook things up at his mosque: "They [the board] said that, actually, Christians are cannibals, since they eat the body of Jesus. It made me aware that you should think things through very carefully." The other man felt frustrated because of the continual worries of his board: "There is so much resistance amongst those first-generation immigrants. They think that the mosque will become ritually unclean if a non-Muslim who has eaten a pork sandwich sets foot on their premises."

Some interviewees reported a never-again experience. When exploring the boundaries, they realized that they had slid too far down the slope, crossing the other's boundary of the sacred. One Jewish woman related that, while attending mass in a Catholic church, she had accepted the wafer for the sake of the interreligious experiment, but confessed: "I would never do that again. Absolutely not. I learned to understand the meaning the wafer has to them ..." A Protestant minister said: "I was impressed [to see] four hundred former guest-workers prostrating in awe, as I wouldn't expect Dutch labourers to do that so easily. I have participated in their *salat* (Muslim prayer), but then I learned that it is something sacramental; it is so *theirs*, and in that sense, holy."

8 A paradoxical outcome: Ritual participation enhances exclusion

All the research participants agreed that rituals are holy; they also agreed that if and when Jews, Christians, and Muslims participate in each other's rituals, guests and visitors are transformed into outsiders. It is a paradox, given the visitors' intention to improve and strengthen the relationship, but the data confirms that, in an interreligious context, rituals create distance rather than nearness.

Rappaport (1999: 40) argues that all those present at a ritual are participating, although they do not have the same roles: "Obviously, a priest has more to do, but congregations sing, kneel, dance or kill pigs. They are not merely watching." The hub of the matter concerns the definition of "presence"—"those present at a ritual constitute a congregation, those present at a theatre are performers or audience" (Rappaport 1999: 39). The attendance of nonmembers—tourists, watching an Indian sun-dance—is experienced by insiders and outsiders as awkwardness, embarrassment, resentment, or shame. "It may even degrade the event to mere mimicry of ritual" (Rappaport 1999: 40). Congregations are usually composed of people who know each other. They stand on common ground. To say *Shabbat Shalom* at a Saturday morning service is to demonstrate who is, and who is not, familiar with the secret language of Judaism.

One of the reasons for accentuating the difference may be the phenomenon of social control. As shown above in the analogy of an Egyptian temple, first encounters take place in an open court. It is there, for everyone to see—an innocuous conversation at a public square. When entering the hypostyle hall—crossing the threshold of a congregation—dialogue participants are attuned to the possibility of co-religionists, and are enabled to wonder at what they are doing.

One Jewish woman admitted that one of the reasons that real dialogue is hindered is that some people in the Jewish community are very frightened: "It's worse than 'leave me alone'. They don't have a computer in order to avoid the demonic Internet. Personally, I am not afraid to enjoy the Christmas Mass in a Parisian cathedral on the television. But I would never attend; we are not allowed to mix with them." She likewise experienced fear—the worry that her community would exclude her for participating in a Christian service. In a similar vein, one Protestant minister decided to go "all the way" and follow the Muslim way of life for a while. From prior experiences he knew that the experiment would not be lauded by his flock; only a small number of members were informed of the nature of his sabbatical. If his congregants were aware of the minister's participation with Islam, they would possibly revoke his pastoral charge, accusing him of *heulen met de beul*, collaborating with the enemy. This charge could likewise be leveled at myself. Though I am Jewish, I participate in the *salat* at regular times; and I am now preparing for a period of profound immersion—incognito—into the Islamic religion and culture. For a couple of months I will not read the Bible or pray my prayers but will focus on the Qu'ran only and study the Arabic language. I hope that the mosque will offer me the opportunity to assist the imam, perhaps as a kind of deputy imam. Regardless, like all interreligious activity, it will be a learning experience.

In either case, long-distance watching on one hand and "going native" on the other, participating in the routines of the dialogue partner is supposed to transform the identity of the participant. The abovementioned interviewees, having been changed by their involvement, are implicated in a parallel, intra-religious dialogue with the skeptics back home.

9 *Rituals and the rejection of novelties*

Theories of identity construction hold that dissimilarities are created to safeguard the continuity of religious identities. Hence, dialogue participants consequently feel that rituals are unassailable. However, we should not overlook the question of whether there is something in the nature of ritual that might elucidate the phenomenon of inclusion and exclusion. Not only the sharing of familiar rituals, but considering new rituals as well made the interviewees feel profoundly uncomfortable. Some had been thinking about the introduction of supposedly neutral rituals, such as the lighting of candles. Many rejected the candle idea emphatically, which is nicely illustrated in the comment of a Jewish man:

> A candle? Come on! Do that at home, will you. We can go to the cinema together, *that* is not a ritual. Mingling around and fraternizing with Christians and Muslims, it's psychological mumbo jumbo. We are adults, aren't we? Either they want to talk to me or they don't. Either you want to befriend me or you don't.

Lighting and/or passing candles during or after an interreligious meeting is thought to be "grossly artificial" (a progressive Jew), "absolute rubbish" (an Orthodox Jew), "way too Catholic" (a Protestant), "not making sense" (a Catholic), "against my faith" (a Moroccan Muslim), and "tantamount to the Protestantization of Islam" (a Turkish Muslim).

According to a British rabbi, the people in the pews need the security of some kind of structure. Rituals are always carried out within a certain frame of reference, hence their deeper meaning is difficult to understand by those who are not familiar with the religious concepts.

> Should Christians be called up for an *Aliyah* (Torah reading)? I don't think so. Mostly because those who are interested in the services have a different kind of commitment from those who are not. If you are interested, you have some sense of the ritual integrity. I'm sure there is a kind of level where you know, this is allowed and that is beyond lawful partaking. An *Aliyah* is something that is totally framed within a Jewish construction. I cannot imagine a Muslim wanting it or understanding how to do it, let alone inviting him. It's the same as the Eucharist. Look, it's not a new problem. I suspect there are *shuls* in America with mixed marriages conducted by a rabbi and a priest together. It exists, and it has become a major problem for rabbis to do it. They can be kicked out for it. So there will always be someone, somewhere, where you can do it. Twenty years later it could become almost normative, for some people. So, I think your boundaries are determined by the particular group that you are talking about, more than a generality about it. But it would be a sensational thing, an ideal: a Muslim doing an *Aliyah*.

Reading between the lines, one could infer from the rabbi's observation that changes will occur, once one is accustomed to the new practice, and the religious authorities relax the ban on it. The question at hand is not the presumed purity, originality, or authenticity of ritual; ritual boundaries are continually being shaped and reshaped.

According to Rappaport, the performers of ritual follow punctiliously established orders or "invariant sequences of formal acts and utterances" (Rappaport 1999: 24), but he is referring here to the formal aspect of ritual. The substance and meaning of ritual, on the contrary, is infinitely various. In Rappaport's theory of ritual, the dynamic aspect of ritual is closely connected to language. Language permits thought to escape from the solid actualities of here and now to discover other realms: the possible, the plausible, the valuable. As a consequence, rituals may both set *and* unsettle boundaries, safeguard continuity *and* make change possible.

10 Magic and the entering of ritual space

Some dialogue participants frame a sudden insight, a moving encounter, in terms of magic. In *The Secret Lore of Egypt*, Hornung (2001) shows that in the Bible, and in the Qu'ran as well, ancient Egypt is portrayed as the outstanding example of magic. The three monotheistic religions make a sharp division between true religion and false magic. The Bible places a relentless ban on magic. It is conceived as a form of causal action to manipulate God. Torah commentator Plaut (1981) draws a clear distinction between the power of speech and extra-human agencies. Whereas the first corresponds with the biblical narrative, the second is equated with the domain of magic.

In *Magic, Science and Religion*, professor of anthropology Tambiah (1990) argues that the Bible accepts the reality and efficacy of pagan magic. The ancient Israelites were familiar with their practices of trying to influence the cosmos: "stand still, o sun (*shemesh*) at Giv'on, o moon (*yareach*) in the valley of Ayalon!" (Josh. 10:12). In the Book of Deuteronomy, Moses instructs the Israelites on a long list of curses—*aroer*— that will fall upon them if they make an idol, dishonor their parents, move their neighbor's boundary stone, lead the blind astray on the road, sleep with their sister, or withhold justice from the foreigner. In ancient cultures, an immediate, "magical," connection is conceptualized between cause (sin) and effect (punishment). Magic is anathema because the Jewish people are bound by the covenant and should not seek to consult other spirits or seek to circumvent the structure of sin/punishment-goodness/reward that the scriptures indicate. The Tenach condemns magic, however, not because of its inability to produce empirical results.

According to Tambiah, magic is based on the metaphorical and metonymical properties of language. In a metaphorical relationship, a person or object A is treated *as if* it were B—the Law of Similarity. In a metonymic relationship, A is treated *as if* it were part of B—the Law of Contact. Frazer (1994/1922) similarly proposed that "like produces like." The presupposition is that similarity indicates the existence of a deeper, magic identity. Qualities and properties are transmitted by invisible but nevertheless real forces. Interestingly, some of the key elements Malinowski observed when conducting fieldwork on the Trobian Islands were *dramatic* expression of emotions, *kinesic* gestures, and movements, and *impregnating* objects and substances with recited words, words of an imperative kind *evoking* certain feelings. "He comes very close to explaining their efficacy in Austinian terms" (Tambiah 1990: 73). According to philosopher of language Austin (1962), "To say something is to do something."

Egyptologist and Museum of Antiquities curator Raven (2010) explains that magic or *heka*—life energy—is connected in a natural way to ancient Egyptian religion. Magical ritual is supposed to convey divine energy. The ultimate aim of the magician-priest is to understand the laws of nature. To be able to mobilize natural forces, the priest had to understand them. He studied natural objects and forces by perusing their color, smell, shape, and sound. Egyptian magic, Raven argues, should be compared to science rather than disqualified as mumbo jumbo. A central tenet of ancient Egyptian ritual is to preserve *ma'at* or cosmic harmony. The primary task of the Pharaoh, in his role as high priest, is to combat *isfet*—the forces of chaos and darkness.

A kind of mass hysteria took possession of Egypt at the end of the calendar year. In this period, the warmest time of the year, the Nile was at his lowest tide. The granaries were empty. Individuals were susceptible to contagious diseases. In most cases, this "annual pest" was seen as a manifestation of the goddess Sachmet. In addition, there was a fear of a cosmic disaster. (Pragt 2014: 9)

One of the Egyptian magical skills was finger-pointing. When a herd of cattle was about to cross a waterway, the shepherd would stand on the bows of a papyrus boat and cast a spell on the crocodiles in the water with his outstretched hand.

Paraphrasing Austin's illocutionary law, I would say that to do something is to transform something. Transformation is scary. The confrontation with hitherto unknown practices is frightening. Yet, under the right circumstances, dialogue participants are willing to consider alternatives and discover new realms. For, in a certain sense, to engage in dialogue with the religious other is similar to entering ritual spaces.

11 To participate without participation: Transgressing boundaries

The dialogue participants of this study contended that the ritual boundaries between Judaism, Christianity, and Islam needed to be preserved and respected. However, as some of their stories evince, ritual practices may be placed "between brackets." Their narratives demonstrate that new ritual meanings arise in new contexts. Traditions will be restudied and reinterpreted because of the compelling, shocking, inspiring, or otherwise thought-provoking nature of these encounters. Some interviewees experienced an overwhelming sensation of profundity and proximity while eating, mourning, and celebrating festivals with their interreligious counterpart.

11.1 Eating together

One Muslim interviewee was invited by a Jewish interviewee to her *Shabbat* dinner on a Friday evening, the meal that ushers in the Jewish day of rest. The Muslim woman was touched and surprised by the amount of hospitality bestowed on her by her Jewish dialogue friend. The Jewish woman explained that, to her, it was self-evident to serve grape juice instead of the usual *kiddush* wine. Both women emphasized the intimacy of their encounter. Eating together creates an outstanding opportunity to discuss food: what is *kashrut* or *halal*, why it is important to live by rules and prescriptions like these, did one encounter any difficulties at business lunches and so forth, and how those kinds of problems are solved. One Muslim said that in the North African town where he was born and raised, it was not unusual at all to be invited by Jewish neighbors on *Shabbat* to share dinner with them. He added that they had picked up and resumed this habit when meeting and living—as Jews and Muslims—together in France. A Christian minister based in the inner city valued shared meals from the perspective of social cohesion:

> In my church we organize meals every month. It's *halal*, so everyone can join. "Everyone" means that we also explicitly intend to invite the homeless and the drug addicts in this neighborhood. Last year during the month of *Ramadan*, a Turkish man came in with a bunch of food. He was divorced from his wife; he

felt lonely, and asked if he could break the fast with us! Eating together is the most basic form of. … Everyone must eat. At the subconscious level it gives you energy. And I think that this makes you more open to the other. You could call it a rite of passage; it helps to open up.

11.2 Mourning together

Funerals confront us with the irreversible traversing of our final boundary between life and death. In our modern societies it is increasingly the case that colleagues, friends, and relatives from different religious backgrounds are involved in or invited to the memorial service. Six interviewees—three Jews and three Christians—reported an interreligious burial they had attended. Two British Jewish interviewees said:

> People are more open in the face of death, but this is common sense. I think it has to do with civilized behaviour. It is the recognition that there are many different cultures around you. It will happen because it is just realistic, but it depends on how multicultural you are. In the UK we have many groupings together, but England is very *laissez-faire*. Holland is a particular story, the Jewish people, they don't trust anybody. There is a kind of Jewish defensiveness which comes out of the fact of being a minority, a history of being both the victims of the Holocaust and using the Holocaust as a kind of weapon, both against others and internally.

> Look, there *are* funerals where all major religions do attend. [For example] 11 September in New York. But that was not the first; there are other places too. There will be a rabbi who will give a sermon, and they'll say some prayers in Hebrew. There will be an imam quoting the Qur'an. And there will be a Christian, be it a Catholic or a Presbyterian or a Methodist and so forth. And they *have* developed interreligious prayers. You will be amazed how much they use what they call the Old Testament. Does Judaism take any component from any Christian religion? I don't know.

Christian comments on interreligious funerals were given by two Protestant ministers and one Catholic priest. One of the ministers had attended a Hindu cremation, where relatives of the deceased asked him to do something: "I decided to read Psalm 23, and they understood." The second minister explained that he was touched by the obsequies of a Jewish acquaintance. A Jewish funeral begins with several readings; Psalm 23 is recited, with its famous verse: "*Adonai* is my Shepherd, I shall not want." At a Muslim funeral, members of the congregation say the *salat al Janâza*, a communal prayer. The funeral involves the reading of the *Fatiha* (opening *Surah*) and a number of *Takbirs* (*Allahu Akbar*). The priest said that:

> I had to bury a young boy once who had been murdered. The entire school was there. Two thirds of them were Muslim, but the funeral was Catholic. So I

decided to explain in the sermon what we were going to do and what it meant: meeting God, in Jesus' hands. They were as silent as a mouse. In deep awe they experienced the ritual. The principal told me afterwards that she had never seen them that respectful. What I had tried to do was to take them seriously. And I must say, it was a powerful experience to me too. I felt a sense of communion through the presence of those Muslim youngsters. In a word: it was beautiful.

Local histories—the element of *couleur locale*—determine to a certain extent what is ritually possible. Yet the message one conveys is that modern times require us to reconsider ritual practices. Some respondents say that the circumstances may require that traditional rituals are put between brackets, for a short period of time, for the sake of interreligious respect and friendship. Although they frame it in different words, these interviewees went through a stage of liminality and experienced something they had never felt before.

11.3 Celebrating together

In my congregation a discussion was ignited, a couple of years ago, about a project that took place during *Sukkoth* and *Ramadan*. Because of the coalescence of a Jewish and a Muslim festival, the dilemma was: Were we going to encourage an unlawful mixture of rituals—boiling the kid in its mother's milk—or accentuate our hospitality—the principle of *hakhnasat orchim*. It was decided that the *Iftar* would be announced as a meal, although from the Muslim point of view it was a *breaking of the fast*, and we all knew that the Muslims would continue to call it an *Iftar*. Gradually, the intra-religious discourse changed; the *Ramadan-Sukkoth* meeting lost its syncretic connotation. From then on, the *Iftar* was simultaneously "theirs"—Islamic—and interreligious. A similar story was told movingly by a Catholic priest about a Christmas event:

> To my surprise the board of both the Turkish and the Moroccan mosques in this neighbourhood attended the Christmas service last year. Many showed up, owing to the grim political atmosphere after the Van Gogh assassination. I was especially stunned when… You know, this was a typical Catholic mass. And when it was time for Holy Communion, I saw my Moroccan friend A. coming up to the altar, where I was conferring the bread, the wafer indeed, and the wine, together with the acolyte. And there was A., standing right in front of me. And I thought: "No matter what Rome thinks, I cannot refuse him." It was so pure; it was so real. It was a sign of interreligious friendship. However, next time I will talk to A. before the mass, and explain to him what it means in our tradition.

For the past couple of years interreligious *Iftars* have sprung up like mushrooms. They have become the preeminent occasion for Islamic congregations to open their doors to local politicians and MPs, neighborhood organizations, representatives of Christian and Jewish communities, and so forth. Muslim groups are reaching out to non-Muslims by offering an *Iftar* on their premises. In the rank and file of Muslim congregations, this policy is sometimes criticized for not being a real Islamic ritual anymore. They feel that an Islamic ritual risks being transformed into a purely social encounter for the sake of local community building. Many of the dialogue participants reported having attended an *Iftar*. The interreligious *Iftar* is a serious attempt at coping with both setting and transgressing boundaries.

12 Conclusion

Once the physical as well as emotional threshold is crossed, dialogue participants are confronted with a soul-searching dilemma: either observation of or participation in ritual practices. The broad consensus among the research participants was that it is unlawful to take part in each other's rituals because they are holy, and the ritual is predictably "doing" something to its participants. Paraphrasing Austin, to do something is to transform something, which can be frightening. However, under the right circumstances, dialogue participants were willing to consider alternatives and to discover new realms, even if joining a ritual may mean experiencing a sense of exclusion. In extraordinary situations, such as "interreligious" funerals, a large minority of interviewees decide to ignore the boundaries and to place the holiness of ritual practices between brackets, if only during a liminal period of time. Dialogue participants coped with the continuation and transformation of traditions by inventing the strategy of participating without participation. In doing so, religious worlds can become subjects of acting, asking, shaping, and considering.[1]

Chapter 15

MOURNING THE LOSS OF MY DAUGHTER: THE FAILURE OF INTERFAITH BEREAVEMENT RITUALS

Anya Topolski

Epitaph Upon A Child That Died
Here she lies, a pretty bud,
Lately made of flesh and blood:
Who as soon as fell fast asleep
 As her little eyes did peep.
Give her strewings, but not stir
The earth that lightly covers her.

— Robert Herrick

1 Introduction

On September 2, 2013 (*Elul* 27, 5773), G-d took back my daughter Hannah, a gift of pure light and joy, just two years after she was born. While I have been very well supported by my community of friends, both locals and expats (like myself), I had to face the jolting experience of planning an interfaith funeral as well as other rituals of bereavement almost entirely on my own. My partner was in shock from the moment I called him from the hospital until the day of the funeral. The continuing responsibility to care for my two other children, and my acute awareness of being part of a minority faith (which means that the default option is never my own), stipulated that I had to keep it together until after the funeral.

Hannah was the youngest of my three children and my only daughter. She was the happiest, easiest child I could have dreamed of having. While my strong feminist inclinations constantly made me struggle to avoid gender stereotyping and the color pink, I was ecstatic to have a daughter. According to Judaism, which is transmitted matrilineally, Hannah was the only child through whom my faith would certainly have been continued. While I had not thought much about this fact during her life, it affected me in a manner I still do not quite understand when planning her funeral. My only possible explanation is that as a Jew who has always believed in Fackenheim's 614th commandment (Fackenheim 1994) to not allow Hitler a posthumous victory (which I see as distinct from support for the state of Israel), her death was not just my own tragedy but also that of the entire Jewish community.

My husband is a practicing Catholic, a former seminarian. We have been together for over a decade, and had an interfaith wedding nine years ago. Since then we have kept our promise, inscribed in our *ketubah* (Jewish marriage contract), to strengthen each other in our respective faiths and to raise our children as both Jews and Christians. Against countless challenges, both familial and societal, we have tried and most often succeeded—until now. Hannah's sudden and unexpected death was the worst moment of our lives, a moment when we most needed our respective faith traditions and their mourning rituals. It was a time when we found no way to weave our two traditions together; moreover, it was a time when our interfaith commitments came into serious conflict.

Concretely, I felt frustrated by Catholicism for its seeming lack of bereavement rituals. The exceedingly well-defined plurality of Jewish rituals of mourning only amplified this seeming Catholic lacuna. Other than the funeral mass, Catholicism did not seem to provide rules, rituals, or relief, and I have often wondered if this lack of rituals also makes it harder to go on living after losing someone. While we chose to mourn Hannah's death by following the Jewish customs, these cannot have the same power for my partner as a Catholic as they do for me as a Jew.[1] This was the first time we had to make such a choice—a choice I hope other interfaith parents do not have to make. While in the grand scheme of things, which one can perhaps only envisage after experiencing the greatest loss a parent can suffer, these tensions are insignificant, the fact that they added more pain to the most painful moment of our lives leads me to conclude that in our time of greatest need, interfaith ritual participation failed us.

2 *When we need rituals most: Death and bereavement*

While once upon a time there were rituals for every aspect of daily life that were practiced by the vast majority of believers, in our current secularizing societies (perhaps with the exception of the most orthodox) only a few rituals are still ordinarily performed—this dwindling is often referred to crudely as the "hatch, match, and dispatch" model. As both my partner and myself consider ourselves observant, the first two of these rituals have been performed with a great deal of care and reflection. At our interfaith wedding we had both priests and rabbis, church and *chuppah* (wedding canopy or covering), *Kabbalat Shabbat* prayers and the breaking of bread. Upon celebrating the birth of our three children, we once again had both Jewish and Catholic presiders at an interfaith ceremony. It thus seemed obvious that this would be no different at our own funeral services. While we never imagined the nightmare of having to say goodbye to one of our greatest gifts, one of our own children, reality has a way of reminding us that we are not in control. When my partner's priest and my rabbi came to our house on the evening of Hannah's death, we sat down to discuss the funeral assuming that it, like all our other rituals, would be interfaith. Yet unlike the joyous rituals of the miracle of new life or the public commitment to married life, the tragic ritual of saying goodbye to a soul one loves seemed not to have a predefined interfaith path to follow.

While the joy of new life is greater than the sadness of its loss, or as Lord Tennyson so beautifully expressed it, "'Tis better to have loved and lost than never to have loved at all," the grief brought by this lost love is overwhelming for even the strongest of communities. As psychological research establishes, "the death of a child may be the greatest tragedy that a parent will ever face [and is in relation to other types of grief], particularly intense, complicated and long lasting" (Miller 2003: 1). It should thus come as no surprise that the bereaved often turn to their faith at this time to find solace and support, as it is at times of loss that we are most likely to turn to faith for answers, for meaning in what—for me—feels meaningless and unjust. There is no doubt that we both desperately needed our faith and community on that day and every day since, and in this we are certainly not alone. Research on religious commitment and adjustment to the death of a child demonstrates that many parents who have experienced such loss, with the exception of those who had no faith before, become more faithful after such an event (Cook and Wimberley 1983: 222–38). This leads me to conclude that while rituals are always a potential source of support and guidance, it is at the worst moments of our lives, at moments of loss and despair, that we need them most.

3 What Judaism and Catholicism offer the bereaved and how these came into conflict

I will now provide an account of what Judaism and Catholicism offer the bereaved, describing both the rituals and the visions or theologies that undergird these practices. While there is a great deal of diversity, both within Judaism and Catholicism, between cultures, religious orders, and so forth, I would like to consider what is generally known to those who are practicing, although perhaps not counted among the most orthodox of their flock, in so-called developed countries that have undergone the process of secularization. In other words, my account is not meant to be comprehensive of all funeral and bereavement rituals but intends rather to outline the most common practices and explanations for them.

Let us begin with what Judaism offers the bereaved.[2] There are two foundational principles as concerns the death of a member of one's family or community. First, from the loss of a loved one to their burial, during the period of *aninut*—which should be as short as possible as stated in Deuteronomy 21:23—the focus is on respect for the deceased (*kevod ha-met*). Second, following the funeral, *avelut* begins as the focus shifts toward the survivors who are in need of comfort (*nichum avelim*) and is clearly divided into three temporal periods: the first seven days (*shiva*), the first thirty days (*shloshim*), and the first year and subsequent anniversaries (*yahrzeit*). The first principle expresses itself in several practices that might strike one as morbid, which is how I perceived them prior to my performance of these rituals. Not only did they feel on an almost instinctual level as necessary, they were existentially comforting and a means to express corporeal care for the last time. The aim is to care for the deceased's body, which had once been the bearer of the deceased's soul, and to show respect for this "bearing" by safeguarding the body (from the moment of death until it is placed in the ground), cleaning it, and returning it to the earth in a very natural and simple state (inspired by verse 3:19 from Genesis, "for dust you are and to dust you shall return"[3]).

While I rationally knew that Hannah's spirit was no longer in her physical body, emotionally I felt otherwise, and it was absolutely necessary for me, as her mother, to hold on to her as long as possible and to care for her beautiful little body. While I did not recite psalms, as is the tradition, I did continue to recite her bedtime prayers and favorite lullabies. I could not leave her alone or with a stranger (such as the hospital or funeral home staff); it felt necessary for me to ask friends, our priest, and her godfather to stay with her body whenever I had to care for my partner and our other children, or make funeral arrangements. In this sense before even having a chance to learn of this Jewish ritual, I performed it spontaneously by creating an interfaith watch (*shomer*).

The second part of respect for the deceased is the preparation of the body by means of washing (*rechitzah*), purifying (*taharah*), and dressing (*halbashah*). Again, I was surprised how instinctually this came to me. The hospital attendant, a man, began to wash Hannah's precious body as I was sitting staring at her in shock and disbelief and I interrupted, much too strongly, and screamed—"stop that, I need to do that." He of course apologized and let me take over. I sang Hannah her favorite bath songs and ritually washed her body and hair for the last time. While the ritual also requires that the body be dressed in a white shroud (*tachrichim*), this did not feel right to me, as Hannah had always been full of colors and joy, so instead I dressed her in one of her simplest but most beautiful dresses.

On the morning of the funeral, during which I was in a shock-induced trance-like state, I was guided by the rabbi and a member of my synagogue, who together formed the traditional society for funeral support (*chevra kaddisha*) that every Jewish community should have. Given that the rabbi was not my regular rabbi, I relied heavily on the other woman, who as a mother also understood my pain and whose presence was an incredible sacrifice and support. Together, as only women are permitted to do to a female body, we wrapped Hannah in a communal prayer shawl (*tallit*). After this we recited prayers together and placed her body into a very simple natural wood unadorned coffin (*aron*), which I accompanied to our home, from where we processed by foot to the cemetery. Before this I rejoined my husband and two boys, as well as the priest and rabbi, in our house for the *keriah* ritual. This ritual requires that one tear a visible part of one's clothing. In our case we tore the material just above our hearts, clothes which we had worn, without washing, throughout the period of *shiva*. The symbolism behind this ritual, which spoke to my partner and I, was that just as our hearts and lives had been torn apart by Hannah's death, so now was our attire. After this we stepped outside from our house and were surrounded by friends, family, neighbors, and so many others, including some strangers who had heard of our tragic loss. I was told that there were over 400 people outside our house, which is meaningful only in that it made us realize we were not alone in our pain and sadness.

The funeral itself was on a Friday morning, a compromise that had its own interfaith and political tensions. Hannah died on Monday, September 2, 2013, *Elul* 27, 5773 in the Jewish calendar, two days before *Rosh Hashanah*, the Jewish New Year. Jewish funerals (or sitting *shiva*) are not permitted on holy days (while biblically *Rosh Hashanah* should only be celebrated for one day, it is most often celebrated for forty-eight hours, thus from Wednesday night to Friday night) or on Shabbat (which begins Friday night and ends Saturday night). This meant waiting until Saturday night—which was not possible according to local Catholic law or the Christian-inspired communal laws that prevent funerals from taking place on Sunday.[4] The idea of waiting until the following Monday was too long to bear emotionally as well as practically unfeasible as all my family had immediately arrived upon hearing of Hannah's death, as the custom is to bury Jews as fast as possible, and many were leaving by Sunday night. Jewish law also permits the funeral to be delayed if family must travel from across the globe. This conflict, which we were aware of on the evening of Hannah's death, was our first realization that our different traditions might lead to both religious and practical difficulties. Fortunately, by means of an interpretive loophole—the visiting rabbi chose to follow the biblical interpretation of *Rosh Hashanah* as lasting twenty-four hours— we were able to set the date for the funeral for Friday morning, allowing all Jews enough time to be home for *kabbalat shabbat* that evening.

The funeral itself was, oddly enough, a moment of beauty and peace in a week of suffering and torture. The shining sun, the hundreds of processors, the children carrying white balloons, the lit candles in every house on the procession route, the eulogies and music, as well as many of the rituals themselves somehow lifted our spirits, if only for a brief time. Yet the planning it involved was far from agreeable. Not only was finding a date difficult, so was locating a Reform rabbi who was comfortable with interfaith celebrations. One of the most painful moments was my local rabbi's claim, while sitting in our living room, less than twelve hours after Hannah's death, that "in principle I am opposed to officiating at an interfaith ceremony." The fact that our rabbi felt the need to make such a statement at such a time was cruelty. We knew his position (albeit one I find odd given that half of my community is composed of interfaith families), but were shocked by his need to express his own discomfort when our hearts had just been ripped out. He knew we were an interfaith couple; if he was not able to support us as we were in such a horrendous moment, why even come to our home? This "problem" was resolved by a practical reality, as my rabbi would be out of the country on Friday morning—the only moment possible to have the funeral given all the intersecting obstacles. The visiting rabbi who was to take his place for the period of the high holidays expressed his full support and sympathy for us both as parents and as an interfaith family, and agreed to participate in an interfaith funeral. It was only then that funeral planning, and the busyness and relief this brings, could begin.

Central to a Jewish funeral ritual is the eulogy, the mourner's prayer (*kaddish*), and the placing of dirt on the coffin. While we chose to have two eulogies, both for linguistic and religious purposes, in theory Catholic funerals do not have eulogies, which made this yet another interfaith disparity. After the eulogy and a few songs, not normally part of the Jewish funerary rites, we invited people to place stones, and for the children marbles, in a bowl at the gravesite. The placing of stones is the Jewish version of what Christians do by means of flowers. Symbolically I find much comfort in stone and marbles, which are eternal, representing the need to rebuild our lives step by step (a process of rebuilding that some Jews associate with the destroyed temple), and providing a means to show the mourner that someone has visited the grave. However, in the days since Hannah's death when I have visited her grave I often feel sad that she is not covered by color and flowers and beauty (especially evident since she is buried in a non-Jewish cemetery, chosen because it was within walking distance from our home). The other aspect of this ritual is that rather than spend money on flowers, we asked people to donate to a Christian refugee charity in Hannah's name—a ritual that we both are pleased to have respected, as it gives meaning to our loss by helping others.

Perhaps the center of the entire mourner's ritual in Judaism is the *kaddish*, the mourner's prayer that praises G-d, about which many books have been written.[5] At the funeral itself I was too devastated to recite the *kaddish*, and only said *amen*, but the *kaddish* became a source of interfaith pain during the mourning days (which I will recount later). After the coffin is interred, the ritual is that all mourners place dirt into the grave. This very physical ritual is both horribly painful and very real. It is a symbol of closure with regard to the symbolic aspect of showing respect for the dead and marks the start of the comforting of mourners.

While the period of *shiva* normally begins after the funeral (and reception), in our case because Friday night is the start of Shabbat, this was delayed by one night, with *shiva* beginning on Saturday night. The second principle of Jewish bereavement comes into effect during this period, with the goal being to comfort the mourners. In the first seven days this means giving them time to suffer, protest, cry, and rest. Mourners are not permitted to cook, clean, wash, or perform other work—this role is taken up by the community. Mirrors are covered so mourners do not look at themselves (a form of idolatry) but instead focus on their loss and sadness. These seven days are referred to as "sitting *shiva*" because mourners often sit on the floor or close to the ground in order to symbolize the experience of being weighed down by grief. Of all Jewish rituals this one was perhaps the most appreciated by my non-Jewish partner. While the goal of *shiva* is to prepare the bereaved to return to the world, for these seven days they are allowed to escape the world—a rare allowance in Judaism, a faith that is focused on the life. Each day during *shiva* (which begins by lighting a candle that burns throughout the period), at a prescribed time, the house fills with people, family, and friends, who come together to reflect, share stories, and most importantly to say the *kaddish*. All Jewish prayers require a quorum (*minyan*), which is a minimum of ten Jews. This prayer, which celebrates G-d and life (not an easy thing to do at such a time), is also recited for the rest of the month (*shloshim*) and as part of every communal prayer for a year (*yahrzeit*).

What was terribly painful for me personally was that my partner, a non-Jew, could not be counted in the *minyan*. While there were more than a dozen Jews present and so there was no fear that we would not have *minyan*, it pained me horribly that the man I love, whose love brought Hannah into the world and whose suffering was so close to my own, was not counted. This bothered me all the more because Jews, after the *Shoah*, should know the pain (and danger) of being excluded, of not counting. While we and our community benefited immensely from the sense of support we experienced each night of *shiva*, this ritual is clearly Jewish, and thus led to non-Jews feeling excluded.

At the end of *shiva*, the entire community leaves the house together (which the mourners have not done for seven days) and accompanies them symbolically back into the world—something any mourner has great difficulty doing. This is also why there is a second proscribed period of bereavement—*shloshim*—when mourners slowly try to enter their new "normal" routines, but continue to say the *kaddish* and are still not required to cook or clean (again roles often taken up by the community). After the first month, mourners are gently pushed to resume their routines, even if they do not yet feel normal. As is the case with most Jewish rituals, it is the doing so slowly that allows for the transformative experience, an experience it is hoped mourners will experience during the first year, or *yahrzeit*, of their loss. This *yahrzeit* is commemorated by once again lighting a candle, reciting the *kaddish*, and often by way of the *yizkor* service during *Yom Kippur* (Day of Atonement).

As I stated at the outset, we were presented with such an abundance of meaningful Jewish mourning rituals that *in comparison* we felt that the Catholic bereavement rituals were lacking.[6] My partner and I have always tried to bring together the best of both traditions, and yet this proved very difficult at this time, which is why we chose to largely follow the Jewish rituals.[7] The Catholic rituals we knew or discovered by talking with the priest and others in our community said very little about the period preceding the funeral. There is a vigil prayer service on the evening before the funeral in which family and friends gather with the bereaved to pray. Without explicitly planning this, our house was indeed full of loved ones the night before, and stories and tears were shed and shared. It is during the vigil that a eulogy is permitted, if desired, as it is not meant to be part of the funeral mass itself. The core of Catholic bereavement ritual is the mass of resurrection, held in the church, during which Jesus's life takes central stage, although in practice the deceased is often related to Jesus (in one way or another). There is also space made for music, psalms, and readings (Psalm 23 is most commonly used by both Jews and Catholics). After leaving the church there is a graveside ritual, the rite of committal or internment, which consists of a final prayer often said by all present and a priestly blessing (often with incense) over the ground to make it holy and ready to receive the body. With regard to the mourning period, there are no prescribed rituals, although mourners will most often wear black clothing for as long as they feel it is appropriate. Nonetheless there are three practices that are still common enough that they are understood by the general public. The *first* is the wearing an armband for a year (traditionally only done by a widow); *second*, the celebration of a requiem mass, called month's mind, in memory of the deceased; and *third*, a mass to honor the deceased on November 2, All Souls' Day. Although neither my partner nor I felt called to wear an armband, the attire we wore for the next month was rather somber. In addition we did have a mass and meal at the end of the first month and again on November 2, which was exactly two months after Hannah died. We also chose, on December 2, to plant a tree in the local park, where Hannah had celebrated her second birthday, which we will watch grow year after year and wish Hannah could do the same.

4 Interfaith Bereavement: The failure of ritual participation

By way of conclusion I wish to end with perhaps the most difficult aspect of interfaith bereavement—the question of our respective beliefs in theodicy and the afterlife. As many philosophers and theologians have argued, "theodicy is both the foundation and final test of all religions" (Pramuk 2013: 67). As my partner is a theologian and I am a philosopher, it should come as no surprise that we have often discussed questions of theodicy—well before having to tackle these questions existentially. Like Harold Kushner, we were forced to reject a notion of G-d as all-powerful, and this very early on in our relationship. We came to this decision when we were discussing the apocryphal book of Judith, which led us to discuss the *Shoah* and how G-d could have allowed such suffering. We agreed that G-d had not allowed it but that we, humanity, were not only responsible for what occurred but that we had not even allowed G-d to protest by refusing to leave space for G-d to appear in our midst. The image of Jews and other persecuted minorities crammed into the trains heading to death camps conveys this sense; there was no air to breathe, no space between people for G-d to appear. Instead, we concluded, G-d suffered with us, and still does, for what happened during humanity's darkest time.

In our darkest time, a time that I often thought of the thousands of parents who saw their children murdered during the *Shoah*, our understanding of G-d was unsurprisingly greatly put into question. Nonetheless, there was one experience during Hannah's funeral that deeply affected us and our notion of theodicy. Just after the funeral was over, when most people were trickling toward their cars and workplaces, on what had been until then the most beautiful sunny dry day in September, it started to rain, a warm but heavy downpour. We were both sure that this was the heavens crying with us. While no one could have predicted or prevented Hannah's untimely death, we both felt that G-d was suffering with our community and us. Neither of us would have ever had such a thought or belief before this day, and yet at that moment—for the first time since her death—we both felt a sense of peace, albeit only fleetingly.

Without wanting to speak in the name of Judaism, or more specifically in the name of reform Judaism, the question of the afterlife has as many answers within Judaism as there are Jews (and maybe even more since many Jews hold two often contradictory beliefs at the same time—I surely do). Judaism in general, with the exception of a few principles inspired by Maimonides and taken as dogma by the orthodox, has very little dogma, and as such many views on the afterlife are accepted on the level of *doxa*. The afterlife, known as "the world to come" (*olam ha-ba*), is written about in the Torah and Talmud but is rarely discussed by Jews who, as a principle, focus on life (*chaim*) in the here and now. Prior to Hannah's passing I did not take much time to consider these questions, often silently laughing at some of the Christian dogma that seemed all too allegorical to me. My feeling, which has only partially changed, is that we will never know if there is an afterlife, so the best bet is to live as good and fulfilled a life as possible, and in this way, if there is judgment and an afterlife, we have lived both here and there as best as possible. While this framework remains, I will admit to having opened myself up, or having been opened up by these tragic events. I feel so strongly connected to Hannah, at every waking and sleeping moment since her passing; and I hear her voice in nature, in events that I cannot explain rationally. I have always believed in the importance of human relationality, a subject I have written on as an academic for over a decade through the writings of Hannah Arendt and Emmanuel Levinas; I just never realized that relationality might even be strong enough to overcome death.

While it is much harder to write about how Catholics view the afterlife, I can only imagine that there are also as many different visions as there are Catholics. Yet, and this is perhaps the strength of Catholicism, there is much more said and written about the afterlife than in Judaism. I can only imagine that this must be a huge strength and solace in times of mourning. To the best of my knowledge, Catholics see death as a form of resurrection (which is why the funeral mass is called the mass of resurrection), as a journey from a finite physical life to an eternal ethereal existence. While not all the deceased will go to heaven, in theory, a good and faithful life is lived as a means to avoid either purgatory or hell. While the latter question offers no comfort to me, the idea that Hannah is now an eternal star or angel, a soul that can still communicate with me if I keep my heart open to her spirit, is extremely comforting. It is also why I continue to obsessively look at her picture, as her smile expresses this eternal love and joy that I so wish to rediscover in myself.

5 Conclusions

While I do feel that we found our way and have managed to respect our faith commitments as well as our marital commitments to keep each other strong in our respective faiths, I do wish we had been better supported. As an interfaith family for the past decade, I saw our relationship as an interfaith success story, a story of how difference is a gift, to be discovered by means of respect and dialogue. This experience was surprising because our interfaith differences were amplified and clashed. I felt that Catholicism did not offer us as mourners enough, and that Judaism was too exclusive. The most painful aspects of this interfaith ritual were that: *first*, a non-Jewish parent of a Jewish child could not be counted as part of the *minyan* (minimum of ten people needed to say the *kaddish*, mourners' prayer). This was exacerbated by the fact that my partner's family and many of our non-Jewish friends felt, even though we stated otherwise, excluded by these Jewish mourning rituals—most had never even heard of sitting *shiva. Second,* our rabbi felt the need, at our moment of greatest despair, to overtly express his "disapproval" of such interfaith rituals—he spoke out of fear and concern over his reputation rather than love—why is there so much fear surrounding interfaith relationships? *Third,* the symbols of commemoration are themselves in conflict, a conflict that we continue to experience each time we visit the grave. *Last but not least,* there is the question of our views of the afterlife. Yet I refuse to allow conflict to have the last word over cooperation. While some of these tensions still hurt me, I am sure that within a few years they will all be forgotten, and all I will remember, or want to remember, is the incredible love and support both our religious and secular friends[8] expressed through their smiles, meals, presence, and shoulders (which we still use for support). For us, and for them, this tragedy brought us closer, and also served to teach others about the traditions of Judaism, which were unfamiliar to so many. While at present this brings little comfort, I know myself well enough to know that the love and learning that came from our loss will one day be a source of strength for me.

Faith is like the force, it feeds on love and hope and fades when faced with fear and anger. It seems to me that neither Jew nor Catholic could disagree with this Star Wars analogy (the one we used to help our boys deal with their sadness), and yet the greatest barrier to interfaith ritual participation is the fear and distrust both religions express toward interfaith partnerships and all that is associated with such choices. While I have focused here on the painful aspects of interfaith, and specifically Jewish-Catholic, bereavement rituals, the heart of the matter is that if faith is about hope and love, there needs to be a new understanding that an interfaith family can be a gift and blessing to both religions. Had there been some model or story about parental interfaith bereavement, my partner and I might have been spared this little bit of additional pain in a time when we were both drowning in grief. It is this hope that inspired me to write this piece just a few months after I lost Hannah, my precious gift.

Chapter 16

PARAMETERS OF HOSPITALITY FOR INTERRELIGIOUS PARTICIPATION: A JEWISH PERSPECTIVE

Ruth Langer

1 Introduction

I am a Jewish liturgist who serves as a professor of Jewish Studies in a comparative theological context at a Catholic and Jesuit university, a position that has brought me into the world of Christian-Jewish relations and, in that context, into interreligious participation. The invitation to write this chapter has created a welcome opportunity to reflect on these experiences and to offer some thoughts about the factors that contributed to their successes or failures. Because interreligious participation often is more a learning or intellectual experience than a spiritual one, this reflection will focus primarily on a set of factors that make that learning experience possible, namely those shaping the hospitality[1] offered. I suggest that when followers of one religious tradition visit the home of another, the success of that experience will be shaped by the ability of the host and guest to discern and meet each other's needs and expectations. What constitutes a genuine welcome requires a nuanced sensitivity, particularly on the host's part.

In what follows, I trace this through a number of themes. I begin with a discussion of the American (mostly secular but implicitly Christian) culture in which I grew up, and its lurking tensions around anything overtly interreligious, especially prayer. Following this, I develop the theme of hospitality, beginning with cases where I was the guest and looking explicitly at examples where hospitality was offered to me, which with my reception resulted in successful opportunities for interreligious participation, and, in contrast, times where hospitality was not offered by the host or refused by the guest, resulting in limited interreligious contact. The final sections reflect on opportunities I have had to be the host and apply some of the principles learned. These include situations of joint interreligious prayer, where this host-guest dichotomy should break down but often does not.

2 Formative experiences: American secularity

I grew up in an assimilated home, in a family that identified with Reform Judaism, with roots so deep in America that the Holocaust touched us only indirectly. Our cul-de-sac, as far as I knew, consisted of Jews and a few Catholics, but, in the immediate post-Vatican II period, only the football players mixed much. As the "smart" kids who took school seriously, children of an academician, my brothers and I were outsiders to the local social scene. On our way to public school, we walked past the local Catholic church and school daily, but never entered. I recall being secretly afraid of the otherworldly looking nuns in their habits. However, if there was anti-Semitism around us, we were not aware of it. Nonetheless, we never had occasion to enter churches except as tourists; we never had occasion to learn what Christianity was about. I certainly had Christian friends from school, including some Catholics whom I remember only for their large families, but our mutual hospitality extended only to occasional play dates, and religion was never a matter of discussion.

This was the era immediately following the 1962–3 US Supreme Court's ban on any religious expression in state-sponsored public schools, especially organized prayer.[2] My parents had grown up reciting the Lord's Prayer in school along with the Pledge of Allegiance (to the American flag) at the beginning of the school day. My teachers, fairly recently deprived of the first, now were expected to begin the day with "opening exercises," armed with a book of supposedly inspirational poetry and readings to replace the prayer.[3] By 1970 or so, perhaps because of its overall superficiality and inability to set a tone for the day, teachers left this book unopened, and we simply recited the "pledge." During the Vietnam and Watergate eras and their consequent challenge to American patriotism, my teachers dropped even that. As a result, we not only had no Christian prayer imposed on non-Christian students, but we had no prayer at all, and eventually no ritual at all. Perhaps for lack of creativity and leadership, or perhaps because interreligious understanding was still in its infancy even in more progressive neighborhoods, an attempt to find a model for public, child-oriented interreligious (non-)prayer died in infancy.

Deeper issues were opened by the extension of this American "wall between church and state" to public schools. What would the program of winter music classes and concerts be? Could we sing about snow and Santa, but not Christmas and Jesus? Could we compromise instead by sharing our holiday rituals and including some Hanukkah songs?[4] I had Jewish classmates whose parents objected to their singing Christmas carols; my parents, in contrast, enjoyed them (although we adamantly did not celebrate Christmas ourselves). As a child, I learned and sang all the carols with gusto and a complete lack of understanding as to their religious content. Thus, it is hard to classify this as positive interreligious participation.

This removal of religion from the schools, one that had begun with issues of prayer, had impact on curricula as well. While we could learn about the (glorious) Crusaders or the abuses leading to the Reformation in history classes, we could never open a theological text, including any part of the Bible. Ancient

History focused entirely on polytheist societies and lost religions, ignoring the contributions of Jews and Christians. Most vividly, I recall a class rebellion when our tenth grade English teacher of Italian Catholic heritage sought to point out the Christian symbolism in Ernest Hemingway's *The Old Man and the Sea*. We, a class dominated by Jewish students, shouted her down as violating church-state separation. As part of our backlash against the historical one-way imposition of Christian values, we Americans gloried in an ignorance that prevented intelligent interreligious participation even in understanding and appreciating cultural icons. As this one-way imposition had historically most often been conversionary in intent, the Jewish (and atheist-agnostic) reflex was and is still to swing the pendulum to the other extreme and remove all religion from the discourse. However, one nevertheless cannot appreciate most Western literature without asking this teacher's question; and I did reread the novella—last year.

My encounters with living Christianity occurred in other settings. I spent four summers at a supposedly nondenominational summer camp in Colorado, one that held services Sunday morning and sundown. A friend describes its chapel as "vaguely Christian" in decoration, but its memorable aspect was its spectacular mountain view. I never felt uncomfortable there, even singing in the choir. I was probably mostly unaware of any Christian presumptions embedded in the worship, as my own Jewish knowledge was rudimentary at best. If songs mentioned Jesus, I skipped his name, as I knew that I was not to pray to him. However, the only song I recall is "Kumbaya," about which we joke now, but which fit the spirit of the times. The messages taught there were indeed simply human, focused on interpersonal ethics. I felt fully an insider to the camp community, and religious differences simply were not an issue. However, in adulthood, with deeper learning about my own tradition, I came to live an observant life where keeping the Jewish Sabbath and dietary laws matter greatly. My own children went to a Jewish camp on a New Hampshire lake.

My first experience attending a regular church service was a Catholic friend's confirmation in ninth grade. I remember clearly my mother's warning not to join the congregation in kneeling. Instead, I was only to slide forward a bit in the pew so that it would not be so obvious that I was a stranger. I cannot recall her explanation for this; I reconstruct it as her transmitting her own childhood lesson against kneeling before the cross. I also do not recall any instruction against joining in the liturgy, perhaps because she did not know about the post-1970 rite's English and participatory nature, perhaps because omitted words might suffice. In retrospect, this was not so different from her instructions about proper behavior when attending a group bat mitzvah for some orthodox Jewish friends. In both cases I was an outsider; in both cases, the goal was ostensibly to fit in while maintaining internal integrity and difference. In neither case do I recall feeling particularly welcomed at the actual service.

It was during my years in university that my Jewish identity and knowledge really began to develop, including a stronger sense of differentiation from Christian society. A secular, assimilated identity does not leave room for interreligious interactions of substance. Most of my identity development took place through the classroom, though, as well as through involvement in the small Jewish community on campus. It involved minimal "real" interreligious experiences. Dialogue between religious groups was not part of the campus extracurricular world, nor was religion an acceptable topic of dining hall or dorm-life discussion—this was a secular world. The study of religion itself was rigorously historical but nevertheless under threat; faculty who left or retired were not replaced, and the department ceased to exist. Perhaps being at a secular university with Quaker roots discouraged other religious groups from participating deeply in shaping the communal identity.

My deepened Jewish identity and passion for Jewish learning led me to rabbinic school, where life continued to be insular, with the exception of the small group of Christian PhD students also living in the dormitory of Hebrew Union College in Cincinnati. Our attempt at some formal dialogue with them resulted in one program—and a failed resolution to do more. I do remember sensing a need to map out for myself the complex contemporary American Protestant reality, but at the time, the only course on Christianity was an elective on the New Testament. Nor did student pulpits, literally flying visits to corners of the country for two weekends a month, leave time for engagement in interfaith work, either at the pulpit or at school. Even our first year in Jerusalem, which did involve many tours, including to Christian and Muslim sites, never involved any interface with the ritual life in them. The emphasis of the program then was on filling in the many deficits in our Jewish knowledge, not on placing this in dialogue with or learning from other religious expressions.[5]

My shift to increased interreligious participation began during my doctoral work and really developed because of my academic appointment. I have now spent almost two decades in the Theology Department at Boston College, a Catholic and Jesuit university, as its professor of Jewish Studies in the Comparative Theology area. One of the significant consequences of this appointment has been not only my ever-deeper involvement in Christian-Jewish dialogue but also my pedagogic reality of teaching Christians about Judaism. As, from the Jewish perspective, study of Torah is itself a form of worship, teaching Torah in the Boston College context becomes, for me, a significant form of interreligious participation, one that is in many ways more accessible, powerful, and authentic than a ritual experience.

In addition, early in my academic career, mentors in the world of liturgy encouraged my joining the North American Academy of Liturgy (NAAL), a group of several hundred liturgists of whom barely a handful are Jews. Often, I have been the only Jewish participant at the annual conference. Only two or three others have been consistent attendees over the years, and only a few of these are Sabbath observant. This conference has been my most consistent locus of interreligious *participation*, even though most members generally would not describe the experience as interreligious.

Thus, my personal reality, as a Jew growing up in America in a fairly assimilated home, included very minimal exposure to actual participation, even in my own tradition's rituals, until I left home for university. Yes, we attended services on Rosh Hashanah and Yom Kippur, we had a Passover *seder*, we lit candles at Hanukkah, and we attended a few hours weekly of religious education at our synagogue that included a brief service. This was superficial compared to my children's experience at a Jewish school from kindergarten until university that dedicated half of its curricular time to Jewish subjects and required daily participation in prayer. Our family attends synagogue every Sabbath and holiday. Specifically Jewish rituals of prayer, of learning, of eating, structure our family life. However, in both my childhood and my children's childhood, participation in other communities' rituals was and is unusual. Learning with members of other communities, though, has been an increasingly important component of experiencing and thinking about how others live their religious lives. Experiencing their prayer or praying with them has occurred in a few contexts, mostly at Boston College and the NAAL. These experiences will be discussed, not chronologically, but by type, in the following sections.

3 Receiving hospitality: A guest at St John's Abbey

My actual involvement in dialogue began while I was writing my doctoral dissertation. Patrick Henry, with whom I had studied early Christianity as an undergraduate, invited me to participate in a series of summer consultations on "Jewish and Christian Understandings of Scripture" held in retreat at the Institute for Ecumenical and Cultural Research, associated with the Benedictine St John's Abbey in Collegeville, Minnesota. This was my introduction to intense dialogue, as we lived interreligiously: in our formal discussions of the announced topic, in our housing in religiously mixed groups, in our leisure time together, and over meals. We ate with the monks, whose meal times were arranged around prayer or mass in the church next door to the refectory. Thus, it was natural to accept the invitation to learn about the religious life of the abbey, including attending prayer.

This was my first really formative experience of liturgical interreligious participation, made positive because of a dynamic that negotiated positively between the abbey's fundamental offer of hospitality and my comfort zone as a guest. Determining and respecting this comfort zone is critical for successful interreligious participation. When we have houseguests, we try our best to make them feel "at home," but this requires our discerning correctly both our limits and the guests' limits. Do we like to accept help in the kitchen or not, and do the guests feel comfortable helping? Misreading the clues can lead to discomfort on either side. In a ritual situation, the details are different, but the dynamics are similar. Numerous factors shape the possibilities of participation. To what extent does a particular community permit participation by guests? The possibilities range from an impossibility of hospitality because no uninitiated may witness the ritual, to an embrace of any visitor as a fully qualified participant, to any point in between. Guests who do not respect the "rules of the house" violate the proffered hospitality. On the other hand, guests come with their own sets of criteria, some received from their own religious training, some more personal. Possibilities here range from those who feel that entering another religion's worship space is *ab initio* sinful, making it impossible to accept hospitality, to others who prefer to remain spectators, to those who feel free to participate fully. Both the host and the guest need to articulate their parameters to determine their point(s) of overlap and determine if and how interreligious ritual participation can occur.

St John's Abbey offered a warm hospitality. In the abbey church, the monks' choir and the pews for everyone else are on opposite sides of the altar.[6] When we were there midsummer and midweek, the monks' community was by far the larger one, and the vast pews were largely empty. Although not designed to do so and perhaps because we did not sit in the front, this made our small number, even the Catholics, seem like guests. I could be an observer without needing to pretend to participate. That the chanting was divided between two monastic choirs with no obvious role for the laity helped this. The relationships built in our dialogic setting meant that it was easy for my housemate, a Dominican sister, to show personal hospitality as well. I could ask the most basic of questions, not only about the mechanics of the liturgy, but even about her personal religious journey. Many of the details of my lessons have blurred with later more formal learning, but I recall clearly her discussion about kneeling and the degree to which "kicking the habit" with its flowing skirts had reduced the power of the practice for her. These, however, were mostly intellectual lessons, teaching me to be an informed observer, like the guest standing at the kitchen doorway.

Not all of the hospitality came from Catholics, though. Another participant in this consultation was the veteran Jewish dialogue participant, Rabbi Leon Klenicki. He helped me begin to struggle with the ins and outs of actually participating in parts of the liturgy, especially the morning and evening prayer that consisted significantly of the chanting of the Psalms, that is, our shared texts. Could I join these monks in singing about Israel, when we did not understand the word to hold the same meaning? He was much more comfortable than I was, as I recall, and indeed encouraged me to learn this side of Catholic life. On the other hand, neither of us took up the invitation of one of the monks, also a priest, born a Jew, whose hospitality extended to offering that we partake of the Eucharist. We did have extensive conversation with him about this (not during mass!), and it was clear that he was not combining this with any overt invitation to baptism. Rather, he apparently found the demarcation of identity created by excluding his people, the Jews, from communion, to be theologically problematic.

However, this transgressed the teachings of his church, which welcomes unbaptized guests to its pews but not to partake of the Eucharist. It also exceeded our comfort zones as guests, not only because we knew it transgressed this basic Catholic rule, but even more because it would constitute a symbolic gesture of our participation in fundamental Christian beliefs. Jews do not accept Christian theological understandings of the meaning of Jesus's life, death, and resurrection; therefore, accepting the Eucharist simply as physical nourishment is far from an empty gesture. It becomes, not an act of communion, but potentially an act of mockery. Thus, this is a situation when "standing outside the kitchen" is the appropriate place for the guest, a stance that respects that which goes on within by not participating.

4 Refusing hospitality

There are other occasions where offers of hospitality misjudge the guests' comfort zones and result in their needing to refuse it. I regularly respond this way at Boston College. The university encourages all community members to participate in its official Catholic liturgies, whether this is the opening element of freshman orientation in the summer (where there has been significant official resistance to announcing or staffing any alternative gatherings), the baccalaureate mass before graduation, or encouraging faculty to join processions in academic regalia. There are hints that they expect parallel prayer to occur in these settings, at least for Protestants. But parallel prayer requires that the greater setting be religiously neutral, and these are not, at least for non-Christians. The university does not recognize that when it comes to religious matters, some community members remain guests who prefer to stand outside. While I will attend a funeral mass or a mass of healing for a colleague as a gesture of caring for the people involved, I personally draw the line at becoming part of a religious procession behind the cross. The cross is a symbol of deep significance to Christians, but it marks precisely those points where Christianity and Judaism differ. In addition, while for Christians, the cross is a sign of love, for Jews it is deeply associated with a history of persecution by Christians.[7] While I am comfortable accepting hospitality as a guest at the religious rituals of others, I am not comfortable if this extends to making me a participant in symbolic actions that are specifically not Jewish.[8]

There are observant Jews who will not enter the place of worship of another religion, in obedience to the biblical and rabbinic prohibitions on participating in *avodah zarah*, literally "strange worship," sometimes inadequately translated "idolatry." This applies even to entering a religious space as a tourist, not only to witnessing a ritual. A colleague passed up a private, night-time tour of the otherwise closed Aachen Cathedral for this reason. Another toured the Vatican Museum but avoided entering the Sistine Chapel. Obviously, I have made different decisions; one cannot study liturgy comparatively without experiencing it to the degree possible. However, this concern about participating in an improper form of worship, especially if it violates the Jewish understanding that worship may not involve any sort of physical imaging of God, does lurk behind much of what I have written here. While medieval Jews found ways to understand Christian Trinitarian worship as permissible for gentiles, for Jews, it was and remains "strange worship." As a theology professor at a Catholic university, I need to try to understand Christian liturgy, but, as a Jew, I cannot participate fully in it. While I went to the Aachen Cathedral and marveled at it, I did not approach the relics. I do not genuflect or kneel. At best, I can be a guest, a spectator, knowing that even that crosses a line. When I find myself at a church service where the preliminary rite includes sprinkling the entire congregation to remind them of their baptisms, I wish I had a place to hide.

This issue affects intersections with other religions as well. In 2010, my husband and I lectured and toured in China. Religious sites were high on our agenda, but that turned out to be a challenge. Apparently, those raised under Communism's antireligious norms either could not or would not be hosts to their own heritage. Many guides did not think them important, resisted taking us into some easily accessible and very important temples,[9] and could teach us little once we entered. The information we received about the imperial worship at the Temple of Heaven was just wrong. The Confucian Temple in Beijing was fully inaccessible. In Nanjing, the graduate student who took us to the Confucian Temple was clearly uncomfortable. But we had an opposite experience with an extremely hospitable Chinese colleague who knew a bit about Buddhist practice and belief from his grandmother. He took us to the only remaining Buddhist temple within the walls of Nanjing. We were glad to see the architecture, to appreciate the statuary, and to learn. This left us comfortably as spectator guests. However, our colleague, seeking to deepen our learning, in his genuine hospitality, decided to buy some incense and demonstrate an incense offering for us. I am unsure if he sensed our discomfort or understood it: watching a stranger make an offering is neutral; in Jewish understanding, causing someone to make an offering implicates us in the offering, which crosses an important line into problematic secondary participation in the worship itself.

A host may also have limits on how much hospitality can be offered—but there are various ways to achieve this. The NAAL deliberately moves around North America so as to explore local liturgical scenes. This used to include many field trips.[10] The memory of one trip endures, mostly because it includes an instructive counter-example to the hospitality necessary for effective interreligious participation. A group of us, probably all Christians except me, visited a Russian Orthodox church for its Sunday liturgy. Fortuitously, as I had never experienced this liturgy before, a colleague served as a guide. I was immensely grateful for his personal hospitality that reduced my sense of being an utter stranger. I do not recall how much of the liturgy was in English, but the opportunity to watch people, to seek to understand their veneration of the icons, to hear the music, was all wonderful. However, when they reached the point of communion, the priest interrupted the flow of the service, announcing loudly in English and seemingly at length, that anyone not baptized in the Orthodox communion was forbidden to partake. Perhaps this was their normal announcement, but given the presence of our group, it felt like we were unwanted, even as guests. Unlike me, perhaps some of these liturgists did indeed plan to take communion, making some intervention necessary. This announcement, though, shattered the precarious balance between being welcomed guests and strangers.

5 Shared hospitality: Joint prayer

A society that thinks about liturgy also does liturgy, and three of the NAAL's conference liturgies—the opening and closing liturgies and the table prayer at the banquet—are meant to be fully nondenominational, welcoming complete participation by people of any faith.[11] In interreligious experiences with an obvious host, the combination of the guests' comfort level and religious beliefs with the host community's rules determines whether the guests remain interested spectators or join in some or all of the prayer. The host's welcome negotiates between maximal hospitality and respecting the guest's degree of desire to remain a guest. In joint prayer, by contrast, this distinction between host and guest ought not to be present. The interreligious experience fails as liturgy if attendees feel like guests. Constructing them, thus, presents a quite different set of challenges.

Depending on the location of the conference and logistics, some of the NAAL's joint liturgies may be held in local liturgical spaces, especially when these spaces offer some element of particular interest. My first year at the conference, that local space was Cincinnati's Plum Street Temple, the historic downtown synagogue. I had been there before many times. Hebrew Union College—Jewish Institute of Religion, my seminary, holds its ordination services there, packing its nave to the gills. This NAAL service was different. The community around me was much smaller and almost entirely Christian. Appropriate to the space, not a single liturgical element was counter to Jewish tradition and, indeed, much was drawn from it, including especially the older traditions of American Reform Judaism which had many roots in this 1865 building. Supplied with the music, though, these liturgists joined in the singing full voice and with harmonies, filling this cathedral-like[12] space in a way that I had never experienced. This introduced a foreign, albeit very welcome, energy into a usually staid sanctuary. Thus while the Jewish setting nominally extended hospitality, what mattered then was the enthusiastic, unified community of prayer. These were guests who went beyond "offering to help in the kitchen." Instead, keeping to the host's recipes, they prepared the meal. On other years, this opening liturgy, without so many specifically Jewish elements, has taken place in beautiful and/or historic Christian liturgical spaces as well.

Many years, for logistical reasons, the academy committee has chosen instead to create its own neutral liturgical space in the hotel, mitigating the host-guest dynamic almost entirely. However, this "almost" remains significant. Frequently, I have been consulted in planning this opening and as well as the closing liturgy.[13] The challenge regularly confronting my colleagues—who genuinely want to construct a joint liturgy that removes the host-guest dichotomy—is to discern what constitutes a structure and content that really invites interreligious comfort and participation in joint prayer. Some elements are more obvious. Symbols and words that reflect obviously Christian faith exclude Jews. When we meet in a church, there will be crosses or crucifixes and Christmas decorations, but the words are under our control. When we meet in the hotel, though, these symbols can be avoided. My colleagues understand that as Jews do not pray to Jesus or the Trinity, prayers and hymns framed to or about God with this language exclude. Scripture readings should come from our shared Scriptures.

However, deeper questions regularly emerge. How does one choose a reading? The Jewish reflex is to look to the weekly cycle; even for Christians who follow the common lectionary, its readings are less likely to be useful interreligiously, especially during the Christmas season. Do customary Christological interpretations of an Old Testament reading matter if they go unstated? And does one structure the service according to the Christian pattern, in which the Scripture reading precedes the most important prayers, or according to the Jewish pattern, in which it follows them? In reality, I never did more than name the last issue to my colleagues, but it is not a trivial matter. Those who participate regularly in liturgy have expectations about its fundamental grammar. When all of the liturgy is strange, it is much more challenging to participate fully and wholeheartedly. Does operating in a foreign ritual structure transform participants into guests? Is this just a necessary prerequisite to joint prayer that, at least at some point, some will inevitably feel like guests? This is a huge unresolved theoretical issue for the construction of interreligious prayer.

The more subtle the issues, the more difficult they were to resolve. Sometimes, a particular prayer or hymn apparently fit all the criteria for being non-denominational—it named or alluded just to God, using non-Trinitarian, non-Christological language; its sentiments seemed universal. However, the person planning the liturgy was unaware that the theology expressed was explicitly Christian, not universal. We had an extended "discussion" one year over my insistence that the lyrics of "Amazing Grace" express a profoundly Christian theology about original sin and salvation, inappropriate for Jewish participation. Jews do not share the Christian reading of Genesis 3, and hence do not accept that the way to salvation is through God's "amazing grace" (expressed in the sacrifice of Christ).[14] While the hymn has a wonderful melody, and I probably sang it as a child at summer camp, I cannot sing it now. I do not understand myself as once "lost," and those who do would not consider me now "found." We found better solutions with hymns that do indeed voice universal hopes, even when in the historic Latin of the church, like *Dona Nobis Pacem*. In this, I can join wholeheartedly. Another year, we discovered that modern Israelis had borrowed a beautiful setting of the final verse of the Psalter from Christian usage, so we sang the words in Hebrew and Latin.

A community of professional liturgists is perhaps likely to be the most successful venue in which to search for innovative ritual paths. There is little precedent for this before recent decades, given the human history of interreligious misunderstanding and use of liturgy as a conversionary tool. However, we have made numerous attempts over the years to construct "multi-religious" liturgical experiences at Boston College. Elements of this have grown out of responses to outside events: a memorial service for Itzhak Rabin after his assassination in 1995, and a subsequent prayer for peace in Jerusalem.[15] Our seminarians held a Holocaust Memorial Service. All of these required discussions not dissimilar to my experiences with the NAAL liturgists. More interesting are the outgrowths of a now-defunded attempt at an Interfaith Initiative on campus, one of whose annual liturgies continues. Conscious that all university-wide liturgies were Catholic, this group developed two services to celebrate the diversity of our community, one near the time of the opening Mass of the Holy Spirit in September, and an ongoing Multi-Faith Thanksgiving Service preceding our November civic holiday. These celebrations consisted of reflections, music, or liturgical snippets from a variety of religious traditions, addressing a common theme, read or performed by representatives of these religions.[16] However, the celebration lacked a shared "grammar" and basis in familiarity. The people gathered felt more like an audience than a community; they did not leave the service inspired, educated, or transformed (though the gospel choirs have been a hit).

This observation speaks to the deep challenge of constructing real interreligious participation. How does a diverse group of people create a ritual that is familiar enough to all that they can go beyond intellectual appreciation of its words and join in its performative levels of communication, thus melding them even momentarily into a united community? Gatherings convened around civic events that include calls to action or a purpose may be the most successful, as long as they are prepared with sensitivity.[17] But at the same time, such events are all too often constructed as a staged series of presentations to a passive audience, leaving them as listeners, not participants. Thus, there is no clear host, and everyone feels a guest. It may be that another model sometimes discussed, that of parallel prayer—where all simultaneously use their native modes of worship—is more effective, but I have not experienced this.

6 *Offering hospitality*

Over the years, there have been various opportunities for me to offer liturgical hospitality both at Boston College and at the NAAL. In both cases, what has been most successful is for me to bring my "guests" into the Jewish setting. As liturgy is a focus of many of my courses, I require my students to experience it. The modes in which this has operated have varied over the years, but generally I have sought out the most hospitable settings in which the students will experience the liturgy, not necessarily with deep comprehension, but with an appreciation for its esthetics and performance. The most accessible service will always be Friday night, and because I am strictly Sabbath-observant, if I am to join the students, it must be within walking distance of my home. I do not take students to my Orthodox synagogue where men and women sit separately, the service is entirely in Hebrew with no pages announced, and liturgical performance is uneven, often uninspiring.[18] From my experiences visiting unfamiliar liturgical contexts, I know how important it is to demonstrate hospitality by guiding guests through the service.

In recent years, I have been able to arrange class visits to a synagogue with a large, demonstrably welcoming congregation, where there is ample space for us all to sit together, and where the liturgy is performed with enthusiasm and professionalism. Even though the liturgy is all Hebrew, they announce pages and use a prayer book with four parallel columns: Hebrew, transliterated Hebrew, English, and commentary. These deliberate, recent, and successful innovations have swelled their own attendance from a few dozen to several hundred. Prior to this, they once asked us not to come because their small chapel would be too full; another year we were welcomed, but to a service geared to preschoolers. We can now show up almost without prior notice, but with arrangement, the rabbis meet with the class afterward and answer questions.

What do my students get out of this? Unless this is a course only on liturgy, they have had only the most rudimentary introduction to the synagogue and its prayers in class. I do not expect them to catch the verbal content of the service.

They comment on the joy of the music, the participation of the congregation and especially its children, the choreography and body language of the worshippers, the welcome, the space and its symbols, and so forth. Whether they participate or not is very much their own choice—their limits as guests are respected—but the opportunity is given to them. While the synagogue does have limits on its hospitality (it counts only Jews in its quorum and only calls Jews up to the Torah), none of these are evident when hundreds of people come to pray, and a Friday night service does not include Torah reading.

I do also regularly teach a class on the Passover *seder*. Especially if the class is spring semester, I invite them to my home during the festival, not for our family *seder*, which involves too much Hebrew (and regularly lasts five hours), but for their own, where they are responsible for leading and teaching sections of the *Haggadah*. Thus, they experience not only the ritual foods, but the festive meal as well. The *seder*, after all, is fundamentally a home-based, table-based ritual.

How to offer hospitality authentically at the liturgy conference has not been a trivial challenge, but as three of the liturgies are always denomination specific, I have been invited to try. A complete public Jewish liturgy traditionally requires a community of ten Jews,[19] a number we have not yet achieved. The traditional liturgy is also entirely in Hebrew, a language most NAAL members do not know. This forces us to abbreviate our services and use much translation, both of which mean not welcoming these guests to my preferred sort of Jewish liturgical practice. One year, with some help, I led a Jewish weekday morning prayer for the group. To distinguish it from the Sabbath and festivals, the weekday liturgy is businesslike, fast-paced, with unimpressive chant, limiting its appeal and making it more difficult to construct a sense of community.

More successfully, another year we gathered about thirty people for a rousing yet restfully paced Sabbath eve service in the hotel, followed by a kosher meal, a complete set of Friday night rituals. A joyful yet simple set of melodies has become popular for the extended set of Psalms introducing this service; using them capitalized on the willingness of this community to sing along enthusiastically. Providing transliterations allowed all to recite the Hebrew. The following year, a small synagogue near the hotel was eager for us to join them for services and allowed us to use their social hall for our dinner. I welcomed these, not only because it allowed me to extend hospitality to my friends and share my tradition, but also because it decreased the existential loneliness of spending the Sabbath away from home, family, and synagogue. The NAAL's interest in supporting these was its own expression of hospitality. While participants welcomed these services enthusiastically—indeed, they had no inhibitions as guests—the logistics in most cities did not allow them to be continued.

7 Conclusion

One final example blends many of the categories of this discussion, describing a rich locus of sensitively offered hospitality. One year my teaching assistant was a local Greek Orthodox priest, and he warmly invited our undergraduate comparative class to experience his liturgical world. We were careful to teach elements of Greek Orthodox practice in class before arranging a Sunday morning visit. It was a remarkable morning, again, primarily because of the hospitality shown to us. Father Tonias asked seminarians whom he mentored to guide us and answer questions throughout the service, substantial parts of which were in Greek. He thoughtfully suggested that our students arrive at ten in the morning, prepared for a two-hour liturgy. However, knowing well my liturgical interests, he invited me to experience everything within the realm of the possible, as defined from both our perspectives, resulting in a four-hour immersive experience. I arrived for the Office of Preparation, and he invited me to stand on the top step at the door of the *iconostasion* to view and learn about the preparation of the Eucharistic elements and the details of the liturgical robing within the sanctuary behind it. Matins (*Orthros*) followed before the students (and most of the congregation) arrived for the main Sunday liturgy; I stayed on to witness the concluding rituals in the sanctuary and join the coffee hour before going out for lunch.

My students and I fully remained guests, but honored, welcomed ones. Even the priest's sermon cleverly included elements of interest to the class while ostensibly being addressed mostly to the young children grouped at his feet. Nevertheless, we lacked sufficient knowledge of the liturgy's words and chants to join in; without Orthodox baptism, Eucharistic participation was out of the question for all. However, unlike my prior experience, there was no announcement about who could participate in communion; had the issue arisen, it would have been handled discretely. After all, the officiating priest knew each guest by name. From the perspective of creating a zone of comfort in which learning could occur, of building relationships, the visit was successful, especially because our roles as host and guest were carefully and thoughtfully defined.

Thus, my experience teaches that hospitality is an indispensable element of successful interreligious participation, but this hospitality must be nuanced and respectful of the guest's own religious concerns and limits. With this sensitivity, a host can welcome others as guests to an experience that will increase interreligious understanding while not threatening the individual's identity. In an ideal world, there could even be situations of mutual, simultaneous hospitality where people of different religious traditions construct a joint ritual experience into which both can enter fully. However, for this to function as religious ritual, it must have a compelling shared purpose which draws a diverse group of people into a community.

Chapter 17

EPILOGUE: INTER-RITING AS A PECULIAR FORM OF LOVE

Joris Geldhof

There is no doubt about the importance of the topics discussed in the present volume. This importance is both of a practical and a theoretical nature; it affects not only many people and the (religious) communities they belong to, but also scholars of religion and their disciplines. Practices of participation in rituals of "other" religious traditions constitute a complex area of reflection and research, which has become increasingly significant—at least in the area typically identified as "the West"—and which is rapidly evolving in many directions. The goal of the present book is to shed light on these multiple phenomena, and to do that not only from the perspective of different religions but also from a variety of scholarly angles. Moreover, one should not forget that scholars of religion are often simple practitioners of their own religion as well. A combination of insider and outsider perspectives is at least very helpful to map the area where ritual participation and interreligious dialogue interfere and overlap. In any case, in order to explore the field of ritual practices in which members of other religious traditions participate, there is no other option but to carefully listen to many voices, whereby personal experiences—both positive and negative—and theoretical reflections are equally important, and whereby the borders between both these discourses are crossed.

The aim of this epilogue cannot consist in attempts at recapitulating, comparing, or synthesizing the individual chapters. No matter which approach I would adopt in doing so would do serious injustice to the richness and profundity of the authors' insights and ideas. Rather, I take the liberty of commenting on some of the overall results articulated by the contributors to this book. I do that with a view to indicating avenues for further research, and I cannot but do that while including my own background, interests, and profile as a liturgical theologian, one who is specializing in the study of the meaning of the ritual and worshipping practices of Christians. The most useful way to structure my thoughts is to center them on four crucial concepts, which I think in one way or another run through the entire book. These categories are complexity, hospitality, contingency, and sensitivity.

1) *Complexity*. If there is one thing that becomes apparent in this book, it is the dazzling complexity of the phenomenon under consideration. There are many

factors, aspects, or dimensions in play when one enters the field of "inter-riting," and there are not fewer layers and degrees of intensity with which the phenomenon is experienced, appreciated, and evaluated. One can think of factors like the size and composition of the communities, the places where inter-riting happens, the concrete occasions and reasons why it happens, the motivations before and the impressions afterward, and so forth. One has to take into account, for example, the form and function of the ritual (life cycle rituals, cosmic rites, seasonal or agrarian rites, prayer services, petitioning and worshiping ceremonies, etc.), the roles ascribed to humans and deities involved, social and cultural influences, and differences between religious leaders and the larger populace.

Another important factor is the nature of the religious tradition itself within which members of other religions are participating ritually. Belief tenets may not entirely grasp what is occurring; traditional rules of conduct may not apply; classical ways of celebrating and customary patterns of behavior may be challenged; and doctrinal statements about one's religious self-understanding may fall short—but all these things do matter. Likewise significant are the mechanisms of authority and group discipline within the communities and traditions that "allow" "others" in their own midst when they celebrate and worship. The authors in this book shed light on many of these factors and dimensions and the intriguing ways in which they can intertwine. In a particular manner, many of the theoretical intuitions of ritual studies scholar Catherine Bell are confirmed: ritual "is not an intrinsic, universal category or feature of human behavior" but "a cultural and historical construction that has been heavily used to help differentiate various styles and degrees of religiosity, rationality, and cultural determinism" (Bell 2009: ix).

Beyond all complexity, however, remains a stratum of perplexity. What one might experience in interreligious ritual encounters is something beyond words and concepts, even if they capture something essential of what is going on. One's own tradition might lack the appropriate framework to give one's experiences a place, and it is likely that the "other" religious tradition is also failing to accommodate the "right" interpretation. This perplexity may paradoxically point to a certain "beyond-contextness" in the midst of variegating situations that are deeply rooted in and informed by the concrete milieu in which they occur. We are no doubt dealing here with a kind of particularity to which our generalizing frames of reference and traditional theologies are no longer adapted. The point is, however, that it seems impossible to create yet another frame, interpretation, or theory within which practices and experiences of inter-riting would perfectly fit, for we are touching a level of existential depth and meaningfulness far beyond the problematizable—or, as Gabriel Marcel would say, a mystery.

In other words, the complexity of the phenomenon under discussion reveals an astonishing perplexity, which is not reducible to an individual fact, an action, a problem, a theme, an experience, a metaphor, a symbol, or whatever; it must always be, as became evident in this book, a combination of several of these *together*. Future reflection about interreligious encounters in and through ritual settings will have to create languages which, on the one hand, further unfold the intricacy of inter-riting but, on the other hand, respect its mysterious nature. This perplexity has, above all, to do with the irreducible specificity of rite and ritual, which can never be a mere object of research.

2) *Hospitality*. The dynamics of hospitality constitutes another central issue that was addressed in many chapters, both explicitly and at an implicit level. The notion of hospitality is a telling and interesting category to conceptualize issues in both interreligious dialogue and ritual studies, although it is not infrequently taken in a cheap and superficial way. Hospitality, when deeply understood, is not just about friendliness and trying to make someone else feel at ease. It is not only about words and simple gestures of welcome. Hospitality evokes and denotes fundamental attitudes toward the real stranger, who is not regarded as an intruder but as someone to whom honors are due. It is more about respect and veneration than about tolerance and accommodation. In the best Levinasian tradition, one could say that the balance between the self and the other is reversed. Hospitality springs from humility, not from pride in one's merits and achievements. Its basis is not mere emotion or affection but the recognition of shared humanness.

Undoubtedly, hospitality is a notion—as well as a reality—which deserves close attention when practices of inter-riting are explored, described, and discussed in the future. One of the reasons for this is that hospitality, as a concept, allows for the flexibility and fluidity of the practices under consideration. On the one hand, there is the hospitality one gives in the capacity of host. In ideal circumstances, one organizes the meeting at which the guests are invited in such a way that they feel comfortable. In the case of ritual settings, however, this is by no means obvious, let alone always guaranteed. For it may happen that there are non-invited guests, or that they behave—innocently or not—inappropriately, or that the expectations of the host community at large are by no means met, which results in anger, frustration, and grousing among the members. How to act as a host in ritual for religious "strangers" is not evident at all. But being a host has certain advantages which one lacks as a guest (and vice versa): the boundaries of the regular and the familiar are somehow always kept. One does not (have to) leave the natural milieu where one's religious self feels at home.

This is no longer the case, at least in principle, if one is a guest in the rituals of another religious tradition. Therefore, this entry into the phenomenon of inter-ritual participation poses another set of challenges. There are different degrees of uncertainty. One is not always sure how far one can go in view of what one's own tradition would allow under "normal" circumstances. It may happen, however, that the limits of the normal are significantly stretched and no longer recognizable, and this can be valued both positively and negatively. It is also possible that it is unclear how far one can go according to the other's standards, rules, and expectations. One can definitely become a border-crosser against one's own will and at the same time regardless of the will of the other. To know how far one can go, moreover, is only rarely a matter of information and documentation. It never hurts to know some generalities and details in advance, but very often the ritual unfolds in a way which surpasses the rationalizable and controllable. One can find oneself suddenly dancing, even if one knows what that means and had strongly admonished oneself not to do it. This raises additional questions, of course, about ritual and embodiedness, but it would lead us too far astray if we developed that issue in some depth.

In any case, it seems invaluable to further explore the hermeneutics of hospitality. Scholars involved in and fascinated by inter-riting are invited to reflect about, and from, both host- and guest-perspectives. This double possibility sheds light on the individual experiences of persons as well as on the dynamics at play in religious communities in a subtle and nuanced way. Insights from sociology, philosophy, and anthropology could be particularly helpful in this respect.

3) *Contingency*. If it is true that religion is, to no limited extent, a fundamental form of *Kontingenzbewältigung* (Luhmann 1977)—coping with contingency—the same can be said par excellence of ritual. Rituals communicate, mediate, and express symbolic meanings, and can probably best be understood as symbolic actions that perform or realize something which invites (or incites) one to partake. Instead of being anticipated by logics, ideas, or vocabularies, rituals do and shape meaning; the minds grasping (something of) their meaning and the bodies living them are always *a posteriori*. Therefore, it is fair to say that there is a priority of ritual over the subjects participating in it. Nevertheless, rites and rituals do not and cannot escape the radical contingency and finitude within which humanity flourishes. The human condition is always embedded in concrete circumstances; one does injustice to human beings if one turns their lives and life conditions into abstractions. This is likely to be the most fundamental reason the chapters in this book display an inalienable devotion to concreteness. The turn to case studies and reported experiences is not an admission of weakness because of some incapacity to construct theories or generally valid knowledge; it is the highest possible proof for the appropriateness of the authors' selected approaches.

The logical opposite of contingency is necessity. But in the field of religion, rite, and ritual, logic and rational deduction are of little use. The strict opposition between the two concepts is blurred (Grube and Jonkers 2008). At the practical level of their (f)actual performance, rituals are definitely bound to contingency. Things may happen or not happen, be foreseen or not foreseen, be provided or not provided. The laws of finitude apply. At the level of their form, shape, or essence, however, one tries to escape sheer contingency and add, protect, or install some kind of necessity. Inasmuch as rituals are symbolic actions, there is a dimension of stubbornness or reluctance toward the merely contingent. Apparently, people have a deep awareness that, in ritual, things somehow have to be as they are and as they have always been, even if they manifest themselves, obviously, through time and in the world. But from within historical confines there is a profound desire for what goes beyond the "timing" of time and hence creates (at least the illusion of) a certain stability in the midst of fragmentariness, arbitrariness, and transitoriness. Symbols and rituals aim at a certain absoluteness; they become obsolete inasmuch as they are no longer absolute.

This tension is important for scholars involved in the study of inter-riting. The life of rituals as symbolic actions seems dependent on their capacity to escape contingency. But, on the other hand, if they do that in a way which completely denies the laws of finitude, they will soon be perceived as inhuman and fall into desuetude anyway. An interesting question is what elements of contingency and necessity are touched when religious strangers are received into the ritual bosom of one's own religion. Is their participation "absolutely not done," "just an accident," or something in between? No doubt that the very vitality of religious traditions is intrinsically challenged when "others" appear in their midst.

4) *Sensitivity*. Finally, it strikes one how crucial sensitivity is, not only at a psychological and emotional level but also as exercising the art of tactfulness. Typical of tact is that it neither obeys strict laws nor follows rigid rules. Just like politeness, there is a pattern or logic, understandable only from a cultural background, but not an elaborate juridical system. Tact and sensitivity are situated beyond the legal and the legitimate. As the contributors have shown, this sensitivity is essential in any act of host or guest in inter-riting. Often, it is not possible to rely on a stable tradition or on clear statements stipulating what to do. Much is left to the individual conscience of people and the spontaneous intuitions of the groups to which they belong. This can be both an advantage and a disadvantage, depending on the occasion. The point is, however, that even if traditions and authoritative bodies within them were more straightforward, still the variety of existing practices would not be covered. The reason is, again, ritual's being irreducible to thought (intelligence), prescription (ethics), and emotion (religiosity). The "ritual rest" of religion is more obstinate than one often assumes, and is approached only truly if one looks at it as something beyond belief contents, moral maxims, and expressions of feelings. One should approach it with due sensitivity.

Interestingly, sensitivity is the appropriate way to solidarity. Solidarity cannot be enforced or compelled unless deeper layers of shared humanity are invoked, the same undercurrents that manifest themselves in ritual. Hence, participation in the rituals of other religions may make one receptive to connections beyond the imaginable. Maybe rituals and inter-riting are capable of achieving things that other typically human actions are unable to realize. Establishing bonds of solidarity where politics, economy, ideologies, religious institutions, and even art fail might be one of them. But then, of course, conditions must be optimal; there must be confidence, openness to exchange, and reverence for the unexchangable. Rituals, however, may not only require such attributes, but also may be the resource for them. Beyond the dichotomy of the possible and the impossible, inter-riting entails a great potential for the future of humanity and the religious richness of the world. It is up to scholars and thinkers to further explore this potential.

In sum, one could draw a striking parallel between practices of inter-riting and the phenomenon of love (Marion 2007; Jeanrond 2010). Just like love, practices of participation in other religions' rituals is complex, both in the sense of being difficult and multilayered. It is a complex of activity and receptivity circling around apt ways to receive the other in one's own intimacy and about being received in the other's heart—very much like hospitality. Further, it is the case in both love and inter-riting that one longs for the other-than-contingent; not everything could always be otherwise. There are limits to how much difference one can bear. Finally, love and inter-riting are not captured by ideas and emotions alone.

Because of their bodily nature and the symbolic way in which they express and communicate themselves, they require above all a fine-tuned sensitivity. The last word of this book, then, may be in the order of a wish: that all women and men may approach and enjoy each other's religious rituals always carefully, receptively, and sensitively.

NOTES

Chapter 1

1 In his chapter to this volume Douglas Pratt makes further distinctions, but for the purpose of this introduction, I will limit myself to these two types.
2 For India, Selva Raj and Corrinne Dempsey edited a volume called *Popular Christianity in India: Riting Between the Lines* (New York: State University of New York Press, 2002). See also Michael Carrithers, "On Polytropy: Or the Natural Condition of Spiritual Cosmopolitanism in India: The Digambar Jain Case," *Modern Asian Studies* 34:4 (2000): 831–61.
3 As I argue elsewhere, religious knowledge is in part explicit knowledge, that is, codified knowledge that can be found in scripture and its commentaries, teachings, and guidelines. This faith can be communicated with relative ease and may even be accessible to outsiders. Marianne Moyaert, "Inappropriate Behavior? On the Ritual Core of Religion and its Challenges to Interreligious Hospitality," *Journal of the Academic Study of Religion* 27 (2014): 1–21.
4 The word "liturgy" is used here in a broad sense to denote the symbolic system as well as the rites, rituals, and gestures, and the structure, shape, and forms of worship that each religious community has evolved in the course of translating its faith into a sustained ritual practice, especially in community. See: W. Ariarajah, *Not Without My Neighbour: Issues in Interfaith Relations* (Geneva: WCC, 1999); A. Chupungco, *What, Then, Is Liturgy? Musings and Memoir* (Collegeville: Liturgical Press, 2010).
5 Etymologically the word "sacred" derives from the Hebrew *qadash*, to be set apart and dedicated for some specific religious purpose and thus forbidden, withheld or removed. The dictionary by Koehler and Baumgartner (KBL) lists the various meanings as "to be holy, withheld from profane use, to be treated with special care, fallen to the sanctuary's share."

Chapter 2

1 See Jeannine Hill Fletcher, *Monopoly on Salvation?: A Feminist Approach to Religious Pluralism* (New York: Continuum, 2005). Michelle Voss Roberts, *Dualities: A Theology of Difference*, 1st ed. (Louisville: Westminster John Knox Press, 2010). Both authors explore the way in which the assumption of either/or identities leads people to ignore the hybridized character of all identities.

2 Receiving transmission from a teacher or acceptance as a member or leader in a given community would be such signs of belonging. Such recognition is a social act and not simply an individual choice. See Catherine Cornille, *Many Mansions? Multiple Religious Belonging and Christian Identity*, Faith Meets Faith (Maryknoll: Orbis, 2002).

3 A summary of these theologies can be found in Paul Knitter, *Introducing Theologies of Religion* (Maryknoll: Orbis, 2002).

4 Jonathan Haidt, *The Righteous Mind: Why Good People Are Divided by Politics and Religion*, 1st edn (New York: Pantheon Books, 2012). The book was much discussed for Haidt's finding that those regarded as political liberals in the context of the United States tend to ground their responses almost entirely on concern for harm, unfairness, and certain types of oppression, largely to the exclusion of the other values. Those regarded as conservative register the pull of all six values in significant ways.

5 A smaller number approved the behaviors in question, arguing in some cases against their own emotional response that since no one was harmed they were acceptable. We are aware that moral intuitions are to some extent variable, formed by the cultural groups we belong to. In the past those intuitions have included some we now condemn (revulsion at those of other races, for instance). With that awareness, in some cases we seek to veto our intuitions through more abstract, universal reasoning. Haidt's observation is that our reasoning serves our emotional intuitions more often than it trumps them. Sustained change in human behavior involves alteration in those intuitions as well as in our arguments.

6 You can take a survey of your own profile on these moral intuitions at http://www.exploringmyreligion.org/.

7 He advances arguments that each of these moral intuitions has a basis in our evolutionary development, a basis that remains valid today. Some of them are weighted more heavily toward protecting the interests of individuals against "free riding" or exploitation by others, and some more heavily toward the good of healthy groups (which is ultimately advantageous for members and their kin).

8 See Chapter 10 in P. Knitter, *Introducing Theologies of Religion* (Maryknoll: Orbis Books, 2002).

Chapter 3

1 For his biography see Ursula Baatz, *Hugo M. Enomiya-Lassalle. Ein Leben zwischen den Welten* (Zürich und Düsseldorf: Benzinger Verlag, 1998). Since 1948 there have been more than 100 publications from Hugo M. Enomiya-Lassalle in Japanese, German, English, French, Italian, Spanish, Dutch, Swedish, and Korean. His German publications include *Meditation als Weg zur Gotteserfahrung* (Matthias-Grünewald Verlag, 1980); *Wohin geht der Mensch* (Benzinger Verlag, 1985); *Leben im neuen Bewusstsein* (München, 1986); *Zen und christliche Mystik*, (Freiburg: Herder, 1986); *Zen-Unterweisung* (München: Kösel Verlag, 1987); *Zen und christliche Spiritualität* (München: Kösel Verlag, 1987); *Zen Meditation für Christen* (München: O.W. Barth Verlag, 1995).

2 The encounter and taking refuge with Shih-fu is described in the personal introduction to the book on pp. 7–51.

3 On the topic of dual belonging see Rose Drew, *Buddhist and Christian? An Exploration into Dual Belonging* (New York: Routledge Critical Studies in Buddhism, 2012), and also Harold Kasimow, John P. Keenan, and Linda Klepinger Keenan (eds), *Beside Still Waters: Jews, Christians, and the Way of the Buddha* (Boston: Wisdom Publications, 2003).

4 On the Museum, see Maria Reis Habito, "Master Hsin Tao's Vision: The Museum of World Religions," in Arvind Sharma (ed.), *The World's Religions After September 11* (London: Praeger Perspectives, 2009), vol. 3, 3–13. www.mwr.org.tw.

5 The website of the Elijah Interfaith Institute is www.elijah-interfaith.org.

6 For the history and teachers of the Sanbo Zen lineage, see www.sanbo-zen.org.

7 On Rabbi Froman, see "Menachem Froman, Rabbi Seeking Peace, Dies at 68," *New York Times*, March 10, 2013, and Yossi Klein Halevi, "Lessons from a Man of Peace," *Jerusalem Post*, March 6, 2013.

8 See H. Klein, "'Allah!' rief der Rabbi," *Die Welt*, March 30, 2002. http://www.welt.de/print-welt/article381654/Allah-rief-der-Rabbi.html

9 *New York Times* article quoted above, p. 26.

10 See Bhikkhuni Liao Yi and Maria Reis Habito (eds), *Listening: Buddhist-Muslim Dialogues 2002–04* (Taipei: Museum of World Religions Development Foundation, 2005); Also, Bhikkhuni Liao Yi and Maria Reis Habito (eds), *Heart To Heart: Buddhist Muslim Encounters in Ladakh* (Taipei: Museum of World Religions Development Foundation, 2012). The dialogues are also featured on the website of the Interfaith NGO Global Family for Love and Peace, www.gflp.org.

Chapter 4

1 My translation from French. Diderot and d'Alembert (2011, vol. 2: 839): "Quant à la question de la nécessité des cérémonies pour un culte, sa solution dépend d'une autre; savoir, si la religion est faite pour le seul philosophe, ou pour le philosophe et le peuple: dans le premier cas, on pourroit peut-être soûtenir que les cérémonies sont superflues, puisqu'elles n'ont d'autre but que de nous rappeller les objets de notre foi & de nos devoirs, dont le philosophe se souvient bien sans le secours des signes sensibles: mais la religion est faite indistinctement pour tous les hommes, comme il en faut convenir; donc, comme les prodiges de la nature ramènent sans cesse le philosophe à l'existence d'un Dieu créateur; dans la religion Chrétienne, par exemple, les cérémonies rameneront sans cesse le chrétien à la loi d'un Dieu crucifié. Les représentations sensibles, de quelque nature qu'elles soient, ont une force prodigieuse sur l'imagination du commun des hommes: jamais l'éloquence d'Antoine n'eût fait ce que fit la robe de César. *Quod litteratis est scriptura, hoc idiotis proestat pictura*, dit saint Grégoire le grand, liv. IX. épît. ix."

2 Compare Martin Luther's *On the Freedom of a Christian* in which he distinguishes the inward from the outward man (Luther 1980: 126). For an English translation, see Lutherans Online: "And so it will profit nothing that the body should be adorned with sacred vestments, or dwell in holy places, or be occupied in sacred offices, or pray, fast, and abstain from certain meats, or do whatever works can be done through the body and in the body. Something widely different will be necessary for the justification and liberty of the soul, since the things I have spoken of can be done by any impious person, and only hypocrites are produced by devotion to these

things." (http://www.lutheransonline.com/servlet/lo_ProcServ/dbpage=page&mode
=display&gid=201203471482779218011111555 [accessed March 6, 2014]).

3   And—in the same vein—a priority of mind over body. Due to spatial limits we will
    leave the topic of embodiment aside.

4   Humphrey and Laidlaw (1994: 267): "We have suggested that ritual action is,
    in a sense, like an object. This is not because people have a common idea of it,
    but because they do not." Also, p. 265: "Ritual itself tends towards a dispersal of
    meaning."

5   Humphrey and Laidlaw (1994: 267): "The patterns rituals take, beyond our purposes,
    beliefs, or intentions, propose their own time, and to step into this, to enact it
    ourselves, is perhaps to defy our transience and death."

Chapter 5

1   See the joint publication *Pro Dialogo/Current Dialogue* (Rome: Pontificium
    Consilium Pro Dialogo Inter Religiones/Geneva: WCC, 1998) in which are contained
    a selection of preliminary papers and the formal reports and findings of the study.

Chapter 6

1   The Catholic Church also teaches the importance of self-examination in preparation
    for the Eucharist: see CCC, no. 1385. In addition to self-examination, some
    Reformed denominations regard unity of faith as expressed in the Reformed
    confessions as the decisive criterion for table fellowship. For example, the
    Presbyterian Church in America (PCA) distinguishes three levels of relationship.
    The highest is "ecclesiastical fellowship," determined by a formal adherence to the
    creeds and confessions adopted by the PCA. At that level of relationship, there is
    intercommunion, pulpit exchange, and delegate sharing at general synods.

2   See *Lumen Gentium* (8): "This Church constituted and organized in the world as
    a society, subsists in the Catholic Church, which is governed by the successor of
    Peter and by the Bishops in communion with him, although many elements of
    sanctification and of truth are found outside of its visible structure. These elements,
    as gifts belonging to the Church of Christ, are forces impelling toward catholic
    unity."

3   "This Bread Of Life," Report Of The United States Roman Catholic-Reformed
    Dialogue on the Eucharist/Lord's Supper (November 2010). http://www.crcna.org/
    site_uploads/uploads/resources/synodical/ThisBreadofLife.pdf.

4   For stronger critiques of Schmemann and Kavanagh's line of interpretation, see
    Marshall 1995 and Berger 2001.

5   For an important recent critique of this way of construing the relationship of liturgy
    and theology, see Aune 2007, esp. 152–6.

6   *Pace* Frits Staal, who argues strongly that ritual is best understood not as a bearer of
    disembodied "meaning," but as pure "doing." See Staal 1975.

7   Hughes' entire project provides a nuanced proposal for how late modern worshippers
    make meaning, drawing from Charles Peirce's semiotic theory to analyze the
    construction, transmission, and apprehension of meaning in a worship service.

8   I use the general term "Eucharistic prayer" here to refer to the practice of praying at the Lord's Supper, before receiving the bread and wine; it is also called the Great Prayer of Thanksgiving, or anaphora. For a comparative chart of the Eucharistic liturgies from four Reformed Churches and the Roman Catholic Church in the United States, demonstrating the convergences of liturgical practice, see "This Bread of Life," 493–510.

9   One version of the classic opening dialogue consists of the following responses, alternating between presider and people: "The Lord be with you / And also with you. / Lift up your hearts. / We lift them to the Lord. / Let us give thanks to the Lord our God. / It is right to give our thanks and praise." One classic text of the Sanctus (or more properly, the Sanctus/Benedictus) is "Holy, holy, holy Lord, God of power and might, heaven and earth are full of your glory. Hosanna in the highest! Blessed is the one who comes in the name of the Lord. Hosanna in the highest!"

10 Recent changes in the official English language version of the mass have made the Catholic version less similar to English language Protestant liturgical resources. For instance, the opening dialogue now begins "The Lord be with you / *And with your spirit*," rather than the previous, ecumenically shared response "And also with you." This shift has complicated the kind of partial ecumenical participation I describe here.

11 "You Satisfy the Hungry Heart," text: Omer Westendorf, music: Robert E. Kreutz, *Glory to God: The Presbyterian Hymnal* (Louisville: Westminster John Knox Press, 2013), 523; "Eat This Bread," text: Robert Batastini and the Taizé Community, music: Jacques Berthier, *Glory to God*, 527; "One Bread, One Body," text and music: John B. Foley, *Glory to God*, 530. These hymns also appear in many other denominational resources, both Protestant and Catholic.

12 For instance, though a direct causal connection will be impossible to prove, it seems clear that there is a correlation between the increased attention to the epiclesis in Eucharistic praying and increased attention to the role of the Spirit in doctrinal reflections on the Eucharist in the past few decades.

13 The reality of "multiple religious belonging," as discussed in recent years by scholars like Paul Knitter, challenges the notion that each person belongs only to a single clearly marked religious community. In the Christian world, there is an analogous and growing phenomenon of what we might call "multiple Christian belonging," or the practice of identifying with more than one Christian community. This poses a challenge to ecumenical dialogue itself, which has presumed clearly defined cultural-linguistic boundaries between communities that are not so clear in lived experience.

Chapter 7

1   http://www.interfaithmarriage.org.uk/resource_packs/Resourcepack.pdf, pp. 59–60.

2   For instance, "Attending a Muslim Funeral—A Guide for Non-Muslims," an undated pamphlet issued by the Muslim Burial Council of Leicestershire.

3   I am grateful to Dr Sejad Mekic for this reference.

4   This normally evangelical technique is controversial among evangelicals themselves, since it appears to be an implicit validation of the revealed source of Muslim forms of worship. See Warren C. Chastain, "Should Christians Pray the Muslim Salat?," *International Journal of Frontier Missions* 12 (1995): 34–40.

5 For Vatican II's implications for Muslim-Christian joint prayer see Gavin D'Costa, "Interreligious Prayer between Christians and Muslims," *Islam and Christian-Muslim Relations* 24 (2013): 1–14.

6 Abu Bakr al-Kasani, *Bada'i' al-sana'i' fi tartib al-shara'i'* (Beirut: Dar Ihya' al-Turath al-'Arabi, 1421AH), I. 225–6.

7 Syrian Christian devotion evolved organically from earlier forms, particularly Jewish Christianity (Arthur Vööbus, *History of Asceticism in the Syrian Orient: A Contribution to the History of Culture in the Near East* [Louvain: Secrétariat du Corpus SCO, 1958]); and nascent Islam is thought by many historians to have substantive precursors not only in Syrian Christian piety but also, ultimately, in Ebionite Christianity, considered as a point of Muslim/Jewish/Christian commonalty by, *inter alia*, Hans Küng, *Islam* (Oxford: Oneworld, 2007), 43–4. For the "dependence of Muhammad on Jewish Christianity" see Pierre-Antoine Bernheim, *James, Brother of Jesus* (London: SCM, 1997), 269; John G. Gager, "Did Jewish Christians See the Rise of Islam?" in Adam H. Becker and Annette Yoshiko Reed (eds), *The Ways that Never Parted: Jews and Christians in Late Antiquity and the Early Middle Ages* (Minneapolis: Fortress Press, 2007), 361–72; for Qu'ranic religion as a version of Syriac Christian ascetic piety see for instance Tor Andrae, *In the Garden of Myrtles: Studies in Early Islamic Mysticism* (Albany: State University of New York Press, 1987), 8.

8 The classic study is Asim Roy, *The Islamic Syncretistic Tradition in Bengal* (Princeton: Princeton University Press, 1983).

9 In later reflection, however, he explains that Christian joining in Muslim *salat*, while "a true and intimate participation," should not involve Christians physically joining the prayer-rows; see Dall'Oglio 2009: 91. See also Guyonne de Montjou, *Mar Moussa: une monastere, un homme, un desert* (Paris: Albin Michel, 2006).

10 Non-Muslim participants who choose not to recite the Qu'ranic text might find comfort in the *fiqh* ruling which permits the recitation of Jewish or Christian scriptures during the *salat*; cf. Kasani, I. 299.

11 For a different, more recent method whereby a faithful Christian may affirm Muhammad's true prophethood see Anton Wessels, *The Torah, the Gospel, and the Qur'an: Three Books, Two Cities, One Tale* (Grand Rapids: Eerdmans, 2013), 53–4.

12 See the discussion among jurists recorded by Ibn 'Abidin, from which he concludes that Christians who participate in canonical Islamic practices should not automatically be considered converts. Even pronouncing the *Shahada* during the call to prayer, for instance, does not constitute conversion, since there are Christians "who believe that Muhammad's ministry was to the Arabs alone." Participation only entails conversion in the eyes of the Shari'a if the non-Muslim participant explicitly renounces his former religion. Muhammad ibn 'Abidin, *Radd al-muhtar 'ala'l-Durr al-mukhtar* (Damascus: Dar al-Thaqafa wa'l-Turath, 1421AH), II. 470-1-5; note, however, the existence of differing opinions.

13 See, for instance, Kasani's Hanafi objection to non-Muslim attendance at the drought prayer (*salat al-istisqa'*): Kasani, I 636: they should not attend because they are the locus of God's curse; this contrasts with Malik's permissiveness in this respect. Note also the Kadızadeli opposition, on grounds of the risk to spiritual efficacy, to the established Ottoman practice of permitting Muslim and Christian congregations to pray side by side for the alleviation of the plague (Madeline C. Zilfi, "The Kadızadelis: discordant revivalism in seventeenth-century Istanbul," *Journal of Near Eastern Studies* 45 [1986]: 264).

14 *Daily Telegraph*, September 15, 2011.
15 As explicitly attested in scripture; see Daniel Gimaret, *Dieu à l'image de l'homme: les anthropomorphismes de la sunna et leur interpretation par les théologiens* (Paris: Cerf, 1997).

Chapter 8

1 Among Anglicans this affirmative attitude was contested. See, for example, Archbishop Carey's concerns in the Synod debate (Carey 1992; see also Kuin 2011: 89–130), on the history of this debate in the thirty-year period of her study.
2 The German bishops encourage multireligious prayer, but reject interreligious prayer (German Bishops Conference 2003). In the United States, President Obama had a multireligious prayer service related to his inauguration. Muslims, Hindus, Jews, and of course Christians prayed and read from their scriptures during the service (Ruggeri 2009). This is likely to become routine in Western democracies.
3 See *Pro Dialogo* Bulletin, 98, 1998, 2, for theological reflections on this matter from a Protestant, Orthodox, and Catholic point of view. The Anglican document, *Multi-Faith Worship* (London: Church House, 1992) also conflates the arguments between multireligious and interreligious prayer as does the subsequent response by the House of Bishops: *Multi-Faith Worship? Guidance on the Situations which Arise*, GS Miscellaneous 411 (London: Church House, 1993).
4 This committee was founded in 1987 by the Conference of European Churches and the Council of European Bishops' Conferences.
5 See Katz 1978 for a powerful critique of such arguments. Too much literature in this field depends on shaky referential commonality, but one must equally admit that reality is not only processed through referential concepts, but through practices and community formation.
6 See http://blog.radiovatikan.de/nein-nein-nein/ (checked August 2014) for the text of that meeting, which was clearly structured to avoid any sense of interreligious prayer.
7 Interestingly the German Catholic bishops give different reasons but do not indicate the cultic problem—see para. 44.
8 Christian Troll (2008) presents another interesting Catholic approach.
9 For a fuller study of the Council's teaching on Islam, see my book (2014). Troll's argument is based on this common agreement (Troll 2008: 367) and, while fully acknowledging differences, he finally gestures toward the "spiritual": "The mystery invites us: not to eliminate the intellect but to exceed what the mind can achieve with its own forces" (Troll 2008: 368). But the intellect then apparently relates this exceeding to interreligious prayer in a way that suggests that it is a point where arguments cannot be given and some other factor is important.
10 *Praeparatio evangelica* is an ancient term meaning "preparation for the gospel" and was used by Eusebius of Caesarea to indicate that Judaism was a preparation for Christ. Vatican II uses this term in a novel fashion to extend it to natural religions including Islam (see Carola 2010). The significance of this extension has not been fully explicated and developed.
11 For Catholic criticisms, see, for example, Dörmann 1994: 21–43.

12 The Benedictine monk, Pierre-François de Béthune, is a case in point. As Secretary
    General of Dialogue Interreligieux Monastique, he argued that what grounds
    interreligious prayer is orthopraxis: one can "become really obsessed with the purity
    of doctrine and simultaneously quite blind about orthopraxis," and again: "If one
    emphasizes the conceptual contents of prayers *communicatio* is impossible. But if one
    pays more attention to experience and *praxis,* the communion of prayers imposes
    itself" (de Béthune 1987: 162). While I take that as a warning against the focus I
    am adopting, it is not possible for orthopraxis and experience to bypass doctrine,
    although de Béthune is right in saying that doctrine should not necessarily be the
    sole engine of the ship. Nevertheless, his arguments in fact support multireligious,
    not interreligious, prayer, although he moves between the two without distinguishing
    between them.
13 See Vatican I, Canons of Chapter II, number 1 (Denzinger 1955: 3026).
14 Some are more optimistic about these differences: see Grose and Hubbard 1994:
    1–44, and Solomon et al. 2005.
15 Adam Sparks (2010) does well to warn against analogy. The analogical trope
    must also face an unforeseen difficulty, found in the Catholic catechism. While
    not explicitly discussing Islam, in § 58, it says of past covenants: "The covenant
    with Noah remains in force during the times of the Gentiles, until the universal
    proclamation of the Gospel." There is a curious irony here, for insofar as
    interreligious prayer may be founded on this covenant, its reality would seem to
    dissolve the very covenant upon which it is founded, for it would assume that
    our partners in interreligious prayer have understood the gospel insofar as they
    pray with us (in the specific sense that the gospel is now known through the
    co-intentionality required by interreligious prayer).

Chapter 9

1 See, for example, Alexandra Cuffel, "From Practice to Polemic: shared saints and
   festivals as 'women's religion' in the medieval Mediterranean," *The Bulletin of
   the School of Oriental and African Studies* 68 (2005): 401–19; Alexandra Cuffel,
   "'Henceforward all generations will call me blessed': Medieval Christian Tales of
   Non-Christian Marian Veneration," *Mediterranean Studies* 12 (2003): 37–60; Dionigi
   Albera, "Pelerinages mixtes et sanctuaries 'ambigus' en Méditerranée," in Sylvia
   Chiffoleau and Anna Madoeuf (eds), *Les pèlerinages au Maghreb et au Moyen-Orient*
   (Beyrouth: Institut Français du Proche-Orient, 2005), 347–78.
2 See, for example, Selva Raj and Corrine Dempsey (eds), *Popular Christianity in
   India: Riting Between the Lines* (Albany: SUNY Press, 2002); Anna Bigelow, *Sharing
   the Sacred: Practicing Religious Pluralism in Muslim North India* (Oxford: Oxford
   University Press, 2010).
3 As Clooney argues, the new comparative theology is different from the older
   comparative theology, as it has become deeply aware of its various biases against
   the other, its underlying agenda of proving the superiority of Christianity, its
   concealed and narrowly conceived missionary impulse, and so forth. However,
   the new comparative theology also shares the older emphases on the faith
   commitment of the theologians and scholarly inquiry. In this regard, the new
   comparative theology stresses the positive and constructive nature of this

comparative project, making it a properly theological enterprise. It pays attention to the ways in which the comparative enterprise affects the practitioners as theologians and their understanding of their own theologies. On this topic see also, James Fredericks' "Introduction," in Francis X. Clooney (ed.), *New Comparative Theology: Interreligious Insights from the Next Generation* (New York: T&T Clark, 2010), vi–xvi. See also Francis X. Clooney, SJ, "Comparative Theology," in John Webster, Kathryn Tanner, and Iain Torrance (eds), *The Oxford Handbook to Systematic Theology* (Oxford: Oxford University Press, 2007), 653–69; David Tracy, "Comparative Theology," in Lindsay Jones (ed.), *The Encyclopedia of Religions*, vol. 13, 2nd edn (Detroit: Macmillan Reference USA, 2005), 9125–34.

4   For a detailed account of this research and its results, see my *Muslim and Catholic Pilgrimage Practices* (Ashgate, 2014); also my original PhD dissertation, *Journeying to God in Communion with the Other* (Massachusetts: Boston College, 2011). This dissertation includes an extended chapter on the construction of a refreshed Catholic theology of *communio sanctorum* as a result of my encounters with the Muslim tradition of sainthood (Chapter 9).

5   In the context of Asian Christianity, I argue that complex identity (rather than "multiple religious belonging"), which stems from sharing the same religio-cultural space, has marked the distinctive ways in which many Asian Christian communities forge their identity. This complex identity can make cross-ritual participation easier and more natural. See my chapter, "Multiple Religious Belonging or Complex Religio-Cultural Identity: An Asian Way of Being Religious," in Felix Wilfred (ed.), *The Oxford Handbook of Christianity in Asia* (Oxford: Oxford University Press, 2014), 493–509.

6   On this Christian Troll writes: "An encounter in prayer can also take place through silent participation in the other's liturgical prayer, admittedly without full accompaniment in speech and symbolic gestures. Here it is a matter of discreet participation in liturgical prayer by the Muslim or Christian as guest, in an attitude of respect and prayerful presence." Troll, "Can Christians and Muslims Pray Together?" *The Way* 50/1 (January 2011): 68.

7   On the "polyphony" of rituals in Muslim shrines in Java, see, for example, J. Jamhari "The Meaning Interpreted: The Concept of *Barakah* in *Ziarah,*" *Studia Islamika: Indonesian Journal for Islamic Studies* 8 (2001): 91.

8   The concept of *īmān* (and its derivation, *mu'min*) is central to the Qu'ran, and it does not primarily refer to "belief" but rather faith, inner peace, absolute assurance, and total trust, granted by God. Thus it is foundational and existential disposition of human being vis-à-vis God. Cf. Farid Esack, *Qur'an, Liberation and Pluralism* (Oxford, 1997), 117–26; also Toshihiko Izutsu, *The Concept of Belief in Islamic Theology* (Tokyo, 1965).

9   On the *tawassul* prayers used in West Java, see Julian Millie, *Splashed by the Saints* (Leiden: KITLV, 2009), 101–7.

10 In south central Java, all Muslim shrines are open to non-Muslims. Only certain shrines in East Java, such as the shrines of Sunan Bonang and Sunan Ampel, put certain limitations to non-Muslim visitors.

11 On the role of Mary, she argues that "the primary angle of vision will be pneumatological, seeing Mary as a graced woman. Since she is embraced by and responsive to Spirit-Sophia, she is a sister to all who partner with the Spirit in the struggle for the coming of the reign of God" (Johnson 2006: 104).

12 It should be noted as well that this spirit of cross-ritual participation can also be
found in Louis Massignon, for example. His spiritual journey was initiated when he
was visited inwardly by the "other," namely Mansur al-Hallaj (a "Christic" Muslim
saint whom he called "the Stranger") during his stay in Baghdad in 1908. Curiously,
it was through his encounter with this Muslim saint that led Massignon back to his
Catholic faith. Together with others in the "cloud of witnesses" (that included his
mother, Charles de Foucauld, J. K. Huysmans), al-Hallaj interceded for Massignon.
In my view, the overall dynamism of Massignon's experience can be understood
within the renewed understanding of *communio sanctorum* as a new and creative
form of the practice. It started off with deep immersion into or communion with
Islam or the world of Muslim saint and sainthood, then continued with the act
of coming back more deeply to the Catholic tradition, but it also led to a deeper
involvement or communion with Islam, including the appropriation of Muslim
rituals. The Badaliya prayer group that Massignon founded adopts the practice of
praying the al-Fatiha (the opening prayer of the Qu'ran) before the crucifix, and of
meditating on the examples of Muslim saints as a way to go deeper into communion
with Christ. See Anthony O"Mahony, "Louis Massignon, the Seven Sleepers of
Ephesus and the Christian-Muslim Pilgrimage at Vieux-Marché, Brittany," in
Craig Bartholomew and Fred Hughes (eds), *Explorations in a Christian Theology of
Pilgrimage* (Aldershot: Ashgate, 2004), 126–48; also Christian Krokus, *Faith Seeking
Understanding: Louis Massignon's (1883–1962) Catholic Conversation with Islam*
(PhD Dissertation, Boston College, 2009).

Chapter 10

1 Composed by Sriram Pidaparti and published in a souvenir (2006) to commemorate
the inauguration of the temple.
2 *Mūrti* is one of the many Sanskrit terms that are difficult to translate easily. It is still
too often problematically translated as "idol," with all the resonances of false worship
and improper association of God with a finite object. We will henceforth leave it
untranslated, hoping that its meaning will be evident from the wider discussion.
3 For a summary of both interpretations see S. Chatterjee and D. Datta, *An
Introduction to Indian Philosophy* (Kolkata: Calcutta University Press, 2008),
365–430.
4 For a description of *mūrti*–making at the Puri-Jagannath temple in Orissa see,
"Creation of the Sacred Image: Apotheosis and Destruction in Hinduism," in
J. P. Waghorne and N. Cutler (eds), *Gods of Flesh/Gods of Stone*, 9–32.
5 Quoted in a commemorative magazine published (2006) to celebrate the opening of
the Hindu temple, Maple Grove, Minnesota.
6 It is revealing that Hindu immigrants from the Caribbean, and especially from
Guyana and Trinidad and Tobago, founded both of these Toronto temples. These
communities have existed in the Western world for over 160 years and reflect a
process of change, adaptation, and transformation of tradition. See Anantanand
Rambachan, "Global Hinduism: The Hindu Diaspora," in R. Rinehart (ed.),
Contemporary Hinduism (Santa Barbara: ABC-CLIO Inc., 2004), 381–414.

7   http://www.hindustantimes.com/India-news/Bhubaneswar/Controversies-over-Jagannath-Temple-s-entry-rules/Article1-907457.aspx (accessed August 26, 2013). Another temple that prohibits outsiders is the Ekambaranathar Temple. This is a Shiva temple in Kanchipuram, Tamil Nadu. See http://www.ekambaranathartemple. org (accessed December 11, 2013).

8   http://www.thehindu.com/news/national/other-states/nonhindus-can-enter-jagannath-temples-except-shrine-at-puri/article2764219.ece (accessed August 26, 2013).

9   http://indiatoday.intoday.in/story/non-hindus-to-sign-faith-form-to-enter-tirumala-temple-in-andhra-pradesh/1/210621.html(accessed August 26, 2013).

10 Traditional prayer of unknown authorship. Cited in Anantanand Rambachan, *The Hindu Vision* (Delhi: Motilal Banarsidass, 1992), 7.

11 For a full declaration see: http://www.hafsite.org/pdf/2nd%20Jewish-Hindu%20 Summit%20Final%20Declaration%2002-27-08.pdf (accessed September 11, 2013).

12 Scholars regard the Ṛg Veda as the earliest of the Vedic texts (ca. 1500 BCE or earlier).

13 The reformist Arya Samaj movement is one exception and has a purification (*shuddhi*) ceremony.

Chapter 11

1   See Abhishiktananda 1998. In what follows I will be emphasizing the deep etymological link between "Eucharist" and the act of "thanking."

2   See report by David Sharrock, "Archbishop fuels row over Irish Communion," *The Telegraph*, London, February 20, 2001.

3   Abhishiktananda (Henri Le Saux OSB) (1910–73) is one of the great twentieth-century pioneers in interreligious dialogue. Having moved to India in 1948 in search of a more radical form of spiritual life, he adopted sannyasa in accordance with Indian tradition and became an inspiring exponent of Hindu-Christian dialogue. Together with his mentor, Fr Jules Monchanin, he founded an ashram at Shantivanam in Tamil Nadu, where he was later followed by Dom Bede Griffiths and others. Multiple contacts with prominent Hindu saints such as Sri Ramana Maharshi and Sri Gnanananda Giri led him to deep advaitic mystical experience. After some years he went to live the life of a hermit in Arunachala and later the Himalayas. His lifestyle, books, and diaries are now the subject of considerable interest, and in recognition of his outstanding contribution, symposia were held around the world in the centenary year of his birth in 2010. The first, at Saccidananda Ashram (Shantivanam) in Tamil Nadu was particularly valuable, as it provided information which was not hitherto accessible about the circumstances of Abhishiktananda's life and the current situation of interreligious dialogue in India. For an account of the research findings of these symposia see Dupuche 2001. Another very useful critical source is Shirley du Boulay's excellent biography of Abhishiktananda (du Boulay 2005).

4   Abhishiktananda 1998.

5   In a 2012 correspondence, Du Boulay informed me that Abhi became less and less preoccupied by the particular doctrinal restrictions on the Eucharist in his later days, in spite of what seems to have been a continuing, and often fertile, tension between his deep Catholic vocation as a Benedictine monk and his passionate

commitment to encountering Christ in other faiths. Several other contemporaries
and friends of Abhi have made similar observations. Bettina Baeumer told me she
felt sure Abhi shared the Eucharist with Hindus, and Joseph Prabhu suggested he
probably engaged in interfaith Eucharists alongside Murray Rogers and Raimon
Panikkar. I still, curiously, have found nothing in Abhi's own writing which explicitly
confirm this; but several entries from his *Spiritual Diary 1948–1973: Ascent to the
Depth of the Heart*, cited above, hint in this direction. It is still, to use Abhi's own
terms, an "open space," over which the Spirit "hovers and beckons." What is sure is
that Abhishiktananda, for all his devotion to his Church, realized that his experience
of interreligious sharing represented a real challenge to the traditional Christian
theology of single church salvation.

6   See also my account of this interfaith Easter ritual in Kearney and Rizo-Patron
    2010: 20–4.

7   Abhishiktananda 1998. All subsequent diary citations below are from this source.

8   King's volume includes the full text of Teihlard's *Mass on the World* and a related
    "Prayer Service Based on *The Mass of the World*" (pp. 145–67). I am deeply indebted
    to King's very insightful and exhaustive research work on Teilhard's texts, letters, and
    diaries for the citations of Teilhard which follow.

9   Joseph O'Leary notes that in its reaction against Docetism, the early Church insisted
    on the reality of Christ's flesh and blood and on the physical reality of the resurrected
    body, and of the bodily presence of Christ in the Eucharist. In his famous work,
    Against Heresies (V, 2, 2), Saint Irenaeus argued against those who wished to deny
    the carnality of Christ and, by implication, the salvation of human flesh: "But vain
    in every respect are they who despise the entire dispensation of God, and disallow
    the salvation of the flesh, and treat with contempt its regeneration, maintaining that
    it is not capable of incorruption. But if this indeed does not attain salvation, then
    neither did the Lord redeem us with His blood, nor is the cup of the Eucharist the
    communion of His blood, nor the bread which we break the communion of His
    body (1 Cor. 10:16). For blood can only come from veins and flesh, and whatsoever
    else makes up the substance of man, such as the Word of God was actually made. By
    His own blood he redeemed us. … He has acknowledged the cup (which is a part
    of the creation) as His own blood, from which He bedews our blood; and the bread
    (also a part of the creation) He has established as His own body, from which He
    gives increase to our bodies."

10 One still finds residual traces and hints in Teilhard of theodicy and, more
    specifically, of a Christocentric theology of fulfillment and sacrifice, especially in
    relation to the celebration of the Mass during times of war and tragic suffering.
    See here Joseph O'Leary's critical commentary on this complex link between the
    Eucharist and ritual blood sacrifice. "We do not know what aspects of the Eucharist
    go back to Jesus himself; all the New Testament accounts of its institution, as well
    as the eucharistic allusions in the stories of the multiplication of loaves and fishes,
    depend on the ritual as practised by Christians. If, as the majority of scholars
    hold, the Last Supper was not in fact a paschal meal, its amalgamation with the
    Pasch was a natural and enriching early Christian development. There is a pleasing
    modesty in the idea that Jesus's last meal was not a Pasch, and that his sharing of
    his body and blood avoided an immediate identification with sacrificial rituals.
    Within the New Testament, Hellenistic elements enrich the original Jewish basis,
    notably the Hellenistic ethics of friendship in John 15" [pointed out by Thomas
    Söding, in Van Belle 2007: 364] (O'Leary 2008a: 169–70). O'Leary goes on to

suggest how research into early forms of sacrificial religion, often based on mystery nature rites, already reveals a rich body of interpretations and practices which defy any attempt to establish some kind of "essentialism" regarding the Eucharistic origins. Accordingly, O'Leary warns against more common cultural forms of the fetishistic cult of blood sacrifice. Though O'Leary does not cite de Chardin, many of these observations are relevant to his considerations on the sacrificial role of the Mass (see King 2005: 96–7, 106–7). See also my critical analysis of the role of the Christian mythology of blood sacrifice in relation to war and political violence in "Myth and Martyrdom" and "The Triumph of Failure" in Kearney 2009, as well as Kearney 1979.

11 See Teilhard de Chardin, "The Spiritual Power of Matter" (1919), cited in King 2005: 129.

12 See the challenging recent work of Catherine Cornille (2008), Marianne Moyaert (2014), and Paul Ricoeur himself (1998). It is helpful to recall here Ricoeur's inspiring notion of "eucharistic hospitality" developed in line with his concepts of "interconfessional hospitality" and "linguistic hospitality," according to the hermeneutic model of translation. Ricoeur's basic point is that a good translation must always respect a certain irreducible difference and otherness in the guest language, which can never be fully subsumed into the host language. Translation as a model for interfaith dialogue means what the Greek term originally said—*dia-legein*, welcoming the difference between host and guest as well as creating bridges and mediations. Complete fusion between religions or persons—or members of the Trinity—would be the end of hospitality. See my introduction to Ricoeur 2004 and my conclusion to *Anatheism* entitled "Welcoming Strange Gods" (Kearney 2010: 166–81).

13 The text of St Timothy's canon is as follows: "If a catechumen child or even an adult person comes forward and, without evil intention, receives of the divine Gifts during the Holy Sacrifice, he should be baptized at once, for he was called [to do so] by the Lord." Timothy of Alexandria flourished in the reign of Emperor Valens, about A.D. 372. He wrote the canons in the form of questions and answers, which are confirmed indefinitely by canon I of the 7th Ecumenical Council, but definitely by canon II of the 6th Ecumenical Council; and by virtue of this confirmation they acquired what in a way amounts to ecumenical force. They are to be found in the second volume of the Pandects, and in volume I of the Conciliar Records, p. 352 (http://faculty. cua.edu/Pennington/OhmeGreekCanonLaw.htm). I am grateful to my friend and colleague, John Manoussakis, for these references. See his forthcoming volume on ecumenical dialogue, *For the Unity of All: Contributions to the Theological Dialogue Between East and West* (Cascade Books, 2015).

14 A symbolic refiguring of this scene is powerfully captured in Andrei Rublev icon of the *Perichoresis*: the trinity of persons feasting around the Eucharistic chalice. See my reading of Rublev's "perichoresis" as a hermeneutic refiguring of the Abrahamic Eucharist (Abraham and Sarah feasting with the three divine strangers) as a Trinitarian Eucharist (the three divine persons around the chalice of bread and wine) in *Anatheism* (Kearney 2010: 24ff) and also in "Eros, Diacritical Hermeneutics and the Maybe" (Kearney 2011). It is important, I suggest, to embrace a hospitable hermeneutic capable of reinterpreting and refiguring the Eucharistic event in terms of multiple scenes of feasting and sharing, bringing together, for example, the primal scenes of Abraham and the strangers in Genesis and the Jewish Passover/Seder with the Christian scenes of not only the Cross and Last

Supper (where service and sharing precede sacrifice) but also Cana, the loaves and fishes, and Christ's post-paschal Eucharistic hosting of the disciple-guests at Emmanus and on the shore of Galilee.

15 O'Leary goes on to make a very cogent case for a pluralist hermeneutics of the Eucharist, which I would endorse.

16 See James Carroll, "Who am I to Judge?," *The New Yorker*, December 2013. O'Leary anticipates Pope Francis' 2013 overture with a useful gloss on the connotations of Matthew 18:20 for a fraternal Eucharist open to creative and recreative "supplements" (O'Leary 2008a: 172). The openness to the possibility of Christic supplementarity in each instance of Eucharistic sharing may constitute a "semantic surplus" (Ricoeur) inviting endless hermeneutic artistry and acoustics. Christ's ways exceed the limits of any single ecclesiastical doctrine, which is why the Eucharist remains a sacred "mystery" and why the sacerdotal work of the priest needs to be complemented by the creative work of the poet. See here Sheila Gallagher's (2013) innovative experiments in Eucharistic art, Sheila Gallagher's *Ravishing Far Near* (New York: Dodge Gallery, 2013), with a catalog introduction by Richard Kearney.

17 See Maurice Merleau-Ponty on this idea of Eucharistic sensation: "Just as the sacrament not only symbolizes, in sensible species, an operation of Grace, but *is* also the real presence of God, which it causes to occupy a fragment of space and communicates to those who eat of the consecrated bread, provided that they are inwardly prepared, in the same way the sensible has not only a motor and vital significance, but is nothing other than a certain way of being in the world suggested to us from some point in space, and seized and acted upon by our body, provided that it is capable of doing so, so that sensation is literally a form of communion" (Merleau-Ponty 2002: 246). See my commentary on this notion in *Anatheism* (Kearney 2010: 89–94); and also the cogent argument made by Joseph O'Leary for a Eucharistics of love and witness which obviates both a sacrificial fetishism of body and blood, on the one hand, and an essentialist metaphysics of substance on the other (O'Leary, 2008a).

Chapter 12

1 The term "Zen" throughout this chapter includes both the Chinese Buddhist Chan school and the Japanese Zen tradition.

2 The Zen school literally means "the meditation school," *zen* being the Japanese form of the Chinese character *chan*, which is a transliteration of the Sanskrit term *dhyana*, meditation.

3 For more on how Zen was presented through this lens, see Albert Welter, *The Linji Lu and the Creation of Chan Orthodoxy: The Development of Chan's Records of Sayings Literature* (Oxford: Oxford University Press, 2008).

4 For an extended discussion of *hongaku* thought in medieval Japanese Buddhism, see Jacqueline I. Stone, *Original Enlightenment and the Transformation of Medieval Japanese Buddhism* (Honolulu: University of Hawai'i Press, 1999).

5 See Hee-Jin Kim, *Eihei Dōgen—Mystical Realist* (Boston: Wisdom Publications, 2004) for an overview of Dōgen's relationship to *hongaku* thought.

6 Dōgen tends to use both terms interchangeably; see Kim, *Eihei Dōgen*, 67.

7 Dale Wright comments, however, that some sense of purpose remains in spite of such disclaimers: "If you lack the purpose of Zen, you will also lack everything else about Zen, including zazen. This is so because the purpose of casting off all purposes in an exalted state of no mind still stands there behind the scenes as the purpose that structures the entire practice, enabling it to make sense and be worth doing from beginning to end" (Dale S. Wright, "Introduction: Rethinking ritual practice in Zen Buddhism," in Heine and Wright, *Zen Ritual*, 3–19, citation at 15).

8 The preceding section appeared earlier as part of André van der Braak, "Zen Spirituality in a Secular Age II—Dōgen on Fullness: Zazen as Ritual Embodiment of Buddhahood," *Studies in Spirituality* 19 (2009): 227–47.

9 In my earlier article, I addressed this problem from a philosophical hermeneutic point of view (van der Braak, *Enlightenment Revisited*).

10 An earlier version of this chapter appeared as André van der Braak, "Meditation and Ritual in Zen Buddhism," *Acta Comparanda* XXI (2010): 109–24.

Chapter 13

1 The word "soteriological" is used in this chapter in its descriptive sense, referring to that which a religion considers to be the problem inherent in the human condition, and its remedy.

2 For reflection on ritual as a way of knowing, see Schilbrack 2004.

3 E.g. Jesus of Nazareth, the idea or experience of awakening, reception of the moral law, submission to divine command, understanding of cosmic balance, etc.

4 This working definition of religion is my own, but is indebted to a critical appropriation of John Hick's body of work on religious pluralism (see Hick 1988), and sparked by Rowan Williams's insights into certain aspects of pre-Nicene Christianity that are in fact visible in all traditions (Williams 1989).

5 For a full account of this methodology, see Clooney 2010.

6 Jn 1:1-16; 15:1-11; 13:1-17.

7 I Cor. 11:17-33.

8 This is a compressed exposition of the Shakyamuni's Four Noble Truths and Eightfold Path. See, e.g., Bodhi 2005: 31–5, 75–8, 239–40.

9 Note the resonance with Seligman's (2008) general account of ritual; see above.

Chapter 14

1 I would like to express my gratitude to Sheila Gogol who so kindly improved the English of this text.

Chapter 15

1 This chapter is being written from my perspective as a mother, Jew, scholar, and mourner. While at times I express emotions and thoughts shared by my partner, out of respect for our differences I am not speaking in his name.

2　D. S. Becvar, *In the Presence of Grief: Helping Family Members Resolve Death, Dying, and Bereavement Issues* (New York: Guilford Press, 2003); K. Kramer, *The Sacred Art of Dying: How World Religions Understand Death* (New York: Paulist Press, 1988); M. R. Leming and G. E. Dickinson, *Understanding Dying, Death, and Bereavement* (Belmont, CA: Wadsworth Cengage Learning, 2011); R. Wolfson, *A Time To Mourn, A Time To Comfort: A Guide To Jewish Bereavement, 2nd Ed. (The Art of Jewish Living)*, (Woodstock, VT: Jewish Lights Pub., 1993); H. Kagan, *Gili's Book: a Journey into Bereavement for Parents and Families* (New York: Teachers College Press, 1998).

3　Jewish Publication Society, *JPS TANAKH/ The Jewish Bible* (Jewish Publication Society of America, 2007).

4　Only after researching this subject (for this chapter) did I learn what was the basis of this practice. Officially, according to the Vatican, funerals are not allowed on Sundays during Advent, Lent, and the Easter Season. While this means that a funeral is permissible on Sundays during the other 130 days of the Christian calendar, many churches—as well as Catholic communes—choose to avoid Sundays altogether to allow everyone a day of rest.

5　A. Diamant, *Saying Kaddish: How to Comfort the Dying, Bury the Dead, and Mourn as a Jew* (New York: Schocken, 2007); A. Ginsberg, *Kaddish and Other Poems: 1958–1960* (San Francisco: City Lights Books, 2010); A. L. Goldman, *Living a Year of Kaddish* (New York: Schocken Books, 2003); M. Smart and B. Ashkenas, *Kaddish: Women's Voices* (Jerusalem: Urim Publications, 2013).

6　J. Cardinal Ratzinger, *Eschatology, Death, and Eternal Life* (Washington, DC: Catholic University of America Press, 2007); L. H. Duquin, *Grieving: With the Help of Your Catholic Faith* (Huntington, IN: Our Sunday Visitor, 2006); E. Kubler-Ross and D. Kessler, *On Grief and Grieving: Finding the Meaning of Grief Through the Five Stages of Loss* (New York: Scribner, 2005).

7　Eastern Christianity or Orthodox rituals are quite a bit more explicit, with several overlaps with Judaism, especially with regard to cleaning and preparing of the body for internment.

8　I have not focused in this chapter on the incredible contribution and support shown by our secular friends, but it is worth recognizing how open and interested they were in learning and respecting my Jewish rituals. As Post-Christians, most were familiar with the basic Christian rituals. Yet in addition they provided a great deal of love by way of lighting candles in every window on our street for seven nights, giving all the children at the funeral white balloons to release as we placed Hannah into the ground, and also several months later helping us plant a tree in the local park in her memory.

Chapter 16

1　I nuance this term here differently from Catherine Cornille in her final chapter of *The Im-possibility of Interreligious Dialogue* (New York: Crossroad, 2008). There, she uses the term "to imply an attitude of openness and receptivity to [religious] differences as a possible source of truth" (177). I do not deal with matters of truth here, but with more concrete gestures of hospitality and a receptivity to religious difference that respects the other's integrity. This is largely because Cornille writes about theological dialogue; my concern here is the dialogue of experience.

2   *Engel v. Vitale* (1962) forbade prayer and *Abington School District v. Schempp* (1963) banished Bible readings, both based on readings of the First Amendment of the Constitution of the United States which says that "Congress shall make no law respecting an establishment of religion." This went well beyond the original sense of the amendment, which was to prohibit any one church from receiving government sponsorship, as was common in Europe. In subsequent clarifications, especially *Lemon v. Kurtzman* (1971), the court ruled that activities in schools had to be fully secular and religiously neutral.

3   I recall nothing of their specific content, just of being called upon to choose or perhaps read something from the book on the teacher's desk.

4   This is ultimately the model of the American public square, with ongoing debates, not about Christmas trees, but about whether a crèche can be erected on public property.

5   There is now a mandatory course on Christianity in the seminary curriculum.

6   For a detailed discussion of the structure of this church, see "St John's Abbey Church Tour," http://www.saintjohnsabbey.org/files/5513/7331/7901/abbey_church_tour_-_8-28-12_small.pdf (accessed January 5, 2014).

7   Mary C. Boys has written about this with great sensitivity in a number of contexts. See her "The Cross: Should a Symbol Betrayed Be Reclaimed?" *Cross Currents* (Spring 1994); or *Has God Only One Blessing? Judaism as a Source of Christian Self-Understanding* (New York: Paulist Press, 2000), ch. 13, "The Cross as a Christian Symbol."

8   Coherent with this, I will not perform Jewish rituals in the presence of a cross or crucifix. When Boston College introduced crucifixes into classrooms a few years ago, I needed to adapt my teaching of liturgy and ritual.

9   We were eating at a vegetarian restaurant run by the Tibetan Buddhist Temple in Beijing, with its huge Buddha.

10 The growth of the academy, a desire to focus more on the work of its seminars, and sheer organizational complexity led to their diminution.

11 The other three—generally the Friday and Saturday morning services and the Friday evening "academy liturgy" presided over by the current president—represent the best or newest liturgical thinking of their sponsors. I find myself attending these less and less, both in order to leave time for my own prayers, but also because the ethos of participation discussed in the following paragraphs makes remaining a guest quite complicated. (N.B. This has recently been condensed so that the opening liturgy is the "academy liturgy" and the meeting closes with the banquet and its table prayer. This leaves only the two morning prayers led by particular groups according to their own norms.)

12 This synagogue is curiously cruciform and was deliberately built in rivalry with the Catholic cathedral across the street, particularly in the height of its "steeples." However, its decoration is deliberately and elaborately Moorish, echoing the romanticized Golden Age of Jews in Spain under Islam. Its steeples are shaped like minarets.

13 The table prayer at the banquet was designed to echo Jewish prayers over wine and bread before a meal and an abbreviated Grace after meals following it. The prayers before the meal include also some influence from the post-1970 "Prayer over the Gifts" in the Catholic Mass. However, it may well be historically incorrect to understand that Jesus used the rabbinic blessing formula at the Last Supper. This banquet setting does not include Eucharistic echoes.

14 For the lyrics, see: http://www.constitution.org/col/amazing_grace-p.html.

15 I was on sabbatical and away from campus in September 2001, so am unable to reflect on responses to it. However, I did hear of hurt from Jewish students at the request that all students place a cross in the window of their dormitory room. The Boston College community in general celebrates its Catholic identity with minimal consciousness of the sensitivities of the students, staff, and faculty who do not participate in it. There are now crucifixes in almost all classrooms; only one university chaplain (of fourteen) serves the 30 percent of students who are not Catholic. There have been steps in the right direction: the designation and appropriate furnishing of a small "multi-faith" chapel; the recent partial funding of a Hillel advisor; and some interreligious dialogues for students.

16 The communities represented have usually been Protestants, Orthodox Christians, Jews, Muslims, Buddhists, and Hindus.

17 See the articles in *Liturgy* 26:3 (2011) and the analysis offered by Stephanie Perdew VanSlyke and me in "Interreligious Prayer: Introduction," 1–10.

18 Orthodox synagogues, while often constructing a wonderful community for those whom they perceive as belonging, can be criticized for being often inhospitable to guests, simply because they presume familiarity from childhood with the complex liturgy and lifestyle. This can leave even non-orthodox Jews feeling lost and disenfranchised. It also affects insiders who lack skills and knowledge, especially women. I was once at a synagogue in Germany, where most of the attendees were recent immigrants from the Soviet Union. Some eagerly arrived the moment the service began, but they did not know how to participate. I am still angry that no one offered them guidance or even announced page numbers during the service.

19 A *minyan*, traditionally of adult men (i.e. aged thirteen and up). Liberal Jews count women, and some communities today seek ten men and ten women. Not all Jewish members of the NAAL would have felt constrained by this, but most do.

BIBLIOGRAPHY

Abhishiktananda/le Saux, H. (1998), *Spiritual Diary 1948–1973: Ascent to the Depth of the Heart*, New Delhi: ISPCK.

Akehurst, P. and Wootton, R. W. F. (1977), *Inter-Faith Worship?*, Bramcote: Grove Booklet on Ministry and Worship.

Albera, D. (2005), "Pélerinages mixtes et sanctuaries ambigus en Méditerranée," in S. Chiffoleau and A. Madoeuf (eds), *Les pèlerinages au Maghreb et au Moyen-Orient*, Beyrouth: Institut Français du Proche-Orient, 347–78.

Amaladoss, M. SJ (2012), "Inter-religious Worship," in C. Cornille (ed.), *The Wiley-Blackwell Companion to Interreligious Dialogue*, Malden: Blackwell-Wiley, 87–97.

Amalorpavadass, D. S. (1988), "Sharing Worship, Its Relevance in a Multi-Religious Society in an Inter-Faith Sharing of Life," in P. Puthangady SDB (ed.), *Sharing Worship: Communicatio in Sacris*, Bangalore: National Biblical Catechetical & Liturgical Centre, 35–58.

Andrae, T. (1987), *In the Garden of Myrtles: Studies in Early Islamic Mysticism*, Albany: State University of New York Press.

Anies, H. M. M. (2009), *Tahlil dan Kenduri: Tradisi Santri dan Kiai*, Yogyakarta: Pustaka Pesantren.

Ariarajah, W. (1999), *Not Without My Neighbour: Issues in Interfaith Relations*, Geneva: WCC.

Aquinas, *Summa Theologica*, Tertia Pars, Q. 73, Art. 3, Reply to Obj. 2.

Asad, T. (1993), *Genealogies of Religion*, London: John Hopkins University Press.

Ashbrok-Harvey, S. (2005), "Locating the Sensing Body: Perception and Religious Identity in Late Antiquity," in M. L. Satlow, S. Weitzman and D. Brakke (eds), *Religion and the Self in Antiquity*, Bloomington: Indiana University Press, 140–62.

Augustine (1993), Sermon 272, in *The Works of St. Augustine*, Vol. III/7, trans. E. Hill, New Rochelle: New City Press, 300–1.

Aune, M. (2007), "Liturgy and Theology: Rethinking the Relationship," *Worship* 81: 141–69.

Austin, J. L. (1976), *How to Do Things with Words*, Oxford: Oxford University Press.

Aydin, M. (2002), *Modern Western Christian Theological Understandings of Muslims since the Second Vatican Council*, Washington, DC: Council for Research in Values and Philosophy.

Baatz, U. (1998), *Hugo M. Enomiya-Lassalle. Ein Leben zwischen den Welten*, Düsseldorf: Benzinger.

Banerjea, N. (1974), *The Development of Hindu Iconography*, Delhi: Munshiram Manoharlal.

Basetti-Sani, G. (1977), *The Koran in the Light of Christ: A Christian Interpretation of the Sacred Book of Islam*, Chicago: Franciscan Herald Press.

Bateson, G. (1972), "A Theory of Play and Fantasy," in G. Bateson (ed.), *Steps to an Ecology of Mind*, New York: Ballantine Books.

al-Bayhaqi, Abu Bakr (1405/1985), *Dala'il al-nubuwwa wa-ma'rifat ahwal sahib al-shari'a*, Beirut: Dar al-Kutub al-'Ilmiyya.

Beal, J. P., Coriden, J. A., and Green, T. J. (eds) (2000), *New Commentary on the Code of Canon Law*, New York: Paulist Press.

Becvar, D. S. (2003), *In the Presence of Grief: Helping Family Members Resolve Death, Dying, and Bereavement Issues*, New York: Guilford Press.

Bell, C. (2009 [1997]), *Ritual: Perspectives and Dimensions*, Oxford: Oxford University Press.

Bell, C. (2009), *Ritual Theory, Ritual Practice*, New York: Oxford University Press.

Berger, T. (2001), "Prayers and Practices of Women: Lex Orandi Reconfigured," in S. K. Roll and A. Esser (eds), *Women, Ritual, and Liturgy*, Yearbook of the European Society of Women in Theological Research, Louvain: Peeters, 63–77.

Bernheim, P.-A. (1995), *James, Brother of Jesus*, London: SCM.

Bhikkhuni, L. Y. and Reis Habito, M. (eds) (2005), *Listening: Buddhist-Muslim Dialogues 2002–04*, Taipei: Museum of World Religions Development Foundation.

Bigelow, A. (2010), *Sharing the Sacred: Practicing Religious Pluralism in Muslim North India*, Oxford: Oxford University Press.

Bodhi, B. (ed.) (2005), *In the Buddha's Words: An Anthology of Discourses from the Pali Canon*, Boston: Wisdom Publications.

Bormans, M. and Jacquin, F. (eds) (2011), *Louis Massignon: Badaliya au nom de l'autre (1947–1962)*, Paris: Les Éditions du Cerf.

Braverman, A. (2003), *Living and Dying in Zazen: Five Zen Masters of Modern Japan*, New York: Weatherhill.

Braybrooke, M. (1989), "Praying Together: Possibilities and Difficulties of Interfaith Worship," *Dialogue and Alliance* 3: 89–93.

Brown, D. (1982), "Meeting Muslims," in *The Churches and Islam in Europe (II)*, Geneva, quoted in *Can We Pray Together? Guidelines on Worship in a Multi-Faith Society* (British Council of Churches, London, 1983: 1).

Buber, M. (1951), *Two Types of Faith: A Study of the Interpenetration of Judaism and Christianity*, New York: The MacMillan Company.

Burrell, D. (2004), *Faith and Freedom: An Interfaith Perspective*, Malden, MA: Blackwell.

Burrell, D., Cogliati, C., Soskice, J. M., and Stoeger, W. R. (eds) (2010), *Creation and the God of Abraham*, Cambridge: Cambridge University Press.

Carey, G. (1992), *Debate on Multi Faith Worship*. http://www.glcarey.co.uk/Speeches/1992/MultiFaith.html (all web addresses checked August 2014).

Carola, J. (2010), "Vatican II's Use of Patristic Themes Regarding Non-Christians," in K. J. Becker and I. Morali (eds), *Catholic Engagement with World Religions*, Maryknoll: Orbis, 143–52.

Carrithers, M. (2000), "On Polytropy: Or the Natural Condition of Spiritual Cosmopolitanism in India: The Digambar Jain Case," *Modern Asian Studies* 34: 831–61.

Carvalhaes, C. (2013), *Eucharist and Globalization: Redrawing the Borders of Eucharistic Hospitality*, Eugene, OR: Wipf and Stock.

Catechism of the Catholic Church (1994), London: Geoffrey Chapman.

CBEW (Catholic Bishops' Conference of England and Wales) (2010), *Meeting God in Friend and Stranger*, London: Catholic Truth Society.

Chastain, W. C. (1995), "Should Christians Pray the Muslim Salat?" *International Journal of Frontier Missions* 12: 34–40.

Chatterjee, S. and Datta, D. (2008), *An Introduction to Indian Philosophy*, Kolkata: Calcutta University Press.

Chau, A. (2006), *Miraculous Response: Doing Popular Religion in Contemporary China*, Stanford, CA: Stanford University Press.

Chau, A. (2012), "Efficacy, Not Confessionality: On Ritual Polytropy at Chinese Funerals," in G. Bowman (ed.), *Sharing the Sacra: The Politics and Pragmatics of Inter-communal Relations around Holy Places*, Oxford: Berghahn, 79–96.

Chupungco, A. (2010), *What, Then, Is Liturgy? Musings and Memoir*, Collegeville: Liturgical Press.

Clooney, F. (2009), *Beyond Compare: St. Francis De Sales and Vedanta Desika on Loving Surrender to God*, Washington, DC: Georgetown University Press.

Clooney, F. (2010), *Comparative Theology: Deep Learning across Religious Borders*, Chichester: Wiley-Blackwell.

Clooney, F. X. SJ (2010), *Comparative Theology: Deep Learning Across Religious Borders*, West Sussex, UK: Wiley-Blackwell.

Colijn, A. (2014), "'Christians do not Perform Traditional Rituals.' Discourse and practice in China's Three Self Patriotic Movement," Paper presented at the Christianity in Asia Summer School in Münster on September 23, 2014.

Congregation for the Doctrine of Faith (2000), *Dominus Jesus: On the Unicity and Salvific Universality of Jesus Christ and the Church (06.08.2000)*. www.vatican.va [accessed December 18, 2014].

Cook, J. A. and Wimberley, D. W. (1983), "If I Should Die before I Wake: Religious Commitment and Adjustment to the Death of a Child," *Journal for the Scientific Study of Religion* 22(3): 222–38.

Cornille, C. (2002), *Many Mansions? Multiple Religious Belonging and Christian Identity*, Faith Meets Faith, Maryknoll: Orbis.

Cornille, C. (2008), *The Im-possibility of Interreligious Dialogue*, New York: Herder and Herder.

Cornille, C. (2011), "Interreligious Hospitality and its Limits," in R. Kearney and J. Taylor (eds), *Hosting the Stranger between Religions*, New York: Continuum, 35–44.

Cornille, C. (2013), "Multiple Religious Belonging and Interreligious Dialogue," in D. Cheetham, D. Pratt, and D. Thomas (eds), *Understanding Inter-Religious Relations*, Oxford: Oxford University Press, 324–40.

Courtens, I. (2009), "Mary, Mother of All: Finding Faith at the Sacred Source of Sendangsono, Indonesia," in W. Jansen, C. D. Notermans and A.-K. Hermkens (eds), *Moved by Mary: The Power of Pilgrimage in the Modern World*, Aldershot: Ashgate, 101–16.

Cragg, K. (1970), *Alive to God: Muslim and Christian Prayer Compiled with an Introductory Essay*, Oxford: Oxford University Press.

Cragg, K. (1999), *Common Prayer: A Muslim-Christian Spiritual Anthology*, Oxford: Oneworld.

Crespo, C., Davide, I. et al. (2008), "Family Rituals in Married Couples: Links with Attachment, Relationship Quality, and Closeness," *Personal Relationships* 15: 191–203.

Cuffel, A. (1997), "'Henceforward all generations will call me blessed': Medieval Christian Tales of Non-Christian Marian Veneration," *Mediterranean Studies* 12: 37–60.

Cuffel, A. (2005), "From Practice to Polemic: Shared Saints and Festivals as "Women's Religion" in the Medieval Mediterranean," *The Bulletin of the School of Oriental and African Studies* 68: 401–19.

D'Costa, G. (2011), *The Catholic Church and the World Religions: A Theological and Phenomenological Account*, London: T & T Clark.

D'Costa, G. (2014), *Vatican II: Catholic Doctrine on Jews and Muslims*, Oxford: Oxford University Press.

Dall'Oglio, P. SJ (2009), *Amoureux de l'Islam, Croyant en Jésus*, Paris: Éditions Ouvrières.

Danielou, A. (2001), *The Hindu Temple*, trans. K. Henry, Rochester, VT: Inner Traditions.

de Béthune, P.-F. (1987), "Situating the Theme within the Context of the Christian Tradition," *Pro Dialogo Bulletin* 64: 159–65.

De Clerck, P. (1978), "'Lex orandi, lex credendi': Sens original et avatars historique d'un adage équivoque," *Questions Liturgiques* 59: 193–212.

De Clerck, P. (1994), "'Lex orandi, lex credendi': The Original Sense and Historical Avatars of an Equivocal Adage," *Studia Liturgica* 24: 178–200.

de Montjou, G. (2006), *Mar Moussa: une monastere, un homme, un desert*, Paris: Albin Michel.

Denzinger, H. (1955), *The Sources of Catholic Dogma*, 30th edn, trans. R. J. Deferrari, New Haven: Loreto Publications.

Deringil, S. (2011), *Conversion and Apostasy in the late Ottoman Empire*, Cambridge: Cambridge University Press.

Derrida, J. (2002), *Acts of Religion*, ed. and trans. G. Anidjar, London: Routledge.

Diamant, A. (2007), *Saying Kaddish: How to Comfort the Dying, Bury the Dead, and Mourn as a Jew*, New York: Schocken Books.

Diderot, D. and d'Alembert, J. (eds) (2011), *Encyclopédie, ou dictionnaire raisonné des sciences, des arts et des métiers, etc.*, University of Chicago, ARTFL Encyclopédie Project (Spring 2011 Edition). http://encyclopedie.uchicago.edu/.

Dogen (1985), "Shoji," in K. Tanahashi (ed.), *Moon in a Dewdrop: Writings of Zen Master Dogen*, New York: North Point Press, 74–6.

Dogen (1985), "Tenzo Kyokun," in K. Tanahashi (ed.), *Moon in a Dewdrop: Writings of Zen Master Dogen*, New York: North Point Press, 53–66.

Dōgen (2008), "Fukanzazengi," in T. D. Leighton and S. Okamura (eds), *Dōgen's Extensive Record: A Translation of the Eihei Kōroku*, Boston: Wisdom Publications, 532–5.

Dörmann, J. (1994), *John Paul II's Theological Journey to the Prayer Meeting of Religions in Assisi. Part I: From the Second Vatican Council to the Papal Elections*, Kansas City, MO: Angelus Press.

Đozo, H. (2006), *Izabrana Djela*, vol. 4, Sarajevo: Elkalem.

Drew, R. (2011), *Buddhist and Christian? An Exploration of Dual Belonging* (Routledge Critical Studies in Buddhism), Routledge: Abingdon.

Du Boulay, S. (2005), *The Cave of the Heart: The Life of Swami Abhishiktananda*, London: Orbis.

Dupuche, J. R. (2001), "Abhishiktananda Centenary Symposium," *Australian Journal of Theology* 18(3): 249–58.

Duquin, L. H. (2006), *Grieving: With the Help of Your Catholic Faith*, Huntington, IN: Our Sunday Visitor.

Eck, D. (1981), *Darśan: Seeing the Divine Image in India*, Chambersburg: Anima.

Eck, D. (1993), *Encountering God*, Boston: Beacon Press.

Eliade, M. (1957), *The Sacred and the Profane: The Nature of Religion*, London: Harvest Book, Harcourt, Inc.

Elison, C. G., Burdett, A. M., and Wilcox, W. B. (2010), "The Couple that Prays Together: Race and Ethnicity, Religion, and Relationship Quality among Working-Age Adults", *Journal of Marriage and Family* 72: 963–75.

Enomiya-Lassalle, H. M. (1980), *Meditation als Weg zur Gotteserfahrung*, Mainz: Matthias-Grünewald Verlag.

Enomiya-Lassalle, H. M. (1985), *Wohin geht der Mensch?*, Zürich: Benzinger.

Enomiya-Lassalle, H. M. (1986a), *Leben im neuen Bewusstsein*, München: Kösel (1988, *Living in the New Consciousness*, Boston: Shambala).

Enomiya-Lassalle, H. M. (1986b), *Zen und christliche Mystik*, Freiburg: Herder.

Enomiya-Lassalle, H. M. (1987a), *Zen und christliche Spiritualitt*, München: Kösel.

Enomiya-Lassalle, H. M. (1987b), *Zen-Unterweisung*, München: Kösel Verlag (1994, *The Practice of Zen-Meditation*, Aquarian Press).

Enomiya-Lassalle, H. M. (1995), *Zen Meditation für Christen*, O.W. Barth Verlag (1974, *Zen meditation for Christians*, New York: Open Court).

Esack, F. (1997), *Qur'an, Liberation and Pluralism: An Islamic Perspective of Interreligious Solidarity Against Oppression*, Oxford: Oneworld.

Fackenheim, E. L. (1994), *To Mend the World: Foundations of Post-Holocaust Jewish Thought*, Bloomington: Indiana University Press.

Fagerberg, D. W. (1992), *What is Liturgical Theology? A Study in Methodology*, Collegeville, MN: Liturgical Press.

Fattal, A. (1958), *Le Statut Légal des non-Musulmans en Pays d'Islam*, Beirut: Imprimerie Catholique.

Fletcher, J. H. (2005), *Monopoly on Salvation? A Feminist Approach to Religious Pluralism*, New York: Continuum.

Ford, D. F. and Pecknold, C. C. (eds) (2006), *The Promise of Scriptural Reasoning*, Oxford: Wiley-Blackwell.

Foulk, T. G. (2008), "Ritual in Japanese Zen Buddhism," in S. Heine and D. Wright (eds), *Zen Ritual*, Oxford: Oxford University Press, 2–82.

Frazer, Sir J. (1993/1922), *The Golden Bough: A Study of Magic and Religion*, London: Wordsworth.

Friedman, Y. (2003), *Tolerance and Coercion in Islam: Interfaith Relations in the Muslim Tradition*, Cambridge: Cambridge University Press.

Gager, J. G. (2007), "Did Jewish Christians See the Rise of Islam?" in A. H. Becker and A. Y. Reed (eds), *The Ways that Never Parted: Jews and Christians in Late Antiquity and the Early Middle Ages*, Minneapolis: Fortress Press.

Gangopadhyay, A. and Fernandez, C. (2013), "Malaysia Rules Catholic Paper Can't Use 'Allah,'" *Wall Street Journal*, October 14, 2013, http://online.wsj.com/news/articles/SB10 001424052702304561004579134493628158288.

Garfield, J. L. (trans. and comm.) (1995), *The Fundamental Wisdom of the Middle Way: Nāgārjuna's Mūlamadhyamakakārikā*, Oxford: Oxford University Press.

George, A. (2011), "Le palimpseste Lewis-Mingana de Cambridge, témoin ancien de l'histoire du Coran," *Comptes Rendus des Séances de l'Académie des Inscriptions et Belles Lettres*, 377–429.

German Bishops Conference (2003), *Leitlinien für das Gebet bei Treffen von Christen, Juden und Muslimen. Eine Handreichung der deutschen Bischöfe*, Arbeitshilfe 170, Bonn. http://www.dbk.de/nc/veroeffentlichungen/?tx_igmedienkatalog_pi1[show]=8.

Gimaret, D. (1997), *Dieu à l'image de l'homme: les anthropomorphismes de la sunna et leur interpretation par les théologiens*, Paris: Cerf.

Ginsberg, A. (2010), *Kaddish and Other Poems: 1958–1960*, San Francisco: City Lights Books.

Goffman, E. (1959), *The Presentation of Self in Everyday Life*, Garden City, NY: Doubleday.

Goldman, A. L. (2003), *Living a Year of Kaddish*, New York: Schocken Books.

Grant, S. (2002), *Toward an Alternative Theology: Confessions of a Non-Dualist Christian*, ed. B. J. Malkovsky, Notre Dame, IN: University of Notre Dame Press.

Griffiths, P. J. (1999), *Religious Reading: The Place of Reading in the Practice of Religion*, New York: Oxford University Press.

Grimes, L. (2002), *Deeply into the Bones: Re-Inventing Rites of Passage*, Berkeley, CA: Berkeley University Press.

Grose, G. B. and Hubbard, B. J. (eds) (1994), *A Jew, Christian and Muslim in Dialogue*, Notre Dame, IN: Cross Cultural Publications.

Grube, M. and Jonkers, P. (eds) (2008), *Religions Challenged by Contingency. Theological and Philosophical Approaches to the Problem of Contingency* (STAR: 12), Leiden: Brill.

Haidt, J. (2012), *The Righteous Mind: Why Good People Are Divided by Politics and Religion*, 1st edn, New York: Pantheon Books.

Halevi, Y. K. (2002), *At the Entrance to the Garden of Eden*, New York: Harper.

Halevi, Y. K. (2013), "Lessons from a Man of Peace," *Jerusalem Post*, March 6, 2013.

Harvey, G. (2013), *Food, Sex and Strangers: Understanding Religion as Everyday Life*, Durham: Acumen.

Heim, S. M. (1995), *Salvations: Truth and Difference in Religion*, Faith Meets Faith, Maryknoll: Orbis.

Heim, S. M. (2001), *The Depth of the Riches: A Trinitarian Theology of Religious Ends*, Sacra Doctrina, Grand Rapids: W.B. Eerdmans.

Heim, S. M. (2012), "Otherness and Wonder: A Christian Experiences Moksha," in J. H. Peace, O. N. Rose, and G. Mobley (eds), *My Neighbor's Faith: Stories of Interreligious Encounter, Growth and Transformation*, Maryknoll: Orbis, 192–6.

Heine, S. (2008), *Zen Skin, Zen Marrow: Will the Real Zen Buddhism Please Stand Up?*, Oxford: Oxford University Press.

Heine, S. and Wright, D. S. (eds) (2008), *Zen Ritual: Studies of Zen Buddhist Theory in Practice*, Oxford: Oxford University Press.

Hick, J. H. (1988), "Religious Pluralism and Salvation," *Faith and Philosophy* 5(4): 365–77.

Hillenbrand, C. (1999), *The Crusades: Islamic Perspectives*, Edinburgh: Edinburgh University Press.

Hoffman, L. A. (1990), "Worship in Common: Jewish-Christian Service: Babel or Mixed Multitude," *Cross Currents* 40: 5–17.

Hornung, E. (2001), *The Secret Lore of Egypt; Its Impact on the West*, Ithaca: Cornell University Press.

Hughes, G. (2003), *Worship as Meaning: A Liturgical Theology for Late Modernity*, Cambridge: Cambridge University Press.

Hume, D. (1985), *Of Superstition and Enthusiasm*, in D. Hume, *Essays. Moral, Political and Literary*, ed. E. F. Miller, Indianapolis: Liberty Fund, 73–9.

Hume, D. (2007), *A Dissertation on the Passions—The Natural History of Religion. A Critical Edition*, ed. T. L. Beauchamp, Oxford: Clarendon Press.

Humphrey, C. and Laidlaw, J. (1994), *The Archetypal Actions of Ritual. A Theory of Ritual Illustrated by the Jain Rite of Worship*, Oxford: Clarendon Press.

Hunsinger, G. (2008), *The Eucharist and Ecumenism: Let Us Keep the Feast*, New York: Cambridge University Press.

Huyler, J. (1999), *Meeting God: Elements of Hindu Devotion*, New Haven: Yale University Press.

ibn 'Abidin, M. (1421 AH), *Radd al-muhtar 'ala'l-Durr al-mukhtar*, Damascus: Dar al-Thaqafa wa'l-Turath.

ibn Hisham, 'Abd al-Malik (1936), *al-Sira al-Nabawiyya*, eds. M. al-Saqqa and I. al-Ibyari, Cairo: Mustafa al-Halabi.

ibn Sa'd, M. (1985), *al-Tabaqat al-Kubra*, Beirut: Dar Sadir.

Inter-Faith Consultative Group (IFCG) (1992), *Multi-Faith Worship? Questions and Suggestions from the Inter-Faith Consultative Group*, London: Church House Publishing.

Irwin, K. (2002), "Lex Orandi, Lex Credendi—Origins and Meaning: State of the Question," *Liturgical Ministry* 11: 57–69.

Islam in Europe Committee (IEC) (2003), *Christians and Muslims: Praying Together. Reflections and Texts*, Geneva: Islam in Europe Committee. http://cid.ceceurope.org/fileadmin/filer/cid/Doc_Interreligious_Dialogue/PrayingtogetherE.pdf .

Izutsu, T. (1965), *The Concept of Belief in Islamic Theology: A Semantic Analysis of Īmān and Islām*, Tokyo: The Keio Institute of Cultural and Linguistic Studies.

Jamhari, J. (2001), "The Meaning Interpreted: The Concept of *Barakah* in *Ziarah*," *Studia Islamika: Indonesian Journal for Islamic Studies* 8: 87–128.

al-Jawziyya, Ibn Qayyim (1997/1418), *Ahkam ahl al-dhimma*, al-Dammam: Ramadi li'l-nashr.

al-Jaziri, Abd al-Rahman (2009), *Islamic Jurisprudence According to the Four Sunni Schools, Volume I: Acts of Worship*, trans. N. Roberts, Louisville: Fons Vitae.

Jeanrond, W. G. (2010), *A Theology of Love*, London: T&T Clark.

Jewish Publication Society (2007), *JPS TANAKH/ The Jewish Bible*, Jewish Publication Society of America.

John Paul II (1987), "Pope's Christmas Address to the Roman Curia, the World Situation Constitutes a Pressing Appeal for the Spirit of Assisi, 22 December 1986," *Bulletin, Secretariat for Non Christians*, 64: 54–5.

John Paul II, *Redemptoris Missio: On the permanent validity of the Church's missionary mandate (07.12.1990)*. www. vatican.va [accessed 18 Decmeber, 2014].

Johnson, E. A. (2005), *Friends of God and Prophets: A Feminist Theological Reading of the Communion of Saints*, New York, London: Continuum.

Johnson, E. A. (2006), *Truly Our Sister: A Theology of Mary in the Communion of Saints*, London and New York: Continuum.

Jordens, J. T. F. (1978), *Dayananda Sarasvati: His Life and Ideas*, Delhi: Oxford University Press.

Judith, S. L. G. (2012), "Hospitality in Prayer," in F. Ward and S. Coakley (eds), *Fear & Friendship: Anglicans Engaging with Islam*, London and New York: Continuum, 132–43.

Kagan, H. (1998), *Gili's Book: A Journey into Bereavement for Parents and Families*, New York: Teachers College Press.

al-Kasani, Abu Bakr (1421 AH), *Bada'i' al-sana'i' fi tartib al-shara'i'*, Beirut: Dar Ihya' al-Turath al-'Arabi.

Kasimow, H., Keenan, J., and Klepinger, L. (eds) (2003), *Beside Still Waters: Jews, Christians, and the Way of the Buddha*, Boston: Wisdom Publications.

Katz, S. T. (1978), "Language, Epistemology, and Mysticism," in S. T. Katz (ed.), *Mysticism and Philosophical Analysis*, Oxford: Oxford University Press, 22–74.

Kavanagh, A. (1984), *On Liturgical Theology*, Collegeville, MN: Liturgical Press.

Kearney, R. (1979), "Terrorisme et sacrifice: le cas de l'Irlande du Nord," *Esprit* 4: 29–44.

Kearney, R. (2006), *Navigations: Collected Irish Essays 1976-2006*, Dublin: Lilliput.

Kearney, R. (2010), *Anatheism: Returning to God after God*, New York: Columbia University Press.

Kearney, R. (2011), "Eros, Diacritical Hermeneutics and the Maybe," in C. Willett and L. Lawlor (eds), *Philosophical Thresholds: Crossings of Life and World*, Selected Studies in Phenomenology and Existential Philosophy, vol. 36, *Philosophy Today*, SPEP Supplement 55.

Kearney, R. and Rizo-Patron, E. (eds) (2010), *Traversing the Heart: Journeys in Interreligious Imagination*, Leiden and Boston: Brill.

Keown, D. (2004), "Trikāya," in *A Dictionary of Buddhism*, Oxford: Oxford University Press.

Kim, H.-J. (2004), *Eihei Dōgen—Mystical Realist*, Boston: Wisdom Publications.

King, T. (2005), *Teilhard's Mass: Approaches to the Mass on the World*, New York: Paulist Press.

Knitter, P. (2002), *Introducing Theologies of Religion*, Maryknoll: Orbis.

Knitter, P. F. and Hick, J. (1987), *The Myth of Christian Uniqueness: Toward a Pluralistic Theology of Religions*, Faith Meets Faith, Maryknoll: Orbis.

Kramer, K. (1988), *The Sacred Art of Dying: How World Religions Understand Death*, New York: Paulist Press.

Kreinath, J., Snoek, J. A. M. and Stausberg, M. et al. (eds) (2006), *Theorizing Rituals: Issues, Topics, Approaches, Concepts*, Leiden: Brill.

Krokus, C. S. (2009), *Faith Seeking Understanding: Louis Massignon's (1883–1962) Catholic Conversation with Islam*, PhD Dissertation, Boston College, Chestnut Hill, Massachusetts.

Kubler-Ross, E. and Kessler, D. (2005), *On Grief and Grieving: Finding the Meaning of Grief Through the Five Stages of Loss*, New York: Scribner.

Kuin, T. H. F. (2011), "'Defender of Faith': Is there an Anglican Theology of Religious Pluralism? The Church of England and Other Faiths, 1966–1996," PhD thesis, University of Bristol, UI.

Kukai (1972), *Major Works*, trans. Y. S. Hakeda, New York: Columbia University Press.

Küng, H. (2007), *Islam*, Oxford: Oneworld.

Labib, M. Z. (2000), *Tuntunan Ziarah Walisongo*, Surabaya: Bintang Usaha Jaya.

Laksana, A. B. (2010), "Comparative Theology: Between Identity and Alterity," in F. Clooney (ed.), *New Comparative Theology: Interreligious Insights from the Next Generation*, New York: T&T Clark, 1–20.

Laksana, A. B. (2011), *Journeying to God in Communion with the Other: A Comparative Theological Study of the Muslim and Catholic Pilgrimage Traditions in South Central Java and Their Contributions to the Catholic Theology of* Communio Sanctorum, PhD Dissertation, Boston College, Chestnut Hill, Massachusetts.

Laksana, A. B. (2014a), "Multiple Religious Belonging or Complex Identity? An Asian Way of Being Religious," in F. Wilfred (ed.), *The Oxford Handbook of Christianity in Asia*, Oxford: Oxford University Press, 493–509.

Laksana, A. B. (2014b), *Muslim and Catholic Pilgrimage Practices: Explorations through Java*, Aldershot: Ashgate.

Langer, R. and VanSlyke, S. P. (2011), "Interreligious Prayer: Introduction," *Liturgies* 26: 1–10.

Lathrop, G. (1993), *Holy Things: A Liturgical Theology*, Minneapolis: Fortress Press.

Leighton, T. D. (2007), *Visions of Awakening Time and Space: Dōgen and the Lotus Sutra*, Oxford: Oxford University Press.

Leming, M. R. and Dickinson, G. E. (2011), *Understanding Dying, Death, and Bereavement*, Belmont, CA: Wadsworth Cengage Learning.

Lemmens, W. (2010), *Spinoza on Ceremonial Observances and The Moral Function of Religion*, in *Bijdragen. International Journal in Philosophy and Theology* 71(1): 51–64.

Levenson, J. (2012), *Inheriting Abraham: The Legacy of the Patriarch in Judaism, Christianity and Islam*, Princeton: Princeton University Press.

Lilienthal, D. (1998), "Avoda, gebed en werken," *Voor Zijn aangezicht; Een gesprek van Joden en christenen*, onder redactie van Reinier Munk et al. Kampen: Kok.

Lindbeck, G. A. (1984), *The Nature of Doctrine: Religion and Theology in a Postliberal Age*, London: SPCK.

Luhmann, N. (1977), *Funktion der Religion*, Frankfurt: Suhrkamp.

Luther, M. (1980), *An den christlichen Adel deutscher Nation. Von der Freiheit eines Christenmenschen. Sendbrief vom Dolmetschen*, Stuttgart: Reclam.

Maalouf, A. (1984), *The Crusades through Arab Eyes*, London: Al-Saqi.

MacCulloch, D. (2010), *Christianity: The First Three Thousand Years*, London: Penguin.

Madigan, D. A. (2004), "Revelation and Inspiration," in J. D. McAuliffe (ed.), *Encyclopaedia of the Qur'ān*, vol. 4, Leiden: Brill, 437–48.

Makransky, J. (2000), "Mahayana Buddhist Ritual and Ethical Activity in the World," *Buddhist-Christian Studies* 20: 54–9.

Marion, J.-L. (2007), *The Erotic Phenomenon*, trans. S. E. Lewis, Chicago: University of Chicago Press.

Maraldo, J. (2010), "A Call for an Alternative Notion of Understanding in Interreligious Hermeneutics," in C. Cornille and C. Conway (eds), *Interreligious Hermeneutics* (Interreligious Dialogue Series 2), Eugene: Wipf and Stock, 89–115.

Markham, I. (2009), *Engaging with Bediuzzaman Said Nursi*, Farnham: Ashgate.

Marshall, P. V. (1995), "Reconsidering 'Liturgical Theology': Is There a *Lex Orandi* for All Christians?," *Studia Liturgica* 25: 129–51.

McClain, E. G. (1981), *Meditations through the Qur'an: Tonal Images in an Oral Culture*, York Beach: Nicolas Hays.

McGuire, M. B. (2008), *Lived Religion: Faith and Practice in Everyday Life*, New York: Oxford University Press.

McLaren, B. D. (2012), *Why Did Jesus, Moses, the Buddha, and Mohammed Cross the Road?: Christian Identity in a Multi-Faith World*, 1st edn, New York: Jericho Books.

Merleau-Ponty, M. (2002), *The Phenomenology of Perception*, London: Routledge.

Miller, M. K. (2003), "The 'Impossible Grief': Working with Couples Who Have Lost a Child," *Currents: New Scholarship in the Human Services* 2(1). http://www.ucalgary.ca/currents/files/currents/v2n1_miller.pdf.

Millie, J. (2009), *Splashed by the Saints: Ritual Reading and Islamic Sanctity in West Java*, Leiden: KITLV.

Miyamoto, K. C. (2010), "Mission, Liturgy, and the Transformation of Identity," *Mission Studies* 27: 56–70.

Mohamed, M. N. (2003), *Salaat: The Islamic Prayer from A to Z*, Fairfax, VA: B 200.

Moore-Keish, M. (2008), *Do This in Remembrance of Me: A Ritual Approach to Reformed Eucharistic Theology*, Grand Rapids: Eerdmans.

Morris, J. W. (2005), *The Reflective Heart: Discovering Spiritual Intelligence in Ibn 'Arabi's 'Meccan Illuminations*, Louisville, KY: Fons Vitae.

Moyaert, M. (2014a), "Inappropriate Behavior? On the Ritual Core of Religion and its Challenges to Interreligious Hospitality," *Journal for the Academic Study of Religion* 27: 1–21.

Moyaert, M. (2014b), *In Response to the Religious Other: Ricoeur and the Fragility of Interreligious Encounters*, Lanham: Lexington Books.

Narayanan, V. (1985), "Arcāvātara: On Earth as He is in Heaven," in J. P. Waghorne,
    N. Cutler, and V. Narayanan (eds), *Gods of Flesh/ Gods of Stone: The Embodiment of
    Divinity in India*, Chambersburg, PA: Anima.

O'Donnell, E. (2012), "Embodying Tradition: Liturgical Performance as a Site for
    Interreligious Learning," *Cross Currents* 62: 371–80.

O'Leary, J. (2008a), "The Eucharist as a Work of Art," *Archivio di Filosofia* 78: 169–76.

O'Leary, J. (2008b), "The Eucharist: A Work of Art," *The Japan Mission Journal* 62: 93–7.

O'Mahony, A. (2004), "Louis Massignon, the Seven Sleepers of Ephesus and the Christian-
    Muslim Pilgrimage at Vieux-Marché, Brittany," in C. Bartholomew and F. Hughes
    (eds), *Explorations in a Christian Theology of Pilgrimage*, Aldershot: Ashgate,
    126–48.

Osborne, K. B. (1999), *Christian Sacraments in a Postmodern World: A Theology for the
    Third Millennium*, New York: Paulist.

Ott, L. (1955), *Fundamentals of Catholic Dogma*, trans. P. Lynch, Cork: Mercier Press.

Padwick, C. (1961), *Muslim Devotions: A Study of Prayer Manuals in Common Use*,
    London: SPCK.

Patai, R. (1987), *Ignaz Goldziher and his Oriental Diary*, Detroit, MI: Wayne State
    University Press.

Paulsell, S. (2012), "Faith Matters: Devotional Difference," *Christian Century* 129(2): 35.

Phan, P. (2004), *Being Religious Interreligiously: Asian Perspectives on Interfaith Dialogue*,
    Maryknoll: Orbis Books.

Pidaparti, S. (2006), Commemorative Magazine Celebrating the Opening of the Hindu
    Temple, Maple Grove, Minnesota.

Plaut, G. W. (ed.) (1979), *The Torah: A Modern Commentary*, New York: Union of
    American Hebrew Congregations.

Polanyi, M. (1958), *Personal Knowledge*, London: Routledge.

Polanyi, M. (1967), *The Tacit Dimension*, New York: Doubleday.

Potter, K. (1963), *Presuppositions of India's Philosophies*, Englewood Cliffs: Prentice Hall.

Pragt, H. "Magische praktijken." Eigen uitgave: zie. www.egyptologie.nl.

Pramuk, C. (2013), "'How Long, O Lord?' Interfaith Perspectives on Suffering, Protest, and
    Grace," *New Theology Review* 17(4): 66–75.

Pratt, D. (1997), "Parameters for Interreligious Prayer: Some Considerations," *Current
    Dialogue* 31: 21–7.

Pratt, D. (2010), *The Church and Other Faiths: The World Council of Churches, the Vatican,
    and Interreligious Dialogue*, Bern: Peter Lang.

Prennthaler, J. (1922–37), *Brieven van Pater J. B. Prennthaler aan Pater Directeur van de St
    Claverbond (1922–1937)*, Manuscript.

Prennthaler, J. (1935), "Open Brief van Pater J. Prennthaler, S.J.," *St Claverbond* 169–72.

Preston, J. J. (1985), "Creation of the Sacred Image: Apotheosis and Destruction in
    Hinduism," in J. P. Waghorne, N. Cutler, and V. Narayanan (eds), *Gods of Flesh/ Gods of
    Stone: The Embodiment of Divinity in India*, Chambersburg, PA: Anima, 9–32.

Raj, S. and Dempsey, C. (eds) (2002), *Popular Christianity in India: Riting Between the
    Lines*, Albany, NY: State University of New York Press.

Rambachan, A. (1992), *The Hindu Vision*, Delhi: Motilal Banarsidass, 7.

Rambachan, A. (2004), "Global Hinduism: The Hindu Diaspora," in R. Rinehart (ed.),
    Contemporary Hinduism: Ritual, Culture and Practice, Santa Barbara, CA: ABC-CLIO,
    381–414.

Rambachan, A. (2006), *The Advaita Worldview: God, World, and Humanity*, SUNY Series
    in Religious Studies, Albany, NY: State University of New York Press.

Rappaport, R. A. (1999), *Ritual and Religion in the Making of Humanity*, Cambridge: Cambridge University Press.

Ratzinger, J. (2004), *Truth and Tolerance: Christian Belief and World Religions*, trans. H. Taylor, San Francisco: Ignatius Press.

Ratzinger, J. Cardinal (2007), *Eschatology, Death, and Eternal Life*, Washington, DC: Catholic University of America Press.

Raven, M. J. (2010), *Egyptische Magie: op zoek naar het toverboek van Toth*, Zutphen: Walburg Pers.

Reedijk, R. (2010), *Roots & Routes: Identity Construction and the Jewish-Christian-Muslim Dialogue*, Amsterdam: Rodopi.

Reinkowski, M. (2007), "Hidden Believers, Hidden Apostates: The Phenomenon of crypto-Jews and crypto-Christians in the Middle East," in D. Washburn and A. K. Reinhart (eds), *Converting Cultures: Religion, Ideology of Transformations of Modernity*, Leiden: Brill, 409–33.

Reis Habito, M. (ed.) (2001), *Weisheit und Barmherzigkeit: Master Hsin Tao*, M Mo Ta: Adyar.

Reis Habito, M. (2009), "Master Hsin Tao's Vision: The Museum of World Religions," in A. Sharma (ed.), *The World's Religions After September 11*, vol. 3, London: Praeger Perspectives, 3–13.

Ricoeur, P. (1998), "Entretien Hans Küng-Paul Ricoeur: Les religions, la violence et la paix—Pour une éthique planétaire," *Sens* 5: 211–30.

Ricoeur, P. (2004), *On Translation*, London: Routledge.

Robbins, J. (1991), *Prodigal Son/Elder Brother: Interpretation and Alterity in Augustine, Petrarch, Kafka, Levinas*, Chicago: University of Chicago Press.

Roberts, M. V. (2010), "Religious Belonging and the Multiple," *Journal of Feminist Studies in Religion* 26: 43–62.

Roberts, M. V. (2010), *Dualities: A Theology of Difference*, 1st edn, Louisville: Westminster John Knox Press.

Roberts, N. (2013), "A Muslim Reflects on Christ Crucified: Stumbling Block or Blessing?" *Islam and Christian-Muslim Relations* 24, 313–31.

Robinson, N. (1990), *Representations of Jesus in the Quran and the Classical Muslim Commentaries*, London: Macmillan, Palgrave.

Roebuck, V. J. (ed.) (2003), *The Upaniṣads*, London: Penguin Books.

Roy, A. (1983), *The Islamic Syncretistic Tradition in Bengal*, Princeton: Princeton University Press.

Ruggeri, A. (2009), "For President Obama, a somber, inclusive inaugural prayer service." *US News*, January 21, 2009. http://www.usnews.com/news/obama/articles/2009/01/21/for-president-obama-a-somber-inclusive-inaugural-prayer-service.

Ryle, G. (1971), *Knowing How and Knowing That*, in Idem, *Collected Papers. Volume II: Collected Essays 1929-1968*, London: Hutchinson, 212–25.

Ryle, G. (1980), *The Concept of Mind*, Harmondsworth: Penguin.

Saliers, D. (1994), *Worship as Theology: Foretaste of Glory Divine*, Nashville: Abingdon.

Santideva (1996), *The Bodhicaryavatara*, trans. K. Crosby and A. Skilton, New York: Oxford.

Schilbrack, K. (2004), "Ritual Metaphysics," in K. Schilbrack (ed.), *Thinking Through Rituals*, New York: Routledge, 128–47.

Schmemann, A. (1972), "Liturgy and Theology," *Greek Orthodox Theological Review* 17: 86–100

Segal, R. A. (ed.) (1998), *The Myth and Ritual Theory: An Anthology*, Oxford: Blackwell.

Seligman, A. B., Weller, R. P., Puett, M. J. and Simon, B. (2008), *Ritual and Its Consequences: An Essay on the Limits of Sincerity*, New York: Oxford University Press.

Şentürk, R. (2002), "*Adamiyyah* and *'Ismah*: The Contested Relationship between Humanity and Human Rights in Classical Islamic Law," *İslam Araştırmaları Dergisi* 8: 39–69.

Sesboüé, B. (2004), *Hors de l'église pas de salut? Histoire d'une formule et problèmes d'interprétation*, Paris: Desclée de Brouwer.

Shapiro, R. (2009), *Recovery—The Sacred Art: The Twelve Steps as Spiritual Practice*, Woodstock, VT: Skylight Paths.

Sharf, R. H. (2001), "Visualization and Mandala in Shingon Buddhism," in R. H. Sharf and E. H. Sharf (eds), *Living Images: Japanese Buddhist Icons in Context*, Stanford: Stanford University Press.

Sharf, R. H. (2005), "Ritual," in D. S. Lopez Jr. (ed.), *Critical Terms for the Study of Buddhism*, Chicago: The University of Chicago Press, 245–70.

Sharma, A. (2011), *Problematizing Religious Freedom*, Studies in Global Justice, New York: Springer.

Smart, M. and Ashkenas, B. (eds) (2013), *Kaddish: Women's Voices*, Jerusalem: Urim Publications.

Smith, W. R. (1889), *Lectures on the Religion of the Semites. Lecture 1*, in Segal (ed.) (1998).

Solomon, N., Harries, R., and Winter, T. (2005), *Abraham's Children: Jews, Christians and Muslims in Conversation*, London: T&T Clark.

Sparks, A. (2010), *One of a Kind: The Relationship between Old and New Covenants as the Hermeneutical Key for Christian Theology of Religions*, Eugene, OR: Pickwick Publications.

Staal, F. (1975), "The Meaninglessness of Ritual," *Numen* 26: 2–22.

Stone, J. I. (1999), *Original Enlightenment and the Transformation of Medieval Japanese Buddhism*, Honolulu: University of Hawai'i Press.

Stein, H. "'Allah'llahH. r Rabbi," *Die Welt*, March 30, 2002, at http://www.welt.de/print-welt/article381654/Allah-rief-der-Rabbi.html.

Sullivan, F. A. (1992), *Salvation outside the Church? Tracing the History of the Catholic Response*, New York: Paulist.

Sure, H. (2001), "Cleansing the Heart: Buddhist Bowing as Contemplation," in B. Barnhart and J. Wong (eds), *Purity of Heart and Contemplation: A Monastic Dialogue Between Christian and Asian Traditions*, New York: Continuum, 92–108.

Taft, R. F. (1992), "What Does Liturgy Do? Toward a Soteriology of Liturgical Celebration: Some Theses," *Worship* 66(3): 194–211.

Tambiah, S. Y. (1990), *Magic, Science, Religion and the Scope of Rationality*, Cambridge: Cambridge University Press.

Tanner, N. (1990), *Decrees of the Ecumenical Councils*. Vol. 2: *Trent to Vatican II*, London: Sheed & Ward.

Tennyson, A. T. Baron (2004), *In Memoriam: An Authoritative Text, Criticism*, New York: W.W. Norton & Co.

Thangaraj, T. (1997), *Relating to People of Other Religions*, Nashville: Abingdon Press.

Thatamanil, J. (2011), "Comparative Theology after 'Religion,'" in S. D. Moore and M. Rivera (eds), *Planetary Loves*, New York: Fordham University Press, 238–57.

Troll, C. W. (2008), "Common Prayer of Christians and Muslims?" *Stimmen der Zeit* 6: 363–76. http://www.con-spiration.de/texte/english/2008/troll-e.html.

Troll, C. W. (2009), *Dialogue and Difference. Clarity in Christian-Muslim Relations*, trans. D. Marshall, Maryknoll: Orbis.

Turner, V. (1974), *Dramas, Fields, and Metaphors: Symbolic Action in Human Society*, Ithaca: Cornell University Press.

Tylor, E. B. (1871), *Primitive Society*, 1st edn, London: Murray.

Ucko, H. (1993), "Inter-religious Worship and Prayer," *Current Dialogue* 24: 35–9.

Ucko, H. (1995), "Report on Inquiry on Interreligious Prayer and Worship," *Current Dialogue* 28: 57–64.

Valkenberg, P. (2006), *Sharing Lights on the Way to God: Muslim-Christian Dialogue and Theology in the Context of Abrahamic Partnership*, Amsterdam: Rodopi.

Vámbéry, Á. (1973), *Arminius Vambery: His Life and Adventures*, New York: Arno Press.

Van Belle, G. (ed.) (2007), *The Death of Jesus in the Fourth Gospel*, Leuven: Peeters.

van der Braak, A. (2008), "Enlightenment Revisited: Romantic, Historicist, Hermeneutic and Comparative Perspectives on Zen," *Acta Comparanda* XIX: 87–97.

van der Braak, A. (2009), "Zen Spirituality in a Secular Age II—Dōgen on Fullness: Zazen as Ritual Embodiment of Buddhahood," *Studies in Spirituality* 19: 227–47.

van Ess, J. (2006), *The Flowering of Muslim Theology*, Cambridge, MA: Harvard University Press.

Van Gennep, A. (1960), *The Rites of Passage*, Chicago: University of Chicago Press.

Van Herck, W. (1999), "The Role of Tacit Knowledge in Religion, in Tradition and Discovery," *The Polanyi Society Periodical* 26(2): 21–30.

Van Herck, W. (2003), "Een primaire religieuze taal? Over tabernakels en brooddozen," in P. Cortois, W. Desmond and I. Verhack (eds.), *Godsdienst/filosofisch bekeken*, Kapellen: Pelckmans, 167–78.

Van Herck, W. (2007), "A Friend of Demea? The Meaning and Importance of Piety," in A. Sanders (ed.), *D.Z. Phillips' Contemplative Philosophy of Religion*, Hampshire: Ashgate, 125–38.

VanderWilt, J. T. (2003), *Communion with Non-Catholic Christians: Risks, Challenges, and Opportunities*, Collegeville: Liturgical Press.

Vishanoff, D. (2013), "Boundaries and Encounters," in D. Cheetham, D. Pratt, and D. Thomas (eds), *Understanding Inter-Religious Relations*, Oxford: Oxford University Press.

Volf, M. (2012), *Allah: A Christian Response*, New York: HarperOne.

Vööbus, A. (1958), *History of Asceticism in the Syrian Orient: A Contribution to the History of Culture in the Near East*, Louvain: Secrétariat du Corpus SCO.

Voss Roberts, M. (2010), "Religious Belonging and the Multiple," *Journal of Feminist Studies in Religion* 26(1): 43–62.

Wainwright, G. (1980), *Doxology: The Praise of God in Worship, Doctrine, and Life: A Systematic Theology*, New York: Oxford University Press.

Welter, A. (2008), *The Linji Lu and the Creation of Chan Orthodoxy: The Development of Chan's Records of Sayings Literature*, Oxford: Oxford University Press.

Wessels, A. (2013), *The Torah, the Gospel, and the Qur'an: Three Books, Two Cities, One Tale*, Grand Rapids: Eerdmans.

Wheatcroft, A. (2003), *Infidels: The Conflict between Christendom and Islam, 638–2002*, London: Viking.

Williams, R. (1989), "Does It Make Sense to Speak of Pre-Nicene Orthodoxy?" in R. Williams (ed.), *The Making of Orthodoxy*, Cambridge: Cambridge University Press, 1–18.

Wingate, A. (2005), *Celebrating Difference, Staying Faithful*, London: Darton, Longman and Todd.

Winter, T. (2011), "America as a *Jihad* State: Middle Eastern Perceptions of Modern American Theopolitics," *The Muslim World* 101: 394–411.

Wittgenstein, L. (1971), Remarks on Frazer's "Golden Bough", *The Human World* 3: 18–41.
Wittgenstein, L. (1979), *On Certainty*, Oxford: Blackwell.
Wolfson, R. (1993), *A Time To Mourn, A Time To Comfort: A Guide To Jewish Bereavement, 2nd Ed. (The Art of Jewish Living)*, Woodstock, VT: Jewish Lights Pub.
Wooden, C. (2011), "Back to Assisi: Pope Benedict to Commemorate Event He Skipped," *Catholic News Service*, January 7, 2011. http://www.catholicnews.com/data/stories/cns/1100061.htm.
Woodhead, L. and Heelas, P. (2005), *The Spiritual Revolution: Why Religion Is Giving Way to Spirituality*, Oxford: Blackwell Publishing.
Woodward, M. (1989), *Islam in Java: Normative Piety and Mysticism in the Sultanate of Yogyakarta*, Tucson: University of Arizona Press.
Wright, D. S. (2008), "Introduction: Rethinking Ritual Practice in Zen Buddhism," in Heine and Wright (eds), *Zen Ritual*, Oxford: Oxford University Press, 3–19.
Wright, T. (2013), *No Peace without Prayer: Encouraging Muslims and Christians to Pray Together: A Benedictine Approach*, Collegeville, MN: Liturgical Press.
Zaman, M. Q. (2002), *The Ulama in Contemporary Islam: Custodians of Change*, Princeton: Princeton University Press.
Zilfi, M. C. (1986), "The Kadızadelis: Discordant Revivalism in Seventeenth-Century Istanbul," *Journal of Near Eastern Studies* 45: 251–69.

Ecclesiastical sources

Book of Order 2011–13, Presbyterian Church (USA).
Catechism of the Catholic Church (CCC).
Code of Canon Law (CCL).
WCC (1982), *Baptism, Eucharist, Ministry*. Faith and Order Paper, no. 111, Geneva: World Council of Churches.

Internet Sources

http://www.ekambaranathartemple.org [accessed December 11, 2013].
http://www.hafsite.org/pdf/2nd%20Jewish-Hindu%20Summit%20Final%20Declaration%2002-27-08.pdf [accessed September 11, 2013].
http://www.hindustantimes.com/India-news/Bhubaneswar/Controversies-over-Jagannath-Temple-s-entry-rules/Article1-907457.aspx [accessed August 26, 2013].
http://indiatoday.intoday.in/story/non-hindus-to-sign-faith-form-to-enter-tirumala-temple-in-andhra-pradesh/1/210621.html [accessed August 26, 2013].
http://www.interfaithmarriage.org.uk/resource_packs/Resourcepack.pdf.
http://www.thehindu.com/news/national/other-states/nonhindus-can-enter-jagannath-temples-except-shrine-at-puri/article2764219.ece [accessed August 26, 2013].
Troll, C. W. SJ (2008), 'Common Prayer of Christians and Muslims?' http://www.con-spiration.de/texte/english/2008/troll-e.html.
Lumen Gentium (November 21, 1964). http://www.vatican.va/archive/hist_councils/ii_vatican_council/documents/vat-ii_const_19641121_lumen-gentium_en.html
The Bhagavadgītā http://www.bhagavad-gita.org.

NAME INDEX

SUBJECT INDEX